FORBIDDEN MEMORIES

FORBIDDEN MEMORIES
A Journey of Healing

By Sandra P. Riggin

EVENING STAR PRESS
Sautee-Nacoochee, Georgia

The details and events of this book have been written according to the author's recollection and without malicious intent. The names of the people and institutions who do not wish to be identified have been changed to protect their confidentiality.

ISBN 0-9742924-0-0

Library of Congress Catalog Card Number: 2003094292

Printed in the United States of America

First Evening Star Press Edition: March 2004

Dedications

To God who loved me and protected me on my journey,

To my inner child who clung tightly to the memories of her past so one day I could experience healing and resolution and know what it means to embrace myself and the world around me,

And to the millions of people around the world who are still suffering because of the pain they endured as children.

Acknowledgements

Thanks to God for His mercy and for keeping me alive so I could share my story.

Renee Evans, Bobbie Pethel and Tom Sieswerda for doing endless hours of proofreading and never letting me forget the importance of my story.

Kim Sutton for donating his brilliant photography skills.

Marlin Geiger for sharing his wonderful talents with designing the book cover and setting up the book.

Jane Grillo for offering her proofreading skills.

It should be noted that all of the above people donated their time and skills so this book could be published. They offered their services, without anything in return, because they believed in the quest of helping survivors of childhood abuse to heal.

Words of Wisdom

Wisdom Keeper, Clan Mother of the Second Moon Cycle, asks us to clear the path to remembering by weeding out all of the past events that hold our attention. In order to reclaim the fragments of our spirits that remain stuck in old traumas, disappointments, and heartaches, we must breathe these lost pieces of Self free from the feelings we forgot to express at the time. In this manner, we free our energy, reclaim the vision we owned before our disappointments, and bring that shard of ourselves home-to the present. Then we have all the attention and focus we need to be in the Now, remembering who we are and why we are here.

Earth Medicine by Jamie Sams

For a while it was necessary to look back and come to terms with what happened to me as a child. In my family there was a lot of emotional abuse and neglect shrouded in denial and minimizing. I still needed to face the truth and climb out of my own denial, which convinced me I would get a chance to relive my childhood and make a better past.

A wise person once said in *Courage to Change* that it's necessary to "look back without staring." As long as I kept staring at my past without experiencing my feelings about it, I stayed mired in fear, resentment, and self-pity. So I continued to root out those defects that kept me from being serene. I couldn't let go of something that I didn't possess. Only after I stopped long enough to feel my anguish, bitterness, and emptiness could I let them go and move ahead.

Hope For Today (Alanon)

Preface

This journey of healing, written from my heart, is an exact account of what happened to me each step of the way. It is not rose-colored for entertainment, but provides an honest account of what it took for me to heal so others might do the same. To break the vicious cycle of self-destruction, I had to learn to be a healthy and self-esteemed adult, capable of loving and caring for myself. I had to delve into the depths of my heart and soul to help my lost and tortured child face the demons that held her prisoner. It required intensive therapy and startling personal insights. My need to succeed and be happy, just once in my life, was the driving force that kept me striving for resolution. It reveals periods of learning and understanding followed by periods of confusion and hopelessness, but in the end, it tells the story of my survival and triumph.

I began writing Forbidden Memories as a means of healing myself from the painful things that happened to me as a child which held me captive even as an adult. This writing took five very long years, yet it was the most cathartic thing I had done on my journey to healing. It was the final step that led to freedom and helped me develop a healthy perspective about the child who lives inside of me.

As I saw the form this book was taking, I also realized I couldn't keep it to myself. There were too many people in the world who were still suffering. Each day that I counseled my clients, I would hear story after story of their childhood abuse and their inability to handle it as an adult. There were stories of people drinking and drugging themselves to death, becoming slaves to eating disorders, cutting themselves, marrying people who were abusers, having difficulty maintaining interpersonal relationships, and those who were constantly on the verge of suicide. Thus, I began applying the techniques outlined in my book. With this I began seeing dramatic results and many people recovering. I saw people breaking the cycle of addiction, beginning to love themselves, and giving up suicide as a means of coping. I saw many who were evolving into the person they had always wanted to become.

It is important for each person who decides to read this book to understand that the road to recovery and healing will not be easy, uneventful, and without pain. This road usually passes through numerous hills and valleys. Strides of progress are often accompanied by difficult setbacks; periods of growth stunted by old behaviors and habits.

I liken this journey of healing to constructing a new road. The land with your current behaviors and way of life have to be cleared away.

Then the remaining sticks, stones, and ruts of your existence have to be exposed and thrown out. As these items are discarded, the surface of your thoughts and emotions have to be scrapped clean and leveled many times in order to support a new foundation. After the foundation is poured and before it dries, it needs to be pressed down many times in order to get the remaining uneven surfaces smoothed out so only the new road remains. Finally, the guardrails need to be added to ensure ongoing protection and progress.

This book may prove to be difficult for many people to read. Thus, I would encourage each person to be gentle with themselves and take this journey one step at a time. There may be sections too painful to be read today. If necessary, skip that part and come back to it when you are ready. But keep reading so you, too, may find the answers you are looking for.

My desire is that this book will open the hearts of survivors so they may speak their truths, heal, and break the vicious cycle of abuse. In addition, I hope it will open the minds of friends of abuse survivors so they may better understand. Finally, I hope this book will open the eyes of anyone who has ever abused another person and will allow them to see how the abuse has impacted that person's life.

Foreword

Sometimes one picks up a book, looks at the cover, and is either intrigued and wants to look further, or is turned off. I hope you will find this book intriguing to the point that you cannot resist adding it to your reading list. Through Sandy's personal life history you will be exposed to the harrowing reality that was the life of a child growing to adolescence and then adulthood, who was severely abused and then thrown away as though she was nothing more than human debris. Few people, if any, are better qualified to walk you through the world of mental, physical and sexual abuse than Sandy. Whether you are a mental health professional, yourself a victim of abuse, or whether you are simply interested in understanding the real life trials of victims of unrelenting abuse, you could not have a better guide than Sandy. She has lived a life one would not wish on their worst enemy. She suffered greatly at the hands of trusted family members, friends, and those who betrayed their offers of help to someone desperate for even a hint of love and acceptance.

Failing to find the human touch she needed to feel alive, Sandy endured extended forays into escapist encounters involving drug abuse and other death defying escapades. Reading her book will bring you face to face with the worst of humanity and with the naked need engendered by the depravation of one our most basic needs—the need for the acceptance and love of other people who are significant in our lives. By reading this book, you will be infinitely better informed about the devastation of the human psyche when all efforts to find such acceptance and love are lost. You will learn about the lengths to which one will go to avoid or hide from the pain of utter rejection by those held closest and believed dearest, even though objective reality offers no support for those perceptions. You will follow Sandy through the worst imaginable childhood, into an even worse adolescence, and finally into adulthood which was it's own special horror because she arrived there totally unprepared to manage the complexities of adult and work relationships.

In person Sandy is a bright, likable, complex person with a penchant for hiding a horrendously wounded inner core with an easy going joviality and a sharp sense of humor. Upon meeting her casually, not even an experienced therapist could guess the cauldron of emotional pain and the immensely wounded psyche lurking behind her social persona. You can only appreciate why that might be true by reading Sandy's story. Her story could never have been written in a Hollywood script. Even with Hollywood's penchant for overstatement and blatant exaggeration, Sandy's real life story extends beyond Hollywood lore and beyond what one would expect to be the limits of human endurance. It seems impossible that any person could endure the physical and emotional pain, the betrayal, the abandonment and the abuse that were an every day part of Sandy's life. And Sandy very nearly did not survive them. In her efforts to deal with the emotional trauma brought about by those issues, Sandy developed myriad maladaptive coping strategies which compounded her plight and which, on many, many occasions, very nearly culminated in the loss of her life. Many people offered help along the way, but many of those offers ended with betrayal of her trust, more abuse, and a further collapse of Sandy's hopes for a better day. Those issues finally brought Sandy to therapy with me.

I would like to tell you that it was my 30 years of experience, or my wonderfully therapeutic persona, or some great therapeutic skill on my part than resulted in Sandy's recovery. I would like to tell you that, but the truth is Sandy recovered from a psychological state that more often than not results in suicide because she is, at her core, a fighter. I relied on that core to keep her alive. Although it was a close call on many occasions, I am happy to say that when she found the proper fight, she won.

In summary, this book is about Sandy's journey to and from a hell that almost defies imagination. For a person of empathy, this book is a painful read. But it is ultimately a tribute to the resilience of the human psyche and to the deep and abiding strength from which a few people like Sandy wring the stamina, courage and determination to fight the demons of a life spent in unrelenting pain and turmoil. If you can read only one book this year, I would encourage you to choose this one. Read it, and despite Sandy's successful recovery, I feel certain you will be thankful it is not a life you had to live.

DR. DAVID BAILEY

Brothers' Introduction

From the pen of Patrick Probst, the oldest brother:

The human spirit is a wondrous thing. It is our life, our energy. A strong spirit inextricably links us to our basic desire to survive. More than survive, our spirit drives us to flourish, to make a mark, and to be more than we had imagined possible. Moreover, our spirit makes us stronger by building upon our life's experiences. At the end of the day, it is our spirit that enables us to create a reason to live, and to create a life worth living.

In my sister's story, you will see that she has a strong spirit and that her life now is worth living. It is an inspiring true story of a journey through hell and healing.

At the age of 38, I finally had the chance to see our childhood through her eyes. I was reluctant to read her book at first. Not because of the shared memories of our life, but because of how awful it would be to learn about everything else – events that were whispered about or never voiced. Also, I was reluctant because I didn't really know my sister or much about what had happened to her. And, for much of my life, I didn't care. Strangely, I only vaguely remembered our past and most of those memories seemed second hand. In her book, there was no escaping the truth. I sat there with her life, and part of mine, spilled out before me. It was a surreal tale of forbidden memories - many memories I had long forgotten, some I never had, and some I didn't want to have. As I read on, I wondered what effect the memories would have on me. Would it bring light to the dark thoughts of my mind that had been locked away, dusty and safely hidden for years? Would it change the relationships I had with my family and others around me? Worse yet, would it change my innocence —a naive innocence where I was taught to believe that people do their best, want to help and are kind? Credit I normally gave without thought to adults, authority figures, teachers and institutions of good will were now turned upside down. It made me angry and sad. I am not sure that I could have survived her struggle, much less have had the strength and courage to turn life into "a journey of healing."

It occurred to me as I read her book, that while trying to make life worth living, many of us often don't see the signs that could have helped us along the way. Many times we don't learn from our own histories, dooming ourselves to repeated dysfunctional practices handed down from generations past. Sometimes we are too young and inexperienced to see the patterns. At other times we just don't care. In our own family, like many others, we fell into the trap of repeating family tragedies. They were all too well rehearsed. And as we grew into adults, those often subconscious, pervasive patterns had a devastating effect on each of us and on those around us. Only now does it seem obvious to me that our family functioned much like drowning people who cannot swim, often taking would be rescuers down with them. No one was spared and least of all, my sister.

Fortunately for me, my experiences were more akin to a glancing blow. I as read on, untold events were graphically brought to light and I wondered why I didn't see everything going on around me. I know I was young and couldn't read the subtle signs. I was just a child. That's what I tell myself anyway. As I grew older, I had only the slightest, mostly unconscious feeling of unplugging from our family, like a vacuum cleaner cord, stretched too far, slowing working its way from the outlet. The next thing I knew, I had little relationship with my family. I had learned to survive by distracting myself in the comfort and safety of school and trusting only myself while the family disintegrated.

My sister took a different route, taking life full on not knowing what dangers lay ahead. She survived the worst that life had to offer. She thought she could protect everyone and in the end, be loved and help create a stable family. She paid a high price for trying to save a drowning family. And to be perfectly honest, many experiences were a set back for her—a drain on her spirit. She tells her story from the eyes of an innocent child who didn't understand the violence of an abusive father or the broken spirit of a mother who had come from an equally tragic past. She felt life tearing her apart in ways that were unimaginable. It was a road of repeated abuse, drugs, incest, rape, wrong influences, denial, rejection and silence. It was simply awful—a path of constantly looking for safe places that were rarely found. And, life happened to her at a time when she was most vulnerable. She wanted to give up many times, but still she lived.

This is her story. There is no right or wrong. No judgments and in many cases, no explanations for events unfolding, just raw emotions and vivid memories that are haunting and at times, disabling. Remarkably, the story has a happy ending. It's a story of closure and growth around wounds that have healed and scars that can't be hidden. She talks about abuses so outrageous you will be tempted to pass judgment and call her story incredulous. Yet, my sister gives this journey to those who can hear what she is saying. It is her hope that this will bring about a journey of healing to others, and that this will allow others to make their lives, and the lives of those around them, better.

I am proud of my sister for living and for making something of her life. I give her my validation and my love—something she will never have to want for again. At the end of the day we can say her life was worth living.

From the pen of Mike Probst, the youngest brother:

I've always had the ability to laugh at life, but now it seems to be laughing back. I never wanted to take it too seriously because growing up everyone around me seemed so stressed out and in their own little world. Everything was so big and such a problem that as a child I often felt left out. I remember thinking about the love, affection and instructions I desperately needed in order to survive, but never got. Because of those experiences, I finally hit a wall, and at the age of 37 everything in my life unraveled. I desperately scrambled to pick up the pieces of my childhood and to make sense of them—hoping they would help me figure out who I am. I started embarking on this path after I ended up in jail and then back in my mother's house because I was emotionally handicapped and unable to take care of myself. This step back in time allowed me the opportunity to re-experience where I came from all over again and to know that I needed to heal and move on in my own way. This was also the time that my sister, Sandy, and I started discussing her book, Forbidden Memories, and how she had recovered.

Reading the pages of her manuscript reminded me of many things, especially the confusion I felt as a child. We lived in so many places that I never knew where we belonged, much less where we were going to end up from one moment to the next. School was difficult. We were in so many of them that I felt as if they were glorified day care centers and I never believed I fitted in. No matter where we lived my confusion was pervasive. There was always some type of drama and then trauma that automatically followed. And when things became too hectic we moved again, leaving me even more confused. There were also the days when I was devastated by the violence, wondering what to do. I would just stand there frozen and helpless. Somehow I felt as if I were the problem. Despite all of this, my existence and need for survival was nothing compared to my sister's. She was the one who truly overcame a great injustice. She had to survive the trials and tribulations that would test her heart and ability to become the person she wanted to be and yet was never intended to be. She was the one who was left to deal with the family problems, bury the secrets and try to act as if nothing bad was happening to any of us.

I now know that each of us has a story, which is individually unique, simply because we experience life in our own way. Our stories become our journey and our lives unfold—every one of us was created for a specific reason. The quest to discover who we are, to know where we came from, and know where we want to go is invaluable. However, this journey requires a willingness to take a risk and courage to fight the fight. Facing our fears and uncovering our wounds can be difficult, especially if there are things in the past that hurt so badly we wish God had never dreamed our name. Sometimes emptiness can be so debilitating that we begin to self-destruct like our family did through alcohol, drugs, and violence. We breathe but we don't exist.

I now believe that Sandy had a journey to complete and a destiny to fulfill. It was one that took much courage, soul searching, and basically what many people aren't willing to do and that is to look at themselves and their past. She took our childhood, stared it in the face and overcame the fear of silence. She answered the hard questions, "How can I find myself, get over what happened to me, and be who God intended me to be?" She then found it within herself to write her story, and mine, so that there aren't any secrets left to be told and nothing left to hide from. From the revelation of these secrets comes hope that other people will learn from her experiences and begin to believe that recovery is possible.

Because of Sandy's book, we have reconnected and are venturing down some of the same paths today. Even though I am still in the process of learning from her, I have a stronger foundation. I am understanding that I, and everyone else, can make our lives what we want and have the things we hold important.

In closing, Sandy is a living testimony of change. She is someone who traded in the traumatic cards she was dealt for a new set and a new life. Sandy is a true warrior with a life that has meaning and value. When you see her, you will know she has a sense of ownership and possession of her life, a sense of purpose and balance. She is a true conqueror who had the courage to go back and relive the past and this time to win. May each person reading this book find the ability to do the same as a result of pursuing their own journey to healing.

CONTENTS

Chapter 1

A Desperate Cry for Help

IN THE EARLY MORNING HOURS of June 16, 1997, I lay on an emergency room gurney, virtually lifeless from a potentially lethal overdose of 180 muscle relaxers.

Every organ in my thin body began shutting down. I was having one uncontrollable seizure after another. My heart rate was virtually non-existent, and my face reflected a ghostly, corpse-like shade of ash white. My skin was cold and clammy, my body temperature dropped too low to sustain life. No longer able to support my own breath, the doctors forced a long tube down my throat so that a machine could breathe for me. Moments later, I lay in a lifeless, fetal position in a coma.

There was nothing left for the doctors to do but wait, so I was transferred to the intensive care unit to see if I would ever regain consciousness. The hours slipped by and then I took a potentially irreversible turn for the worse: while experiencing hallucinations in an extremely combative unconscious state, I tried to pull out the IVs, and the tube in my throat. Although the medical staff prevented me from ripping out the tubes, there was now deep concern—my actions and unresponsiveness to pain were clinical signs of brain damage. To make matters worse, aspiration pneumonia had developed from the charcoal used to pump out my stomach.

On the fifth day, I finally awoke from my coma, reasonably intact. For a few moments, I wasn't sure what had happened, and why I was lying in the hospital hooked up to machines in an intensive care unit. Suddenly, I remembered the overwhelming need to kill myself, and the overdose in the bathroom at work with my supervisor and employee assistance counselor sitting in the next room. I was instantly horrified and disappointed that I hadn't died

I remembered thinking as I took the pills, surely I'm about to die. I was glad my pain and misery would soon be over. At the same time, my heart was filled with fear and panic because I was about to face death on its terms, and I must have been a bad little girl who was going to hell for her transgressions.

Lying in the hospital bed, I was consumed with a resurgence of memory about why I had tried to take my own life at a mere thirty-three years of age. I remembered the intense feelings of worthlessness; fear that things in my life were never going to be different; and the exhaustion from the constant strain of trying to survive emotionally from one day to the next.

The memories kept rolling over me, as did the fear that I might do or say something wrong. I was afraid that I would never fit in anywhere, and would always drown in loneliness because I didn't know how to have a "normal" relationship with anyone.

Finally, the most painful memories resurfaced: believing that I would never know how it felt to be loved in a good way, and that I would never be able to forget the terrible pain of the child who resided inside me. It was her pain and memories of unspoken secrets that I couldn't bear for even one more day.

After remembering why I chose death over life, a small voice within me spoke: This isn't supposed to be happening again...I am supposed to be dead this time. I don't want my life back, to continue living with my past hurts, or to be alone anymore. I don't want to be alive!

I was afraid of being in trouble now that I had survived my worst suicide attempt. Would I lose my job? Who was mad at me? How would I explain what had happened? Would I be locked up again? I felt alone, with the sinking feeling in the pit of my stomach that I would have been better off if I had died.

My body felt as if it had been beaten and left for dead on the side of the road. There were bruises all over my arms from the IVs, and every muscle in my body ached from the convulsions and vomiting. My throat was swollen and raw from the breathing tube, and my lungs were tight and full of mucus from the pneumonia. I wasn't able to talk because of the rigid tube that had been down my throat for almost a week. I was so weak and physically sick that I could barely get in the police car to be taken across the street to the psychiatric unit where I was placed on a 24-hour suicide watch.

I knew my desperate act would leave my work associates, friends, and the psychiatric hospital staff wondering what could possibly have happened to me that would make me feel as if I had no other option but to end my life. Pondering that question, my life flashed before me.

PART I

THE EXPERIENCE OF SURVIVAL

Chapter 2

In the Beginning

My story began on October 24, 1963 in Jacksonville, Florida, when I was born to Peyton and Hilda Lowden. Dad was an overweight and overbearing bald man. Strangely enough, I never knew very much about him, and even less about his family and background. At some point in my life I learned that he was adopted, and never knew his real parents. I vaguely remember the woman who was his adoptive mother and my grandmother. Dad was an ill-tempered man who liked to control and hurt people. Perhaps that explains his choice of career as a police officer— a niche in society where he thought his behavior might be more tolerated. I remember hearing him brag about how the people he arrested were afraid of him because he beat them up before he took them to jail. His temper caught up with him though—he was eventually dismissed for brutality. After that, he struggled to find employment, until he became a projectionist at a local movie theatre.

When my mother met my father, she was an eighteen-year-old who had just run away from a miserable and abusive childhood in Hampton, South Carolina. She grew up in a home with nine brothers and sisters, a hard-working father, and a mother she described as "crazy." Hilda Lowden was small in stature, had beautiful features, and a smile of innocence that would make you think nothing bad had ever happened to her.

When I was a little girl, I remember my mother ingraining in me the memories of her frightening childhood. Many children she grew up with had to work in the cotton fields because of extreme impoverishment. Mom was also left with no option but to perform hard labor in order to buy food for her survival and clothe herself for school. There were many stories of her hunger because there was nothing but potatoes to eat, and she often had no shoes to wear. The cotton fields weren't kind to anyone, and they left my mother with many emotional scars and a sense of being alone and helpless.

My mother struggled with terrible nightmares, and often told me of their awful contents. She confessed that as a little girl she was afraid she would never graduate from high school, and that she would never be able to escape from Hampton. She said her biggest problem was that she had been deprived of life's basic necessity—love.

The unusual part of my mother's childhood was her memories of her parents' constant fighting. Families in that era usually argued in private so no one would ever know of the family's imperfections. Women tended to be rather submissive, thereby maintaining their false sense of harmony.

A pivotal moment in my mother's life occurred during one of these "private" arguments between her parents which escalated so wildly out of control that her dad stabbed her mother. It completely changed Mom's perception of her father. She had always believed he was special— now she had to face his horrible act of violence.

She also told stories of things that had happened to her that left so much unexplained. I could only surmise as to the true nature of the events. For instance, once as a little girl she awoke in her father's bed, unable to see or walk. She was taken to a doctor, but no medical explanations could account for the sudden onset of this physical malady. Whenever she told me that story, I could hear the fear and sadness in her voice, and I wondered what had really happened to her. I felt sorry for her, but I knew of no way to ease her pain. Later, as an adult, I wondered if she had been sexually abused.

There were many stories about how Mom and her mother, Ruth, never really got along. One of the stories I heard repeatedly was about how Grandmother Ruth reacted when Mom, who was 18 years old married my 34 year old father, and became pregnant with me. They were standing at the top of a staircase when Mom proudly revealed her pregnancy. Upon hearing the news, Grandmother Ruth became so enraged that she shoved her pregnant daughter down the stairs. Mom never said why Grandmother Ruth got so angry.

I was the eldest of three children, with two younger brothers, Pat and Mike. We lived in a small, quaint brick house. It had a tiny fenced-in backyard, and a barbecue pit and garage my dad had built. My room was tucked away at the end of the hall, adjacent to my parent's room. My brothers shared a room at the other end of the house.

Because my room was beside my parents', I often heard them fighting. They didn't just have disagreements—they screamed, broke furniture, and physically hurt each other. Every time they started quarreling, my heart sank to my stomach in pure fear, and I would hide in my room and pray that my father wouldn't hurt my mother.

In order to cope, I would clutch the stuffed, pink kitty my mother had given me when I was born. It was the most precious thing I had—it made me feel safe. I carried it around by the tail, sucked my thumb, and rubbed its tail on my upper lip. My pink kitty and I were inseparable, and I loved it with all my little being. There were occasions when I lost my kitty, or just its tail, and I would become distraught until I found it again, or Mom sewed the tail back on.

My life was held together by my pink friend. I clung to it during the difficult times, like my first experience with my Grandmother Ruth. When I was about two years old, my mother was seven months pregnant with my youngest brother, Mike. She took me, and my younger brother, Pat, to stay at my grandmother's house while my dad went to the Army Reserve for two weeks. For some reason, Grandmother Ruth wouldn't let us stay in her house, so the three of us stayed in the cramped quarters of her 13-foot travel trailer in her yard.

One morning, Mom and Grandmother Ruth started fighting over some diapers. Grandmother Ruth became so angry that she started beating my mother with a broom. I was panicked with fear—it was obvious Grandmother Ruth was out of control—and I had no idea how to make her stop hitting my pregnant mother.

Grandmother Ruth pounded heavily on Mom, while I stood paralyzed and crying in the corner of the room. Finally, one of my uncles ran in and stopped the incessant beating. Since Grandmother Ruth could no longer vent her anger on Mom, she quickly turned to me and pushed me down a flight of stairs. I landed at the bottom of the stairwell, with my mouth bleeding and my body bruised. Confused, I cried out with gut-wrenching fear. I had no idea what had just happened, or why, and I was terrified of my grandmother from that moment on.

My grandmother wasn't the only person I had to fear. There was my dad who had returned home from the reserves. One day he took my brothers and me to the store with him and made us wait for him in the car. Being typical children, we started exploring everything in our encapsulated environment until we found something that fascinated us— a book of matches. We had no idea what they were, but we were curious and wanted see what they did. Being the eldest, I figured out how to light one of the matches. Surprised by the strong charred smell it produced, I wanted to light another one to recapture that wonderful smell, until I saw Dad coming toward the car. I panicked because I knew I was going to get in terrible trouble for exploring and lighting the match.

Dad climbed back into the car where he could easily smell the remnants of the match. His face turned bright red as he spun around to the back seat and began hitting all three of us. I put my hands over my head to shield my face, but he struck me solidly several times, leaving marks on my face and tears streaming from my eyes.

Then there was the garage my dad had built adjacent to the house. There was space to park the cars, to work on projects, and a bathroom with a shower located in the far corner of the cinder block building. Void of any windows, the bathroom was an eerie place, especially to a little girl. It had a peculiar musty smell, like a damp closet that had been closed off for years, growing mold and mildew as it aged with time. With no direct sunlight, the dank environment attracted spiders and other insects that made their homes in the shower.

I especially remember the shower because Mom became upset when my brothers and I got dirty from playing outside. She was a perfectionist about her precious house. She didn't want us to trample any dirt into it, so she insisted that Dad take us to the garage to shower. As I stood there cold and naked, I could barely breathe for fear that the insects would crawl on me or bite me.

Much later, I learned from my brother Mike that it wasn't just the insects that bothered me, but the fact that my father insisted on showering with me. As a child, the things that likely occurred in that shower caused me to block out the true nature of those disturbing experiences.

I repeatedly begged Mom not to make me shower in the garage, but she never questioned why I was so terrified. Instead, I was forced to shower in that awful place wondering how long I was going to be able to maintain my sanity.

I was now about five years old, and I tried to stay as close as possible to Mom because she was the most important thing to me. Whether it was out of a sense of responsibility, or love, I cherished her more than anything in life. I wanted Mom to love me and to think I was special. But also because I thought it was up to me to protect her from my abusive dad, because she couldn't take care of herself. And, I was the only one of us three kids she had entrusted with her painful feelings and childhood memories.

Despite my perception of her as helpless, there were occasions when she took charge of her life. Like the time she decided to go to night school at the local junior college to study nursing. She had to learn to be something if she was ever to escape Dad and his physical abuse, and her childhood. I didn't like the fact that she went to school in the evening because it left us kids alone with Dad. There was no way of telling if he was going to be in a good mood or not, or if he might thrash me for no apparent reason.

One evening, I knew Mom was going to be home late, so as I often did for security, I crawled into her side of the bed and fell asleep before she got home. In a dreamy state, I heard her voice, but continued drifting back to sleep until Dad picked me up and carried me to my own bed.

I must have drifted back off to sleep again before I was re-awakened by Mom crying and screaming, "Please stop hurting me!" I quietly sneaked around the corner to see what was wrong. I was stunned to see the bedroom in complete disarray with clothes thrown all over the room, lamps broken, and knick-knacks strewn all over the bed. I then looked up to see Mom standing wide-eyed, on the bed, as Dad threw dresser drawers at her. She was screaming and crying for him to stop, but he just kept on.

I stood there crying and in complete shock, with my heart aching for her. I ran recklessly into the room and begged Dad to stop hurting her. He turned and glared at me in an all-too-familiar fury, while Mom attempted to escape to the hall between our rooms. When he saw her trying to flee, he ran after her, grabbed her, and began punching her in the face. As he repeatedly bashed her, bright red blood ran out of the corner of her mouth. I stood there in disbelief as he yelled, "I'll kill you!" Then I saw the knife in his hand and the rage in his eyes.

I was crying and kept screaming, "Stop! Stop! Why are you doing this? Why?" For some reason, Dad found it necessary to turn around and face me to answer my question.

He said that Mom was sleeping with her professor at the junior college! I had already met this professor, Gene, and thought he was only a friend, so I kept telling Dad, "That's not true! And I can prove it." I ran into my room and dialed Gene's telephone number, praying that God would let him be home. Within seconds, I heard Gene pick up the receiver. My trembling voice pleaded with him to talk with Dad. Without waiting for his response, I laid the phone down and ran back into the hall and told Dad that Gene was on the phone so he could ask him if he and Mom were sleeping together.

I don't know why, but he quit hitting her just long enough to go and yell at Gene. I thought that was our opportunity to get out alive, so I ran into my brothers' room, woke them up, and gasped to them, "Get in the car!" On shaking legs, I ran to get Mom. I told her we needed to leave before Dad got off the phone. Once in the car, she sat there with her hands shaking and a look of fright flooding her face, while I anxiously kept watch for Dad to explode out of the house toward us.

I screamed at Mom and a few seconds later she sped away. All four of us were crying. We didn't know what to do, or where to go. So, we drove around hoping we could figure out what to do.

Just when we thought we were out of immediate danger, Dad pulled up behind us, and tried to run us off the road. My brothers cried loudly in the back seat. Fear engulfed us again.

Mom's hands gripped the steering wheel tightly, as she tried to avoid veering off the road. But Dad obviously intended to stop us—no matter what the consequences. So she pulled off the road, and with a mask of terror covering her face, got out of the car. I was afraid he would kill her right there, but instead, he told her, "I'll kill you if you don't come home now!" Mom bowed her head in submission, and drove us back to the house we had fled only minutes earlier.

The fights and trying to protect my mother and brothers became the norm for me.

The fighting and abuse from my dad weighed heavily on me, as some very strange and unsettling things began happening to me. When I became scared, I literally saw things change before my eyes. I would be standing there looking at the person who was yelling or threatening me, and all of a sudden, they would seem as if they were way down a long corridor or tunnel. They seemed so distant and looked so small, as if I were looking in the wrong end of a pair of binoculars. My hearing would become distorted and faint, as if people were talking to me from miles away and I could barely hear them. Then my skin had the sensation that something was crawling on it, while my face and scalp tingled. Finally, things seemed to move in slow motion—as if time were standing still. I didn't understand what was happening, and I never told anyone about this because I was too afraid of getting into trouble. I later learned this was called, "dissociating."

At the same time the physical manifestations appeared, I also started having disturbing nightmares, which left me crying and in cold sweats. One nightmare visited me over and over again for many years. I dreamed there was a large white wall and one part of it wasn't solid, even though it looked like it was. I would stand at that one particular section of the wall, fearful because I could put my hand through it and watch my body disappear into nothingness. I was even more afraid I wouldn't be able to get back out again. I would then walk by a section of the wall where I could hear a voice coming from inside, but I was unable to see who it was. Sometimes I thought it was me behind the wall crying for help, for someone to let me out, but I was too afraid to go into the wall to find out. Other times, I thought it was my mother crying for someone to rescue her—but I was too afraid to go in after her because I was terrified that I would be lost in there forever and no one would know where to look for me. It was like I was in The Twilight Zone.

With my family falling apart and the fighting between my parents escalating, an event happened that changed my life forever. I was six years old and my brothers and I went to play at a neighbor's house. This was unusual for us, because the whole neighborhood knew how abusive and volatile my father was, thus scaring away any children, and especially, their parents. Since my father wasn't home we made our way over to Riley's place. We chose his home because he was one of the only kids in the neighborhood who would play with us, and it seemed as if his dad let him do whatever he wanted. We started off wrestling around and playing games in the yard, but soon became bored and decided to go exploring in his dad's garage.

I was amazed to find that his garage wasn't like ours: void of the damp musty smells, it was bright and full of stuff to play with. Most of all—it didn't scare me. After looking around and exploring for a while, we found a dartboard and several darts lying in the middle of the room. My brothers and I had never seen anything like darts before and we were excited, as if we had just discovered the toy of the century. After Riley got permission from his dad, we took the darts outside and began throwing them at the trees, up in the air, and anywhere we could find to throw or stick them. We soon grew tired of this too, so we went back inside the garage to find the dartboard.

As I walked into the garage, I saw a door to the far right-hand side of the wall where the dartboard hung, and an old ragged couch sitting to the left of it. In the center of the room sat a long narrow bench that we used to stand on to throw the darts at the dartboard. We each took turns throwing the darts, while someone else leaned on the couch waiting to pull the darts out of the board. With great excitement, I had just finished my turn and ran quickly over to sit on the arm of the couch so I could take my turn retrieving the darts. It was my brother, Pat's turn and he threw his first dart. After it landed securely on the board, I reached up, pulled it out, and then sat back down on the arm of the couch, awaiting the next throw.

The next dart left his tiny five-year-old hand, but instead of landing on the dartboard, it hit me in the middle of my left eye. I had no idea what had just happened, but all of a sudden, everything turned black and agonizing pain shot through my face. Without thinking, I reached up, felt the dart in my eye and quickly pulled it out. Everything became intensely bright, and the light caused excruciating pain to well up and shoot through my eye. I felt something warm running down the side of my face: it was the fluid draining from the center of my eye.

Terrified, I began screaming for someone to take me home so Mom could help me. Everyone just stood there in shock. No one moved—not even to breathe. They just left me standing in the middle of the room, sobbing. Since no one did anything, I put my hand over my eye and took off running down the street, crying, and yelling, "Mom!"

I finally made it home and opened the door to see Mom on the telephone. She turned around and looked at me, and became white as a ghost as she hung up the telephone. Without hesitation, she picked up the phone again, but she couldn't get her hands to stop shaking long enough to make the call for help. Instead, she loaded me into the car and drove me to the doctor's office. The nurse immediately escorted us into an examination room where we sat for what seemed like forever. I was suffocating with fear of the unknown and dread of what my punishment would be once we got home. The doctor finally came in and anxiously explained to Mom that she needed to rush me to the hospital for emergency surgery. The words "emergency surgery" scared me, as I wondered what that truly meant, and if it would hurt. With no explanation or comforting, I was taken into surgery for a procedure which lasted hours: my lens, pupil, and cornea were punctured; debris was floating around in my eye; I had lost almost all of the vitreous fluid inside my eyeball; and I needed stitches.

After surgery, I was in excruciating pain. When I tried to open my "good" eye to see my hospital room or to eat, immense discomfort shot through my now, "bad" eye, as if I were being impaled with the dart all over again. I couldn't sit up or lean forward, as the pressure on my face and eye was too great. Since there was nothing I could do to avoid the pain, I learned to just keep both my eyes shut and lie perfectly still. There were many days when I wanted to cry because of the accident, and because I was now legally blind, but I couldn't even do this because the salt from my tears would seep through the stitches and burn my eye.

I went home about a week later and was confined to bed because the doctors were afraid the stitches would pop loose if I put any pressure on my eye. I was terribly frustrated being a child and having to stay still so long. I wanted to go outside, play, and forget this whole thing.

The only redeeming memory that stands out for me during this whole incident was Gene—Mom's secret boyfriend—trying to help take care of me. I was confined to lying perfectly flat in the bed. I found it extremely difficult to eat and was reduced to ingesting nothing more than soup. This was particularly aggravating because I always seemed to spill the hot liquid, soaking my clothes and bed. I was so frustrated with the whole process that I almost gave up hope of ever being normal again. Somehow,

Gene recognized my frustration, and this led to us having a little secret that we never told anyone: he allowed me to drink my soup out of a straw. Because Mom forbade it, for reasons I didn't understand, we would sneak around using the "forbidden straw technique." He made a joke of it, which made things a little easier and more fun for me. It was a trivial thing, but it was the first time in my life I could remember anyone treating me as though I were special.

I don't know what the accident represented to my mother, but afterwards she began treating me like there was something wrong with me. I could see it in her eyes that I was different in some way, but I didn't understand how. Inside, I was still the same child who needed my mother to love me, but everything changed now that I was a six-year-old girl with an ugly eye. I later learned that Mom indeed viewed me differently when she said, "You were no longer my perfect little girl. I had to step away from you."

This was just the beginning of numerous surgeries and a complete change in how Mom treated me. After this, the days grew lonelier as I ached for my mother's love. My agony was further complicated when my brother, Pat, was severely punished for hurting me. Dad beat him senselessly in the middle of the street while the whole neighborhood watched. When I heard of the anguish Pat suffered because of the accident, I was filled with immense guilt and grief, and felt responsible for his pain and embarrassment.

Mom's relationship with Gene continued, and I hoped that he would be the one who would change our family's future. I thought he must have been Mom's dream come true, especially since I believed he was the neatest person I had ever met. He was a very quiet man, caring and kind—the opposite of my father. One evening when my brothers and I were spending the night at Gene's garage apartment, I became sick with a fever and vomited. Much to my surprise, he stayed up all night with me in the bathroom, even while I threw up. I couldn't believe that anyone would do something like that for me. In some way, it made me feel special again, as it kind of reminded me of our "forbidden straw" secret.

However, Gene always seemed to be a very lonely person, and I never saw him with any friends or family. I didn't understand it, but we seemed to be his only connection to the outside world. Somehow I picked up on his sadness, and I could feel his loneliness when he was around us, like he wished he had a family to call his own. He used to talk about wanting a little dog, so that he wouldn't have to be alone. We all thought that a little cuddly creature would be great company for him. So, on his birthday, we surprised him with his very own little Pekinese puppy. When we gave him the little bundle of joy, Gene seemed so happy that he immediately bonded with the little dog. It was like he had found a safe person to be with, and one who would love him, no matter what.

After Mom and Gene met and fell in love, things at home became more confusing and stirred up than usual. Then a strange event occurred that should have been a clue to Mom that all was not well with her new-found love. It happened one afternoon when Mom and Dad were fighting. The yelling, punching, and threats were explosive, and eventually escalated to the point of violence. For safety reasons, Mom threw us kids in the car and drove to a local hotel for the day. I remember this vividly because I still had the patch on my eye and the hotel had a pool I really wanted to swim in. I hadn't been able to play like other kids since my accident, so I begged Mom to let me take a dip in the pool. She wouldn't let me swim until nightfall for two reasons: my patch would get wet if there were other kids in the pool, and my dad could drive by and see us if it were daylight. Although I was disappointed with the delay, I was filled with great anticipation for my chance to be a kid again, even if for just a few precious moments.

After nightfall, she kept her promise by letting me get in the water to wade around. I couldn't enjoy myself though because I was afraid Dad would drive by and see me in the pool, and then know where to find, and possibly kill, Mom. After all, I'd already learned that Dad could find us no matter where we went.

Later that night Mom explained to me and my brothers that Gene was coming to get us from the hotel, and we were going to run away with him to live "happily ever after." Her fear of my father finding us was apparent, but so was the hope that now filled her eyes, as she awaited her "prince's" arrival. I was so excited that we were finally going to be rid of my father that I forced myself to sit up all night and wait with Mom. But, at dawn Gene was nowhere to be found. Defeat completely encapsulated my mother's face while my child's heart had to bear one more of her disappointments as well as my own.

By late morning, Mom realized there was no other option but for us to return home. Terrified, she called the police to escort us to the house to make sure that Dad wouldn't kill her or us kids. When we pulled into the driveway with the police, my heart pounded with such fear that I thought my chest was going to explode, while Mom looked as if she were going to pass out. We slowly walked into the house where we saw beer cans lying everywhere and Gene sitting there, helping my dad get drunk! I stood there confused, not understanding why Gene had done this. After the police left, an ugly fight ensued and life was back to it's normal chaos.

Time continued to pass in much the same way until I was eight years old and Mom explained that she had spoken with my father several years earlier about getting a divorce. With tear-filled eyes and a trembling voice, she said, "He swore that if I ever left him, he would hunt me down, kill me, and bury me!" Hence, she maintained the role of the obedient wife, while the fighting escalated in frequency and volatility.

Then one day, during that same year of my life, with the support of Gene and the police department, Mom found the courage to file for a divorce, even though it was done deceptively. She created a story that led my father to believe that them divorcing would be like a fresh start for them and it would one day lead to them remarrying. This deception was needed because women of that day could not divorce their husband's without their consent and signature, and it bought my mother both.

Despite the promise of remarrying my mother, Dad did everything he could do to prolong the process, and it took almost six months before the divorce was final. He then moved out of the house and into a tiny, dilapidated apartment. I wasn't sure why, and it confused me greatly, but I felt sorry that he was reduced to living in what appeared to be a shack with shabby furniture. I wasn't sure how to make the pity I felt for him co-exist with the fear, anger, violence and abuse I had endured when he lived with us.

Despite the fact that Mom and Dad were divorced, he kept coming to the house to start fights, beat on Mom, and terrify us kids. He always managed to incite a huge argument, resulting in Mom, or a neighbor, calling the police. It was during one of these fights that the police finally admitted to Mom that they knew about Dad's violent temper because there were records of at least 15 domestic violence calls on him when he was married to his first wife! This information sparked the beginning of Mom and Gene devising a plan that I would soon experience firsthand.

Chapter 3

A Fresh Start

MY BROTHERS AND I CAME HOME from school one day to find our clothes packed in paper grocery sacks and Mom demanding, "Get in the back of the car!" I could sense that something was terribly wrong, but I didn't know what. This felt different. It wasn't filled with the same fear and desperation I felt when Mom and Dad argued, only worry about what was getting ready to happen. My thoughts quickly turned to the idea that maybe we were finally going to run away from my father, and, if we were, would he be able to find us?

Mom drove us to the Jacksonville Airport where Gene was waiting for us in the parking lot. As soon as he saw us coming, he jumped out of his car to make sure no one was following us. Mom briskly shoved us and our paper grocery bags into the back seat of Gene's little red and black Caprice, and told us to keep quiet and sit still until they finished packing the car. I was afraid because Mom was nervous, acting as if we would get in trouble if someone discovered what we were doing. The sound of the trunk slamming shut was my cue that our journey was about to begin— to where—I had no idea.

Seconds later, I saw Mom run back to her car, nervously place a note on the dashboard and lock it. Speeding out of the airport parking lot, it was clear that we were leaving Jacksonville, and my father, for good. Once we were clear of the city limits, Mom turned around and announced, "We're going to be living with Gene from now on, and we're going to Hawaii so we can get married! We're then moving to Australia so we can get as far away from your father as possible. Surely he won't be able to find us if we are on the other side of the world."

I didn't know what was going to be worse—taking the chance of running away from dad, or riding from Florida to California in the back of Gene's tiny car without going crazy. We were typical children with short attention spans and a need to be constantly entertained, but in our cramped "capsule" we were only given a few pieces of paper and ink pens to color with. We soon ran out of paper to draw on, and boredom set in with only ink pens to play with. We were left with nothing to occupy our little minds and hands except the white seats and white side panels of Gene's car. By the time we were halfway across the country, the white interior was quite a masterpiece of artwork, featuring ink drawings by three budding young artists! Gene was angry and tried his hardest to get the ink stains out, but to no avail. It was our contribution to the journey—unappreciated as it was.

There were many stops at motels and hotels before we reached California. At each one, I was afraid to go outside to play because I was terrified I would run into Dad, and seeing him meant death. I remember one little motel out in the middle of nowhere where I fearfully hid in the room. Mom, noticing my new fear of being outside, tried to convince me that it was safe to at least walk around the motel. In my child-like naivete, I tried to act brave by venturing to the small pool located in the middle of the complex. I looked around for a long while to make sure it was safe before I settled in for a short stay by the pool, soaking in the warm rays of the sun.

A few minutes later, I thought I saw Dad standing on the other side of the pool. My breathing immediately stopped and my heart started racing as I tried to figure out a way to get around the pool without him seeing me. I bowed my head, hiding my face as close to my chest as possible, while I bolted to the room to warn Mom of our immediate danger. With tears running down my face, I stuttered, "Da—Dad's at the pool! He's here to kill us!"

She tried to persuade me that I was mistaken, but she wanted to be sure, as one mistake could cost her, and us, our lives. With each step back to the pool, my legs shook violently and my hands trembled. We hid behind a wall and peered around the corner so I could point out the person I thought was Dad. But, much to my surprise, it was only a man who looked like him. Despite my mistake, I maintained a vigilant watch for my father, while praying that God wouldn't let him find us.

We finally made it all the way to Arizona and stayed overnight in an old, run-down hotel that was barely habitable. I don't remember much about Arizona, only the morning we were to leave. I was weary from running from Dad, wondering whether he was going to catch up with us and kill us. I was especially tired that morning, but I still got up early with the family and packed my paper grocery bag, and hoped that Dad wasn't standing outside, waiting to blow us away.

Without incident, we got in the car and proceeded to drive to California so we could catch a plane to Hawaii. Two hours down the road I woke up from a hazy sleep, only to panic because I couldn't find my pink kitty. I frantically searched the car, but pink kitty wasn't there. Terrified, I shook Mom's shoulder, and screamed in a panicked voice, "I can't find my pink kitty!" Amazingly, she didn't seem too concerned and just ignored me. "Mom—please, please, help me find my friend. We gotta go back to the hotel—pink kitty must be there!"

But Mom looked at me with a blank expression on her face and, without any explanation, unemotionally stated, "We can't go back." I looked at Gene for help, but he just sat there and didn't say a word.

I felt as if my heart was literally being ripped out of my chest, and the core of my being was cut wide open, leaving it completely exposed and vulnerable to the world. I just lay on the back seat and cried uncontrollably, wishing that someone would either help me find my friend or kill me.

Hours later, Mom admitted, "I think your kitty was put on top of the car when we were packing at the hotel. It probably blew off when we drove away."

I kept crying and felt worse than ever now that my only friend in life was lying all alone in a parking lot, or on the side of the road.

We ended up at the next hotel in the next unknown town with me still lying in the back seat, sobbing uncontrollably. I managed to drag my weary and broken spirit into the hotel room where all I could do was lie on the bed in a fetal position and cry, while Mom did nothing to comfort me. I found myself retching with such emotional and physical pain that I couldn't eat or sleep. I felt as if I was dying on the inside, as if I had lost a part of myself. I desperately needed someone to help me cope with this, but instead, I was left alone, wondering if I was going to go crazy from the feelings of hurt and abandonment. I had lost my only security and the only safe thing in my life. I had no defenses in my hateful, hurtful world. Choked with emotional pain, I wondered, who was going to take care of me now that I had lost my only friend and confidant? And, how was it that Mom could have known how much pain I was in and not have gone back to get my kitty? Why didn't she comfort me through this? Why was I left alone in my hour of greatest need? But, most of all—how was I going to survive without my pink kitty?

For several weeks I was devastated. I felt as if all my life energy had been drained from my body. I didn't care anymore. Why should I? After all, it was obvious that Mom didn't care about me anymore.

We finally made it to Hawaii relieved that we had reached our destination without interference from Dad. We lived in Honolulu and Waikiki Beach for about three months and Mom and Gene got married. I remember the wedding ceremony like it was yesterday. I was uncomfortable watching my mother get married, especially since it wasn't a traditional wedding. Mom wore a plain brown dress and Gene a suit and tie. The wedding was kind of eerie as it reminded me of one of those Justice of the Peace ceremonies, but in a church. However, this was a wonderful time for Mom because she really believed Gene loved her, despite his getting drunk with Dad in Jacksonville. This was what she had been looking for all of her life—someone to love her enough to rescue her from her miserable existence; run away with her; marry her; and live happily ever after.

With Hawaii now our new home, we rented an apartment near the magnificent beaches. It was a wonderful place with its warm, blue tropical water, the grass a shade of green I had never seen before, and people with perfect tans.

After Mom and Gene were married, it seemed like things were finally going to be all right, even though my devastation and depression continued from the loss of my pink kitty. I basically retreated far into myself, so I could try to live with the deprivation of the only thing that had made me feel safe. Then one day, Mom decided she knew the solution to my problem: we would buy another pink kitty and all would be well. I didn't want a replacement—I wanted my friend back! In my six year old mind it was hard enough for me to want to keep living, without being forced to walk around looking for something to replace my pink kitty—especially with the person who wouldn't comfort me or go back to get my friend. Despite my resistance, we walked the streets of Hawaii for hours, going in and out of stores and looking through mounds of stuffed animals.

We finally came to a store where we found a pink kitty which sort of resembled my lost friend. But, it was different in a lot of ways: its face looked the opposite way; it wasn't worn out; the tail hadn't been repeatedly sewn on; the pink hair wasn't rubbed off; and it smelled different. I finally just gave up and let Mom buy the new pink kitty for me since it seemed so important to her, and it appeared to help relieve her guilt. However, I wasn't ever able to attach myself to this new pink kitty as I had my lost friend.

We left Florida in such a hurry that there wasn't much time to pack our paper grocery bags. This was also true for Mom, as she only took a few clothes and even fewer prized possessions. One of those prized possessions was her most valued object in the whole world—a black pantsuit my dad had given her. It was the first nice thing anyone had ever given her and it seemed to make her feel special.

After a month or so, the bliss of the marriage and hanging out on the beautiful Hawaiian beaches with my new and improved family vanished in Mom and Gene's bedroom in the midst of a horrible fight. Mom was screaming and crying hysterically, and her swollen face and tear-filled eyes let me know that she was in pain. I looked over at Gene, and was shocked to see that he was very cold and calculating, showing nothing but a face of stone. Mom just stood there crying while Gene spewed profanities and called her every curse word he could think of. Then, out of nowhere, he pushed her against the closet door and began slapping her. I then saw something in Gene's eyes that showed me he was trying to figure out what he could do next to hurt her in the most profound way.

A sense of euphoria seemed to glaze over his face as he went directly to her closet and pulled out her black pantsuit. Staring intently at Mom, with no remorse and only cold determination, he ripped it apart. I watched the devastation come over my mother's face, the disbelief that this was happening again. I couldn't believe it was happening either, and at that moment in time, I felt as if my mother and I became one. My heart ached for her, and I wished there was something I could do to take her pain away, but I didn't know how. History was repeating itself—the only thing I knew how to do was to carry her pain for her.

As time went on and the fighting continued, I learned to isolate and hide myself from the world and everyone around me. This was the only way I knew how to deal with the saddened and confusing feelings of my return to hell, especially without the comfort and safety of my pink kitty and my alienation from Mom because I was no longer "perfect." I discovered a hiding place at the apartments in the fenced area where the trash was stored. In sadness and despair, I would sneak through the door and sit alone in the corner for long periods while the fighting continued. I was so confused, so hurt, and so lonely that I believed I was only safe and acceptable when I was hiding behind a trash-can. It was too hurtful to be around my family, much less other people.

Meanwhile, we knew Dad would be looking for us, so it was time to head to Australia, a place clear on the other side of the world—a place where Dad hopefully couldn't find us. However, Mom was afraid that Dad, being a former police officer, had leveraged old contacts and convinced the authorities to place a warrant out for her arrest for fleeing the state of Florida with us kids. And if that were true, the background check for the passports would alert the police to our whereabouts. Thus, we decided not to go to Australia, but packed our few belongings and headed back to California hoping to find a place to call home.

Chapter 4

On the Road Again

LOS ANGELES, CALIFORNIA, was a huge city, and we drove around all day looking for a cheap place to rent. We ended up in Santa Monica driving through some of the poorest and dirtiest parts of the city. I sat quietly crying, afraid that we would end up living in this morbid place. Hours later, we drove by a house that was over-grown with shrubs and vines and looked as if it should have been condemned. To my embarrassment and dismay, we rented that place with its haphazard front yard, faded pink paint, and broken-down garage.

My bedroom was located in the back of the house overlooking a jungle masquerading as a backyard. Vines and over-grown shrubs were everywhere; you would have sworn you were out in the middle of the rain forest. In my childish view, I thought the backyard was great because it hid us from the rest of the world and provided me with plenty of places to explore. At the same time, I felt ashamed because it didn't look like other people's yards.

For the first time, I knew we not only looked poor, but that we were poor. The entire neighborhood was a destitute and low-class area, with dirt-poor families who had virtually no money or resources. Not only was I disappointed, but I also wondered how everything had gotten progressively worse since we had left Jacksonville. And, would the rest of our lives be like this?

In many ways, I thought I ended up with the best room in the house, because my closet was neatly tucked away under a stairwell. God must have been looking out for me since that closet became my hide-out and my escape from the world. It also kept me from having to reduce myself to hiding behind trash cans.

In my closet, I put the only prized possession I had left in the world—my little red and white 45-rpm record player. It was the only thing of mine, besides my clothes, that had survived the trip from Jacksonville. I didn't have toys, my pink kitty—nothing else of my own. I took my precious commodity and a light and began forging my secret place in the wonderful closet that reminded me of a hidden cave. By the time I was finished, I had a pillow to sit on, a couple of books to look at, and some cookies hidden in the corner for special occasions. This was truly my sacred place and I spent many hours in my closet. It was like my secret world where I could escape all of the fighting and pain—a world where I could be safe.

I was in the third grade in Santa Monica and I hated the school and the kids. I was new and definitely didn't fit in with anyone. Again, my injured eye made me different and left the kids playing cruel jokes and making fun of me. They thought it was funny that my bad eye drifted out as if it was staring off into space, that I couldn't play like normal kids because I didn't have any depth perception and that my once blue eye was now a strange shade of green. They didn't quite know what to think of a kid with one blue and one green eye, and frankly, neither did I.

When it was time for recess, I wanted so badly to play with the other girls, but I wasn't usually invited to play. So I ended up watching while my heart silently yearned to fit in. I wanted to be liked and accepted. Instead, I was afraid of everyone and everything. It was a good thing we didn't stay in any place too long because I don't think I would have ever liked it at that school.

Mom and Gene's unhappiness with each other persisted in Santa Monica, much like it did in Hawaii. Gene became more agitated by the day because Mom got a job at one of the hospitals working as a registered nurse on the three-to-eleven shift, and this left him at home to play surrogate mother. His angry demeanor showed us that he resented every second of his "motherly" duties to us kids, and I became afraid of doing anything that would possibly upset him. Getting enough sleep was also out of the question for all of us because we only had one car. Gene woke us around 10:30 p.m. each night to drive over an hour to pick Mom up from work.

The tension in the house was almost more than I could bear. Seeing Mom and Gene arguing, and her being physically hurt by him, left me fearing that he was going to hurt her like my father did. This left me scared and wondering if we would end up leaving Gene like we did my father. It was obvious that they weren't happy with each other. I wondered if it was because Mom was still upset and bewildered about what had happened in Hawaii with her pantsuit. Or was Gene feeling trapped because he had rescued a woman and her three kids and knew that he would always be on the run from her ex-husband?

All I knew was that Mom started taking her moods out on me, and only me. She yelled at me, and pushed me around until I began to fear her and to feel anger stirring in my soul. So I spent more and more time alone in my closet, trying to escape the pain and hurt through the comfort of the music from my little record player. I listened to sad songs over and over again. With no one to talk to, the songs expressed what I felt. I especially understood the songs about longing for love. I was on the same quest—I needed someone to love me.

The fighting persisted between Mom and Gene, and every day I would securely tuck myself away in my refuge, savoring the quietness, while eluding the misery of my family and way of life. Then, to my utter dismay, I came home from school one day to find the door to my veiled world slightly ajar. Nervously, I walked into my precious hide-out to see that someone had gone through my stuff, sat on my pillow, played my records, eaten all of my cookies, and then left the door to my secret world open for everyone to see! I was furious and felt completely exposed. Until that very moment, I had never experienced the emotional confusion of being angry and crying at the same time.

In panic, I ran and told Mom that someone had been in my closet. She looked at me as if my plight was no big deal, and confessed that she was the one who gave my brothers permission to play in my closet. I was so upset that I could hardly respond to her invasion of my privacy. All I could do was stand there with tears rolling down my face like a wounded puppy who had been kicked one time too many. Seconds later, I managed to get the words out, "But this is my private place."

Again, she acted as if I was blowing this whole thing out of proportion. It was clear she had no idea what I was talking about and didn't care about my feelings, just like she didn't care about them when I lost my pink kitty. I was crying uncontrollably and begging Mom to please explain how she could have done that to me, and why she couldn't understand what I was trying to tell her. Without any emotion whatsoever, she completely dismissed what happened.

My emotions shifted and I now understood rage: the feeling of not being heard and having no one to understand me. I felt like I was going to explode from the hurt and devastation running through me because I knew my secret place would never be the same and I was left with no place to hide—I had lost yet another pink kitty. Would I ever be able to trust that any of my safe places would ever be truly safe? Would the adults in my life ever stop hurting me?

As the months went by, Mom and Gene's fighting escalated and my relationship with Mom became almost non-existent. Nothing in Santa

Monica was working out. Everyone was miserable and we all remained fearful that Dad would catch up with us soon. So, at the end of the school year, we packed our bags again and moved to Pasadena, Texas, to hopefully find salvation and refuge.

In Pasadena, we lived in a small apartment at the Cedar Grove Apartment Complex. There were two distinct sets of apartments finished in a stucco-type material, giving the buildings a Spanish look. A stone tunnel divided the apartment blocks and I hung out there because it was definitely the "cool" thing to do. It became a separate world for me where I could go to get away from everything.

These apartments, even though nicer than the pink house, were in a very seedy neighborhood and were filled with very street-wise kids. Almost everyday of the week, my brothers and I got beat up by bullies and were crushed because we didn't understand why. When we got tired of getting beat up, we succumbed to them and learned how to be cool, smoke cigarettes and be tougher.

We lived on the second floor in a small, three-bedroom apartment. My folk's bedroom was downstairs, while my brothers and I had rooms upstairs in our usual delegation of space with me in one room and my brothers in another. We still only had a few pieces of furniture, but overall the place wasn't too bad. At this point, anything was better than what we had left behind in Santa Monica.

My mother got another job as a nurse, while Gene began working in a cancer research center. We finally had two nickels to rub together.

I attended fourth grade here, and again, I was picked on because I was the new kid with an eye problem. A straight "A" student, I always wanted to do well so that someone might think I was good at something; maybe even I would think I was good at something. I also found that if I could hide myself in my schoolwork, I could stay out of whatever was happening at home, and this suited me just fine. Then, all of a sudden, I began failing school—I was falling asleep in the middle of my classes: couldn't retain any information; and basically, just couldn't learn anything. That wasn't good because I was trying my hardest to make it into a particular class the next year: the class with the smartest and "coolest" kids in school. I truly wanted to be a part of that. I thought that if I could get into that class, then I would finally be someone important and would finally fit in somewhere.

With my grades dropping, Mom became infuriated with me, beat me, and then sent me to my room to study in "solitary confinement." No matter how much she yelled, or punished me, I continued to fail exams I could have passed earlier in the year. Instead of trying to find out what was wrong with me, she continued to beat me for not doing well, and not being able to learn. Night after night, I lay in my room crying from the physical pain of my body, and the emotional hurt of my heart. I wondered, What is wrong with me? Why can't I learn anymore? Why would Mom rather hurt me than find out what was wrong with me? I found no answers.

My teachers also started complaining about my lack of performance. Mom's beatings intensified with my continuing inability to stay awake, concentrate, and learn. I was more afraid than ever to come home because I was guaranteed a thorough thrashing. The vicious cycle went on for months before the school insisted that Mom take me to a doctor. The local physicians didn't know what was wrong, so they sent me to the hospital for a myriad of tests.

The tests revealed that I had copper poisoning. Oddly enough, my youngest brother, Mike, had it as well. I asked Mom how I had gotten the rare form of poisoning, and she said it was from the "pollution in the air." Mike and I went through some type of treatment and soon I was able to learn again and resume passing all my tests with A's. However, I was still beaten by my mother if she was unhappy with any aspect of my school work, even for something as unimportant as the way I held a pencil. I was forced to feel inadequate and unlovable until I could learn to hold my pencil like she wanted me to do.

One of the reasons we moved to Pasadena was that Gene's mother and sister lived there. I had no idea that he even had a family, much less a mother and sister. When I saw them, I was surprised at how old both of them looked. His mother's face was full of wrinkles and even his sister looked like an old lady.

Rachel, my new step-grandmother, and Stacey, my new step-aunt, lived together in a house in a very quiet and somber neighborhood. The house was small and full of stuff, much like any old lady's home: filled with lifelong treasures. I still remember the old lady, perfumed smell that permeated the air. I hated that smell. It made me sick to my stomach.

By now, I was lured into a false since of security since my dad hadn't caught up with us yet. I started hoping that he had just given up. I was becoming comfortable with the idea that he was gone forever, never to terrify or beat me again.

Soon after my false sense of safety became familiar to me, the principal called me into the office one afternoon at the end of the school day. She sat me in one of the glass rooms next to her office and told me that I wasn't going to ride the school bus home that day because Mom was coming to pick me up. Confused, I patiently sat in the office and awaited Mom's arrival, and for her explanation.

The principal was very nice. She gave me some markers and some paper to keep me occupied. I especially remember the markers because they each smelled like fruit. I had no idea they made markers that were scented because we could never afford anything like that. I sat in the office waiting patiently for Mom and sniffing all the good smells out of the cool markers. Hours passed by slowly until I started getting anxious, bored, and wondering if Mom had forgotten about me. I gathered the courage to approach the principal and asked, "Where is my brother, Pat? When is Mom coming to get me?"

Looking uncomfortable and sympathetic, she replied, "Pat is waiting in a different building." I didn't understand why she looked so distraught until suddenly the police rushed into her office. I was immediately afraid and knew something was wrong.

Several police officers in dark blue uniforms and heavy belts filled with guns and handcuffs then came into the room and sat down. They explained that my real dad had found us, that he was outside in the school parking lot with Mom and Gene and he was trying to take us kids back to Jacksonville with him. They also said that Dad wanted to see me. Terror rushed through my body until I could hardly breathe. I didn't know what to do because I didn't want to see him. But, I was also afraid of making him mad, so I let the principal and the police escort me outside. It looked like a stakeout with Mom and Gene standing by their car with the police, and Dad standing alone by his car across the parking lot from everyone else.

As I was escorted to my dad's car, I felt as if my knees were going to buckle under me, and my lips trembled with fear. I stood in front of him in sheer terror, wondering if he was going to grab me and force me back to Florida with him. He then bent down and whispered, "Mom is crazy and mean and she had an affair with Gene while we were married." My mind raced with confusion. I wanted to declare him a liar and scream, "No!" but I couldn't get the words to come out of my mouth. I was terrified that he would get mad at me and hurt me if I stood up for myself and for Mom. I kept looking across the parking lot, praying that someone would read the expression on my face and rescue me from this horrible man and terrifying situation. Seconds later, I blacked out and I don't remember how I got away from him.

The next thing I knew I was in the car with Mom, Gene, and my brother, Pat, heading home. All of a sudden, Mom yelled at Gene that she had forgotten that my youngest brother, Mike, was still at the day care center. Gene sped over to the center to find that my dad had already been there and tried to convince them to let Mike go with him. To our relief, the day care center didn't let Mike go.

Dad was ordered by the police to leave the state of Texas. Instead, he decided that he wasn't quite finished with us yet. None of us had any idea he was still hanging around until one day when he called Mom demanding that a deal be struck or he wouldn't ever leave us alone. Neither Mom nor Gene told us about the so-called "deal" until it went down at Grandmother Rachel's house early one morning.

We drove to Rachel's where my brothers and I were told to go to the spare bedroom and be as quiet as possible so that Dad wouldn't know we were there. We were given specific instructions to hide on the floor and not make a sound because Gene was going to secretly meet with Dad and give him money to leave us alone. I was as nervous as I was in the school parking lot just a few days earlier. I was especially afraid that someone was going to get hurt. Lying on the bedroom floor, my curiosity and nerves got to me. I crept up to the window and peered through the sheer curtains to see what was going on. I held my breath as I watched Gene slowly walk outside and place a brown paper bag filled with money under the back tire of the car. The money signified that my father wouldn't only leave us alone, but that he would let Gene adopt us.

Moments later, Dad arrived and slowly drove by the house to make sure the police weren't there to arrest him. After circling the block, he parked his car next to the curb. He walked cautiously toward the back tire of our car, slowly bent down and took the paper bag out from under the rear tire. After quickly counting the money, he slipped back into his car and left as quietly as he came. Much to my surprise, there was no scene made, but I felt like I was a piece of property that had just been sold on the "black market" to the only bidder available. All I could do was hope that this would be last time I saw my father.

After this tense event occurred at Grandmother Rachel's house, Mom began having problems with Gene's family. Rachel expected Mom to be the picture-perfect wife, like back in the 1950s: evening meal, newspaper, and slippers waiting for her husband every night. The only problem with this was that Mom worked and she, too, was tired when she got home. It now appeared that it was Rachel's and Stacey's mission in life to make her feel bad about herself and to hopefully convince Gene to divorce her for a better woman. Despite my grandmother and aunt's obviously inappropriate behavior, he never stood up for Mom. This only infuriated her further and became another source of many arguments.

With the increased arguing also came an escalation of Gene's temper until he began losing control with us kids. Any little thing we did wrong resulted in him literally beating us, usually with a belt, until we were black and blue.

In order to have more control over us kids, especially since we were now bought and paid for, Gene and Mom came up with a list of rules they wrote on a yellow legal pad. The list of do's and don'ts were taped to the kitchen door to be seen by all. If we broke any of the sacred rules, we automatically got a severe beating. There was no discussion—just brutal punishment. It got so bad that I was afraid to go home; afraid I would do something wrong; afraid I would break one of the cardinal rules and get another beating. I was also afraid for my brothers because they, too, were being beaten on a regular basis. I felt bad for them each time Gene took them upstairs to whip them savagely. Every time I heard Pat or Mike cry out for Gene to stop hurting them, and with each sound of the belt against their bodies, my spirit sank with desperation and a need to run upstairs to make him stop. But I knew if I did, I would have gotten it worse than they were already getting it. It didn't seem that I could win with Gene, no matter what I did or didn't do.

The beatings became an issue when the school called Mom about the bruises on Pat's body. Gene then developed methods to punish us unmercifully without leaving any traces of his abusiveness. Oddly enough, this was also the time I realized that my brother Pat was a bed-wetter and had been so even when we lived in Jacksonville.

By the end of fourth grade, we were off again to another city for yet another fresh start. Mom wasn't convinced that Dad would leave us alone, even after the clandestine exchange of money. This time we were moving to Lexington, Kentucky, because Gene was offered a job from the doctor he worked for at the cancer research center. The doctor was moving to Kentucky to set up a new cancer research facility. The only problem with that was it left Gene temporarily without a job.

While we were waiting for Gene to get the confirmation to start work in Kentucky, we left Texas and went to Indianapolis, Indiana, to stay with Mom's sister, Brenda. As Gene was now unemployed, we had no place else to go. I had never met my Aunt Brenda, her husband or any of my cousins. I didn't even know what a cousin was until we got to Indianapolis. I couldn't believe we were going to stay with these people whom, although they were supposed to be my extended family, I had never seen or heard of before.

At first, Aunt Brenda was nice in that she let us stay with them for awhile in their town house. I was amazed at how wonderfully they lived compared to us. They lived in a spectacular place with a huge pool, tennis courts, saunas, and steam rooms. It was like living in a rich person's house.

While we were at Aunt Brenda's place, Gene was supposed to be receiving paychecks from the cancer research center while waiting to start work. That didn't make sense to me, but I accepted it because it was what Mom told me. However, instead of Gene being paid, a freeze was put on his checks until he actually started working. We were now in a terrible situation where we had no money and were at the mercy of Mom's family.

I didn't know why fate or karma would have it this way, but Mom's sister turned out to be just like the rest of her family. Instead of Aunt Brenda being the nice person I had imagined, she was a spiteful woman who insulted my mother and acted as if she didn't want any of us in her home. She especially didn't like us kids being in her fancy town house for fear that we would mess it up. Whenever she looked at my brothers, or me, I could feel hatred oozing from every pore of her petite body.

To top it all off, Aunt Brenda and Gene were also caught sexually messing around with each other! Mom actually witnessed Aunt Brenda walking around naked in front of Gene when they thought no one was home! I didn't know if Aunt Brenda sought Gene out or if it was the other way around, but when Mom found out about them, she had us pack our few belongings and rushed us out to the car. But then, to my surprise, she didn't have enough common sense to leave Gene behind with his new lover—she took him with us.

We headed to South Carolina to stay with Mom's other sister, Relaine. Again, we were going to a relative's house because we had nowhere else to go and no money. She was also another aunt I had never heard of. I didn't understand why we were driving from Texas to Indiana, and then to South Carolina, when our destination was Kentucky, especially when we didn't have any money. Why not find a cheap place for us to stay in Lexington, if that was where we were going to live? Why waste all our time and resources running all over the country without the financial means to do so?

We left Indiana and drove to South Carolina with barely enough money for gas and no money for food. I was so hungry that I sat in the back seat of the car wondering when we would be able to eat again and envisioning how good it would taste to have a burger and a large order of fries. But, my mouth only drooled while my stomach growled loudly with imagined anticipation. We didn't have anything to eat all the way from Indiana to South Carolina.

When we arrived at Aunt Relaine's house, we found that she was just as hateful, if not more so, than Aunt Brenda had been. I didn't understand what was going on with our so-called family, just that we were staying with a bunch of people who were supposed to be our kinfolk, but who didn't seem to like or want us.

After spending a couple of days with Aunt Relaine and her family, the truth finally came out and it scared me to death. Aunt Relaine confronted Mom in a very hateful and derogatory tone of voice and said that my dad had been in contact with her and he told her that Mom was a habitual liar. He also told her a bunch of lies about all of us. Thus, she had a decision to make—to believe my father, or to help us. She chose to believe my dad and made it perfectly clear that she didn't want to help us at all. She immediately got on the phone and called my dad to let him know we were there. The shock of Aunt Relaine's betrayal hit my mother and she had us pack our few belongings to run away again, even though we truly had no money and no one else to turn to for help. Everywhere we had turned was a dead end.

As we drove out of South Carolina, the atmosphere in our car was permeated with fear and panic and no one dared break the silence. Everyone was afraid of what would happen next and worried about what we were going to do for gas money, a place to stay, and food. Finally, in pure desperation, Gene pulled off the road, called Aunt Stacey, in Texas, and told her what had happened. He then humbly asked her if she would help us. Reluctantly, she wired him just enough money to put gas in the car to get back to Texas, but she wouldn't send any money so we could eat or rest in a hotel. We were left digging around behind the seats of the car until we finally scraped up enough change so we could have one chocolate milkshake each from South Carolina to Texas.

We finally made it back to Texas to listen to Gene's mom and sister rant and rave about how he had gotten himself mixed up with the wrong woman and wrong family. They tried mercilessly to convince him of the seriousness and error in his judgment. Listening to them made me feel as if we were the worst people in the world, and not worthy of anyone's kindness or compassion. I wondered if anyone would ever be willing to give us a break and to help us get on our feet again. After hours of arguing, Gene told them that we would only stay long enough for him to write to the labor board to tell them that the research center hadn't been paying him. Not long after that, the research center sent Gene some money and we were off to Lexington, Kentucky for yet another fresh start.

After arriving in Lexington, we went back to living in old, run-down houses that screamed to everyone who passed by, "We're poor again!" When I saw the house we were going to rent, my heart sank. It was a dilapidated, two-story farmhouse with the paint peeling off it and weeds growing up to six-feet tall, engulfing the front and backyard, and hiding any grass that might have once stood there. To the left of the house was an old rotten barn. In the backyard was an old wooden fence covered with nothing but thickets and weeds. Beyond the wooden fence, there was a feeble shack that barely remained erect. It looked as if it would fall over or cave in on itself if a gentle breeze brushed against it.

Moving to Lexington didn't change our luck, and this became evident when Gene learned that the cancer research center wouldn't open because the doctor's wife had developed cancer and was about to die. Gene was still out of a job. What were we going to do? How were we going to survive?

Because no one was employed, Mom and Gene spoke to the old man who rented us the farmhouse and told him of our dire situation—no money, no food, and no way to pay the rent. The owner took pity on us. His compassion and sympathy allowed us to live rent-free in the old house. Although a relief to everyone, I was thoroughly embarrassed because an outsider now knew that we were destitute and only worthy of pity.

Since we spent so much time moving from one place to the next and there usually wasn't much money, we didn't have any furniture or possessions, only the clothes on our backs. This left the inside of the house looking as desolate and disparaging as the outside of it. We couldn't afford a dining room table like a normal family. Instead, we ate off a picnic table with benches. Every time I walked into the kitchen, I thought the picnic table looked as if it were lost and wanted to be outside where it belonged. The living room and dining room had absolutely no furniture in them at all, only a telephone and telephone book lying on the floor next to one of the windows. The only rooms in the house that had furniture in them were our bedrooms. We only had that little bit of furniture because we went to the Salvation Army where they screened our poverty level and supplied our five-person family with three beds and three chests of drawers. Without them, we wouldn't have had any furniture in our rooms at all.

Gene finally managed to get a job at one of the local technology centers selling telephones, while Mom remained unemployed. Gene wasn't particularly happy with his job because he considered it "beneath" him since he had a graduate degree in microbiology, had taught nursing and did research at several universities. It was disconcerting to him that he couldn't find any other jobs which reflected his level of intelligence and education and it seemed to greatly fuel his temper.

We stayed poverty-stricken the rest of our time in Kentucky. We shoved towels under the kitchen door to prevent the infestation of fleas that lived in the utility room from getting into the rest of the house. There were wharf rats living in the walls of the house. One time, the stench in the house had grown so foul that Gene pulled some of the boards off the side of the house to find out what was causing the smell. He was shocked to find dead rats filled with maggots being eaten by other rats. We couldn't afford to heat the house much in the winter, despite the extremely cold and snowy winters. I found it fascinating that when I sat on the floor of the house, I could see my breath slipping its way past my lips and forming a misty white cloud in front of my face. Since we couldn't afford heating fuel, Mom had us go to the old barn to chop pieces of wood off it to burn in the fireplace. When we made those precious fires, everyone stood as close as possible to the flames so that none of the warmth escaped, or was wasted. When the day came for us to leave that house, Mom and Gene had to finally confess to the kind old man that to stay warm during the winter months, we had almost burned up his entire barn.

We were also hungry a great deal of the time and were restricted to repeatedly eating the same type of things. Most of our meals consisted of homemade biscuits with either gravy, honey, or stewed tomatoes. Since we couldn't afford any other food, we ate those damn biscuits day in and day out. I absolutely grew to hate them!

The house was out in the country, in the middle of nowhere. All the other places we had lived in were in the city with plenty of kids and neighbors around us. But now we were isolated, and there was nothing for my brothers or me to do, and no one for us to play with. In many ways, this was all right with me, especially since none of the kids at any of the schools had ever liked me because my damaged eye made me look different from everyone else. I was used to being alone, so I spent a great deal of time by myself, exploring in the barn and the old shack. I guess it reminded me of the exploring I did in the jungle of a backyard we had in Santa Monica. I didn't know what it was about being in these old places, but I sure enjoyed playing the role of an explorer. I loved looking for ancient treasures and seeing what I could find that would make me feel good about myself and would help me forget about the things that were going on in the house with Mom and Gene.

Just because we had moved didn't mean our problems went away. If anything, our troubles greatly multiplied as Mom and Gene's fighting and cruelty exacerbated with ferocious intensity, and Mom was taking everything out on me.

To make matters worse, my dad complicated everything when he found us again. This time he wasn't just looking to take me or my brothers back to Florida with him, he was looking to cause serious trouble for Mom. He went to the courthouse in Lexington and had Mom charged with some type of credit card fraud. Because he had been a police officer, he managed to convince the court system to issue a warrant for her arrest, even though the allegations were false. He convinced the police that she had made several charges on their credit cards while their divorce was in process.

So the police arrested Mom and took her away. I wondered how many more times we would have to go through this with my dad. I couldn't understand why he kept showing up, especially after he had sold us. I was so scared I didn't know what to do.

The warrant couldn't be settled in Kentucky since the alleged crime happened in Florida. So Mom and Gene had to go back to Jacksonville while they shipped us kids off to stay with some people we barely knew. They lived in a trailer in a park full of other long, aluminum-box type homes sandwiched together to conserve space and money. Granted, they lived better than we did, but that was my first experience living in a trailer. It was strange staying with them because no one would tell us what was going on with Mom and Gene in Florida, or when they would be back. Instead, my brothers and I were left wondering if we were ever going to see Mom and/or Gene again, or worse, would we end up having to live with Dad if Mom went to jail?

We were there for days and I kept asking when we would be allowed to go home, but no one answered my questions, or cared about how afraid I was. Not only were we staying at a stranger's home and being ignored, but we weren't allowed to go outside because everyone was afraid Dad would try to kidnap us again. We were like prisoners cut off from the world in an unfamiliar land.

Mom and Gene finally came back from Florida because Dad had to drop the charges, and we were allowed to go back home to the old farmhouse. Mom tried to explain to us what Dad was trying to do by having her arrested, but as I was only ten years old, I was still a little too young to completely understand. She also explained that the only way to get rid of my dad was to have Gene legally adopt us. She asked if it would be all right. Being young children, all we could focus on was the thought of making Dad leave us alone, so we said, "Yes." I knew that neither Gene nor my dad were great choices as fathers, but I figured I would be better off with Gene, even though he hurt us, too.

As soon as we agreed to allow Gene to adopt us, we were dressed up and taken to the courthouse where he legally became our dad. I remember thinking how the court must see him as an angel, my mother as the protector of her children, and my real dad as an asshole. In reality, they had no idea who they were dealing with.

Things progressively worsened the longer we remained in Lexington, especially with Mom. Something in her snapped, and she became a person I no longer knew, one I wasn't prepared for.

One night I was already in bed because it was a school night. I must have drifted off to sleep for a short while before I was suddenly awakened by sounds of horrifying screams and crying. Panicked, I jumped out of my bed and bounded downstairs to see who was getting hurt, and why. With each step down the long wooden staircase, I heard Mom's angry voice become louder and louder, and was followed by deafening slapping sounds. At the bottom of the stairs, I carefully peered around the banister to see the bathroom door slightly ajar. I saw Mom standing in the middle of the bathroom, but I couldn't yet see who she was yelling at. I could sense the tension in the air as I meekly walked toward the bathroom to see what was causing such a commotion. Approaching the door, I saw my brothers standing in the bathtub, naked and wet. They were crying and holding their hands and arms in front of them while Mom ferociously beat them with a belt. I instinctively knew that I had to do something to make her stop, so I ran into the bathroom and begged, "Mom, please stop hitting them! Tell me what's wrong."

She swung around and looked at me with rage in her eyes. She looked as if she were out of control. All of a sudden, she seemed to forget that my brothers were in the tub, and in a menacing voice she commanded, "Take your shirt off." When I understood her words, my heart drowned with embarrassment that my brothers would see my naked ten-year-old body. My breath grew shallow and momentarily stopped out of fear of what Mom was about to do to me. But I obeyed her by slowly removing my shirt and gently placing it on the floor.

"Turn around and grab hold of the sink," she continued. With my hands and arms violently shaking, I reached for the cold porcelain basin and grasped it for dear life as I anticipated the first blow to my back with the thick leather belt, still wet from the strikes against my brothers' bodies. When the belt landed firmly on my back, I tried not to cry, but the tears came anyway. With each blow, I could hear my brothers crying in the tub and somehow it gave me a sense of relief because I knew that now she wasn't hitting them.

We all wore long-sleeved shirts to school the next day so that no one could see the welts and bruises that marred the surface of our small bodies. But nothing could hide the pain hidden in the depths of our hearts. I dared not look at anyone that day, especially my teachers. When changing classes, I saw my brother, Pat, at his locker, and I whispered, "Have you told anyone about last night? Has anyone seen your bruises?"

Looking nervous, he replied, "Some of the kids in gym class noticed, but I said I got hurt when a belt flew off the lawn mower." He appeared proud of his ingenious cover-up and relieved that they believed him. I, on the other hand, was disappointed and surprised that the kids fell for such a lame story. I guess I was hoping that someone would notice our marks and help us.

The next morning, someone from the school called Mom and Gene. They said they knew about the beatings because of the marks on Pat's body and because he couldn't dress out for gym class because he was trying to hide the bruises. Despite this phone call nothing changed.

I was afraid because things like that had been going on for years with Gene, and I didn't know how I was going to be able to handle it if Mom maintained the same violent course. I was used to her yelling at me, pushing me around and not loving me. But I didn't know if the physical violence was something I would be able to get used to—especially from her, as she was still the only person in my life whose love I needed.

As it turned out, I had no choice but to get used to the violent beatings from Mom because they became a constant for years to come. As she became more infuriated with Gene, and her life in general, I became the official scapegoat of the family. Mom would throw my brothers outside to play all day long so they wouldn't know what she was doing to me.

I was afraid to be around her because we couldn't be in the same room together without her getting upset about something. When she got upset, she hit me with whatever she had in her hand: a broom handle, a long handled spoon, a belt, wire clothes hangers, or the metal vacuum cleaner tube.

It seemed like most of my thrashings occurred in the kitchen, the place where I spent a lot of time cleaning up after meals and the family in general. She would stand there screaming at me for something I didn't do. My legs would shake and my breath would grow shallow because I knew she was going to start hitting me at any moment. For some reason, the first blow always seemed to take me by surprise, as if I didn't know it was coming. My fear would become a reality when Mom started violently swinging at me, with most of the blows landing haphazardly all over my body. She would swing that broom handle so quickly, and with such force, that I would crawl into the nearest corner I could find. I would put my hands over my head to shield myself from her wrath while I cried and begged, "Please, please stop!"

My fleeing into the corner for safety only seemed to infuriate her even more. I could see the rage and anger in her eyes grow as she would scream, "Get up!" Trembling, I would gather the courage to move my battered body out of the corner, only to find that she would begin hitting me harder and with such intensity that I often believed I would never see another tomorrow. I eventually learned to just stay in the corner, while she continued to hit me.

Every time Mom beat me like that, it did something to me. I felt absolutely violated and vulnerable, lost and without hope. I truly didn't know how I was going to be able to survive from one day to the next, or figure out how to protect myself from this person who was supposed to love me.

The beatings from Mom occurred almost daily, and as my desperation grew, I walked and talked in my sleep almost every night. This was my only means of being able to express what was happening to me. It was very frightening to wake up downstairs, or outside, not knowing how I had gotten there or what I was doing. I was now afraid to go to sleep at night, and to live during the day.

I was in fifth grade and really didn't have any friends, mainly because I was afraid to bring anyone home for fear that my folks would start fighting, or that I would get beaten in front of someone. I was also embarrassed about where we lived. This left me alone a great deal of the time, so I whiled away the lonely hours hiding in my room with my little red and white record player listening to the same records I had listened to in California. I sat in front of my window with the old, worn out drapes and listened repeatedly to the few records I possessed. I was very sad, depressed, and lonely, and I didn't know what to do with those feelings, so I just stayed alone and listened to my music. I could visualize the songs in my head and it was like I was wherever the songs were talking about. I was the person who was standing alone in the rain feeling the gaping hole in her soul over the loss of her lifelong love. But, the loss of my lifelong love was my mother, not some romantic and handsome man who was my soul mate.

With the passage of time, I spent more and more time exploring the barn "ruins" and the old shack in the field behind the house. The barn was huge and it reminded me of an old tobacco barn. I walked around and explored in it for hours, hoping I would find something old or valuable, something that would make me feel good about myself. Despite how cool the barn was, I liked the little shack behind the house better. It was really small and I liked that feeling of closeness. I had to climb through a broken window to get into the shack, but once inside, there were old broken tables, battered chairs, and junk everywhere. It was also full of dust and cobwebs. One day when I was out there exploring, I found some old books covered in an inch of dust, and one of them was the story of Pinocchio. I thought I had really found something special. I was so elated about my find that I smuggled the book back to my room so I could be close to my new-found treasure.

On occasion, Mom would surprise us kids with reading Pinocchio to us in front of the fireplace. It was one of the few times we could escape reality and experience a morsel of closeness all at one time.

I used to dream that I lived in the little shack all by myself and that no one knew I lived there. That way no one would ever be able to find me, and no one would ever be able to hit me again. I spent hours in the little shack, especially when I felt sad, or when I needed to hide. I went there to get away from everyone because no one would ever look for me there. It became like my closet in Los Angeles, and the trash-bins in Hawaii.

The fighting, beatings, lack of love and understanding, and my desperate struggle for survival continued through the school year. Because we always followed the same rocky path, and our history always repeated itself, we stayed true to form by not living in one place for more than a school year. The next place we moved to was Cincinnati, Ohio.

Chapter 5

The Abyss

AftER we moved to cincinnati, Mom said, "I promise you can make friends here because we're never going to move again."

I felt such relief in believing that we could finally stop running and hopefully become like other families. Maybe I could fit in somewhere. Maybe have a friend, and participate in some of the school activities for the first time.

But, my dream wasn't going to be accomplished very easily. Even though I believed we weren't going to move anymore, I didn't possess the social skills, self-esteem, or self-confidence needed to participate in everyday life. I was nervous around the other kids my age. I felt like they could see right through me, all the way down to my insecurities. Because the pain and fear of hanging out with kids my age was so great, I only spent time with adults.

We lived in a place called White Oak Town Houses near the local university. They appeared relatively new, and we rented a two-story town house with a finished basement. My bedroom was upstairs across the hall from Mom and Gene with only a bathroom separating us. My brothers shared a bedroom in the basement.

My whole life changed in that Cincinnati town house.

Gene was working two jobs: a microbiology professor at the university; and a respiratory therapist at a local hospital. I especially remember his job at the hospital because of the gory stories he used to come home and tell us. One of his infamous stories was about a little girl whose parents scalded her in hot water until the child's skin peeled off her body liked a blanched tomato.

I was now in the sixth grade and this was my fourth school since beginning my education, and my third school since we left Jacksonville about three years ago.

Mrs. Henry was my homeroom and English teacher. I really liked her and we got along really well. It felt like she could read my thoughts. And somehow I knew she could see that I wasn't like the other kids because everything was harder for me, and I was easily upset when the other kids picked on me about my eye, or even looked at me in a funny way. It was like she understood that something terribly wrong was going on at home. I was fragile in her class and became easily upset whenever I made a mistake or, even worse, a bad grade. I hated feeling that I had to be perfect, or I would be punished for my inadequacies.

The fear that I lived with at home came out at school through small and insignificant incidences. The eye doctor had placed me on some eye drops because I was having continued problems with my bad eye. I didn't understand what the medicine was; I just knew I had to use it. One afternoon while on a class field trip to the park, I lost the drops. Panicked, I began crawling around on the ground, desperately searching for them. Even though Mrs. Henry didn't understand my response, she immediately started helping me look for my drops. Much to my despair, we couldn't find them. With this, I became more upset and started crying. Mrs. Henry asked me what was wrong. My shaky voice confessed, "I'm really going to get it when I get home for being so careless." I could see that she was infuriated that I would be punished for losing my eye drops, which I later learned were only artificial tears and very inexpensive. Despite the fact that she didn't understand why I would be punished for something so trivial, I was glad that she now had a clearer picture of what was happening to me at home.

I continued having difficulties with my eye and had several operations since leaving Jacksonville. This left me with a very misshapen eye that was no longer round or smooth, but wavy and jagged. I had to wear a hard contact lens on my bad eye—why—I didn't know since I was legally blind in it. Even though I complained on a daily basis that it hurt my eye, I was forced to wear it. On several occasions, the school sent me home with my eye blood-red and watering, but that still wasn't proof enough for my mother that I wasn't fabricating my pain. Finally, the eye doctor discovered that the lens was scratching and cutting my cornea. I then had to put a greasy ointment in my eye and wear yet another patch, which made all of the kids poke more fun at me. The doctor also said that he wanted to do more procedures on my eye because it had become lazy, drifting way out to the side. Mom, however, opted not to have anything else done.

My savior that school year was Mrs. Henry. I wished she were my mother. I knew she was a lady who loved and took care of her kids, so I daydreamed about how wonderful it would be to live at her house, and how great it would be to feel loved. Even though I hadn't yet reached the point where I understood that what was happening to me wasn't okay, and that everyone else wasn't living like I was, I wanted Mrs. Henry to know what was going on at home, even though I couldn't tell her. Since I couldn't tell her or anyone else what was happening, I began writing it all down in a journal. This was the only way I had a voice.

The physical abuse from Mom intensified and I felt helpless. I didn't know what it was about me that pissed her off so badly, but she constantly beat me with whatever was close by. She continued to use the vacuum cleaner's metal tube, the broom handle, wire coat hangers, mop handles, even books. I flinched anytime she raised her hand to me, even for something other than punishment.

Mom soon became quite sadistic with her moods and what she did to me. I remember her insisting that I let her cut my hair. Every time she cut it I was afraid to go to school because all the kids would tease me. I hated her for that. I already felt bad enough about myself without her making me more ugly.

One day Mom offered to give me a hairdo and then style it with the curling iron. I really believed it was going to be different this time, that she was going to make me beautiful. She promised that she was only going to trim my hair and then curl it so I would be pretty. My innocent and naïve self believed that she would keep her word, and that I would have the "hairdo of the century!" Everyone would think I was beautiful.

Mom started cutting my hair and I could feel that she was taking off a lot more than she had promised. The reflection in the mirror of my short, ugly hair left me so upset that I begged her to stop. But, of course, she wouldn't put the scissors down. She continued chopping away at what hair I had left, while I tried to sit quietly in my chair and not cry in front of her. Then she reached for the curling iron. I couldn't hold back the tears anymore, and that left Mom seething. She picked up the curling iron and purposely burned my neck, the searing pain caused even more tears.

My uncontrollable sobbing resulted in Mom demanding, "Look at yourself in the mirror!" But I was too embarrassed to comply with her demand. So she grabbed my chin and forced me to face the mirror while she sneered, "Look at how ugly you are when you cry." I was completely devastated by the tear-filled eyes and red swollen face staring back at me— she was right—I was truly ugly.

I finally graduated from the sixth grade and was promoted to the seventh where I entered middle school. Middle school was a whole new world for me with its towering, multi-level school building. It was like being in a real school and I was excited about being in the "big league" with the older kids.

I don't remember a thing about what happened at school during my seventh grade year: who my teachers were; who I had for homeroom; or what I did. I apparently blocked out anything to do with school because of what was going on at home. All of my attention was focused on just surviving from one day to the next.

The summer before I started the seventh grade was unforgettable because I fell into an abyss of even more intense and intolerable abuse. I was eleven years old when it began. I was in the kitchen getting something to drink when Gene sneaked up behind me, picked me up, and sat me on the counter next to the refrigerator. I didn't understand what he was doing, but I saw something creepy in his eyes. Fear gripped me and I prayed that he wasn't going to hurt me. Gene started touching my body in a way that was unfamiliar to me. I was struck with such immense fear that I couldn't move. He put his dry, scaly hands under my shirt and began rubbing my breasts. He then ran his hands all over my body in a way that seemed to mesmerize him. He raised my shirt and began kissing and sucking on my breasts. Moments later, he worked his way up to my face and began kissing me. I felt trapped as he held me really close. He checked that no one was coming into the room, then spread my legs apart and slid my shorts to the side just enough so he could insert his fingers into my vagina. I wanted to scream for help, but I couldn't get the words to come out of my mouth. I could tell that he was trying not to get caught, and I was afraid that he would hurt me if I made a sound, especially since Mom was sitting in the living room. I was also afraid that Mom would blame me for what was happening and it would result in another beating. I knew I couldn't let him see me cry, so I wept silently inside while praying God would make him stop.

When he was done, I felt dirty, like I had just done something wrong. I was bewildered because it felt wrong emotionally and morally, but from a physical standpoint, his touching me excited parts of my body in a way that I had never felt before. I had been desperate all my life for someone to pay attention to me and to love me, but this wasn't the way I wanted it to happen. The guilt paralyzed me, while my physical self was now awakened. I didn't know what to do with my new inner conflict. I wondered, "Is this what it means for someone to love another person? Is this how a dad is supposed to love his daughter? Who can I tell? Who can answer these questions?"

The more Gene did to me sexually, the bolder he became: he cornered me in my room; made excuses to get me alone; made up reasons to get Mom out of the house; made me run errands with him; and took every opportunity he could to fondle and touch me. I especially hated the nights when he came into my room and forced his penis into my mouth just so he could have an orgasm.

Some nights I tried to act like I was in such a deep sleep that I couldn't wake up. But every time I was brave enough to try this, fear consumed me because I was afraid he would get angry and hurt me. I cringed every time he kissed me. I wanted to crawl into a hole and throw up with disgust because of the bridge he wore and his pungent breath that reeked of cigarettes and alcohol. I especially hated it when Gene made me touch him. I hated the feel of his genitals in my hand and wished that someone would kill me.

Gene took every opportunity to molest me. There were many days when I was innocently doing my chores or hanging up my clothes in my room and I would begin feeling scared for no apparent reason. It felt like an evil presence had entered my room. When I turned around, I saw that it was Gene standing there staring at me. I knew by the look on his face what was about to happen. I tried to make him leave and not to touch me, but he wouldn't listen. I was so scared. I wanted him to stop, but I couldn't get the words out of my mouth. So he continued sexually molesting me, and there was nothing I could do about it.

Gene also started fondling and touching me when Mom was in the same room or in the same area. He must have been sure about her supposed ignorance and felt like he was invincible.

I remember the family going on a vacation to Canada. It was the first time we had ever done anything like that as a family. I couldn't imagine we were actually going to go somewhere for fun, and not because we were running. We camped out at a public campground where Gene and I were sitting on a picnic table, talking. I wasn't afraid because I didn't think he would try anything with me since we were out in public and I had prayed to God that none of the bad stuff would follow us on our trip. Much to my dismay, Gene began his usual stuff, right in front of God and everyone.

Gene started touching me. He got up and stood behind me and started rubbing his genitals against my back. He grabbed my hand and placed it on his penis and motioned for me to stroke it. I was embarrassed and sure that everyone around us could see what was happening. I was consumed with despair as there was no place that was safe from him and his constant need for sexual contact.

Without his realizing it, Mom started walking right toward us. At the last second, Gene spotted her and tried to act casual. Mom must have sensed something because she asked what was going on, but Gene said nothing while I hung my head in shame and utter defeat.

Just a few hours later, we were all sitting at a picnic table in our camp. Again, Gene stood up behind me and made me touch his penis while he rubbed himself against my body. Still no word was ever said by Mom.

After returning home from the so-called "vacation," Mom left me alone in the town house with Gene. I was in my room trying to stay out of everyone's way when the sexual abuse turned from a bad dream into a nightmare. I believed that if I remained out of sight, I would be out of everyone's mind, including Gene's. But the next thing I knew, Gene came into my room with that same look on his face, and I was filled again with fear and panic because I knew what was about to happen. He grabbed my hand and took me across the hall to his and Mom's bedroom. I was afraid about what was getting ready to happen because he had never taken me into their room before.

I just stood there paralyzed as he started taking off my clothes. I was filled with embarrassment as I stood in the middle of the room with him staring at my naked eleven-year-old body. He began taking off his clothes, and I could see it in his eyes that he was getting excited. I was so scared I couldn't move. I wished I could have made him stop, but the fear of him becoming angry took control. It was like I became immobilized. I wanted to tell him to stop, but I couldn't utter the words.

He then laid me down on their bed and he climbed on top of me. As the weight of his body fell upon me, I felt like I was being smothered: I couldn't breathe. I then felt his penis growing in size as it lay between my legs and I prayed that he wouldn't hurt me. I felt pinned down without a means of escape and I feared the insertion of his penis into my small body. As he began penetrating me, everything turned black and silent. I couldn't see or hear anything as I went away somewhere deep inside my mind. I don't remember when it was over; getting up out of the bed; or putting my clothes back on. I don't remember anything about the rest of that day—Mom coming home, having dinner—nothing. I don't know where I went, or when I came back.

The sexual abuse worsened by the day, so I tried to stay away from home as much as possible. I believed that was the only way I was going to be safe, free from the beatings and the sexual abuse.

While roaming around the apartment complex, I met Miguel and Lucinda, a couple who lived in the same town houses. Everyone thought they were "cool" because they didn't care how we dressed, how we acted, or how we talked. With them, it was all about having fun. Miguel was a singer and I don't remember what Lucinda did, but I thought they were the coolest adults I had ever met. They spent a lot of time and did great stuff with the neighborhood kids, like going swimming with us and having everyone over to their apartment for snacks and parties. This was a great reprieve from my family and my life, and I immediately fell in love with them. In many ways, I wished that Mom and Gene treated me like they did. I enjoyed feeling like I belonged and that someone cared about me. I liked having someone to hang out with and someone to do things with me—they were my new family.

One day I didn't have anywhere to go, so I went over to visit Lucinda to see if we could hang out together. Miguel answered the door and invited me in. He told me Lucinda would be home shortly and asked me to wait for her in the living room. I plopped down on their couch and made myself comfortable. Moments later, Miguel started walking toward me with the same look in his eyes that I had seen in Gene's. He pulled me close to him and started touching my body. I froze and thought to myself, "Please, God, don't let this happen to me again!" As Miguel touched me, I felt my body tremble with fear and my heart drown with shame, much like it did with Gene. I didn't know how to make him stop, and I couldn't force the issue because I was afraid he would hurt me just like all the other adults in my life.

I remember the smell of his cologne and how it made me feel sick to my stomach. And, that he wore a gold Italian horn around his neck, with his shirt slightly unbuttoned to show off his hairy chest.

Somehow, I made it out of their apartment, but not before feeling utterly dirty and disgusting all over again. I couldn't believe what had just happened. I needed to tell someone, but I didn't know who. I didn't know who would believe me, and I didn't know how badly I would be beaten if Mom or Gene ever found out.

My new family was no longer safe and I wasn't able to have fun with my new friends anymore. My new life was cut short because every time I went over to Miguel and Lucinda's, he touched and fondled me. Nothing I did made him stop. At the same time, I couldn't go home either because the same thing was happening there with Gene. I had no place to go where I could be safe.

Because I was about to explode from the shame and guilt that was running around inside me, I told a girlfriend about what Miguel had been doing. I told her to relieve my own feelings of guilt and shame, but also to see if she could help me figure out how to make him stop. After telling my story, she laughed at me and said she didn't believe me. I was disappointed and bewildered by her lack of understanding, so I told her some of the things that Miguel was doing to me so that she would believe me. To my amazement, the more I talked, the more she acted like what Miguel was doing was a cool thing because he was good looking and he was a popular singer! I finally figured out that she wasn't going to believe me, so I tried to cover up my awkwardness and vulnerability by pretending I was something special because he chose me instead of her. My being the chosen one now left my friend believing me and promising me that she wouldn't tell anyone, especially Lucinda.

The next day, my friend told me that Lucinda wanted to talk with me about something. I didn't think much about it, so I went over to their town house to see what was up. As usual, when I arrived there were several other kids from the neighborhood there. When I walked into the kitchen, Lucinda's expression changed to a look of anger and I instinctively understood that my friend (who had promised utter silence) had betrayed my confidence. With an angry and threatening tone of voice, she confronted me about my allegations and demanded to know if they were true. Although I was afraid the truth would earn me another beating, I bowed my head in submission and whispered, "It's true."

When Lucinda heard my words, rage filled her eyes. "You're a liar," she declared, "and if you don't apologize to Miguel for saying those bad things about him, I won't be your friend anymore!"

I was stunned that she didn't believe me and that I was faced with alienation at the price of the truth. In the end, I was too needy for Lucinda's love and acceptance and I didn't want the other kids to think I was a bad person, so I gave in to Lucinda's demands and did what she asked.

To apologize to Miguel, I had to go upstairs to find him. With each step I took, I shook from head to toe because I was afraid that Miguel would hurt me because I had told our secret. I saw the seriousness on his face as I rounded the corner. I could smell his cologne as I stared at the floor and said, "I'm sorry."

He smirked and then hissed, "You'll come over here every day, and I'll kill you if you ever tell another person."

By trying to get someone to help me, I made things worse for myself—Miguel's abuse worsened. The daily routine began with Miguel taking me upstairs to a spare room so we'd be alone. He would start kissing me and touching me all over my body, while I stood paralyzed in fear and praying that God would make him stop. Miguel touched me just long enough to get himself excited. He then grabbed me by my head and forced me to my knees. Once my knees were firmly planted on the ground, he held my head in his hands and thrust his penis in my mouth with vibrant force. He held my head tightly while he pumped his penis back and forth in my mouth; I silently cried to myself. As he became more excited, he shoved his penis deeper and deeper into my mouth until he was almost penetrating the back of my throat. When he started to ejaculate, he held my head even tighter as he shoved his penis so far in that I began gagging. I couldn't breathe and felt like I was suffocating. As I struggled to get air, Miguel rammed his penis in farther so I would have to swallow his semen. With his semen pumping into my throat, I began choking and just when I thought I was about to die, he shoved me to the floor like a used prostitute. I lay on the floor in the spare room gasping for air and wishing I was dead.

The thrashings from Mom, the fighting between her and Gene, the sexual abuse from him, and the new form of sexual torture from Miguel took a serious toll on me: I was turning into a person I didn't know. I was desperate to tell someone what was happening to me, but there was no one to tell. I needed someone to love me like a child should be loved, but no one was available.

I don't know what happened to me, but I ended up having sex with several different men. It seemed like every man I knew at this point in my life was abusing me and I was acting out what they were doing to me. I got into situations I didn't know how to get out of, and started believing that what these men were doing to me was normal and that all men were like this. I didn't think it was possible to have a relationship, much less a friendship, with a man that didn't involve sex, no matter how much I tried not to let it happen.

One day I was swimming with a boy my own age in the pool behind the town houses. We were flirting with each other like normal kids our age since we sort of liked each other, like boyfriend/girlfriend. While swimming, he started touching me in a way that a boy his age had never done. I immediately panicked and was afraid that someone might see us. After I was sure no one was watching, I wondered if his touching me meant that he liked me. After all, I was taught that if someone liked me, that was how they showed it. As we got out of the pool, I was excited at the possibility of someone liking me as a girlfriend. To my surprise, he asked me to come over to his apartment so we could hang out together. His invitation left me feeling warm inside and like I was special, especially since I had never had a boy my age ask to spend some time with me. I happily agreed to visit him in hopes that he would end up being my boyfriend.

I went over to his apartment with a smile on my face and a new sense of hope only to find him alone. He had invited me over so I would have sex with him, in particular, oral sex. Again, I was afraid to say "No." Instead, I went into some kind of automatic mode where I tried to disconnect myself from the world so I could reluctantly do what he wanted. I hated it! It was nasty and disgusting, and I felt just as dirty and shamed as I had with Gene and Miguel. The only difference between them was this boy gave me things, almost like a man would give a prostitute money. So I started focusing on what I could get materially out of it, rather than what was happening to me. However, I quickly got to a place where I couldn't do it anymore, so I started avoiding him.

I soon found myself lured into the apartment of another man who I thought was totally cute. Kurt was quite a bit older than I was since he was in his early twenties. I didn't care about his age because I had a crush on him and I thought I was special because he invited me over to his place. I really liked him, but I was a little scared that he was going to hurt me like everyone else had. I didn't want him to hurt me—I just wanted him to like me and make me feel good about myself. Instead of being made to do things I didn't want to do, he was gentle with me when he touched my body and kissed me. I immediately found myself getting excited and felt my body glow with a warmth I had never felt before. We fell into hours of heated passion that was only stopped by my need to get home before my tardiness would earn me another beating. Being with him felt very different to the rest of the encounters I'd had with men because he allowed me to feel things sexually, rather than making me do things to him. For the first time, being with someone in a sexual way didn't feel wrong—it seemed fun.

However, continuing to see Kurt wasn't worth the beatings and further torture I would endure if Mom and Gene found out about my moments of pleasure. When I told Kurt that I couldn't be with him like that anymore, he became enraged and said, "You come back tomorrow, or I'll find you and hurt you bad!" His threat left my moment of happiness blowing away as fast as it came. With each step I made on my way home, I tried to figure out what I was going to do; I was afraid and felt trapped.

Terrified, I went back to Kurt's apartment the next day. As I stood there shaking and wondering what he was going to do to me, he pulled the curtains shut. He sneered, "You're gonna have sex with me or I'll hurt you—your choice." I lay in the pitch-dark room while he threw himself on top of my body and forced his penis inside me. I wanted to scream because it hurt, but instead, I silently cried to myself. When I got up and put my clothes back on, I ran out of Kurt's apartment knowing that I couldn't let him do that to me again. It was already bad enough that Gene and Miguel were doing that to me—I couldn't take anyone else hurting me like that. I knew I had to hide from him.

I successfully hid from Kurt for a couple of days before he tracked me down. Some of the neighborhood kids and I were using the shortcut through the woods to go to the local store to buy candy. When we were about halfway, Kurt jumped out of the woods and startled us. He grabbed my arm and demanded that the rest of the kids go on. My heart pounded with fear as I saw the kids turn away and leave me. He dragged me deep into the woods. He started touching and kissing me. I begged and pleaded with him to stop, but he threw me to the ground, held my hands and forced himself inside me. The more I begged him to stop, the harder he thrust his penis inside me. When he was done with me, he left me lying in the woods sobbing and half-naked. I blacked out from the pain that ripped through my body. I don't know how I got out of the woods, or how I got home. I don't know how I got past Mom and Gene without them saying anything to me. Kurt must have thought that he punished me enough that day because he never bothered me again.

I didn't want anything else to do with boys or sex—I'd had enough of it. I couldn't make Gene and Miguel stop what they were doing, but I sure could stay away from all the other males in my world.

The sexual abuse continued and Mom never addressed it, not even once. She was too busy fighting with Gene and lashing out at me to have time to deal with the possibility that her husband was having sex with her daughter. I was left alone to fend for myself and try to survive.

The nightmares continued, as did the sleepwalking. I was exhausted from trying to survive the life that existed for me during the day and the unconscious battles my mind fought at night. I was repeatedly having the same dreams. I remember one particular dream where I was running down the streets of a town that had been left in ruins by a nuclear bomb. I was looking for someone to help me, but there was no one. I was always amazed, yet disturbed, by that dream because parts of it were in black and white and other parts in color.

I was now entering the eighth grade, and there was a teacher, Mrs. Tinsley who taught a different eighth grade class who caught my attention. That whole year I wished that I had been in her class because she was a very nice lady who paid me a compliment one day. She told me that I had the most perfect and articulate speech she had ever heard from a kid.

That was the first compliment I had ever had. Her words filled my heart with warmth and joy. I desperately needed to hear those kind words.

Mrs. Tinsley lived with her husband in the same town houses we lived in. I frequently visited with her and her husband. I wanted her to like me so I could feel as if I belonged in her family. But, I also wanted her help so badly that I latched on to her for dear life. I wanted her to see and understand what was going on in my home, to make it all better, to make me feel worthwhile as a person, and to help me deal with everything that was happening in my life. I spent a lot of time dreaming that she rescued me from my family; became my mother; and that we lived happily ever after.

Mom and Gene's fighting escalated to an explosive level and Gene was drinking just about every day. The interesting thing about his drinking was that he wasn't one of those falling down drunks who couldn't keep a job. Instead, he was one of those functioning alcoholics who could hold down a job and not appear to have a problem or be drunk until someone made him mad. Thus, people didn't usually catch onto the fact that he had a drinking problem and was violent when he drank.

I was also afraid to come home from school because I never knew what I was going to find. Usually, the apartment was torn into pieces because Gene was drunk and broke anything he could get his hands on. There would be dishes, glass, furniture and food lying everywhere. Several times the police were called and my brothers and I spent hours at the police station hoping for a reprieve, but one never came.

One night Gene had gone into a rage and was arguing with Mom, I begged him to stop, but he continued ripping up everything in the house and beating up Mom. Once again, our neighbors called the police, and Gene was handcuffed and taken to the police station. It was late at night, but Mom piled our tired bodies into the car and we followed. I was so tired I could barely keep my eyes open. As usual, she didn't press charges. Even though it was a school night and we had to get up early the next morning, we spent all night at the police station while Mom tried to get Gene out of jail.

There was never any consideration for us kids. No one ever thought about how we were handling anything, or how afraid or embarrassed we were. That became all too apparent one New Year's Eve when my brother's friend, Philip, spent the night with us. Mom and Gene got into yet another fight. They were yelling, and Gene was breaking furniture. I was embarrassed for my brother and I couldn't believe that Mom and Gene couldn't find a way not to argue for just one night while my brother had company. Running into the living room and seeing the rage in Gene's eyes, I could sense that this was going to be a terrible fight. He slapped Mom in the face and dragged her by her hair up the stairs to their bedroom. He slammed the door shut behind him with such fury that my body quivered. I was afraid that he might kill her this time. I ran upstairs to my room so I could hear what was happening. Mom's screams were blood-curdling, like the cries of someone who knew they were going to die. All of a sudden, the crying stopped and it sounded like she was struggling. I stood in the hall with thoughts of her death racing through my mind before I ran into their room. I saw Mom lying on the floor with Gene holding her by her hair and shoving pills into her mouth. He was trying to kill her!

Gene screamed, "Get out!" I didn't move. He then said, "Your mom is trying to kill herself."

I stood there, silent and unbelieving. Suddenly, he pushed me aside and ran out of the room to get drunk.

That new level of volatility became a daily occurrence in our house. With the feeling of not fitting in at school, all of the beatings, the fighting, the sexual abuse, not having any self-esteem, and not feeling loved, my grades at school went downhill and I started my unconscious search for help.

When Mom and Gene started to fight and I felt like I couldn't stand there and watch it anymore, I would often find myself at Mrs. Tinsley's home with my knuckles hurting from frantically knocking on her door. I kept hoping she could help me and make the fighting stop—after all, calling the police never got us anywhere. Unfortunately, Mrs. Tinsley didn't know what to do either.

With each day that passed, I felt more and more helpless. I was sad because I didn't know what to do with what I was feeling, but I was also angry because I had no way to retaliate against my abusers and their transgressions. Since I couldn't strike out at anyone who was hurting me, I desperately wanted to kill myself so all the pain in my life would magically go away.

My need to hurt myself was so great that I wrote Mrs. Tinsley a note and told her that I was going to kill myself. My hands literally shook as I threw the note on her desk and ran out of her room. Part of me was relieved that I had told someone what I was going to do, but I also feared what the consequences would be for my confession. My note apparently got her attention because she came and got me out of my next class to talk to me about it.

She said, "I'm sorry about what is happening at your home, but I don't know what to do about it."

"I want to go home with you," I implored.

She replied, "That's not possible."

I was consumed with despair because I knew there was nothing she could do to make my pain disappear. I felt just as empty on the inside at the end of the conversation as I did when it began.

Since I was too afraid to kill myself, I fantasized about it. I ran scenarios through my mind about how I would try to kill myself and how someone would rescue me. I fantasized that Mrs. Tinsley would leave the school building and would see me passed out on the grass from an overdose. I imagined her rushing me to the hospital with a look of worry on her face. I dreamed that I looked into her eyes and knew that everything was going to be okay because she would take me home with her to a place where love was waiting for me. These scenarios of being loved and cared for made my life at home temporarily disappear.

My fantasies of being rescued by Mrs. Tinsley never came to pass, and my relationship with her slowly faded away. She began avoiding me and only occasionally talked with me. It seemed that my family and I were more than she could handle.

The loss of my only friend left me, once again, resorting to isolation. I began hanging out in the woods next to the apartments. I made it my job to explore everywhere I could within walking distance so I wouldn't have to be at home in the midst of the fighting, drinking and beatings. I loved to be in woods, so much so that I pretended that I lived so far back in them that nothing else in the world existed.

I was truly becoming a different person and it showed at school. I went from being a straight A student, caring about what other people thought, wanting to be liked by other kids, and wanting everyone to think I was a good kid, to doing some really stupid things. I skipped school dances to hang out with the wrong crowd. I started stealing pills out of Mom's medicine bottles to take to school so the other kids would think I was cool. The kids I was passing drugs to asked me if the stuff I was stealing would give them a buzz and if I could get more. Since I had no idea what I was stealing, I just played it up as much as possible. I thought I was finding a way to have friends and I wasn't about to blow it. I was making an impression with the drugs, but not to the people I wanted to notice my desperation. However, being part of something felt great, even though I was terrified of getting caught. But history repeated itself as usual when Mom cut short my new endeavor.

It was the last days of my eighth grade year. I was about to graduate and go to one of the coolest high schools in Cincinnati. I was convinced my whole life was going to change at the new school and I couldn't wait.

One afternoon, three days before the end of the school year, I came home from school and Mom broke the news to me that we were moving again to a very small town in the middle of nowhere. I couldn't believe what I was hearing. It was like someone reached into my soul and ripped out every bit of hope I'd had left. I couldn't take another move to another school with different kids just so Mom and Gene could continue fighting and pretending as if nothing was wrong. I was being yanked out of yet another place I had gotten used to, just to start all over again. The solemn promise of "never moving again" was being broken. I don't know what happened to me at that very moment in my life, but I felt my whole personality change. I emotionally "snapped." I was changed forever, never to return to the innocent and hard-working child I had been.

It was the last day of the school year and there was a big graduation event for all of the eighth graders. It seemed like the entire school was there, and after the formalities there was a huge celebration. Everyone was roaming around, talking to each other and having a great time. I, on the other hand, had no one to talk to because I didn't have any friends. I didn't belong to any group: the "in" crowd, the "bad" crowd or the "geeks." I was left alone to struggle with the thoughts about our moving again and I was utterly depressed. I didn't feel like I could breathe, much less socialize with a bunch of people I would never see again. I literally wanted to lie down and die—there was no one to tell what was happening; no one who could help me get through it; and no one to stop it from happening again.

Chapter 6

The Geographical Cure

Our new destination was Felicity, a very small town located about an hour outside of Cincinnati, in the middle of absolutely nowhere. One Saturday afternoon, Mom and Gene put us in the car and we drove up to Felicity to see our new home. As we cruised slowly down the main street of the city, I was devastated that the town looked so poor, with only one school, two bars, a grocery store, a couple of small restaurants, and a traffic light.

I sat in the back seat of the car, silent and sad, as we drove to the house we were going to live in. It was located about four miles outside Felicity on Chilo Hill. Chilo Hill was the name of the road that connected Felicity to a little community called Chilo. And, yes, the road was actually on a hill. Chilo was even smaller than Felicity with its solitary convenience store, bait and tackle shop, and a locally-owned ice cream and fast food type place. It wasn't more than a spot in the road.

While we drove up Chilo Hill, I saw nothing but a couple of old run-down houses with abandoned cars sitting in the front yards. About a mile or so up the road, Gene took a left-hand turn onto a gravel drive that crossed over a small creek and faced a decaying farmhouse. Mom's eyes beamed with excitement as she told us, "This is it! It will need a lot of work because chickens and pigs used to live in it, but we can make it pretty, and it'll be our own home."

Mom's enthusiasm was confusing because my heart only held disappointment at how ugly the house was. I couldn't believe we were going to live in yet another embarrassing place that Mom and Gene would expect us to renovate. I didn't know how many more times I could fix up a broken house. And why did we live like average people in one place, and like paupers in another? The inconsistency was baffling.

The driveway stopped at the back of the house as the back door was used as the main entrance. To enter the house we had to step over a large concrete hole in the ground that caught rainwater. Since there was no city water that far out, we had to rely on Mother Nature to provide us with water. When she decided it was time for a dry spell, we had to scrape up money to pay someone to bring us water in a truck.

Looking around the old farmhouse, it was obvious that just about everything needed renovating. The floors smelled and were ruined from the chicken and pig excrement. The ceilings were falling in and the walls were rotten and buckling. There was mold and mildew in every room, and the tin roof had rusted all the way through from years of not being painted. The front porch sagged from not having enough creek rocks under the corner posts to keep it leveled, and the old floor was rotten and rippled. The exterior was almost hopeless. Some sections of the house were only covered with tarpaper, while other sections were shedding old white paint. There was nothing in the house that wasn't antiquated and in need of repair. To use my mother's own word, the house was "dilapidated."

In relation to our assigned rooms, we pretty much had the same set-up as before with my room being upstairs and across the hall from Mom and Gene's, while my brothers shared a bedroom downstairs. As always, I was assigned a room near Mom because I was her protector.

It seemed like Mom thought all her problems, including those with Gene, would disappear if we moved to that house in the country. In many ways it was like a "geographical cure" for whatever ailed her. Her philosophy was, "If life gets tough—move!" It would have been nice though if she had stopped and thought about how the constant moving was affecting us kids, especially me. I needed her to understand how everything was making me feel, that I was on the verge of giving up at only thirteen years of age.

We spent the next several weeks driving up to Felicity to work on the house. Our family problems moved right along with us, despite Mom's dream of a magical geographical cure. I hated every drive we made to the house, and every minute we spent working on it. I was tired from the strenuous labor we endured. And, I was distressed because the more we worked on the old farmhouse, the more Mom and Gene fought. They couldn't complete a project or task without a major blow out, or intentionally hurting each other. The atmosphere was so tense that neither my brothers nor I even dared to breathe in the wrong direction.

Even the normal developmental stuff that kids go through was too much for Mom and Gene to handle. It didn't take much to get them riled up and that was evident one day when we were getting ready to leave the old farmhouse to go back home to Cincinnati. We had spent the entire weekend trying to make the old place livable. I was absolutely exhausted and every muscle in my body ached from hours of strenuous labor. The only thing that kept me going that horrible weekend was Mom's promise that she and Gene would start teaching me how to drive when we finished our work that weekend. I was excited when I knew it was time for my reward. As we stood in the driveway getting ready to leave, Mom asked Gene to take me out for my first lesson. Anger immediately covered his face. He looked at Mom like he could have ripped her face off. He flew into a fit of rage, spun around and began yelling at me, "I don't want to waste my time with something as trivial as a driving lesson!"

After Gene was finished verbally bashing me, the argument with Mom escalated into a major fight that resulted in Gene taking Mom's car keys and ordering us to walk back to Cincinnati. My heart sank with guilt because I believed the whole argument was my fault. If I hadn't wanted a driving lesson, then we wouldn't be walking back to Cincinnati, which was over 45 miles away. What was I thinking?

Mom refused to give in to Gene, so we took off walking. Eventually we found the main highway, where we walked for hours. I was afraid that we wouldn't be able to see when the sun went down, and was embarrassed because I thought everyone driving by had to know that we were walking because of a family fight. It felt as if each car that passed us could see right through me.

Close to sundown, Gene drove up behind us, stopped the car and told Mom to get in. She refused to respond to him. So another fight ensued right there on the highway with God and everyone watching. When it looked like Gene was going to hit her, Mom gave in, and we rode back to Cincinnati with him in silence.

We finally moved into the old farmhouse, even though we had to continue working on it every day. There were many days when I didn't think I was going to be able to drive another nail, plaster another wall, or lay another piece of flooring without going crazy.

I wasn't only exhausted from the arduous work and constant fighting, but from hunger. Gene was the only one working at that time because Mom had supposedly developed agoraphobia. Her alleged fear of open places made her a prisoner of herself and shut her off from the world. At the same time, it allowed her to torment me in silence. The money and food were very limited and there were many days that my brothers and I were hungry. Mom and Gene became so desperate, that they bought chickens to raise so we could slaughter and eat them. That idea horrified me. My brothers and I were given the responsibility of feeding the chickens every day and I made the mistake of becoming attached to them. When the chickens reached maturity, I braced myself for the killing ritual that was to follow.

I remember standing in the backyard as I watched Gene chase the chickens. As soon as he caught one, he broke its neck and cut the head off with an ax. The headless chickens flailed around before falling to the ground in silence. Gene handed Mom the freshly killed bird to submerge in boiling water. My stomach churned from the smell of scalding flesh and wet feathers. After boiling the chickens for a few minutes, they handed them to me and my brothers for us to pluck the feathers. I sat there and cried during the whole affair, horrified at touching my dead friends. I was unable to eat the chickens, no matter how hungry I became.

About a month later, I realized I was tired of everything and I was never going to adjust to Felicity. Mom and Gene were never going to stop fighting; Gene was never going to stop drinking; and they were never going to stop abusing me. I just couldn't take it anymore. I wanted out. I wanted to be happy and free from my life of hell. So I conned Mom into letting me go to Cincinnati with Gene one day so I could visit fabricated old friends at the old town houses while he went to work at the university. I was supposed to meet Gene at the apartments at five o'clock to return to Felicity with him. Instead of visiting friends, especially since I didn't have any, I walked around and tried to muster up the courage to run away. I knew it was the right thing to do or I was going to end up dead or insane. Thoughts of freedom ran through my head and I made the decision to do it—to run away.

I went to the pizza place across the street from the apartments to get something to eat before heading out on my long journey. After I ate, I thought it was safe to leave because nighttime had set in. But, just as I walked out the door, Gene came up behind me, grabbed by the back of my neck and dragged me to the car. He threw me in the car with such force that I was afraid he was going to injure me. He yelled at me the whole way home and promised that he and Mom were going to kill me. He kept yelling, "Were you planning to run away?" I wouldn't answer him; I feared his response. I didn't trust that he wouldn't kill me right there and dump my body somewhere.

After we got home and I walked in the back door, Mom was standing there holding a long, thick belt in her hand. She was screaming, "You were trying to run away weren't you?" She started pushing me around and demanded that I tell her that I was running away. The more she pushed me around, the more I cried, until I finally snapped. I was angry because she was asking me all those questions, and yet she wasn't willing to hear the truth without punishing me for it.

I finally screamed, "Yes, I was running away—I hate living with you and Gene—I hate what you're doing to me!" No sooner than those words flew out of my mouth and I realized what I had said, I knew I was dead. My truthful statement resulted in Mom and Gene both throwing me against the couch and taking turns beating me with the belt until my flesh was screaming for a reprieve or death.

The hell continued.

With my ninth grade school year quickly approaching, Mom, my brothers, and I went shopping for school stuff. We didn't have much money so, we shopped very carefully and made every penny count. I always liked it when I got my new pencils and paper because it made me feel special. After we finished our shopping late in the afternoon, I was excited that we were driving back home so I could show off my new school supplies to Gene. I breezed into the house where my enthusiasm quickly dissipated by the look on Gene's face that told me he was mad about something. I was instantly filled with terror when he started yelling at Mom. I knew that a big fight was inevitable. Mom yelled back and his face grew distorted with rage at her defiant words. In one quick swoop, he punched her in the face. Several more blows followed.

In order to protect Mom, I jumped into the middle of the argument and started yelling, "Stop hitting her!"

He took one look at me with his frenzied eyes and began pushing me around and telling me, "I'm going to kill you if you don't get out of my face!"

The hollowness of his eyes and the feel of his angry words told me he was serious, so I bolted outside. He ran after me and chased me into a corner between the oil tank and the house. He picked up a snow shovel and swung at me several times. I cowered away from him—I was truly afraid he was going to kill me. As he readied the shovel for another swing, I broke away and ran back into the house. Since he wasn't able to find me, he went back to arguing with Mom with a new vengeance.

The arguing escalated until I became so afraid that Gene was going to hurt Mom that I ran upstairs and got the shotgun out of their room. I ran back downstairs with the gun and pointed it at him. I was so scared that I couldn't get any words to come out of my mouth. I could only stand there with the gun nervously aimed at him. I was literally shaking all over and thought I was going to wet my pants. When he saw the gun, his look told me that he was going to hurt me if he ever got his hands on me or the gun. He started running toward me and I froze—I couldn't breathe; I couldn't move.

Before I knew what had happened, he grabbed the shotgun, pointed it at me, and shouted, "If you ever point another gun at me, I'll kill you!"

I could see it in his eyes that he was debating whether he should go ahead and kill me right then and there. I stood there in utter silence and didn't make a move—I had learned my lesson. I don't know what made him stop, but instead of shooting me, he took the gun and started breaking up the rest of the house with it. I was still so frightened that I could hardly move for the next several minutes. It was like my world was moving in slow motion.

I returned to my senses and realized that I needed to get help. I quietly sneaked upstairs again, crawled out of my bedroom window and ran down Chilo Hill to call the police. I stood in a phone booth shivering with fright. After calling the police, I gathered the courage to return home and crawled back through the same window. Moments later, the police showed up and saw what had happened in our house. Their concerned voices suggested that Mom let them take us kids so we would be safe. They also told her we could end up being removed from the home if the domestic violence continued. I could see that Mom was afraid, but she insisted we weren't going to a foster home, even temporarily, and she wouldn't let anyone help us either. As usual she refused to press charges against Gene, but instead tried to act like everything was all right. Nothing changed.

Another school year commenced and I was nervous about going to another new school. It was small and it wasn't as cool or modern as the high school I was supposed to be attending in Cincinnati. All the grades were on the same grounds. I was afraid I was still going to be an outcast and all the kids would tease me about my eye. I wasn't sure I could go through that again.

The first person I met was a girl named Pennie. She had short blonde hair, wore wire-framed, octagonal shaped glasses, and was also in the ninth grade. I didn't know what it was about her, but we seemed to like each other, and I was elated that I might have a friend. We talked in the hall for a few minutes after class and I was surprised that she invited me to my first party. I had no idea what I was about to get myself into, but I was so excited that I didn't care.

Surprisingly, Mom let me go to the party, and with great joy I got ready before Pennie and her brother, Joseph, picked me up. They drove far back into the woods to a place called "the farm." It was an isolated and abandoned farmhouse located in the middle of a field and the place where all the local kids partied. There was a huge tobacco barn, much like the one in Lexington, which stood next to the house. The inside of the house was filled with old tattered chairs, old cushions, seedy mattresses, and other broken furniture to sit and lie on. It was like I was in a time warp back to the 1960s, at a secret psychedelic party—I loved it!

By the time we arrived, there were a lot of people there. I was filled with an exhilaration and anticipation I had never felt before, even though I was still worried that I wasn't going to fit in. Those feelings were put aside when I saw bottles of liquor lying all around the house: screw drivers, salty dogs, and tequila sunrises pre-mixed in bottles. Before I knew it, someone handed me a bottle and my first drink of alcohol. As I took a large swallow of the sweet flavored drink, my whole body glowed with warmth. I immediately felt like I belonged somewhere, like I was in heaven. Someone lit up several joints and started passing them around. I had never seen a joint and didn't know what to do. But I pretended I had been smoking pot all my life so I wouldn't seem square. I immediately loved its smell, and more importantly, how it made me feel. I had never felt such ecstasy as I did that night. I forgot all my pain and no longer felt the loneliness and desperation of my life—the hole that lived inside me was full for the first time. I felt free and wanted to hold on to that feeling as long as I could.

To enjoy my new sense of invulnerability, I kept drinking and toking until I blacked out and then passed out. Sometime later, I woke up vomiting on the floor in one of the back rooms. Pennie and Joseph stood over me telling me they couldn't take me back home in my inebriated condition. So they convinced me to call home to see if Mom would let me spend the night with them. I don't know how, but I managed to call home and got permission to spend the night with Pennie. Since I was literally, "home free," I continued to celebrate my new-found freedom.

I blacked out again and came to outside a local bar where Pennie and Joseph could buy black market liquor. I was afraid we were going to get caught and thrown into jail. I knew I would never be able to explain that kind of thing to Mom and it would earn me another beating. Despite my fear, we went into the bar through the back door and got a fifth of Sloe Gin. While we were there, Pennie and Joseph spotted my folks sitting in the bar, getting drunk. I was so scared that I froze, and my body shook from the imagined beating I was about to get. I was snapped out of my trance when Pennie grabbed my arm and dragged me out of the bar so we didn't blow my fabricated story. We finally ended up at Pennie and Joseph's house where they smuggled me, and the fifth of liquor, into her room. I lay in her bed and stared up at her ceiling not fully understanding what had transpired that night. I eventually drifted off to sleep from too much liquor and too much dope.

The next morning, I woke up with my first hangover. I forced myself out of bed to hurry home. Afraid that Mom and Gene saw me at the bar, I walked slowly into the house and checked to see how everyone's mood was. I tried to act like nothing had happened, but I smelled like booze and looked like hell. Strangely, Mom and Gene never said a word to me about anything. I wondered how they couldn't have known.

I didn't realize it at the time, but this was the point where my life and that of my brothers began taking on a different direction. It was as if we were looking to Mom for love and protection, and when she couldn't provide it, we went our separate ways. My way was trying to stay away from the house and anesthetizing myself while my brothers sought out other people who could be surrogate parents. It was a shame that we had looked to Mom for survival and never thought about looking to each other.

After I discovered alcohol and pot, I learned there was something special about the school because it afforded me a great deal of freedom. Everyone in the high school was allowed to leave the school grounds and go across the street to the Black Crow Café for lunch. It was a really cool place with a jukebox, dance floor, pin ball machines, and a fooze ball table. None of the straight-laced churchgoers or momma's boys hung out there, just the cool and bad crowd.

The freedom of leaving the school grounds was a blessing, but also a nightmare because it opened up a new area in my life where self-destruction prevailed. About three months into the new school year, I was terribly upset about the fighting and drinking at home and that I had no one to talk to. I felt like I was going to explode if I had to endure another day of fearing for my life, watching Gene beat Mom or tear the house up. As I crossed the street to the Black Crow Café, I became apprehensive because I couldn't bear the thought of being around other people. So I kept walking until I found myself at the same bar where Pennie and Joseph got the liquor that first night we partied at the farm. I was worried that they wouldn't sell me the booze and terrified that they would turn me into the police. But surprisingly, I acquired the fifth of Sloe Gin I so desperately needed.

I quickly left through the back door of the bar and took the isolated secondary streets back to the school. My hands shook as I clutched the freedom that was hidden in the brown paper bag. I could hardly wait to tear open the bottle that held my escape and sanity. I kept a watchful eye out to make sure no one was following me, and that no one saw me drinking the liquor. By the time I had gotten back to the school, I had consumed the entire fifth and was quite drunk.

I had forgotten that the high school was scheduled to have an assembly that afternoon in the gym. That was fine with me because it meant I didn't have to see any of my teachers the rest of the day. I sat down on the bleachers and became overwhelmed with feelings of not fitting in anywhere and I was so depressed that I could hardly breathe. I didn't know what was wrong, and why the alcohol wasn't doing its usual trick with helping me to escape my thoughts and feelings. I quietly slipped out of the assembly and went into one of the classrooms to sit in the dark so I could be alone in my suffering. Surely, no one would miss me. The longer I sat in the dark room, the more depressed I became. I was dying for someone to talk to, but I knew it was forbidden to tell the family secrets.

Suddenly, the classroom door opened and one of my teachers, Mrs. Tristin, entered the room and demanded to know what I was doing. Through my alcohol-scented breath and slurred words, I told her I needed a little space from everyone else for a few minutes. Looking concerned, she sat down and asked, "Have you been drinking?"

"Absolutely not, I don't drink—really!" I said loudly.

"There's no point in lying because I can smell alcohol on your breath. Sandy, what's wrong?"

My heart ached because I couldn't believe that someone was finally asking me that question. I wanted to tell her everything. I wanted her to make my pain disappear. I looked directly at her and saw in her eyes that she wanted to help me. But, as soon as I realized what the consequences would be for exposing the family, I retreated into my shell of shame, just shook my head and looked away. Since it was apparent that I wasn't going to share my secrets, Mrs. Tristin escorted me to the principal's office for punishment.

The principal was a tall, thin, quiet-spoken man. I trembled with nervous anticipation as I waited outside his office for what seemed like an eternity. He finally called me into his office and I felt the same fear that Mom always elicited in me—the fear of unspeakable chastisement. I tried to cover up my drinking, but he smelled the alcohol on my breath and saw my lack of coordination. He told me he was going to suspend me for five days for being intoxicated during school hours. His words stung my ears and filled my soul with panic because I knew Mom was going to kill me or, worse, beat me senseless.

"Please forgive me. Please give me another chance," I begged. He ignored me and kept writing notes. Not knowing what else to do I asked, "Can I please go to the bathroom while you call my folks?" He nodded as he picked up the phone, so I got up and went in the girl's bathroom, knowing that I had to escape before Mom and Gene showed up. I was afraid and had to run—to where—I didn't know. My heart pounded as I ran out the back door of the school.

As soon as I got outside, the cold air slapped me in the face and I saw that several inches of snow had accumulated on the ground since my walk to the liquor store. I had no place to go so I wandered around town for hours on the back streets, contemplating what was going to happen to me. I was chilled to the bone and only knew of one place where I could get warm— the Black Crow Café.

The lady who owned the place told me to wait at her house next door. Minutes later she walked in and told me she knew what happened at school because the police were looking for me. I sat there crying and told her I was sorry, that I didn't mean for it to happen, but I needed the alcohol to help me feel better inside. To my dismay, she didn't seem to care much about what I was saying, kept interrupting me and telling me that I should turn myself in so I could go home. Her words that I needed to "go home" absolutely terrified me. She then left the room for a minute and my heart knew that she hadn't heard anything I'd said. No one understood what I was saying. I felt helpless and like I had no other way out, so I took the knife I had out of my pocket and cut my left wrist three times very deeply, hoping I would bleed to death.

The police and my parents walked into the room and saw my wrist bleeding profusely. The look of anger in my mother's eyes pierced my sinking soul, while the police told me they were going to arrest me and charge me with carrying a concealed weapon. They confiscated my knife, and tried to get me to tell them where I had bought the alcohol, but there was no way I was giving away my secret. Then they said they already knew, and that I would have to appear before a judge because of the concealed weapon and the fact that the bar had sold alcohol to other minors.

But instead of arresting me, the police had Mom and Gene escort me back to the school so the principal could tell me how disappointed he was in me and then suspended me for ten days, instead of just five days. I just bowed my head in shame.

My folks took me home without saying a word. When we got home, Mom looked at my cut wrist, but said nothing as she cleaned out the wounds and put gauze around it. She muttered, "You might need stitches," but never offered to take me to the doctor. She never said anything to me about the suspension, about cutting my wrist, or anything. I was shocked and didn't know what to think or believe about her silence, so I hid myself in my room and prayed that God would let me die.

Drinking and drugging were now my only escape from all the feelings I was having: the bad stuff going on between Mom and Gene; the sexual abuse; the beatings; and from myself. I latched on to drinking and drugging like I had latched on to Mrs. Tinsley and other people—it was my only saving grace.

Gene also continued drinking just about every day. He was mainly a beer man who liked putting away lite beers by the quarts. I hated it when he drank, and especially when he got drunk because it was always a sign that something bad was about to happen. I remember one day when he drove the car off a 100-foot embankment in a drunken state during an argument with Mom. When the police and emergency units showed up, they found neither of them seriously injured, just bruised and scraped up. The most unbelievable thing though, was that Mom told the police that she was the one who was driving! As a result, no one was arrested or charged with anything. After Mom drove them home, she told me what happened and admitted that Gene drove off the embankment on purpose—an attempt at suicide and murder.

There still wasn't any regard for how everything was affecting us kids. My brother Pat, who was in the eight grade, was still wetting his bed. I was sick a lot, and had been for several years. Despite my illnesses, we didn't go to any doctors for help or medicine. We barely had any contact with the outside world, much less any physicians. After all, Mom couldn't risk anyone knowing what was really happening at our house.

One day, I had to stay home from school because I was sick with strep throat. I spent the day in my room and in bed feeling awful. I could barely move and wished that someone would give me some medicine to make me feel better, but I knew that was out of the question. In my feverish sleep, I heard Mom and Gene downstairs fighting, so I forced myself to wake up out of my disoriented state to make sure she was okay. I found them in the middle of another explosive argument with Gene breaking windows and what little bit of furniture we had left. Mom stood there crying with the usual look of disbelief on her face. My soul ached for her. I begged Gene to stop and to tell me what was wrong so I could fix it. He looked hatefully at me and stormed out of the house, slamming the back door so hard the glass in the door shattered all over the floor. My heart was broken, but I tried to comfort Mom and to let her know that everything was going to be all right. However, her grief was too great for consolation. Instead, she went into her room and left me to clean up the mess. I was completely bewildered with what had just transpired. All I could do was stand there and cry at the task that lay before me and because I couldn't even get anyone to care for me when I was sick.

To top everything off, the physical abuse from Mom worsened. What little bit of a relationship we once had was completely destroyed by now even though I still felt responsible to protect her and silently held onto the childish hope that she would love me one day. I still fantasized about her holding me and telling me that she loved me. Instead, I was afraid to go home each day after school because I never knew how I was supposed to act or feel around her. I always stopped at the door, checked the tension and atmosphere in the house so I would know how I was supposed to act and feel and then adjusted my mood accordingly. If Mom was in a bad mood, then I was quiet, stayed out of her way and hid in my room or closet. If Mom and Gene were fighting, I took care of Mom and the house. If Mom was in an occasional good mood, I talked to her and soaked up how good it felt to be with my mother. The troubling thing was that I couldn't be myself and I wasn't sure who I was anymore. *I had lost me a long time ago.* I was now like a chameleon who waited to see what color to change to so I could fit in and be safe.

I really needed Mom to listen to me and to help me, but she was so wrapped up in her own problems that she didn't have time for me. I was left out in the cold to deal with my thoughts and feelings the best way I could. I also appeared to be Mom's personal venting arena because she picked on me all the time and I could never do anything right. She started fights and arguments with me, not because I did anything wrong, but because she was in a foul mood or was angry with Gene. I never knew when she was going to strike so I remained constantly on guard. What always amazed me was it didn't take much to set her off.

One morning, she accused me of breaking a glass measuring cup she used when she made her precious biscuits. Despite the fact that I tried to tell her Gene had been using the cup, she accused me of lying. She started slapping my face and then pushing and punching me. I begged her, "Please stop hitting me—it's not my fault!" My words only infuriated her more. Her anger turned into rage and she was now kicking me as hard as she could. I was so afraid that I assumed my usual posture in the corner of the kitchen to protect myself.

She snatched me out of the corner by my hair and screamed, "You'd better find my cup, and find it fast!" My voice shook as I continued to tell her that Gene had it, but she kept beating me until exhaustion finally set in.

I stood there devastated and crying. Mom looked at me with hate in her eyes and screamed, "Get out of my house and never come back!" I stood there for a minute in shock, and wondered if I heard her words correctly. Then I felt her hands pushing me out the back door. As soon as the frigidly cold air hit my face, I saw several inches of snow on the ground. I didn't have any choice but to start walking to Felicity, even though it was about four miles away. The long and arduous walk was very cold and very difficult because it was mostly uphill and I didn't have any snow boots on. I walked and cried—I felt alone and had absolutely no idea what I was going to do.

The more I walked, the colder I became. I finally made it to Felicity and was relieved to see that the school was open for a basketball game. My plan was to sneak into the school, hide in there until everyone was gone, and then kill myself. That way I could make the bad stuff go away permanently and no one would find me until it was too late.

I sat in a classroom in the dark with my knees pulled tightly to my chest for several hours. I cried because I didn't really want to kill myself; I just wanted Mom to love me and not to hurt me anymore. I wanted someone to help me and to listen to me.

After the ball game was over, I was too afraid to stay in the school, so I ran out of the classroom back out into the snow. I had nowhere else to go, so to stay warm, I huddled under a tractor trailer outside the closed Black Crow Café. I felt completely lost and devastated as I sat there shivering under the tractor trailer. I didn't know what to do. I looked up and saw the pay phone outside the café. I cried, as I only knew one person who might help me, Mrs. Tristin, the teacher who busted me when I got drunk at school.

After getting over the initial embarrassment of calling her, I managed to get the words out of my trembling lips that I needed her to help me. Without hesitation, she came to pick me up and took me to her house. We sat on her couch where I told her about the argument with Mom, the beating, and getting thrown out of the house. But, I was also a good little girl in that I didn't divulge any of the other family secrets. As I told her about the fight with Mom, I saw tears welling up in her eyes. She reached over, hugged me and said that I could spend the night with her and her family. I was relieved that someone had listened to me and it felt like a ton of weight had been lifted off my weary shoulders.

I woke up the next morning happy that I was going to spend time with my new confidant and friend, Mrs. Tristin. Instead, she sat me down and told me that she had called Mom and Gene to tell them where I was and she arranged for them to come over to her house so everyone could talk. I was devastated and wondered if she had heard anything I said to her last evening. Didn't she know she was digging my grave?

Mom and Gene arrived at Mrs. Tristin's house and played their usual game of "we are such loving and caring parents and we care a great deal about our daughter." I sat there with my insides shaking while Mrs. Tristin told them what I had said.

Mom looked at Mrs. Tristin with a somber look on her face and said, "Sandy is a liar, a 'disturbed child' that no one should believe."

As Mom spoke those horribly untrue words, I was filled with despair as I watched Mrs. Tristin's face change from one of compassion to exasperation. She sent me home with my folks where I got another beating and learned the invaluable lesson of never trusting another soul.

Mom's beatings continued and were always accompanied with accusations of things that I hadn't done. The more she hit me and wouldn't let me defend myself, the more frustrated and angry I would become. But I figured that what Mom was doing was trying to make me mad so she would have a perfectly good excuse to hurt me.

When she couldn't get me to fight back, she would push me and start yelling, "Hit me! Come on, you know you want to hit me!" She continued pushing me around and hitting me as hard as she could until one day I snapped. My body became rigid, my hands turned into fists, and I was seething until every cell in my body wanted to hurt her. I felt like I wanted to explode. I wanted to scream at the top of my lungs everything I had always wanted to tell her. It was then that Mom said, "I can see in your eyes that you want to hit me back."

She was right—I was so angry I wanted to slug her a good one, but I couldn't bring myself to do it. I could never physically hurt my mother because I loved her. Instead, I ran up to my room and slammed the door shut. Not a second later the door flew open and she was standing there with a look of rage on her face. I stood there trembling and cried, "I don't want to fight with you—please leave me alone." My pleading fell on deaf ears. As I continued begging and pleading with her to leave me alone, Mom grabbed a handful of wire coat hangers out of my closet and began hitting me with them. She repeatedly hit me in the face until one of the coat hangers cut me under my bad eye. Blood began to run down my face, so I ran into the hallway. Mom ran after me and then proceeded to push me down the stairs. I lay at the bottom of the stairwell for a brief moment in disbelief, wondering who the woman was standing at the top of the stairs—she no longer resembled my mother at all. Mom screamed, "Leave my house!" So I forced my aching and battered body to get up and I ran out of the house.

I was back on the road again, walking to Felicity in the snow. This time I ended up walking around town all day trying to figure out how I could kill myself. There was no one to talk to, and no where for me to go. So, when night came, I walked back home and crept into the house after everyone had gone to bed.

I went to school the next day where all the kids asked me what had happened to my face and my eye, but I couldn't tell them. I was embarrassed and completely humiliated.

My life continued on that hurtful path and was further compromised by Lucinda. She called and asked me to come and visit her and Miguel as they had moved from the town houses in Cincinnati into a brand new house. She had also invited Philip over, a boy I had a crush on in Cincinnati. She knew I liked him and that I couldn't resist coming to see her if Philip was going to be there. I didn't give her a quick answer because I was afraid to see Miguel, but somehow I convinced myself that he couldn't mess with me if Lucinda and Philip were both there. I accepted the invitation and dreamed of seeing Philip.

I packed my bags and made sure I took a stash of liquor and pot with me—I couldn't go anywhere now without my safety net and my only means of coping with the world. After I prepared my stash, I was off to Miguel and Lucinda's house for the weekend.

Mom and Gene drove me, and I couldn't stop shaking the whole way there. So I forced myself to concentrate on the fact that I would be free to party and that Lucinda and Philip would both be there to protect me. As we pulled into their driveway, I was totally amazed at how beautiful their new house was and how they had really moved up in the world. Lucinda met me at the car to help me with my bag and to pay casual greetings to my folks.

After they left, Lucinda proudly took me on a grand tour of the house, showing off their new fancy things. With each room that was visited, I feared when Miguel would surface and how I would respond to him. We finally made it downstairs to the basement where Miguel was shooting billiards. I took one look at him and started trembling. My throat closed up and I couldn't breathe. For a split second, everything appeared as if it were in slow motion and I was back on my knees in their spare bedroom with Miguel's penis shoved so far back in my throat that I was suffocating. I was forced back into the present moment when Miguel muttered, "Hello." I looked at his face and was surprised that he didn't have that look about him that he used to when he saw me. Maybe things between them were better. Maybe they were now happy with each other.

Lucinda and I went back upstairs and I told her all about the farmhouse, the school, and that I was now drinking and getting suspended from school. She didn't seem too shocked that I drank and gave me permission to drink at their house. Her blessing to stay anesthetized was ecstasy for me and a major relief because I wasn't sure if I would be able to make it all weekend without a drink. Much to my surprise, she also let me get high.

All seemed to be going well except for one thing, Philip wasn't there. I was worried he wouldn't show up and I would be disappointed because I desperately wanted to see him again. While we awaited Philip's arrival, Lucinda had me go downstairs to the basement with Miguel to play pool. Since she still didn't believe that Miguel had messed with me sexually in Cincinnati, I had no choice but to do as she told me. I went downstairs where Miguel offered me a drink. I was amazed that everything was going smoothly and he didn't make any threats or sexual innuendoes. Just when I became comfortable and thought that Miguel was truly going to leave me alone, Philip showed up. I was so happy to see him—it was just like old times. We all played pool together and enjoyed each other's company.

Evening came and I was quite successful blocking out my nervousness and fears by getting drunk. I must have passed out on the couch in the basement because I was awakened out of my drunken stupor to a semi-conscious state to find someone sticking something in my mouth. I frantically looked up to see Miguel standing over me with that all-too-familiar look. My body became rigid with fear when I realized what was about to happen. I wanted to cry because I knew I couldn't live through that again, but I had no way of screaming out for help. My eyes begged him to stop, but my look of fright and dismay seemed to only fuel his excitement as he placed his hands on my head and thrust his penis farther into my mouth. He violently thrust his body back and forth until his semen began to flow. He shoved his penis to the back of my throat, cutting off all breathable air, while forcing me to swallow his bodily fluids. Tears flowed as I struggled to get away from him before I passed out or went crazy. After I swallowed every last bit of his semen, he threw me aside and grunted, "You ever say anything about tonight to Lucinda, I'll deny it and hunt you down and kill you."

I felt so dirty, and so ashamed, that I immediately got up and drank as much alcohol as I could gulp down while I cried silently to myself.

The next morning I got up and started drinking again. Lucinda took me aside and told me she was disappointed in me and she wanted to know why I was drunk that early in the morning. Because I couldn't tell her, she called my folks and sent me home early as a punishment. I never returned to see either one of them again.

I was staying drunk and high on a daily basis, on anything I could get my hands on. Joseph and I were partying together all the time and everyone, including him, thought we were a couple. We pretty much partied non-stop with his sister (and my best friend), Pennie. They were my partying mentors and I learned a great deal from them. I learned how to smoke pot out of pipes and bongs, how to smoke hash from under a glass, how to drink moonshine, how to pop speed, and so forth. I quickly became known around town as a drunk and druggie. Parents didn't want their kids hanging out with me and the good kids didn't want to have anything to do with me either.

So, despite wanting to be liked by the good kids and wishing I were part of their happy, well-adjusted families, I said to myself, "Okay, I don't give a shit—I'll hang out with Joseph and Pennie and their friends."

I pretty much struggled through my entire ninth-grade year. Mom and Gene continued to do their usual stuff and I continued to cope in whatever way I could find. But by the end of the school year, Joseph no longer hung out with me and he wouldn't let his sister hang out with me either because I was now trying to shoot drugs. I was alone in my self-destruction and my addiction.

The last few days of the school year proved to be extremely difficult. I went to school early one morning because Mr. Murdock, my teacher, asked to see me. He questioned, "Is there anything wrong? It's obvious that you don't have much money because you always wear the same clothes to school, and I've heard you don't have much to eat at lunch."

I tried not to answer his questions because I didn't really know if I could trust that he wouldn't tell Mom. I was relieved when he said, "You can talk to me any time, but I won't press the issue if you don't want me to."

I wanted to stand up and scream, "I want to tell you everything, but how do I know I can trust you? How do I know you won't hurt me?" However, saying nothing, I left his office, but not before catching a glimpse of a bag full of assorted pills in his top desk drawer.

Mr. Murdock and I left his office at the same time, but I couldn't get my mind off the pills in his desk drawer. My mind and my body cried out to be anesthetized, so I went back to his office to steal his valuable pills. Anxiety ripped through my body as I dug through his desk drawer and stole what I could. Running out of his office, I was devastated that I had stooped to such a level. I felt guilty and afraid.

It was pouring rain that day, so everyone had to run from one building to the other to get to classes. As I ran, I saw Mr. Murdock standing outside the door. I panicked and assumed he was waiting for me. I stood in front of him waiting to be chastised when I noticed that one of the pills had fallen out of my jacket pocket. I bowed my head in shame. I was convinced he knew what I had done. Although fearful, I tried to act cool about the whole thing, and Mr. Murdock didn't say anything to me.

I couldn't stand the silence, so I quickly ran to my next class. I sat there and became filled with paranoia that Mr. Murdock was going to tell the principal what I had done. So I ran out of the classroom to find a place to hide until I could figure out what I was going to do. Before I knew it, I was on the school roof, contemplating how I was going to get out of this mess. I was used to sitting on the roof and getting stoned with other kids during ball games. The longer I sat up there, the more I wished I had the guts to jump off, so that my horrible life would disappear.

The people across the street at the Black Crow Café called the principal and told him I was on the roof and it looked like I was going to jump. I heard voices and realized it was the principal and several other teachers coming to get me. I panicked and ran from them until I found myself standing on the other side of the roof. I stood at the edge and knew that Mom would kill me anyway, so I jumped off the three-story building.

I hit the ground hard but only managed to hurt my wrist and get scraped up. After I realized that I hadn't died, I forced myself to get up and ran into the woods to hide. I couldn't let myself get caught and be sent home. I hid for a long while and tried to stay off the roads because past experience taught me that the police would be looking for me. In utter exhaustion, I wandered up to a house and asked the people who lived there if I could use their telephone to call the principal. With tears running down my face, I said to the principal, "I'm so scared."

In a very reassuring voice, he promised, "I'll help you, but only if you came back to the school." I trusted him and went back. But, instead of helping me, he looked at me with disgust, threw me out of school again, and called Mom and Gene to pick me up.

I waited outside the school building for Mom and Gene and their wrath that would soon follow. Even though I wished for death, I found that I was afraid that my life was about to end. As I stood there contemplating the extreme consequences of my behavior and the beating that was about to ensue, Mr. Murdock approached me and said that he wanted to take me home for the summer to see if he and his wife could straighten me out. I couldn't believe that he still wanted to help after what I had done. I began crying and told him, "Mom and Gene are going to kill me."

He looked into my eyes and said, "I know. But I promise I won't let them hurt you if you agree to come home with me."

Tired of what was happening in my life, I agreed to go with him. Maybe he could show me how to make everything stop, and maybe he could help me get off the drugs and alcohol. And maybe, he could make Mom stop hitting me, and make her love me.

To my surprise, Mr. Murdock kept his promise and talked to Mom and Gene. Since Mom couldn't show her true colors in front of him, she played the role of the "caring mother" who only wanted the best for her "disturbed" child. Thus, she let me go to Mr. Murdock's house for the summer, rather than beating me.

Chapter 7

Summer Storms

I DIDN'T SAY MUCH TO MR. MURDOCK as we drove to his home in Bethel, a small town about 13 miles outside of Felicity. I was stunned from the day's events and was nervous about meeting his family. As he turned off the main road, we drove down a gravel driveway for what seemed like miles to a beautiful, rustic log home in the woods. The house was absolutely gorgeous with its combination of light and dark hardwood floors and walls. The vaulted ceilings with cedar beams were majestic and breathtaking, as was the fireplace made out of beautiful river rock. There was also a large wooden deck in the back of the house that was easily accessed through smoked glass sliding doors. The loft was just as beautiful as the rest of the house, and it was Mr. Murdock and his wife, Daphnie's, bedroom. I had never seen a house like that one before, and I was enamored with everything in it. My room, which I shared it with their infant baby, was downstairs in the basement.

Daphnie wasn't impressed with me and was very quiet, almost cold, toward me. She seemed to resent my presence. I tried to win her over by doing things like helping cook dinner, washing the dishes every night, cleaning up the house, and helping Mr. Murdock with chores. But, no matter what I did or how hard I worked, she just didn't like me. I felt absolutely horrible—I was stuck for a whole summer in another place where I wasn't wanted, another place where I didn't belong. I desperately wanted their approval, so I worked extremely hard. I worked in the garden early in the morning and late in the afternoon. In between the gardening, Mr. Murdock and I bush-hogged, cut wood, put up fences, and did other strenuous activities around his house. It was very hard work, but I really enjoyed it. Mr. Murdock and I spent a lot of time together, talking while we worked. He acted like he liked me as a person, so I answered his questions when he asked me things about home. I thought he was really listening to me and believed what I was telling him. I felt close to him and I wanted to be a part of his family.

I was doing well at the Murdock's until one day when I was standing in the kitchen washing the evening dishes and heard Mom and Gene at the front door. I dropped one of the dishes in the sink and broke it as my hands trembled in fear. I was afraid they were there to hurt me or tell lies to my new family about me. The longer Mr. Murdock and Daphnie talked with them, the more frightened and panicked I became. Without anyone seeing me, I grabbed Mr. Murdock's gun out of the kitchen drawer and ran out the back door deep into the woods. I sat in the woods and cried with the gun pointed at my head, and my index finger resting on the trigger. Just as I was about to pull the trigger, Mr. Murdock came up behind me and grabbed the gun. He looked at me with immense sadness in his eyes and said, "Everything's okay…your folks have left." I started crying and threw my arms around him as I begged him to please help me. Saying nothing, he helped me to my feet and then gently escorted me back to the house. He now understood just how messed up my life was.

I wore a marijuana leaf and a roach clip on a chain around my neck. They were my favorite possessions in the whole world and they screamed to the other kids at school, "I'm cool." One night after dinner, Mr. Murdock brought in a really beautiful, rustic cross on a chain. I thought it was the coolest thing I had ever seen. He told me he would give it to me to wear if I would give him my pot leaf and roach clip. For a moment I hesitated at the thought of giving up my identity and security blanket, but somewhere inside I really wanted to be different. So, I slowly reached up and took off my prized possessions and exchanged them for the cross. I was happy that someone actually loved me enough to give me something. I felt like I was important to at least one person in the universe, so I wore it proudly.

Shortly after the incident with the gun, we traveled to Columbus to see Mr. Murdock's parents for the Fourth of July weekend. There was going to be a big fireworks show that evening and I was excited about it. They lived in a cute little house in a quiet neighborhood and it sort of reminded me of Gene's mother and sister's house in Texas.

Just like in Bethel, Mr. Murdock took me for long walks so we could talk. I really enjoyed our walks together—it was nice to have someone to talk to. I cherished the time we spent together and how he always seemed willing to listen. That particular day led us to an old set of railroad tracks that went far back into the woods. As we were walking and talking, Mr. Murdock showed me how marijuana grew naturally in the woods. I couldn't believe all the pot that was growing out there and it was all I could do not to pick it so I could get high.

We walked for hours until we finally stopped and sat on the ground to take a break. I leaned back into the grassy field and closed my eyes to soak up the sun's warm rays. My communing with the sun was abruptly interrupted when Mr. Murdock leaned over and kissed me. I froze. Was he going to hurt me like Miguel did? My breathing came to a screeching halt and my body grew rigid with fear and anticipation as he started touching my body. I was afraid to tell him "No" because past experience taught me that it always made matters worse. I didn't know what else to do, so I stayed quiet. Seconds later, he took off my clothes and laid his heavy body on top of mine. The feel of his penis between my legs scared me and reminded me of Gene and that awful day in the bedroom. I was filled with shame and embarrassment as he spread my legs apart so he could penetrate me. He tried several times to get his large, adult-sized penis into my child-sized vagina, causing me excruciating pain. Tears rolled down my face as he panted, "Has anyone ever made love to you?" I didn't understand what he was asking because I had never heard that phrase before, so I didn't answer him. I didn't bother to volunteer that Gene had been doing that to me since I was in the sixth grade.

I silently put my clothes back on. I was stunned at what had just happened. One part of me was confused because what Mr. Murdock did to me felt very different from the other adults who had sexually abused me. Although painful, it wasn't violent. I wondered if it meant that he loved me. The other part of me was filled with despair and hurt because I wanted someone to love and care for me without physically violating me.

We walked back to the house where Daphnie immediately acted like she knew something had happened between us. I could see it on her face. The atmosphere became thick with anger and tension and I felt like dirt. I was so scared that I ran back to the woods to the patch of wild marijuana, picked a bunch of it and rolled it up in a paper towel to take back to the house. I stashed it away in hopes of drying it out and getting stoned so I could cover up my shame one last time. I then felt guilty that I was about to start using drugs all over again. I was also afraid that I would disappoint Mr. Murdock and he would send me back home. So I ran into the bathroom and flushed the pot down the toilet. Of course, the wad of pot caused the toilet to overflow. Mr. Murdock's mother was furious and yelled that she knew I had stuffed something down her toilet, even though I denied it. She hated me.

His parents also had a house full of prescription drugs. I didn't know what the majority of the medications were, but I did know what Valium was. They had a bunch of it stashed away in huge bottles, so I stole one just in case of an emergency.

The weekend was over and so was the visit. Not a word was said between Mr. Murdock and Daphnie during the entire trip back to Bethel. I felt guilty, like it was my fault.

The hard work continued in Bethel, and Mr. Murdock spent more and more time with me while his wife's resentment of me grew by the day. It felt good for someone to pay attention to me, but I was confused when Mr. Murdock touched and fondled me. I yearned for him to spend time with me because I wanted to feel loved, but without him touching me and having sex with me. But the more I wanted him to just love me, the more he touched me. Things progressively got worse and he started having sex with me each night after everyone went to bed. I was afraid to fall asleep because I knew he would soon be at my bedside kissing me and touching me, causing me to feel both guilt and pleasure. I then became afraid that he would make me do the things that Miguel did. I wondered what I was doing wrong that made men want to do those things to me?

My behavior, and the way I spent my evenings, drastically changed after we returned from Columbus. Each night after dinner, I washed the dishes, while Daphnie threw glaring looks of hostility at me. I couldn't take it anymore, so I escaped each night by swallowing several Valium. I inevitably passed out on the couch, and Mr. Murdock carried me downstairs to bed. I didn't realize it at that time, but it turned out to be more convenient for him because he could molest me while "tucking me into bed." No one ever questioned the passing out, or Mr. Murdock's late night visits to my room.

During the previous school year, he had taken pity on me by letting me join the drill team because none of the other teachers in the school would let me try out for anything. They didn't want a drunk and drug addict on their team. The drill team always went to camp during the summer months in Columbus and that summer was no exception. It was good for Mr. Murdock that the camp was held there because I could stay with the other girls at the dorm, while he and his wife avoided an expensive hotel bill by staying with his parents.

That first night at drill team camp, I felt like a fish out of water. No one talked to me and I was assigned to a room by myself, while all the other girls had friends and roommates. I was alone and felt like an outcast. I was sitting in my room, depressed and lonely, when I came to the conclusion that life wasn't worth everything I was going through. I remembered the bottle of Valium I had stolen and thought to myself that swallowing a bottle of pills and not waking up would be a painless and easy way to die. That idea sent a feeling of relief and warmth through my body that I had never felt before, as if I was given a reprieve. I said my good-byes to myself, asked God to forgive me, and took the bottle of Valium—100 pills in all. As soon as I swallowed them, I lay down on my bed with the sensation that I was free—I would never be beaten; never be sexually abused; never be hungry; and never feel like an outcast again.

I don't know what transpired after that, only what I was told. One of the girls, Penelope, came to my room and found me nearly unconscious. After seeing the empty bottle of Valium lying in the trash-can, she knew I had overdosed. There were no phones in the dorm to call for help, so she tried to keep me awake as long as possible. With several of the other girls, she walked me up and down the halls nearly all night long. After hours of pacing the cold tile floors, Penelope pulled the mattress off my bed and dragged it into her room for me to lie on, hoping I would survive until morning.

I woke up the next morning in a foggy haze, drifting in and out of consciousness. I was confused and couldn't figure out why I was still alive. I was barely able to put one foot in front of the other, but I made it downstairs for the morning gathering, which was held before breakfast. I was sitting in my chair feeling nauseous when I glanced up to see Mr. Murdock walking toward me looking angry. Without a word, he grabbed my arm and escorted me to his car while I leaned on him for stability and coordination. He put me in his car and immediately drove me to his parents' house. Out of pure fear, I didn't say a word to him. He carried me inside and laid me on the bed. When I kept passing out, he must have realized that I wasn't out of danger yet. But he wanted to avoid the hospital, so he tried to keep me awake by talking to me. I must have drifted off into unconsciousness again because he was shaking me and yelling at me when I came to. He was yelling, "Why are you doing this? Why are you trying to kill yourself?" Not knowing what to say or how to answer his questions, and trying to hide my desperation, I remained silent.

Then I remembered that Mr. Murdock had amphetamines in the bathroom in his shaving kit. I thought if I could just get in there, I could finish what I had started. I convinced him that I needed to use the restroom, so he helped me into the bathroom and left me alone just long enough for me to find the pills and swallow them. I staggered back to the bed to lie down, while he continued asking me, "Why are you trying to kill yourself?" I just lay there and cried. In frustration, he finally gave up and left me alone. I was almost unconscious again when he stormed back into the room and screamed at me because he figured out I had taken his pills. He shook me and shouted the same questions over and over again. I cried and finally told him, "I don't know why I need to kill myself—I just need to!" I saw his face grow soft with understanding and he reached over and hugged me as I passed out.

I came to in the hospital with a doctor standing over me trying to convince Mr. Murdock to put me in the psychiatric unit of the hospital because of the "serious nature of her suicide attempt." I cried because I knew I was in trouble, and surely Mom was going to arrive at any moment. To my relief, Mr. Murdock went against medical advice and took me back to his parent's house.

I don't remember much about the next several days, only that I floated in and out of consciousness. I was all too aware that Mr. Murdock's parents and wife were extremely angry with me. They wouldn't talk to me, and acted like they wanted me to leave. I couldn't understand why they didn't grasp that I was just trying to make my pain stop.

I didn't know what to do with myself, especially since no one wanted to be around me. So I hid in the basement of their house and explored all of Mr. Murdock's parents' old stuff just like I did in the little shack in Lexington. That was fine with everyone since it kept me busy. While looking around, I found several more bottles of pills stashed away. I had no idea what they were, but I swiped a large bottle of them. I was scared to death that someone was going to figure out I had stolen them, but I did it anyway. I hid the pills and planned on taking the whole bottle when no one was looking. This time I would succeed, and no one would have a chance to be angry with me.

The next day, Mr. Murdock said we were going back to Bethel. I knew that was my last chance to end my pain, so I went for a walk. I planned on swallowing every last pill, lying down in the car, and pretending to take a nap, never to wake up again. As usual, Mr. Murdock crept up behind me while I was deep in thought with my plan. He startled me so badly that I could barely answer his question when he asked, "What are you doing out here by yourself?" I wanted to tell him, but I didn't know how to share what was going on inside of me—my immense need to kill myself. So he talked while I listened. His words filled me with sorrow and a sense of hopelessness because I now understood that I didn't know how to stop what I was doing. I started crying because I wanted him to put his arms around me and hold me, like a father would his daughter.

As I cried, I confessed, "I don't know how to stop drinking, drugging, and wanting to kill myself." I then held my hand out, gave him the bottle of pills and begged, "Please help me not to do this anymore."

I could see by the look on his face that he knew I was not only desperate, but I was also serious in my cry for help. It was at that point that he promised to help me. He returned the bottle of pills I had stolen to his parents without revealing what I'd done. We never discussed what happened that day again.

We made it back to Bethel and I really tried not to do any drugs and not to think about killing myself. It was really hard, but I managed to make it for several days. The difficult thing was surviving Mr. Murdock's insatiable sexual appetite.

My efforts to straighten up, and not kill myself, were short-lived. I don't know what prompted Mr. Murdock to betray me, but one night when Mom and Gene visited, he told them the secrets I had revealed to him about my home life. Mom and Gene pasted on their "we are kind and loving parents" faces and proceeded to convince Mr. Murdock that I had lied to him, that nothing I said was true, and that I was nothing but a disturbed child. After they left, Mr. Murdock said, "You're a liar and I will never believe you again!" I was crushed and felt absolutely abandoned. I couldn't understand how he no longer believed me, especially after he saw how suicidal I was. I now had no one to talk to, and no one to believe me. Mr. Murdock then told me that he was going to send me home because he had a family emergency to attend to. Despite my begging him to let me stay, he insisted I go home. It was like his heart had turned to stone, so I had no option but to pack my bags and return home to my folks.

Chapter 8

The Return Home

THE DAY I WENT BACK HOME, I immediately discovered I was back in hell. Mom was running around the house frantic, and screaming, "Your dad kidnapped your brothers!" Dad had apparently made a surprise visit to the house to terrify the family, much like he did at the school in Texas, and the house in Lexington. Mom had allowed my real dad to manipulate her into letting my brothers go back to South Carolina with him for a visit. I was amazed that she had given in to him, but, then again, I didn't know what to expect from her anymore.

My brothers were supposed to have flown back to the Cincinnati airport from their so-called "visit" with Dad, but when they didn't get off the plane, Mom realized that he had kidnapped them. She acted surprised that he would do something like that and I couldn't understand why it was such a shock to her. After all, wasn't that who he had always been?

Weeks went by, and my dad still wouldn't let Pat and Mike return home. We were all worried about them. I was terrified I would never see them again, and feared for their safety. My brothers' abduction only proved to be another excuse for more violent arguments between Mom and Gene. Mom eventually forced Dad, through the court system, to return my brothers home before the new school year started.

As for me, I was feeling abandoned by Mr. Murdock, worried about my brothers, and trying to cope with Mom and Gene's fighting. I knew I had indeed returned to hell and there obviously wasn't any incentive for me to stay clean and sober anymore.

Mr. Murdock returned to Bethel from his supposed emergency and invited Mom, Gene, and me to go to a church event with him and his wife. I jumped for joy at the thought that maybe he had changed his mind about me and finally understood that I wasn't the one who had lied. I hoped that I would be able to live with him again, but this time without the sexual abuse.

While we were in church, they played really sad songs that reminded me of how lonely I felt and how I longed for someone to love me. My heart was crying, even though I dared not let one tear fall from my eyes. When church was over, we stood outside in the parking lot, uncomfortably exchanging pleasantries. I looked at Mr. Murdock with desperation in my eyes that silently begged him and Daphnie to rescue me and to take me back home with them. He then looked at my parents and invited us over to their house for a visit. I smiled because I believed that was the sign that they were going to ask me to move back in with them. Mr. Murdock then suggested that I ride back to their house with him on his motorcycle.

As we drove down the streets of Bethel, I was celebrating my new freedom, and hoping that Mr. Murdock had left his sexual fantasies behind in order to be my friend. Before I knew it, he cruised past the city limits and far out into the country so we could have a long ride. As we drove around, he pointed out all the places he thought were beautiful. It made me ecstatic because he seemed like he was my friend again. We rode around for about thirty minutes before he pulled off the road into a remote place where there was nothing but a huge field and a large oak tree. It was absolutely beautiful.

We got off the motorcycle and sat down under the majestic tree. I was mesmerized by the view and was happy that we could spend time together talking about nothing in particular and everything in general. I felt happy and safe, but as I stared out into the beautiful meadow, Mr. Murdock placed his hand on my leg, and leaned over and kissed me. His touch startled me and my body shook with fearful anticipation at what was about to happen. I was paralyzed with fear. I couldn't get the words out of my mouth to make him stop. So I sat there bewildered as he took my clothes off, moved his hands all over my body and laid me down in the grass. My breath grew shallow when his heavy body lay on top of mine and his penis touched the insides of my legs. My eyes begged him not to do this. I silently cried as my vagina exploded with pain when he tried to force himself inside of me. When he couldn't make it fit the first time, he tried several more times to penetrate me. When he was done, I put my clothes back on with the same shame, guilt, and embarrassment that always plagued me. I was confused and felt like it was my fault that he kept doing that to me.

It was dark by the time we walked in the front door of the house and everyone was standing around waiting on us. They glared at us, and in one angry voice asked where we had been. I felt transparent as Mom, Gene, and Daphnie looked at me with fire in their eyes. I didn't know what to say. I was confused because Mr. Murdock stood there looking at me, expecting me to answer their questions. I mumbled, "We've only been riding around." I knew they didn't believe me because I couldn't get the words out of my mouth without trembling.

Mom asked in one of her angry voices, "Did Mr. Murdock touch you?" I was too afraid to reveal my secret because I knew the adults in the room would blame me and I would get an unforgettable beating. Despite the fact that Mom knew I was lying, she didn't press the issue with Mr. Murdock. Instead, we abruptly left their house, never to return again. I was devastated that my new hope was snuffed out in a matter of a few hours. I felt like I had the whole world on my shoulders.

By now, my brother Pat spent all his time at a teacher's house so he wouldn't have to come home. And Mike locked himself away in his room playing loud music to drown out the dysfunction of our family. The fighting between Mom and Gene was more frequent and more lethal than ever. I never knew if I was going to come home to find the house destroyed, someone threatening to leave, or someone dead. Because of that, I had to do something to keep from going absolutely insane. I had to get some help and I had to stop drinking and drugging. I was tired of being the local alcoholic and drug addict, the kid that no nice mom would let their son or daughter hang out with. I needed someone to help me. Since there was no one who could help me figure out what I needed to do to change, I thought getting a job might be the answer. That way I wouldn't have time to get in trouble and it would keep me away from home.

I met Marie when I was looking for a job. She ran the local quick-stop type of restaurant in Chilo. That place was my last chance at getting a job since no one else would hire me because of my reputation. Marie was very up-front with me and told me she knew who I was and she knew I was a partier. But she gave me a chance by letting me interview with her. I did everything but beg for the job. My sincere desire to do better must have shown through because she said she would give me a chance, as long as I promised not to come to work drinking or high. I wanted that chance more than anything in this world. I wanted to be a good kid. So I promised, and she gave me the job. I was so excited that I could now prove to everyone that I wasn't a bad person.

I showed up to work every day clean and sober. I worked hard and really tried to please Marie because I wanted her to like me. Each night I walked home and prayed with each step that it was too late for anyone to be up arguing and fighting, and for anyone to take out their anger and frustration on me.

After I proved myself to Marie for a couple of weeks, she finally started relaxing around me. I was so comfortable with her that I allowed her to see a side of me that not too many people were privy to. One night it was really late when I got off work, so Marie asked if she could give me a ride to the house. A warm glow that only came from feeling special surrounded me, so I accepted her offer. On the way up Chilo Hill, I asked Marie to let me off in the driveway instead of at the house. I didn't want her to see where we lived and I didn't want to be embarrassed if she heard Mom and Gene fighting. After she pulled into the drive, Marie turned the car engine off and looked at me in a way I had never seen before. Her soft voice asked me what was going on at home. She said she heard things from other people and wanted to know if they were true. A horrible sick feeling filled my body. I was afraid to tell her the forbidden family secrets; I was afraid of Mom's retaliation. So I sat there in silence and prayed that she already knew the answer to her question without me having to betray myself and my family. As we sat there in silence, she reached over, touched my hand and said, "It's okay to tell me—it'll be our secret and I'll never tell your Mom."

My insides yearned for the truth of her words, so I finally broke down and told her some of the things that were happening. When I was finished disclosing what little I felt safe to reveal, she looked at me with sadness and understanding on her face. At that moment I wanted her to hug me and to tell me that everything was going to be all right. Instead, she said she was going home to talk with her husband to see if I could come and live with them. Tears came to my eyes, as I couldn't believe that she would want to do that for me. Although confused about why she would let someone as bad as me stay in her home, I was excited that I might get a chance to live with someone normal, someone who would love and care for me, and where no one would sexually abuse me. With excitement about my possible liberation, I ran up the driveway that night, already feeling free.

While I awaited the decision from Marie's husband, I got a second job babysitting at a neighbor's house. The Talbot's really didn't know who I was because their kids weren't old enough to be in school, so they hired me to baby sit their kids while they worked. They had a lot of money, a huge house, a barn, horses, and farm equipment. I couldn't believe that people actually lived that well in Chilo.

I took the job and did well until I saw that they had hundreds of bottles of different prescription drugs in their bathrooms. I couldn't believe my eyes; I was in a drug addict's heaven. Because I remembered that I was trying to stay off the drugs so I could go home with Marie and her husband, I tried my hardest just to stay out of their bathrooms and not to think about all the beautiful pills that would relieve my enormous pain. Even though I tried really hard not to take any, I couldn't resist stealing a bunch of them and stashing them in my bedroom just in case I needed them in an emergency.

Marie continued trying to convince her husband to let me live with them, while I continued to work hard at the restaurant. One Saturday after a long day at work, I began my customary walk home, preoccupied with thoughts of the day. I was almost home when I heard blood-curdling screams coming from our house. I ran to the back of the house, and saw Mom running down the hill from the garden with Gene close behind carrying a gas can and matches. She was covered in gasoline and he was trying to strike a match to set her on fire! For a brief moment, I stood there in disbelief, wondering what I was going to do to get Mom out of this one. I ran after Gene and pleaded with him to please stop and to tell me what was wrong. He wouldn't pay attention to me, so I picked up the snow shovel and started hitting his car with it so he would come after me. He stopped and looked at me with vengeance in his eyes—I was now his new target.

I was absolutely terrified as Gene chased me around the car, and then the yard, swearing that if he caught me he would kill me. I ran as fast as I could, hoping his old alcoholic body couldn't catch up with me. That only seemed to infuriate him. Then I saw that he had quit chasing me and had gone into the house. Within minutes he was bringing everything out and throwing it into the backyard. Looking vengeful, he set our few precious belongings on fire. I didn't know what to do. Mom was crying uncontrollably and was about to fall apart. I felt helpless and angry with myself because I didn't know how to take her pain away. I didn't know who to call, or who to tell what had just happened. I tried desperately to figure out what I should do to fix the situation. Otherwise, I knew I would end up taking some of the drugs I had stashed away for an emergency such as this one.

I jumped on my brother's dirt bike and rode as fast as I could down to Chilo. I recklessly raced up and down the streets, hoping that I would crash the bike and kill myself. Maybe then someone would stop and look at what was going on at home. But no one even noticed me. The only thing I could think of then was to call the police. I told them Gene had tried to kill Mom and he had burned everything in our house. The police responded, but nothing was done. Gene wasn't taken to jail and as usual, no one rescued us kids from this awful existence.

The next morning, I was emotionally hung over and wanted to take some of the magic pills I had stolen. I couldn't do it though because I was still hanging on to the hope that Marie would take me home with her. Instead, I went to work and *acted* like I was stoned so Marie would ask me what was wrong. If she would only ask, then I would have a good reason to tell her what happened last evening. However, she didn't ask me what was wrong, but had someone fire me and then sent me home without talking to me. I was so mad at myself for pretending I was stoned and for disappointing her. I felt like a complete failure, and an absolutely worthless human being. I couldn't believe that I had messed up the only good thing in my life because I was too afraid to ask for help. I felt hopeless, bewildered and deeply depressed.

I walked up Chilo Hill one more time, dreading the moment I would have to tell Mom I had lost my job and the punishment I would have to endure for my desperate cry for help. As anticipated, Mom asked me why I lost my job. I couldn't tell her the truth that I had faked being stoned so Marie would allow me talk about our family secrets. So I told her that I had taken a Valium before work and that was why I was fired. Rage flared up in her eyes and she demanded to know where I got the pill. I had never lied to Mom before this so it didn't occur to me to start now. Before I realized it, the truth emerged from my lips that I had gotten the Valium from the Talbot's house. Mom snatched me up, threw me into the car and took me to the Talbot's. Looking down at the floor, I confessed that I stole the pills from them. Without hesitation, they fired me, too.

No one ever asked why I was doing those things—no one cared. So I resorted to my self-destructive behaviors with a new vengeance. After all, I had no hope of working, or going to live with Marie. I had to remain in hell until Mom or Gene killed each other or me.

Soon after, they got into another huge fight where I watched them almost kill each other. Then I heard Gene say he was leaving, never to come back. He packed his bags and raced to Cincinnati to catch a plane to Texas where his mother and sister still lived. I was glad he was gone. At the same time, I was terrified because I didn't know how we were going to survive. I didn't know who was going to take care of us since Mom didn't work because she said she was agoraphobic. I never understand the alleged agoraphobia because she drove to the grocery store and went out to other public places. I wondered if it was a way that would allow her to justify not working and gaining people's sympathies.

The next day after school I walked into the house and immediately sensed that something was wrong with Mom. She had a look on her face that told me she was about to drop another bomb in my lap. She said, "I'm leaving and it'll be up to you to take care of everything, including your brothers." My 15 year-old heart almost stopped beating. I couldn't breathe. I just stood there looking at her with a blank look on my face. I wanted to cry and beg her not to leave me, tell her that I would be a good girl if she would just stay. But I didn't get the chance—she just walked out, put her bags in the car, and drove off. I was shocked. My whole world had just come to a screeching halt. I stood there staring at the door for a few minutes, then I completely broke down. I wondered how I was supposed to take care of my brothers. Who was going to help us? How would we eat? How were we going to survive?

I had to do something, or I was going to go crazy. So I walked out of the house and headed down Chilo Hill. As I walked down the hill that held so much pain for me, I took a joint out of my pocket and quickly lit it. I held the magical smoke in my lungs until I felt momentary relief from my mother's abandonment and the enormous burden that was thrown in my lap. I walked for what seemed like forever, getting stoned and trying to figure out what I was going to do.

Some time later, a car started up the hill toward me. I tried to hide my means of escape by cupping the joint in my hand. I recognized the sound of the car and was shocked when I turned around and saw it was Mom. She demanded that I get in the car and we drove home. Nothing was ever said about her leaving, or the joint. She acted like nothing ever happened, and I was expected to do the same.

I don't know how, but we managed to survive while Gene was gone. There were many days we were hungry, but we had a roof over our heads.

Word had apparently spread that Gene had left us, so Jackie, a neighbor, introduced himself to Mom. I thought he was one of the strangest men I had ever met with his skinny body and handle-bar mustache. He wore thick black, horn-rimmed glasses and dressed like a man from the 1950s. He also drove an old, black GTO that he thought was absolutely cool. Everyone thought he was in a mid-life crisis. I didn't trust Jackie from the start, especially when he told Mom he was a Christian man who wanted to help a family in distress. I think he knew that Gene had left, and he was using his position of being a God-fearing man as an excuse to get close to her. As usual, she bought into his façade without question. So Jackie started spending a great deal of time at the house with Mom, and I continued partying my ass off so I could cope with life.

Jackie knew of me by my reputation. He thought he could convert me away from my life of drinking and drugging by offering me a job working around his house doing yard work, painting creosote on his fence posts, mowing the lawn, and so forth. That was fine by me because the extra money meant I could afford more alcohol and drugs. I must admit that Jackie was nice to me and he never tried to mess with me sexually. Because of that, I started to trust him and actually looked forward to working at his place. I worked very hard and did my best. But, just like most of the adults in my life, he soon blew my trust in him.

I came home from school one day to find that Jackie had told Mom that he saw me smoking a joint outside a gas station. The problem was that it wasn't me. I now knew that I could never trust him again, so I stopped going to his house to work. However, the day before I quit working for him, I stooped to an all-time low. I had to stay high and drunk in order to cope with my life and that meant that I needed money. So I spent hours going through every closet, drawer, book and possible hiding place until I stumbled upon a stack of tithe envelopes stuffed in his dresser drawer with money already in them. I carefully opened the envelopes and took a little bit of money out of each of them. I was filled with guilt at stealing money from Jackie and God, but my need to escape out-weighed my guilt.

While I continued trying to survive, it was time for a new school year to begin. The tenth grade wasn't any different. I still didn't fit in with anyone other than the bad crowd, and some days that was even questionable. My only true friends were alcohol and drugs.

It was during that year that Mom found my journals, read them and destroyed them. We never talked about what was in them; she just got rid of them.

I also met a new friend, Preston. He was like me in a lot of ways because he didn't fit in with the other kids either and he was partying to escape his own set of problems. Preston wasn't someone I considered to be a boyfriend, we just enjoyed getting stoned together. I thought it was really something that he had his own van. It was absolutely cool. It was painted a beautiful shade of blue, had shag carpet all over the walls and floors, a curtain divider separating the cab from the back of the van, and a serious stereo system. We partied in his van every day. He picked me up every morning so we could drink and smoke dope all the way to school. We hung out in it at lunch and partied so we could tolerate the rest of the school day. And, he drove me home after school so I could get stoned in order to cope with home. I didn't draw a sober breath the entire time we hung out with each other.

For some unknown reason, Mom liked Preston and didn't show her angry and hostile side when he was around. Her "hanging out" with Jackie also afforded me a great deal of freedom with Preston as we were allowed to go and do as we pleased. That meant we ended up doing some pretty outrageous and dangerous things which almost got us killed, but that was what attracted us to each other. We were wild and didn't care whether we lived or died.

One time, Jackie gave Preston and me permission to take his car for a drive. So we went to Bethel and bought a huge stash of liquor. We hid all but one of the bottles under the back seat. I could hardly wait for the sweet tasting alcohol to hit my lips and make me warm and comfortably numb.

On the way back home, Preston and I managed to drink the entire bottle and opened up another one. In our drunken state we didn't care that it was winter and the roads were slick with snow. The more alcohol I consumed, the more confident I became. I jumped behind the wheel and drove us home as fast and as reckless as I could. As I gunned the engine to get up the driveway, I spun the car out of control and landed in the creek that led up to our house.   Preston staggered out of the car, stood in the icy water and told me that the back wheel was stuck in the creek. I panicked because I knew I was about to get in trouble again: Mom would see that I was drunk and that it was my fault that Jackie's car was stuck. I was afraid this would surely earn me another thrashing.

I tried with all my might to get the car out of the creek, but it wouldn't move. Preston stood there screaming, "Get out of the car!"

I screamed back, "I can't, Mom will kill me if I don't undo this bad thing."

I frantically revved the engine over and over again, trying to get the car to move so I could save myself. My head began hurting and I was having problems thinking, but I wasn't sure why. I felt like I was going to pass out. I could barely keep my eyes open and I wanted to throw up.

Suddenly, the door opened and a pair of hands yanked me out of the car and laid me on the cold ground. As I breathed in the fresh air and became more lucid, I saw Mom standing over me and yelling that I almost killed myself with carbon monoxide. I had no idea what she was talking about—I'd never heard of carbon monoxide. Enormous pain shot through my head and Mom said it was a sign of carbon monoxide poisoning, but nothing was done. I wasn't taken to the hospital or to a doctor to get checked out. Instead, she just went back into the house to socialize with her new boyfriend, Jackie.

Since Mom liked Preston and she was now dating Jackie, it wasn't a problem if I drank. On New Year's Eve, for instance, Mom let Preston and me go out and get absolutely ripping drunk, while she and Jackie went to his house to do the same. I remembered wondering how she could have gone to his house if she was agoraphobic.

I enjoyed the partying and companionship I had with Preston, but somewhere along the way he began seeing me as a girlfriend and he wanted all the things that went along with it. From past experience, I knew it wasn't safe to tell a man how I felt because it always made things worse. So every day that went by, my fear of him wanting me to have sex with him grew by leaps and bounds. I wasn't comfortable being around him anymore.

The day finally came when we were partying in the back of his van and Preston started kissing me. I lay there paralyzed, disappointed and afraid. I wanted him to stop, but I didn't know how without having to admit all the things that Gene, Miguel, and the other men did to me. I was also afraid that Preston, like Miguel, would hurt me if I resisted. I lay there in silence as I had always done, until Preston put his penis in my mouth. My eyes filled with tears and I felt as if I was dying. I was overtaken with guilt and believed I was the worst person on earth.

I continued to reluctantly have sex with Preston and did whatever he wanted as long as he made sure that I had enough alcohol and drugs to annihilate my feelings and to remain blacked out. There were many days though when the black out didn't last long enough and I awoke with Preston shoving his penis in my mouth while I lay there crying. I hated myself because I needed the alcohol and drugs to stay sane, and I could only accomplish that by slaving out my body and soul.

I knew that Preston really wanted me to love him, but I just couldn't. I was too afraid of the sex. I was flashing back to previous times of abuse when I feared for my life. Sex may have been a normal part of a relationship for other girls my age, but I couldn't stand what it reminded me of, and how dirty I felt when I did it. It just wasn't worth it.

Then one day, Preston came to me and said that he wanted me to meet his family. I really didn't want to, but I knew I couldn't get out of it without hurting his feelings. I always knew there was something that bothered him, but I couldn't figure it out until I went home with him.

He lived in a filthy, dirt-poor house. His parents, and most of his brothers and sisters, were toothless and dirty. There were a few pieces of furniture, and as much dirt on the floors in the house as there was outside on the ground. Chickens ran around everywhere, and the yard was full of rusted-out cars. I looked at Preston and saw the embarrassment that he had been trying to hide. I wanted to cry for him because I could feel his pain. I now understood why he worked every day as a mechanic to earn extra cash to get out of Felicity and away from his family.

I must have been Preston's only friend because we went everywhere together and we partied with each other all the time. I must have been his escape from his family as he was mine. We shared that common bond.

One day, Preston showed up at my house unannounced with a strange look on his face, like he was in shock. He looked at me with a joyful, yet fearful face, as he told me that he had been accepted into the Marines at Paris Island, SC, and he was leaving within the week. I could hear the excitement in his voice, but I could also feel the apprehension. He looked at me seriously, hugged me and said, "I wanna give you a car I've been workin' on." It was an old, beat-up 1968 candy apple-red Chevy Nova with rust spots all over it. It was the only thing he had to offer, but with pride and love, he gave me the car as a farewell present. It was a mess, but it didn't matter to me—I was just happy that someone liked me enough to give me anything. As we hugged each other good bye, I thanked him for the car and for being my friend.

I started working on the car immediately because I knew it was my only way out of the house, just like Preston knew the Marines was his only way out of Felicity. I put carpet on the floor to cover up the holes in the floorboard, and tried to make the inside look new. Now that I had my own car, I began driving myself to school and going to all kinds of places to party. The days became a blur as I spent most of them in black outs, and waking up in unknown places. There were so many drugs and so much alcohol in my system I was barely able to stay in reality for any length of time.

Several months later my life changed again when Gene returned home. I don't know what prompted his return or what motivated Mom to take him back. Almost immediately, everything went back to the way it used to be with Gene drinking, and them fighting. I came home from school one day and stopped at the back door to check everyone's mood so I would know how to act and how to feel. Strangely enough, I couldn't find anyone. Then I heard Mom and Gene going at it in their bedroom, and it was my cue to switch into my emergency, protector mode. Panicked, I ran upstairs and found Mom lying on the floor in a fetal position. Her face was swollen and her eyes were red from crying. Gene whispered, "Your Mom has gone crazy." I stared at her, wondering if she had finally gone over the edge. He touched my chin and raised it up just enough so I was looking at him and said, "She's gone crazy because of you and your brothers—you kids made her snap."

That thought absolutely horrified me. I was afraid he was right—it was my fault that Mom was insane. Gene kept telling me over and over again that he was going to have her locked up because of me. I was so afraid for her and for us. He then screamed at me and my brothers to go to our rooms.

It felt like an eternity until the next morning. At first light, I sprang out of my bed and ran downstairs to make sure that Mom hadn't been locked up. When I got downstairs, she saw the expression on my face and asked what was wrong. I was surprised that she didn't seem to remember anything about last night, so I told her what had happened. As I anxiously awaited her response, her face took on a look of fury. She screamed, "Gene and I had been drinking, and I acted like I did because I was drunk—not because I was crazy!" Needless to say, another fight ensued.

Even though my home life wasn't normal and I was terribly disturbed, part of me still wanted what the other kids at school had: I wanted to belong, to fit in somewhere. I was tired of being alone and feeling like an outcast. I thought if I tried out for one of the team sports it would solve my social problem, prove I wasn't worthless, and help me to stop drinking and drugging.

I signed up for the track team. I'm sure the coach, Ms. Carlyle, let me on the team as an act of mercy. Even though pity got me on the team, I was proud and excited that I was a part of something. I went to practice every day and tried my best to impress Ms. Carlyle, even though my body could hardly run around the block from all the poisons I was putting into it.

Several weeks into the season, she called me into her office and told me that during a locker search she had found small liquor bottles in my locker. I sat there staring at the floor, just like I did at home. I tried telling her it wasn't alcohol in the bottles, but she knew better and became angry as she said, "You're no longer on the track team, and you will probably be suspended from school after I speak with the principal."

Not because I felt a need to stay on the team, but because I couldn't fathom the trouble I would be in with Mom, I pleaded, "Please give me another chance. Mom will kill me if I'm thrown off the team or suspended again!" She just ignored me.

Realizing that my fate was sealed, depression and suicidal thoughts crept in. I left the school and went to a school mate, Ben's house. He could see that I was upset, but I was too ashamed to tell him I had been thrown off the track team. After we hung out for a few minutes I excused myself to his parents' bathroom where I raided their medicine cabinet and swallowed every pill I could find. Because I was afraid of getting caught, and knowing that I needed to find more drugs to take, I left Ben's house and went to see a local drug dealer, Fran. She and some other people were tripping on a bunch of painkillers and muscle relaxers and invited me to join in on the journey into oblivion. I was all too glad to accept the offer, so I took a handful of the pills and chased them down with several beers. Beginning to experience the effects of what I had taken, I stumbled back to the school and sat on the sidewalk, hoping I would die.

The assistant track coach walked by, turned, and offered me a ride home. Since the school was being closed up for the night and I had nowhere else to go, I graciously accepted her offer and staggered to her car. My emotions and overwhelming need for help welled up inside of me. I wanted to cry and tell her how sorry I was for the alcohol they found and that I didn't know how to stop what I was doing. I didn't know how to get off the roller coaster. I wanted to tell her that I needed someone to help me and that I would probably be dead by morning. I wanted to scream, "I'm frightened—why won't anyone listen to me about what's happening at home?" But, as I had been taught, I remained silent. As I got out of her car, I slowly took off the necklace Mr. Murdock had given me. I dared not look at her while I whispered, "I'm sorry." I then handed her the necklace that had once signified acceptance, and hope since I would likely be dead in a few short hours.

I stumbled up the driveway and stood outside the back door for a few minutes as I tried to gather my composure before facing the family. When I walked in the back door, I was relieved that everyone was watching television in the living room. My mind raced with thoughts about what I supposed to be doing so I wouldn't draw attention to myself. I looked around the kitchen trying to orient myself when I saw the dirty dishes piled in the sink and I remembered it was my night to do the dishes. So I stood at the sink with my legs weakening and feeling like I was about to pass out. I tried to wash the dishes quickly without breaking any of them, but I could hardly feel my hands. I managed to finish them, only dropping a few of them on the floor and in the sink.

To get upstairs to my room, I had to walk through the living room. I leaned against the kitchen sink for a moment practicing in my mind how my legs were supposed to move. I gathered the courage and kept my thoughts focused on the mental image of my legs as I walked past everyone sitting on the couch. I was relieved that they were so enthralled with the television that no one acknowledged my presence.

Once in my room, I turned on my record player, lay on my bed and began crying because I knew I wouldn't survive the night and, yet, I couldn't tell anyone what I had done. I started hallucinating, so I crawled into my closet where I could hide and feel safe. I sat there in the dark praying that if my death was coming, that it would come soon so I could stop being afraid. Then I threw up all over the closet. My room now reeked of alcohol. I opened the door to see if I could smell it in the hall and, to my dismay, the smell of alcohol filled the air. Mom would surely smell it and say something to me when she came up to bed. Panicking, I put myself to bed and prayed that any punishment would pass me by, and that I would quickly pass to the other side. It was hard to maintain that prayer since I was afraid that if I closed my eyes, I wouldn't wake up. Some time later, I fell into a deep sleep.

I woke up the next morning surprised that I was still alive. I was also surprised that neither Mom or Gene said anything about the smell of alcohol, nor why I came home and stayed in my room the rest of the evening. No one had checked on me or said good night. My body felt so bad that I didn't know how I was going to function or get around. Then I remembered, I was to be kicked out of school again that day. I was almost immobilized with fear, but I forced myself to school anyway— after all, it was safer at school than it was at home.

After I arrived at school, Ms. Carlyle called me into her office. She looked concerned when she saw me, but she didn't ask what was wrong. Instead, she took pity on me and decided not to tell the principal. Being kicked off the team was my sole punishment. I was relieved that I didn't get suspended, but I hated myself because I had managed to mess up one more thing.

My history with extra-curricular activities became a nightmare, and the next one began when I joined the basketball team. Ms. Carlyle was also the basketball coach, and she gave me one more chance to clean up my act so I could play sports. I didn't understand how she thought I was going to change when no one wanted to help make things better at home, but I jumped at the chance to play basketball.

I had begun selling drugs at school so I could support my own habit and to make sure I had enough money stashed in case Mom ever left again. It was much cheaper for me to buy drugs, take out what I needed, and sell what was left over for an outrageous price to some unsuspecting school kid. I was dealing a lot of drugs to a girl in junior high. It was easy because she was young and more naive. I could stay in constant cash and drugs with her as a frequent customer.

After I managed to make my way onto the basketball team, we went away for a game. As always, I had all my drugs and money stashed in my pants pocket—in case I needed to run away, or the family had an emergency and we had to leave quickly. When the game was over, I discovered some of the money had been stolen out of my locker. I was so mad! I couldn't believe that someone would steal my only way out from my awful family and life. I felt violated! As I raged, the other girls on the team watched and laughed. I then realized that several of them were the culprits. Not only was I angry, but their actions confirmed that I didn't fit in. I was enraged and wanted to literally kill someone. I threatened, "If you don't return my money, I'm really going to hurt someone!" Before they could do anything, Ms. Carlyle came into the locker room and found out what we were fighting about. Again, I stared at the ground in resignation.

After we got back to our school, Ms. Carlyle called me into her office. I dared not look at her, afraid that I would fall apart and confess everything: Mom and Gene's fighting, my physical and sexual abuse, Gene's alcoholism, and our poverty. Instead, I stared at the floor while she skipped all the questions about home and continued her line of questioning about how I came to have so much money, and if I was selling drugs to a junior high kid. A part of me was hoping that I would have the courage to tell her the truth so maybe she could help me, but I sat there in fearful silence and said nothing. Because I said nothing, I was given until the next morning to decide what I was going to tell her. She also added a small caveat in that I would be kicked off the team if the rumors were true.

I slowly walked out of Ms. Carlyle's office, racking my brain for a way out of this mess. I was too scared to go home without a plan, so I hid in the dark school while she locked up the building. I wandered around the building with my thoughts vacillating between killing myself and trying to figure out what I was going to tell her. I paced back and forth for hours trying to determine what I was going to do—kill myself, or tell the truth? I felt absolutely helpless and alone. In my heart I didn't want to be as bad as I was, but I didn't know how else to deal with home. Why wouldn't anyone listen to me?

Hours later, I went home, still not knowing what I was going to do. Unexpectedly, Mom and Gene asked about the game. Afraid that they knew I was in trouble again, I quietly mumbled, "I quit the team tonight because I was falsely accused of lighting a cigarette lighter on the bus." I stood there shaking, and praying that Mom and Gene would believe me. Surprisingly, they did.

The next day Ms. Carlyle asked me again if I was selling drugs and if that was why I had so much money. For a brief moment I bowed my head and told her that I couldn't lie to her. I never actually said the words, "I sold drugs," but she understood the message I was conveying. I quickly glanced up at her face and saw the anger in her eyes. She threw me off the team and took me to the principal's office to be suspended again, this time for five days.

I headed home, knowing I would have to lie about the suspension. Fortunately for me, it was a good day at home—no one was fighting— Mom and Gene were in a good mood. I told them about my suspension and stuck to the story about the lighter on the bus. I don't know if they didn't care anymore, but they bought the story in its entirety.

Surprisingly, Mom told everyone that she needed help with her alleged agoraphobia and went with Gene to see a psychiatrist. After the initial evaluation, it was suggested that she see her own psychiatrist for the agoraphobia, and that Gene see a different one for his volatile temper. It was also recommended that the family participate in family therapy, especially since I was continuing to get into trouble at school.

The first time I walked into Dr. David Kniskern's office for a family session, I was surprised to see that he was a person just like anybody else, and not the monster I had imagined. He was a short guy with thinning brown hair and a sweet smile. It only took him a few family sessions to realize that Mom and Gene were the problem, and that I was merely reacting to what was going on at home. It was then that Dr. Kniskern recommended that he see me individually.

Each time I saw Dr. Kniskern, my heart ached because I wanted to tell him the truth about home and how I felt. However, it had been instilled in me that everything I knew to be true was a lie—that I had fabricated everything because I was a disturbed child—so I said nothing. Instead, I acted out and avoided revealing the family secrets. Hiding from the truth left me feeling frustrated, so I decided it would be easier to survive therapy if I got stoned before each session.

At one session, being stoned wasn't enough. My heart hurt so much that I almost told him the truth. I sat on his couch in stark terror, as I prepared the words. But when the truth reached my trembling lips, my insides exploded with years of being hurt and unloved. I ran out of his office and to the bathroom so he wouldn't see my tears and my weakness. I sat there crying and realized that I was at a crossroad—I could either go back in Dr. Kniskern's office, or I could continue running. My heart pounded with fear and my breath almost non-existent at the thought of divulging the family secrets.

Instead of running to the elevators, I slowly walked down the long hallway back to Dr. Kniskern's office. I sat down on the yellow vinyl couch with tear-filled eyes. But no matter how hard I tried, I couldn't say the forbidden words. He looked at me with compassion and said that coming back was my first step in the right direction. His words gave me hope that maybe I could reveal my hidden secrets at our next visit.

As soon as I got comfortable with Dr. Kniskern and I was getting ready to unload my enormous burden, Mom and Gene managed to pull the rug out from under my feet again. My brothers and I came home from school to find Mom and Gene standing outside, yelling at each other with all their might. I held my fragile spirit in my shaking hands and begged Mom to tell me what was wrong. She looked at me with fury in her eyes as she told me that Gene was having affairs with his college students. She knew it for a fact because she found several love letters in his car. I took one look at Gene and his expression told me that Mom was telling the truth. I was devastated and wondered what this meant for the family.

While I stood there watching the scandalous argument, Gene said he was leaving. In my child-like way, I begged him to please tell me where he was going and if he was coming back because I desperately needed to know if I was going to be left alone again to take care of my brothers. Looking sad, he put his belongings in his car and said he was going to the university to sleep in his office. Before he could tell me if he was coming back, Mom threw the rest of his clothes outside and screamed, "Get out!"

He left, and Mom yelled, "Go and pack your bags—now! We're moving to South Carolina to be with my family."

I was stunned at her demand. I stood there looking at her in complete shock because I wasn't sure I was hearing her words correctly. Realizing she was serious, I begged, "Please think about what you're saying, what you're about to make us do—please…"

Instead of listening to me, she dragged me upstairs to pack, screaming, "Hurry, you must hurry!"

I felt myself breaking into pieces, as if I was about to go crazy. I was crying frantically and trying not to slip off into insanity. I packed my few belongings into paper sacks, wishing that someone would make this stop. My thoughts then turned to the fact that we were leaving without any warning and without anyone knowing where we were going. I was afraid that something bad would happen to us and no one would know we needed help if they didn't know where we were.

In desperation, I knew I had to find a way to let someone know what was happening. I decided to write a note and leave it in the mailbox so the mailman would call the police and have us rescued, but Mom rushed us out of the house before I could get down to the mailbox. I then thought of Dr. Kniskern. Surely he could make this bad thing stop! But, I couldn't get to the phone without Mom yelling at me to get in the car.

As we drove from Felicity to Cincinnati, all I could do was cry and beg, "Mom, please don't do this." She just kept telling us how great South Carolina was going to be and how we could stay with her sister until we got on our feet. I was confused and I didn't understand what made her think that Aunt Relaine was going to help us, especially after what she did the last time we needed help.

On the way out of town, we stopped at a Chinese restaurant to eat. My brothers and I sat at the table with our swollen faces and bloodshot eyes as the waiter took our order. Mom told me that she was going to call Gene on the pay phone to tell him we were leaving. That was my opportunity to sneak over to the other pay phone to call Dr. Kniskern. My hands trembled as I dialed his number. I was immediately relieved when his soothing voice answered. Crying, I told him what was happening and that I was barely holding on emotionally. I begged him to talk to Mom and to make this bad thing stop before we ended up leaving for real. After Mom finished talking to Gene, I convinced her to talk with Dr. Kniskern. She reluctantly agreed, and talked with him for a long time and seemed to greatly calm down.

With a completely different look on her face, she hung up the telephone and said that Dr. Kniskern knew where we were, and that Gene was on his way to the restaurant. I panicked because I was afraid that Gene would make Mom mad again, that he would cause a scene, and we would still end up leaving.

Gene arrived at the restaurant and humbly sat down at the table. I was consumed with so much fear about what was going to happen that I blacked out. I came to, sitting in the car with Mom telling me that we were going back home to Felicity. As we drove home, I sat in the back of the car, relieved, but feeling drained and exhausted from the day's events. I lay in bed that night wondering how much more I could take.

The next day, my brothers and I were expected to go to school and pretend that nothing happened. It was only something "we had made up in our minds" and I was never allowed to go back to see Dr. Kniskern again.

Now that I had walked so close to insanity, tasted my own death, felt the sting of domestic violence, and the guilt and shame of physical and sexual abuse, I was staying in oblivion more than ever by doing any, and all, drugs I could get my hands on. I was smoking hash from under glasses, sniffing glue, doing whippets, popping speed, smoking pot, dropping acid, and occasionally shooting dope. I stole and continued to sell drugs to support my habit. I only hung out with the partiers so I would always have access to getting stoned. I was lost to myself, and to everyone around me.

Shortly after this incident, Mom and Gene started taking me out to party. One night we went to an enormous, crowded bar in Cincinnati. I was excited that Mom took me out because I thought it meant that she liked me. She and I danced, and as there was no limit to how much I could drink, so I drank until I was drunk. I blacked out before we left the bar and came to when I was throwing up on the side of the highway.

Everyone thought it was funny.

The family alcoholism, violence, and abuse clicked along like this in Felicity for a total of three, very long, years. Nothing ever changed, it only got worse. And, as history always repeated itself with my family, our time in Felicity came to an abrupt halt.

By the time I finished the eleventh grade, Mom told us we were moving again. This time to Georgia, even though neither Mom nor Gene had arranged a job or a place for us to live—we were just going. I was absolutely devastated at the thought of another move, especially during my senior year in high school. Not only did Mom and Gene take away my childhood, but now they were taking away the most important year of my adolescence.

Chapter 9

Four Months of Hell

I PREPARED FOR THE LONG JOURNEY AHEAD by hiding enough drugs in my car to get me from Ohio to Georgia and until I could find another dealer. I stashed anything and everything I could get my hands on, including pot, amphetamines, Quaaludes and hash.

I took one last, tearful look at the old white farmhouse where I had changed into a person I didn't know. Apprehension and sadness filled my heart, not because of any fond memories, but because I was embarking on yet another unknown trek I wasn't sure I could handle.

We arrived in Savannah, Georgia, in August of 1980. It was a very different city than I was used to. It had old Victorian homes, concrete medians, and squares in the downtown areas that were named after famous people. Palm trees, dedicated to war veterans, lined the main road, Victory Drive. Overall, the city was pretty amazing. We drove around the city and I noticed I was getting a little excited about living here because it reminded me of my love of exploration. Maybe this place was what I needed in order to change and find myself again. Maybe it would give Mom and Gene permission to stop fighting, and to stop hurting me.

After driving around the city for hours, we ventured out to several remote rural areas about 30 minutes outside the city limits. I couldn't understand why we were leaving the beautiful city and going to poor, run-down, country towns. We finally ended up in Springfield, a small town that was a little larger than Felicity. As we drove through it, Mom announced, "We're going to live here."

That one sentence destroyed any excitement and enthusiasm I had and replaced it with sadness and frustration. Part of my discontent was the understanding that living in another small town meant that we would end up in yet another shack that we would have to renovate. My guess was almost accurate: we rented a trailer. I guess I should have been used to it by now, but I wasn't.

The trailer was in a dirt poor, seedy trailer park that had no grass, cars parked on cinder blocks, rusted out trailers, and dirty kids running around unattended. It was the Springfield ghetto. We lived there for several weeks until Mom and Gene came up with the idea of buying a piece of land and putting a trailer on it. I wondered how we were going to pay for it since neither of them had a job. In the meantime, I got a job at Williams' Restaurant in Rincon, and met a drug dealer who lived a couple of trailers down from us.

Despite the fact that we had moved again, it didn't mean that everything was going to be the way Mom imagined. It was merely another attempted geographical cure. The fighting, drinking, abuse, and helplessness came right along with all of us to Georgia. When the fights erupted again, I sat in disbelief and prayed to God, "Please don't let this be happening again...not in Georgia."

Everything was back to status quo, and it was during that time that I realized just how far apart Mom and Gene had grown. I was at work one day and remembered that it was August 25, Gene's birthday. I didn't know what to do for him. Even though he had hurt me many times, I couldn't hurt him by ignoring what should have been his special day. So, after I got off work, I stopped and got him an ice cream sundae. I knew my pitiful ice cream sundae wasn't much, but it was all I could afford. I rushed home hoping it wouldn't melt. I walked in the front door of the trailer, smiled proudly, and handed Gene his ice cream sundae and wished him a happy birthday. I saw a tear come to his eye and I was confused. I looked at Mom and the expression on her face told me that no one else had remembered it was his birthday, not even her. I felt sorry for him and for the first time I understood his loneliness.

By now, no one was exempt from any of these feelings. Mom and Gene fought all the time, and Gene continued to drink like there was no tomorrow. I continued to fall deeper and deeper into my addictions and feelings of helplessness. I didn't know what path my brothers were on because it was all I could do to take care of myself.

Mom and Gene finally financed thirteen acres of wooded land in a tiny, tiny, place called Clyo. It was about forty-five minutes away from Savannah, another fifteen minutes past Springfield, and had a population of 98. It was so small: only one caution light, a post office, and a family-run, quick-stop type of store. The store was so small that it couldn't even be called a convenience store. The property we bought was way back in the woods, off a dirt road. An old, unused roadbed meandered through the property. I couldn't figure out just what we were going to do with that land with no house, no jobs, and virtually no money.

I was afraid that the hard labor was going to resume, and I dreaded the day Mom would tell us her plans for the property. As expected, we started clearing the land by hand. There were no bulldozers, backhoes, or tractors—just one chain saw, an axe, a swing blade, and our bare hands as we worked outside in the hot Georgia sun. Just like in Felicity, there were very few breaks from the arduous work, even during the middle of the day in the 100-degree heat. I was exhausted from cutting down trees, dragging them off, cutting underbrush, and hand-digging a well. While I worked and sweated, I would ask myself if our moving from one place to another, and doing hard work, was ever going to end. I always came up with the same answer though, because I knew deep in the core of my being that it would always be this way. That realization made it even harder for me to keep going.

We eventually cleared a large enough piece of the land to put a mobile home on. The thing I hated most was the shabby well that Gene supervised us in digging. It wasn't deep enough, so the only water available to use and to drink was sulfur water. It smelled like rotten eggs and felt slick. It also turned everything in the bathrooms and sinks a strange brown color. It was absolutely disgusting, and almost impossible to drink. Having to live that far away from civilization magnified my anger.

Once again, my room was separated from Mom and Gene's by only a bathroom, while my brothers shared a room at the other end of the trailer.

After we got settled, Mom and Gene did the usual thing by taking us to see the new school. All of the schools were in Springfield and were named after the county—Effingham County. As we drove into the parking lot of the high school, I couldn't believe how old and shabby the school was, with several small one-story buildings and trailers with awnings. I wondered if this was a cruel joke and what I had done to deserve being put in another school like this one. The only advantage was that I only had to go to classes in the morning because I had already earned most of the credits I needed to graduate. The afternoons were left free for me to work.

My struggle with school continued here as it was obvious that I didn't fit in here either. No one seemed to like me, and they looked at me like I was some kind of transplant from a faraway planet. Since all the seniors had been living in the same town and going to same school with the same people all their lives, they didn't have time for an outsider. So, I pretty much kept to myself. My drugs and alcohol were my company.

The new school had something called drug raids on an unannounced basis, complete with drug dogs. I had never heard of this before and it really frightened me because I never went anywhere without my stash. I was forced to hide my alcohol and drugs in my car. Every day I went to school, I was terrified that I was going to get busted and suspended again.

Despite the raids, I didn't stop getting drunk and high before my classes. I didn't know how not to use anymore, or how to cope with life on its terms. I didn't know how to deal with home. I had to drink and take drugs in order to survive and remain sane.

The ironic thing about us attending school in Effingham County was that Gene got a job working as a middle school teacher with another local school system.

As Mom and Gene continued to fight, I tried to stay away from home. It was also my means of coping with Gene's sexual abuse because if I wasn't there, he couldn't hurt me. However, it failed me one day when I came home from work really late and stoned. It was obvious that there had been an argument because Mom was sleeping on the couch. That was my cue to stay in my room so I wouldn't get dragged into the middle of whatever was going on. I sat on the side of my bed and wondered, How much more of this can I take? Why don't I just go ahead and run away? Then I remembered the horrible beating I got after running away the last time. I forced myself to put those thoughts aside while I changed into a tee-shirt, quietly crawled into bed, and turned the lights out.

My bedroom door opened ever so slightly and I panicked at the thought of who might be coming into my room. I saw the silhouette of Gene's face as he sat down on the edge of my bed. My heart started beating fast and I was terrified at what was about to happen. I couldn't breathe and I was afraid that I was going to have an emotional breakdown if he started touching me again. He sat there looking at me with that same look he always had, and tried to pretend that he was just coming in to talk to me—I knew better. After all, when was the last time he had come into my room for anything except sex? Gene spent maybe a minute talking before his hands began moving all over my body. I felt like I was about to die on the inside, and I couldn't move. As he touched me and kissed me, my mind and body started to slip away into another dimension— into another time.

I woke up the next morning not remembering anything that happened to me after I slipped into my mind, but I knew from the way my body felt what had happened. I walked out of my room, struggling to hide the shame, guilt, and dirtiness I felt. All of my energy was directed into trying to hide the truth, so I didn't speak a word to anyone for fear that I would break down and cry. I was too afraid to be around Gene, so I rushed to the door to get out of the house so I could get stoned as soon as possible. As my hand touched the doorknob, he looked at me like nothing had happened and asked in a sullen voice, "Will you drive me to school?"

He had never asked me to take him anywhere before, so I stood there frozen in my tracks. My tense body and pounding heart knew that he wanted me to drive him to school so he could touch me, and have me do horrible, sexual things with him that would make my skin crawl with revulsion. I was trapped because I couldn't say, "No." I was afraid he would hurt me, and I didn't know what excuse I would provide to Mom for my refusal.

In the car, Gene didn't waste any time before he started touching me and making sexual innuendo. He said, "We should skip school and go to the beach to spend time together." My level of anxiety escalated and I was more frightened than ever. All of a sudden it was like I couldn't talk, so I just drove without saying a word. The closer we got to his school, the more he pressed the issue of the beach.

In desperation, I finally mumbled, "We can't do that." Gene raised his hand, and I shuddered in fear that he was going to hit me. But, instead, he put his arm around my shoulders and insisted, "I want you to skip school, so I can be with you." I was deathly afraid that he was going to make me go with him, so I just kept driving and praying that I could get him to work before he hurt me.

Thank God, we finally arrived at his school and he had no choice but to get out of the car and go into work. As he got out, he glared at me like I had done something terrible to him. He was definitely angry with me and I knew the next time he would make me pay for my resistance.

I was very relieved when he got out of the car and I left his school. I was so nervous that I could barely drive to my own school, so I pulled over on a dirt road and smoked a joint. I couldn't get high quick enough to get rid of that dirty feeling.

I started staying away from home as much as possible to avoid being around Gene and the fighting. Everything started taking a toll on me and I began having difficulty functioning in school. All I could do was get stoned each day before class and pray that I could manage to sit there. I couldn't stand everything that was running around inside me. I always felt like I needed to crawl inside myself and die. My insides were constantly filled with shame, guilt and loneliness. There were many days when I would be sitting in one of my classes and, without warning, I would become so consumed with suicidal thoughts that I couldn't sit still or pay attention. I would run out of my class with the overwhelming need to hurt myself.

I eventually got sent to the principle's office for my classroom disruptions, but no one ever asked me what was wrong. They only threatened me with not graduating if I couldn't control myself.

It amazed me that again no one ever asked what was wrong—especially since Gene was eventually fired from his job at the Middle School for allegedly sexually molesting some of his students! It was Mom who divulged the reason for his being fired, and she seemed really nervous that he was going to have to go to court. Then, out of nowhere, Mom started making excuses for his behavior with the school kids and blamed it on how his mother had raised him! I couldn't believe what she was saying, and I now knew that she would make up the same kind of excuses if she ever had to face what Gene was doing to me. I was relieved for the kids at school that he had lost his job, but I also feared that it would get worse for me now that his other outlet was cut off.

Even though things were awful at home and at school, I continued working at William's Restaurant. I met Gloria there, a woman in her late thirties who was married to a pipe fitter, and had a six-year-old son. Gloria seemed like a good mother and wife, and she gave her family what I had longed for. Every time I was around her, my insides ached because I wanted to be her child and be the one she loved. She and I hung out together because she loved to party and smoke dope as much as I did. Our common interest made us like each other immediately. Our partying knew no limits. We spent most of our time getting stoned at work because it made time pass quickly, and gave us something to laugh about. Eventually, we began partying together after work at her house and I usually ended up spending the night. Being with her made me feel good because I felt like she wanted to be my friend. I became dependent on Gloria's place as a safe haven away from my home. It was a good place since there wasn't any fighting or arguing, no one there messed with me sexually, and I could have fun getting stoned with my friend.

I don't know what happened, but it seemed like after Gene started molesting me again, the cycle of sexual abuse was set in motion once again in every area of my life. One day while I was working at the restaurant, William called me into his office under the pretense of discussing something about work. I felt like a schoolgirl who was being called into the principal's office for doing something wrong. It was an all-too-familiar feeling for me, and one that I dreaded. I thought he was going to tell me I was smoking too much dope at work, but as soon as I walked into his office and he closed the door, I could tell it was going to be more serious. He walked over and sat behind his desk, while I tentatively sat in a chair across from him.

William said, "You're doing well and I like having you here, but you and Gloria need to cut down on the amount of pot you're smoking during work." He then walked over to the door and locked it as he continued, "I'm not going to fire either of you just yet."

I was relieved since I knew what Mom would do if I got fired again. But almost immediately, the atmosphere in the room changed and it was then that I noticed that he had the same look on his face that Gene and Miguel always had when they were getting ready to make me do something I didn't want to do. I became short of breath and my heart started pounding. He walked over to me, stood me up and started kissing and touching my body. I begged him, "Please, please stop," but he told me that he would fire me if I didn't do what he wanted. So I stood there motionless while he poked and prodded me. I felt like the lowest person on earth.

That went on just about every day, and I didn't know how to make him stop without losing my job and risking Mom's wrath.

I started wondering if I had a sign on my forehead that read, "Mess with me…I am so afraid I'll do anything." That thought became all too apparent one night after work. I was sitting in my car and smoking a joint so I could deal with the night that was ahead of me at home. After I got sufficiently stoned, I began driving home. I then saw blue lights flashing behind me. I panicked, but pulled over to the side of the road. As I tried to sober myself up, I saw a cop walk toward me, all puffed up like he was a big shot. I rolled down my window, and the officer looked at me and smirked as the smell of pot wafted toward him. Instead of putting me in the back of his car, he demanded, "Follow me." Because I had never had an encounter with the police like this one, I didn't know what to expect or what proper protocol was. I knew his wanting me to follow him seemed a little strange, but I assumed it was because he didn't want me to leave my car on the side of the road.

I followed him until we ended up at a trailer in a mobile home park. I had no idea where we were because I had never been to that part of Rincon before. I sat in my car, frightened and wondering what I was supposed to do. The young officer barked, "Get out of your car and remember, you'll be in a heap of trouble if you don't do what I say." His sharp tone of voice frightened me. I was so afraid that I said nothing, and hid my face in submission like an obedient dog.

"Go into the trailer, sit down, and don't make a sound," he continued. I did what I was told. The officer lit up a joint and I thought, well, cool— he just wants to party. After the room was filled with the sweet smell of marijuana smoke and the joint was gone, the atmosphere resumed its sense of imminent danger. The officer got a crazed look on his face, pulled me out of my chair and threw me to floor. He towered over me, pulled his pants down and yelled, "Go down on me!"

As I lay on the floor in a fetal position, my trembling voice pleaded, "Please don't make me do this!"

"If you don't—I'll put you in jail," he grunted. With one quick jerk, he pulled me to my knees, grabbed my head, and forced his penis in my mouth. Tears were rolling down my face as I envisioned all the times this had been done to me in the past, and I agonized over how I would survive it again.

He thrust his penis back and forth in my mouth while he held my head so tightly that I couldn't breathe. I struggled for air as he forced his penis to the back of my throat and ejaculated the all-too-familiar salty contents into my mouth. I was choking and gagging when his grip tightened around my head and he forced me to swallow his semen. After his climatic moment, he first shoved me to the floor and then out the front door of the trailer. I lay on the ground ashamed and disgusted as he stood at the trailer's door and said, "I'll kill you if you ever tell anyone about tonight!" I crawled to my car on my hands and knees with shame emanating from every pore of my body.

I drove home thinking I would never be able to stop crying. I thought I was the worst person in the world. I was worried about how I was going to get past Mom without her seeing what kind of shape I was in. I wanted to die, but all I could do was light up another joint and pop open a fifth of liquor hoping I could get stoned quickly enough to block out everything that had happened. I finally made it home, feeling like a wounded animal. I walked in the front door of the trailer, greeted everyone, and immediately went to my room. I lay there crying for hours, but no one said a word to me about anything. I was completely alone and every part of my being knew it.

I had been in Georgia only two months when all those bad things began happening to me. I had no safe place to go, except for Gloria's home when we partied. So I just tried to put one foot in front of the other and continued working so I could support my habit and only means of escape. Then to my utter dismay, William closed the restaurant without telling anyone. I was now out of a job and had to find another one to support my addiction. There were no jobs to be found in our little town, and all of the spare time on my hands left me partying more than ever.

On October 23, 1980, the day before my seventeenth birthday, and just two and a half months after we moved to Georgia, I spent the night at Gloria's house as I had done many nights before when I was too messed up to drive home. I woke up the next morning, on my birthday, on the floor in Gloria's living room with her handing me the phone and whispering, "It's your Mom." One part of me hoped it was her calling to wish me a happy birthday, but the more realistic side of me panicked and wondered what had happened at home with Gene to make her call me.

She blurted, "I don't want you to come home anymore." I sat there in shock. I couldn't believe that my own mother was throwing me out of the house for no apparent reason, and on my birthday.

"You're a bad kid who never follows my rules, so I don't want you anymore," she continued. The core of my being crumbled with the pain of abandonment. My mind raced trying to figure out what rules I had broken to warrant her doing this to me now, when I didn't have a job or any money. Fear silently welled up inside my heart and I felt like I was about to fall apart. I knew my home wasn't anything special, but when I actually heard that I wasn't wanted, it did something to me.

I begged, "Mom, please love me—." She hung up the phone. When she left me hanging like that, it reminded me of all the times she never listened to me and I became infuriated. I wanted to jump in my car, race to Clyo, and yank her up by the scruff of her neck, tell her off, and then kill her. I wanted to hurt her as much as she had hurt me in the past seventeen years. I felt nothing but pure rage.

After I got off the telephone, I couldn't believe what had just happened and that I was homeless. I fell into a pit of despair and numbness. I gave up on life. Gloria came into the room and I told her that Mom had thrown me out, and I was going to end up living in my car because I had no where else to go. She looked at me with compassion in her eyes and told me that I could move in with her and her family. My heart was still hurt, but relieved.

I was so desperate for a job that I drove almost thirty minutes to Garden City to look for work. I began working at a convenience store, frying chicken. It was a long drive for a minimum wage job, but necessary for my addiction.

A quick downhill spiral began after Mom threw me out of the house, and it was complicated by a man I met while living with Gloria and Ronnie. Jeffrey was a short balding man in his late thirties who worked at the local correctional institution. A friend of Gloria and Ronnie's, he lived alone in a trailer outside of Guyton. He seemed like a nice person I could trust and party with, especially since he was old enough to be my dad. In many ways, he seemed harmless.

We spent a lot of time together partying since he stayed well supplied in pot, pills, and liquor. Whatever I wanted or needed, he had. My drinking and drugging was so out of control that I stayed in black outs, even around him. It was during one of my black outs that I realized that Jeffrey wasn't the nice, safe person I thought he was.

I would party with him in his trailer and he'd wait until I was unconscious before he would take me into his bedroom and lay me on his bed. I would awaken to a semi-conscious state from the excruciating pain of his large penis forcing its way inside me. I felt trapped with his body lying on top of mine, like I was going insane and like I needed to burst out of my skin. I wanted him to get off me so badly, but I didn't know how to make him stop. So I lay there helpless, crying, and praying to God that I could get through it just one more time.

I was drinking two fifths of hard liquor every day, smoking pot and popping pills. When they didn't put me far enough out of consciousness, I tried to shoot drugs again. I say "I tried" because I could never get the feeling I was looking for from shooting up, and I knew I had to be doing something wrong.

It got to the point where Gloria and Ronnie were concerned that I had a problem. One night when I came home after partying, they looked at me with concern on their faces and said, "We need to talk." I immediately flashed back to being at home with Mom, and I was afraid: I thought I was in trouble for doing something wrong and that meant extreme punishment; that they probably didn't like me anymore and would make me move out. I was scared because I had nowhere else to go.

I sat on the couch waiting to be punished. Gloria and Ronnie looked at me compassionately and said, "We're worried about you." As I heard their words, I felt like crying. I could feel everything I was running from creeping to the surface, everything that needed to be heard. I wanted to tell them what was bothering me, but I couldn't. My soul ached for their understanding and love, but I couldn't risk Mom finding out about my betrayal of the family.

So I tried to stuff my feelings further down inside and said, "I've got everything under control, don't worry." Even though I knew I was good at hiding things and this was the furthest thing from the truth, I assured them, "I can quit anytime I want." But they knew that I was beyond being able to control what I was doing.

Ronnie said, "You gotta get straightened out, or you'll have to move. We can't have this kind of thing around our son."

I begged, "Please don't throw me out. Give me a chance to prove to you that I can stay clean and sober. I promise I won't drink or do anymore drugs. I promise I'll be good!"

The next night I stayed at home with Gloria and Ronnie trying to keep the promise I had made to them the night before, even though I knew there was going to be a party there that night that had been planned for weeks. I knew I had a much better chance of not drinking and drugging if I wasn't hanging out in the streets. When the large number of people showed up, I felt uncomfortable; I didn't know how to act around them without being high. Everyone, except me, was having a great time listening to music, smoking pot, and drinking. As I smelled the sweet aroma of the marijuana, and imagined the taste of the alcohol on my lips, I thought I was going to lose my mind. The longer I sat there feeling like an outcast, the more my old feelings of being abandoned, abused, and unloved started overwhelming me, to the point that I wanted to hurt myself. The only way I knew how to make those feelings go away was by anesthetizing myself. I resisted as long as I could and then begged Gloria and Ronnie to just let me have one drink. Gloria finally gave in and said, "Okay, but one, and only one!"

It was the next morning, and I was still drunk when I woke up. My head was splitting with pain and I felt like I had been run over by a tractor trailer. As I walked out of my bedroom, I saw the look of disappointment on Gloria and Ronnie's faces. I bowed my head with shame because I knew I had messed up again, but I didn't remember how. They told me, "You got drunk, smoked a bunch of pot, blacked-out, got in a fight with us, and embarrassed the hell out of us in front of our friends."

I had no idea that had happened—the last thing I remembered was being sure that I could stop after one drink. I was so disappointed in myself, and I hated what I had done to my best friends. At the same time, I was also scared because I didn't understand what was happening to me. Why couldn't I control how much I used? And where were all the bad feelings coming from? I was lost and had no idea how to make it all stop. I fell over myself apologizing to them for my terrible mistake and pleaded with them to give me another chance.

Because I promised once again that I would quit, my surrogate family didn't throw me out. I was also presented with the perfect chance to prove myself to them since I was going to a Charlie Daniel's concert in Savannah that night with a guy who didn't drink.

I was proud of myself because I didn't drink or do any drugs all day long. However, as the time drew near for Marshall to pick me up, I began feeling nervous and shaky. I was afraid of going out with a guy, and I needed something to take the edge off. I thought I was going to jump out of my skin or hurt someone if I didn't get something into my system. Desperate, I ran into Gloria's bathroom, rolled up my sleeve and started shooting up some amphetamines. As I stood there with the needle hanging out of my arm, she walked in and saw me. For a brief moment I was paralyzed with fear as I anticipated the fate that awaited me on the other side of the bathroom door. I sat on the commode for a long time, disappointed in myself. Finally, I gathered the courage to walk out of the bathroom, but Gloria was so angry with me that she didn't say a word. She just turned around and walked out of the room. At that very moment I knew I had blown any trust I had left with them, so I ran out of the house and went to the concert with Marshall with the intent of getting blasted into oblivion.

The concert was a disaster. I managed to get drunk, popped some Quaaludes and convinced Marshall to have a few drinks. I woke up lying on the front seat of the car, alone and terribly frightened. I didn't know where I was, or where Marshall was. I opened the car door and fell out onto the sidewalk in, what appeared to be, downtown Savannah. I stopped people who were passing by and asked them to please help me, but no one would get near me, no doubt because of the smell of booze and marijuana.

I walked down the dark streets of Savannah looking for Marshall or the civic center. I then came out of another black out at the police station with a police officer talking to me. He had found me roaming the streets of Savannah. When I realized it was a cop I was talking to, I thought I was going to have a heart attack. I couldn't breathe and my chest hurt from my heart pounding so hard. When I gained some composure, I confessed that I had no idea where I was and that I was trying to get to the concert. He looked sternly at me and told me he was going to put me in a cell if I didn't call someone to come and get me. I stood there immobilized as I didn't know who else to call except Gloria and Ronnie. My hands nervously dialed the phone, and I begged them to please come and get me before I was thrown into jail. I was surprised and relieved at how calm they both were, and that they would come to get me.

The next day, Gloria and Ronnie sat me down one last time and told me they were concerned that I couldn't stop drinking and drugging. They seemed like they really wanted to help me, but I didn't know how to let them. That evening as I sat in my bedroom feeling utterly depressed, I heard Mom and Gene's voices in the kitchen. I jumped off the bed because I knew that something big was about to happen and it had to be about me. Gloria came to tell me that she called them because she was afraid I was going to end up killing myself, especially after she saw me trying to shoot up in the bathroom. She sent me into her bedroom where Mom and Gene were waiting to talk to me.

I stood in the middle of the room afraid that I was going to get the beating of my life, while Mom sat on the bed and demanded, "What's your problem? Why are you doing this?" I stood there trembling, not knowing what to say, even though I wanted to scream everything that had been bottled up inside me for years. But, past experience taught me that it wasn't safe to tell the truth, so I sat there in silence while my heart quietly broke. Mom kept firing the same questions at me over and over again while Gene stood against the wall acting calm, cool, and collected. The more I saw how omnipotent he was acting, the madder I became. I also got angry with Mom because of her insistent questions that she didn't really want to hear the answers to. Despite my anger, I stood there helpless and not saying what needed to be said.

Again, I looked over at Gene and saw that he was convinced I wouldn't tell his secret. With fierce anger, and stark desperation to unload my burden, I looked straight into his eyes and said, "I'll confess what my problem is."

Instantly, he turned as white as a ghost. He lost his smugness and look of invincibility. Mom took the cue from me and turned to look at Gene. Her facial expression told me that she could see the fear written all over his face. Tears began streaming out of my eyes, and I cried to Mom, "I can't tell you what's going on unless Gene leaves the room."

Even though he reluctantly stormed out of the room, I was left wondering how I was going to say the words, especially since I had never spoken them out loud. I confessed to Mom, with great shame and embarrassment, that Gene had been sexually abusing me. Strangely enough, she didn't seem surprised, just angry. I then felt guilty because I thought the abuse was my fault. I was terrified and fearful of what the consequences were going to be for what I did, instead of what Gene did to me. To my surprise, Mom sat there and said nothing. So I asked her, "Do you believe me? And please, please, don't tell my brothers...I'm afraid of what they will think of me."

Mom finally said, "I believe you, and I promise I won't tell your brothers under any circumstance. *It'll be our secret.*" Mom then got up and walked out of the room.

The next morning I was physically and emotionally hung over, but I went about my regular routine of getting drunk and stoned before going to work because I thought everything had been settled last evening. Because my car was broken down, I grabbed enough drugs to keep me comfortably anesthetized all day and borrowed Gloria's car to go to work. I smoked pot all the way to work to make sure that last evening was sufficiently buried so far beneath the surface that it had no chance of seeping out during the day.

When I got to work, I went inside and started my daily work duties while trying to hide how stoned I was. The next thing I knew, the police showed up at my job, handcuffed me, and escorted me out to their squad car as they said, "You're being arrested for possession of drugs."

Since I didn't understand how, or why, it was happening, I begged an officer, "Please call Gloria and Ronnie so they will know what is happening." The officer just looked at me like I was just another juvenile delinquent who needed to be put in a cage. That was on January 4, 1981.

Chapter 10

The Hospital

THE LONG RIDE TO SAVANNAH in the back of the police car didn't end at the police station, but at a place called Turning Point Hospital. I pleaded with the police officers to tell me what was going on and what kind of hospital it was, but they remained silent. They escorted me into the building where several nurses greeted me. They took me to a very small examining room that contained only a metal examination table and a chair. I stood in the middle of the sterile room, crying and afraid. Moments later, a couple of nurses came in and strip-searched me to ensure I didn't have any drugs or anything I could hurt myself with. I was completely humiliated. Satisfied that I didn't have any contraband, they gave me a physical examination, took blood, and put me in another tiny room. My stomach churned as I sat alone, terrified that Gloria and Ronnie weren't there to help me, and they didn't know where I was.

Eventually, another nurse came into the room to explain that I was in a psychiatric hospital and I would be there for at least seventy-two hours for observation. I thought I was going to die. I cried and pleaded with her, "Please let me go home, please call Gloria and Ronnie and tell them what is happening to me. I'm begging you, please tell me how all of this happened."

Her sad eyes looked at me and she said, "Your mother went to the courthouse and swore out a warrant for your arrest. The charges filed against you were for possession of drugs. She told the judge you were a manipulator."

I understood her words, but I was furious and hurt. I felt betrayed since I finally told Mom what Gene had been doing to me, but I was the one being punished for it! I felt helpless—like there was no way out.

The first night in the hospital, I was put on the second floor in a room with another lady, who clearly had mental problems. She lay in her bed, motionless, telling me she had a shock treatment that day. I wondered if they would also try to shock me with electricity. I was so afraid. I didn't know what to do with myself. Filled with impending doom, all I wanted to do was run away.

I thought I would go crazy the next few days, especially since it was the weekend and I really needed a drink or something to get high on. I felt like I was drowning and like I would explode out of my skin. I didn't understand that I was going through withdrawals, so I didn't tell anyone what was happening to me. To make matters worse, I really wanted to see and talk to Gloria and Ronnie, but no one came to see me that weekend—not my mother, not Gene, and not one doctor. So I sat in my room with the crazy lady, wishing that God would go ahead and kill me and get it over with. I needed Him to put me out of my misery. I couldn't stand the feelings of abandonment and isolation, not for one more minute.

Monday finally arrived and I was taken to a small, carpeted room. The door opened and a doctor named Jack Simmons, came in and sat down without saying a word to me. I was surprised that he was the doctor because he was an overweight, hippie-looking guy with long brown hair. He was wearing blue jeans and a denim jacket, and he was the coolest doctor I had ever seen. I was relieved because I was sure I would be able to convince him to let me go home. However, Dr. Simmons caught me very much off guard. He looked right at me and said, "You have a problem with drinking and drugging; you are a manipulator; you are running away from everything that bothers you; and you will probably end up dead within a month if you don't elect to stay in the hospital. Even though you can't see your behavior and your problems, I can help you if you let me. It's your choice—stay or die."

His words pricked my heart and somewhere inside I knew he was right. It really scared me. I didn't want to end up dead or crazy, or like my mother. I just wanted someone to help me. I considered my choices— if I left, I could end up dead or crazy in a very short period of time; if I stayed, I might be able to get over my past, but I wouldn't be able to drink or drug. I mumbled to myself, "How can I choose life and help if my safety net of alcohol and drugs is yanked out from under me?"

With a stern look on his face, Dr. Simmons said, "You've only got a few minutes to make up your mind." I was afraid I would end up dead because I didn't know how to stop drinking and drugging and because I wanted to hurt myself all the time. A few minutes later, Dr. Simmons asked me, "For the last time—are you going to stay, or are you going to die?"

For a moment I couldn't breathe and my legs shook, but I didn't know what else to do so I whispered, "I'll stay."

It was one of the hardest decisions I'd ever made in my entire life…to give up the security of my addiction in order to trust someone to help me and not hurt me.

I was admitted to the adolescent unit with a bunch of other troubled teenagers from broken homes and juvenile detention centers. We were pretty much kept away from the adult psychiatric patients, except during meals. My room was on the second floor of the hospital in a locked ward for the severely mentally-ill patients, and where all the new kids started the program. I wasn't allowed telephone calls, any visitors, or any contact with the rest of the hospital. I had to earn my way off that floor in order to be given more privileges, freedom and a room downstairs with the other teenagers.

The adolescent program was based on a point and level system. There were four levels and everyone started out on Level I. Discharge from the hospital was given at Level IV. The way a person moved from one level to another was by doing things like getting up on time, making their bed, following the rules, going to, and participating in, group therapy, and so forth. The whole concept sounded easy enough and I was confident that I could quickly "earn" my way out of there. My first concern was getting on Level II so I could get day and weekend passes.

Gloria and Ronnie eventually found out where I was after getting into an argument with Mom about her having me arrested. Gloria called me and said, "We didn't know your Mom would have you arrested. She also told us that she doesn't believe what you told her about Gene, and she told your brothers everything you said." I felt utterly embarrassed and was even more ashamed now that my secret was public knowledge.

Desperate to see my surrogate family, I earned my way onto Level II by the next weekend. I also chose to spend my weekend pass with Gloria and Ronnie because no one in my family had come to visit me in the hospital. I later learned from my brother Pat that after I was hospitalized it was if I had died because neither he nor Mike were allowed to talk about me or ask how I was doing. They weren't allowed to visit me or send a get well card. My name was never mentioned.

I was so happy to see them, so thankful that they didn't give up on me. As we drove out of the hospital parking lot, I knew that these people were truly my new family. I also made the decision that I wouldn't get high on my weekend pass, or ever again. I wanted help so I wouldn't ever lose them.

After arriving at their trailer, we sat around talking and enjoying our reunion. Spending time with each other was great, even though I was a little uncomfortable because I didn't know how to act around anyone without being drunk or high. To my surprise, I did pretty well—until Jeffrey showed up. As soon as he walked into the trailer, I was seized with fear because I knew there was no escaping him. I was disappointed because my being good at the hospital and deciding to stay clean didn't get me a reprieve from people like him. My eyes begged him to leave me alone, but he told Gloria and Ronnie that he wanted to spend some private time with me. I didn't want to go with him, but what choice did I have when I was a frail seventeen-year-old girl who was afraid of her own shadow?

Fearfully, I walked into Jeffrey's place where I saw a bunch of joints and a couple of fifths of liquor sitting on the coffee table. I was surprised that he had this stuff sitting there since he knew I had been in the adolescent program for partying too much. I sat on the couch trying to make idle conversation and not look at the pot and booze. When Jeffrey realized I wasn't going to use and end up unconscious, he started touching and kissing me. My body cringed and my breath vanished. I tried to make him stop, but my words only fell on deaf ears. When I realized that he wasn't going to let me up, I panicked. The same feelings of shame and entrapment I always had around men resurfaced. The bad feelings I had been running from reappeared. So I lit up a joint and opened a fifth of liquor.

As I felt my mind and body slipping off into an altered state of consciousness, Jeffrey picked me up, carried me into his room and laid me down on his bed. He was breathing heavily and was touching my body. I couldn't do anything but lie there silently with tears rolling down my face. I must have drifted off into a black out because I was brought back to a state of semi-consciousness from the excruciating pain of him penetrating me.

My body screamed with pain. My heart broke with shame as I lay there in silence as I had been trained to do so for so many years. He violently pumped his body up and down until he obtained his magical orgasm, while I desperately tried to hold on to reality by drifting off into another dimension in my mind. When he was done with me, I smoked as much pot and drank as much liquor as I could before he took me back to Gloria and Ronnie's. I felt absolutely horrible about what had happened and I felt even worse now that I was using again.

The next day, Gloria and I hung out with each other and for a moment everything seemed better. Because she didn't really understand what I needed and how smoking pot led to other things, we got high together. We laughed and enjoyed spending time with each other until it was time for me to go back to the hospital. I relished our time together and was sad that I had to leave my friend to go back to my personal prison.

On the way back to the hospital, Gloria and Ronnie took me to get my car so I could leave it parked in the hospital parking lot. Since I was using again, I made sure I had a bunch of pot and alcohol stashed in my car for easy access and several joints to sneak into the hospital.

I walked back into the hospital where the nurses took one look at me and knew I was stoned. The anger on their faces was obvious, but there was nothing they could do except search me for more drugs and then report me. Thankfully, they didn't find the pot, but they did put me back upstairs and on Level I.

After this incident, my life became a living hell and it seemed like forever before I got off the second floor again. The staff became frustrated because they couldn't figure out how I was getting high, so they locked me up in the Maximum Care Unit. I had no idea what I had gotten myself into.

The first time I ended up in the Maximum Care Unit, I was scared to death. It was a really small room with only a bed, and it was located across from the nurse's station on the second floor. The bed had leather straps in case I needed to be restrained. There was no other furniture in the room, just a thick, black, wire mesh covering a single window that allowed a very small amount of sunlight into the room. The room was sterile with its commercially tiled floor and sheet-rocked walls. The bathroom door was always kept locked for my "protection." In essence, it was like a small padded room without the padding. After the staff threw me into that tiny hole where the door was always kept locked, I was afraid that they were never going to let me out again…that I would be lost in there forever. I couldn't understand why they were locking me up when all I was trying to do was hide from my feelings of being abused, abandoned and unloved. *All I wanted was for someone to show me some kindness and to give me permission to tell my forbidden family secrets…not punish me.*

The Maximum Care Unit became my home away from home. No matter how hard I tried, I couldn't get out. Each time I ended up in that tiny room, I was automatically put back on Level I and wasn't allowed to see anyone else in the adolescent program or participate in any activities, except group therapy. I just stayed locked up in that room. The only time I saw anyone was when the nurses unlocked the bathroom door and when they brought me food or medication.

No one, including me, seemed to know what to do at that point. I was spending so much time isolated from the rest of the world and behind locked doors that I felt hopeless—a lost cause.   As I spent my long days in the barren room, I began feeling that the people at Turning Point were just like Mom and Gene: punishing and hurting me for things I didn't understand. I began to feel as if I was suffocating because the feelings I was running from began to resurface. I felt alone in my pain with no one to listen to me. My need to hurt and kill myself reared its ugly head.   I was so afraid.   I wanted to cry out, "Someone please help me…please love me…please hold me and make me feel safe."

My only saving grace through the long months in the Maximum Care Unit was getting to know Melina, an occupational therapist. I was surprised that she actually came in my room and sat down on the edge of my bed so we could talk. She didn't seem to be afraid of me, or view me as a hopeless case like the nurses did. I really liked her and enjoyed our time together. I didn't know what it was about her, but I could see in her eyes that she had something I didn't: she seemed to like helping people and appeared to enjoy life. Even though it confused me, I wanted some of what she had—I wanted to feel good, and like life.

During Melina's visits, she frequently asked me what was bothering me and why I kept doing things that wouldn't allow me to get out of the Maximum Care Unit. She wanted to know what had happened to me that made me want to self-destruct. Each time she asked me those questions, I became sad. I wanted so badly to tell her everything, but I was too afraid of my own feelings. I was terrified that Mom would find out that I had betrayed the family secrets and she would hurt me or take me away from Melina. So, she brought me a yellow legal pad for me to use as my voice. I was allowed to write down anything I wanted. When she handed me the legal pad and told me it was safe, I wanted to hug her and tell her, "Thank you." But I remained silent, yet filled with hope.

I sat on my bed with my legal pad and tried really hard to figure out what was wrong with me, why I was doing what I was doing, and how I was feeling. There was such a whirlwind of emotions running around inside me that I could hardly make sense out of anything. So I just started writing with the hope that something meaningful would come out. Sometimes, I remembered things that were hidden deep in my heart and would pray that God would give me the courage to put them down on the paper.

Melina's visits were the only thing I looked forward to each day. I would timidly hand her my precious legal pad, containing words that were written as if with my own blood. As she read my thoughts, I anxiously sat on the edge of my bed, so embarrassed and ashamed that I could hardly look at her. Every so often, she would glance over at me with tears in her eyes. It was then that I knew she understood my pain. Then one day, she rewarded my efforts by taking me downstairs to her office for a visit and so we could talk about the things that were on the legal pad outside of the Maximum Care Unit. I had been locked up for so long that it felt strange to be out in the world. I cried because I couldn't believe I was worthy of her kindness.

I was surprised that Melina's office was like a little cubbyhole. I really liked it though because it reminded me of my little closet in Santa Monica, small and detached from the world. I sat down in one of her chairs and gazed at my friend with feelings of warmth and joy as she read my unspoken words aloud from the legal pad. After talking about my thoughts and confessions for a short while, I was even more amazed that she seemed to really be listening to me. But, just as I was becoming comfortable, she stood up and motioned that it was time for me to go back to my room. I was saddened at the thought of my return to my den of isolation, but as we started out of her office, Melina turned around, looked at me compassionately, and gave me a hug. As I felt her arms around me, I melted: that very act was what I had been missing all my life.

I eventually got out of the Maximum Care Unit, but frequently found myself back in there for drinking and drugging because I didn't know how to handle my feelings of self-hatred. I was overwrought with guilt and shame because I thought that what happened to me was my fault, that I caused it.

The only thing I managed to do well in the hospital was my schoolwork. I took my regular high school classes each day at the hospital from a teacher named Cynthia. She was a very tall, slender lady with short, curly brown hair. She was always dressed professionally like a real teacher, and I thought she was wonderful. I don't know why, but I took pride in my schoolwork and it resulted in a great relationship with Cynthia. She liked the fact that I did my assignments without being prompted. I always felt good around her because she seemed impressed that I wasn't stupid, that I could actually think for myself, that I was an A student.

Since I was doing well in school, and kept enough points to at least stay on Level II, I was allowed to go out on passes with Gloria and Ronnie, especially since no one in my family had come to see me. The time I spent with them was the only thing I was holding on to in the real world. Although I loved spending time with them, the same thing always ruined it: every week, Jeffrey showed up to take me to his trailer. He would get me drunk and stoned, and then have sex with me after I blacked out. I had no idea what to do or who to tell. Even though Gloria was the most important person in my life, I still didn't feel safe enough to tell her what was happening. I also couldn't tell anyone at the hospital because I was afraid of being punished and not being allowed to see Gloria or Ronnie anymore. The longer it went on, the more I drank and drugged. I couldn't take the shame, guilt, and filthiness I felt.

The day finally came when I panicked—I might be pregnant. I didn't know what to do, so I sat in my room and contemplated how I was going to kill myself or make myself abort without anyone finding out. As the fear of pregnancy grew, I asked a nurse, "Could you help me because I don't know how to tell if I'm pregnant, only that I've missed my period."

The nurse jumped up out of her chair and frantically ran down the hall to the social workers office. Judy, the social worker, calmly walked out of her office and motioned for me to come and talk with her. Each step I took towards her office left my knees shaking with fear, and my heart beating so hard that I could feel my chest vibrate. She looked at me with concern in her eyes and wanted to know who had been having sex with me, especially since I had been living at the hospital for several months now. I stared at the floor and could barely force a whisper that said it was Jeffery and he was doing it to me when I went out on my weekend passes. Shame oozed out of every pore of my body. I was afraid of what was going to happen to me. I was terrified that Mom was going to find out, and that Judy would put me back in the Maximum Care Unit.

She stood up in anger, looked at me and declared that she was putting a stop to it. I jumped up and pleaded, "Please don't take away my time with Gloria and Ronnie…just make Jeffrey stop having sex with me—I just can't take it anymore." She told me that all my passes were suspended. I didn't understand how she could do that to me when she knew that Gloria and Ronnie were my only family, my only connection to the outside world. Even though I was relieved that Jeffrey couldn't hurt me anymore, my heart was broken that I had now lost my surrogate family.

I stood in the hall for a few minutes trying to comprehend everything that had transpired in the last hour. I felt dirty not only because of what Jeffrey had done to me, but because the staff now knew my secret as well. I was also angry because I felt as if I was being punished once again for something someone else had done to me, much like Mom did when she put me in the hospital after I told her about Gene.

The hospital took me to see a doctor to determine if I was pregnant. Thankfully, the pregnancy test came back negative and I was immediately placed on birth control pills.

My luck in life had always been awful, and things weren't about to change now. I was finally becoming comfortable with the staff and starting to make some progress when I was told that Melina wouldn't be working at the hospital anymore. I felt like my heart was being ripped out of my chest. Despite my tears and my begging the hospital not to let her leave, the only person I cared about had left. My weary spirit collapsed in defeat. I was distraught, and confused about what I had done to make Melina leave without even saying good-bye.

After that, things got worse: I didn't care whether I lived or died—I just knew that I couldn't keep trying to open myself up to people, when all they did was leave me.

About a month after Melina left, the other kids and I were on the second floor in the group room building models in recreation therapy. I was still so depressed from losing my friend that I excused myself from the group to go huff model glue in the bathroom. Once I was sufficiently done inhaling the chemicals, I left the tiny cubicle, only to find Valerie (another occupational therapist) standing at the door, waiting for me. When she saw my lifeless eyes and smelled the glue wafting from me, she looked dismayed. At that moment, I realized I was in trouble again and wondered if it would be enough to land me back in the Maximum Care Unit.

Valerie sat me down, confronted me with my crime and lectured me about what huffing glue was doing to my brain cells. At that moment someone abruptly ran into the room and said that Melina was downstairs, visiting. In pure excitement, I jumped up because I knew Melina had come back to see me, and to tell me how much she had missed me! I was elated that my friend didn't abandon me after all. When Valerie saw the excitement on my face, she motioned that it was all right for me to go downstairs to see my lost friend. I raced downstairs with lightning speed, thinking about all the things I was going to tell Melina, and how I would give her a big hug. I rounded the corner from the elevators and begged the nurses to tell me where she was. One of the nurses looked sadly at me and quietly said, "Melina has already left."

I was absolutely crushed that my best friend in the whole world left me again, without even a word. I stood there for several minutes wondering how many more times I would have to go through this. I wanted to lie down and die. Valerie came downstairs, and seeing the look of devastation on my face, put her arm around me and took me back upstairs to finish our discussion.

By the time we got back to the group room, I didn't care what my punishment would be for huffing the glue. I just knew that my world had finished falling apart and there was nothing else anyone could do to hurt me.

Somehow, during all the chaos, I managed to stay out of the Maximum Care Unit and was allowed to go out on passes as long as I didn't go see Gloria or Ronnie. So I spent all my time driving around Savannah, drinking, popping pills, and smoking dope.

My increased freedom brought with it a wake-up call that I thought would set me straight and ease my addiction. While visiting another girl in the program, who was confined to the second floor, I fell to the floor having uncontrollable seizures. The next day I woke up in my bed, wondering why I was so tired and why I felt like I had been beaten up. The nurses told me that I'd had several grand mal seizures and I was going to Hope Hospital for tests to determine the cause. They found that the seizures were caused by the combination of alcohol and drugs I had been putting in my system, especially the mass quantities of pills I was ingesting during my weekend passes. The doctor said, "If you continue to use, you could end up having another seizure that will leave you brain damaged, possibly a vegetable." I was absolutely terrified and was left wondering how I was going to survive without drinking and drugging. What was I going to do?

After sleeping almost non-stop for five days, I slowly resumed my schedule with the rest of the kids. But, all I could think about was what the doctor had said. Even so, my body cried out for just one joint, or one drink, to take the edge off. I felt like a caged animal with nowhere to go, like a snake needing to shed its skin, but not being allowed to. Desperate, I tried to figure out why I needed to use so badly, but I couldn't figure it out. I finally got to the place where I couldn't stand it anymore—I had to use.

Despite the fact that I was afraid of ending up a vegetable, I scored some pot from someone in the program and went into a small utility closet to hide. My hands shook as I rolled up a joint and lit it. I took one last deep breath and prayed that God would protect me as I took a long drag. I held the smoke in my lungs for a brief moment, anxiously waiting to see if I was going to end up brain damaged. But nothing happened, and I celebrated my success with smoking the rest of the joint. Even though I was greatly relieved that my safety net was still available, smoking that one joint put me back on the roller coaster of addiction.

The longer I stayed in the hospital, the more I could get anything I needed to stay anesthetized and at no cost. The staff brought me pot, while the adult psychiatric patients kept me well supplied with pills and powders from their weekend passes. Basically, I was using anything I could get my hands on.

One night, a girl who was in the adolescent program with me, came back from one of her day passes with a little treat that neither she, nor I, had ever done before. I was so excited about our new adventure that I could hardly wait to get the new substance into my body. We met in the laundry room where she showed me the beautiful, yellow powder called "Tea." We didn't know how much was safe to do, but without fear, Tonya opened the package and split it in half. We stood watch for each other as we snorted the powder up our noses. Immediately after snorting my portion, something began happening to me: the walls looked like they were breathing; the room was moving in all kinds of directions; and I couldn't make out anything Tonya was saying to me, even though I could see her lips moving. Then I blacked out. At first the rest of the kids in the program thought it was funny, that is until I lost the ability to see and to hear. Afraid, they told a nurse I was in trouble. I was immediately taken to my room where the nurses tried to figure out what I had ingested, but I couldn't tell them, and the other girl wasn't about to confess. My face turned bright red, and my temperature was so high that I was taken back to the medical center.

I briefly came to in the emergency room and had no idea where I was until I saw three IV's sticking out of my arms and heard a doctor yelling, "If you're going to keep trying to kill yourself, don't come back to my emergency room anymore!" He continued screaming at me, "You're extremely lucky because the stuff you put up your nose causes people to have temperatures so high that it literally fries their brains." He yanked the IVs out of my arms and then shipped me back to Turning Point. I was put back in the Maximum Care Unit and demoted to Level I to start all over again. I wondered if I was ever going to get out of that place.

Despite the Tea incident, I was still in self-destruct mode. There was a wealthy older man who was constantly in and out of the adult psychiatric program. He and I had become good friends, so on one of his re-admissions, he smuggled me in a paper sack full of pills. I had never seen so many different colors and shapes of pills in one place and I was comforted by the thought that they were all mine.

I hid the bag of pills so I wouldn't get busted and only took what I needed to stay anesthetized. Then one day I woke up feeling severely depressed and wanting to kill myself. So I swallowed a handful of the pills to see if I could make the feelings vanish. When I didn't get the response I wanted, I took another handful of pills until I blacked out. I awoke the next morning in a semi-conscious state, surprised and saddened that I didn't die during the night. I took another handful of pills.

I succeeded in covering up what I had done until I got on the elevator with Valerie, my occupational therapist. I tried to lean against the elevator wall so I wouldn't fall over, but Valerie looked at me strangely and asked, "Are you all right?" Barely able to utter any words, I motioned that I was fine. She obviously didn't believe me because she asked, "What have you taken?"

As soon as the elevator door opened, I retorted, "Nothing's wrong!" I then lost my ability to accurately perceive where the ground was and took a giant step into the air to get off the elevator. It wasn't until my foot hit the ground that I realized what I had done and intuitively understood I was in trouble again.

After Valerie and I escaped our unpleasant encounter on the elevator, I staggered to my occupational therapy class. I quietly sat down and tried to act normal to avoid getting in trouble. Then suddenly, my vision became blurry and I was having trouble swallowing. I was frightened and didn't understand what was happening. My tongue felt like a piece of wet rawhide, and it was difficult to talk and stay conscious. As I looked across the room, I could sense that Valerie was still watching me. When I started having difficulty breathing and swallowing, she ran over to me and demanded to know what I had taken, but I honestly didn't know what I had mixed together. So she picked me up, loaded me into the hospital van and took me back to the medical center for one more emergency room visit. My stomach was pumped out and I was loaded up with Benadryl to stop the allergic reaction I was having to the mixture of pills.

That sort of thing went on for a long while, until the hospital staff made it their business to figure out where I was getting my alcohol and drugs. I had to really try hard to out-smart them, and I must admit I was ingenious with my methods of deception.

I would hide my contraband in bushes along the hospital perimeter, in the ceiling of my room, and in the maintenance envelope in the heating and air conditioning unit. Rolling papers were hidden in my pillow. An ounce of pot stashed in my pants, and so forth. The staff couldn't keep up with me, and didn't catch me until they did a hospital-wide search for contraband. They found a ton of contraband in the hospital, and, yes, they found some of my stash hidden in my room. Again, I was sent back up to the second floor and thrown back in the Maximum Care Unit. I did my time there and was eventually sent to a regular room on the second floor until I could earn enough points to get back downstairs.

The same day I was placed in a regular room, a nursing assistant, Shawnda, was sent to my room to strip-search me. I was surprised that she was so serious about it because she liked to get high as much as I did, and she was one of the staff who let things slide when I got stoned. Despite the fact that she stood there glaring at me in an unsettling way, I absolutely refused to let her search me because I didn't want to end up in the Maximum Care Unit again. My refusal told Shawnda I was hiding something, so she let me in on that the fact that the hospital staff figured out I was keeping the pot hidden on my body. I could either give her some of it or she could strip-search me and take it all. Reluctantly I agreed. Our agreement made everyone happy: Shawnda got credit for being the one who found my drugs; the nursing staff was happy because they thought they had gotten the best of me; I didn't have to be strip searched; and I still had enough drugs to get high.

Several weeks later, while I was still on the second floor in a regular room, I really messed up big time, to the point that even I realized I had crossed way over the line. Another wave of depression hit me when I realized that I still didn't have anyone to talk to, I was still hurting on the inside, Mom still hadn't come to visit me, and I still wasn't allowed to see Gloria or Ronnie. All I could do right was stay in trouble and hurt myself. This time I felt so hopeless that I tried to kill myself by taking every drug I had on me. Predictably, I ended up getting my stomach pumped out again at Hope Hospital and was put back in the Maximum Care Unit where the door was left open because I was on a 24-hour suicide watch.

I didn't have any drugs left to ease my pain and I needed to use or hurt myself in a really bad way. I stood at my door watching everyone else walking around like they didn't have a care in the world, I was immersed in self-loathing. I was tired of everything. I was tired of hurting. I was tired of feeling alone and unloved. I was tired of battling my past, but I didn't know how to make it stop. As I watched the nurses giving the patients their medication, I saw my ticket to an altered reality in the form of two vials of medication and a set of drug keys. When no one was looking, I slipped out of my room, into the nurse's station and stole the vials of medication and the keys. My heart raced as I quickly returned to my room, hid the stolen items under the bathroom sink and pretended that I hadn't left my spot in the doorway for even one second.

In a matter of minutes the nurses figured out the drugs and the keys were gone. The hospital went on panic mode, confined everyone to their rooms, cancelled all passes, and did a complete sweep of the hospital. Of course, the first person they came to was me, and in a trembling voice, I denied my involvement. I knew that if they found me with the drug vials or keys, it would literally be the end of me. I knew they would send me back home to Mom. I contemplated my terrible transgression until I was consumed with such fear that I threw the vials of medication away and hid the drug keys in the ceiling. I stood there perplexed that I had done all of that just to get high. What in the world was I thinking?

The staff couldn't find the medicine vials or the keys, so they pleaded with everyone to turn over the stolen items. They also promised that if anyone would tell them where the stolen items were, no one would get in to trouble. Judy and Valerie made another trip back to talk with me one more time. I looked at their agonized faces and realized that I was out of control and I needed help. I wanted to stop running and to stop hurting myself. My soul ached for their help. I was overwrought with a sense of extreme sorrow because I loved them and I didn't want to hurt them. I finally confessed, with a new heart-felt conviction: "The keys are in the ceiling and I've thrown out the vials." Their faces lit up with relief. I knew I had done the right thing and that this was my first step in the right direction.

From that moment on, I tried as hard as I could to do better, not only for myself, but also for the people standing around me whom I loved and whose help I needed.

My new desire to be free from my old self and my past, resulted in Valerie spending a lot of time with me. It was time that I very much needed with another human being who was kind, gentle, and, most of all, safe. The more time we spent together, the more I wanted to be just like her. She was very pretty and had a great inner peace and strength about her. She was in perfect physical condition and had shoulder-length, jet-black hair and beautiful Greek olive skin. I always knew there was something special about her, and I desperately wanted her to like me. She was also a student of Tae Kwon Do. I felt special when she allowed me, and only me, to work out with her when she was getting ready for her Brown Belt test. A great guitarist, she also spent time showing me how to play songs and how to pick the guitar. The biggest surprise of all was when she asked me if I was interested in learning how to run because she ran five miles every morning. I was definitely interested because I thought it would make me more like her, and I would get to spend more one-on-one time with her. I craved that kind of attention so badly that I would have done anything for it.

I had no idea what I was getting myself into, but Valerie woke me up early every morning for our daily run. I hated getting up before everyone else, but it felt good that she came in early just to spend time with me. So I dragged myself out of bed each morning and forced myself to learn how to run. Our physical jaunts took place at a local park that had a little quarter-mile circle in the middle. I was in such bad physical shape from the alcohol and drugs that Valerie started me off on the little quarter-mile circle. At first, I couldn't get around the track to save my life, and it was then that I knew I was in pitiful shape for a seventeen-year-old. I eventually worked up to being able to run the little quarter-mile circle and then the larger perimeter, which was approximately 1.6 miles. I really enjoyed spending time with my new friend and was amazed that I grew to love running.

One of the other great things about Valerie was that she introduced me to some very cool music, which changed my life. My favorite was a group called Heart. I immediately fell in love with their music because I could totally identify with them. As one of my special privileges, Valerie let me sit in her office for hours listening to several Heart records. I mostly listened to their Live and Dog and Butterfly albums because of a song called Mistrial Wind. I couldn't listen to it often enough; it triggered the place inside of me that needed to be figured out. It tapped into the core of my being and reminded me how badly I wanted someone to love me, just to touch and hold me once in a while in a good way. It wasn't so much the words they sang, but the way they played the music and sang the lyrics with such feeling and compassion. That song made me want to tell my secrets so I could get better and do things right.

Despite my being in the program with these great people, we didn't talk about the real issues that caused my pain and I wasn't able to voluntarily disclose them. I wanted so badly to change myself, but I didn't know how to unload my burdens and face my demons. It was during that time that I found a new way to express my pain.

I had always been concerned about how I looked, especially after all the eye surgeries. Then I met Erin, a new girl who was brought into the program and assigned as my roommate. She was absolutely beautiful with her blond hair, blue eyes, and powdery light skin. She was also quiet and seemed to have it all together. It was also obvious that she came from a rich family, and it made me wonder how she ended up in a place like this. One day, while we were talking, she told me that she was admitted to the hospital because she didn't like to eat. I looked at her in confusion because I couldn't believe she considered that to be a problem, especially since I was trying to survive being beaten, sexually abused, and almost killed several times. I was also surprised because Erin was very beautiful, had the perfect body, and everyone liked her. I wanted to be her. I wanted to be pretty and thin so everyone would like me.

Because of this, I started controlling how much food I put in my body, while Valerie and I continued to run each morning. With each day that passed, it got harder and harder for me to eat without feeling guilty.

I picked at my food and was consumed with self-hatred for how I looked and, more so, for who I was. As I starved myself, I began equating who I was as a person with how I looked. I began to feel as if there was no way I could starve enough or become thin enough to make me feel worthy as a person. What I did know was that I was desperate for someone to love me, yet no matter how much I wasted away, I was still alone and still felt like a bad person. The more alone I felt, the more obsessed I became about my weight. Even when it became apparent that I was thinner than Erin, weighing in at 95 pounds, no one seemed to care. Not a word was said to me about it. In one sense I was happy because it meant that I could starve in peace, but on the other hand, I ached for someone to see that I was crying out for help.

I had been in the hospital for over five months now and was working hard to deal with the issues surrounding my mother. It was extremely painful, but at least I was trying to trudge my way through it. Then one day everyone in the program thought it was time for me to see if Mom and I could re-establish some type of relationship. The idea completely terrified me, but somewhere inside I knew I missed seeing her and I wanted to know why she hadn't been to see me. So, I reluctantly agreed to let my social worker, Judy, call Mom to see if she would be willing to spend some time with me on a day pass. I sat nervously in her office trying to be brave about the telephone call and the possibility of seeing the person I needed most to love me, but who always ended up hurting me.

Judy advised Mom that if she agreed to the day pass, she could take me to a restaurant for lunch and then bring me back within four hours. Judy's face grew pensive and exasperated as she listened to Mom's long, drawn out response. I had to smile at her because I recognized that look I had worn so many times myself. At the same time, I also wondered what kind of lies Mom was telling and how many times she used the phrase "disturbed child" during the conversation.

Moments later, Judy nodded, indicating that Mom had agreed to the day pass. As I comprehended that I was about to go out with my mother for four whole hours, my insides started to shake. Although a little excited about seeing her, I couldn't forget the bad things she had done to me, and had let happen to me. After hanging up the phone, Judy sighed heavily and had a strange look of confusion on her face, but she assured me that everything was going to be okay. After all, what could possibly happen if we were only going to lunch and spending a little bit of time together?

The day of Mom's visit finally arrived, and I was excited, yet afraid. When she walked in the front door, I was immediately torn between wanting to run up and hug her, and wanting to run and hide behind Valerie and Judy for protection. I stood there for a few minutes looking at Mom and wondering what I should do. I wanted her to love and hold me, but at the same time I wanted to scream at her for hurting me. Somehow my desire for her to love and accept me outweighed my fear and anger. I slowly walked over to her, greeted her and pretended that nothing bad had ever happened between us.

I took one last look at my friends as Mom escorted me out of the building to her car. While driving to the Chinese restaurant, I could intuitively sense that she was nervous, but I sat there amazed that she tried to make casual conversation and seemed glad to see me. Her efforts helped me to feel comfortable enough to let my guard down, so I jumped right back into the relationship with her, forgetting everything I knew to be true.

We went to a Chinese restaurant not too far from the hospital. I was glad she had chosen that place because they really had good food. We both were trying to act normal as we stared intently at our menus and anxiously awaited the waitress to break the silence by taking our order. As I ordered some of their wonderful Chop Suey, Mom asked if I wanted one of the mixed drinks with the little umbrellas in it. For a moment I was nervous about drinking because I knew everyone at the hospital would be disappointed in me if they found out. But, because her offer made me think that she loved me, I proudly ordered one.

When the beautiful red and pink drinks with cherries and umbrellas arrived, I was surprised to see they were the size of fishbowls. The tension between us greatly subsided as we drank the tropical drinks and she ordered us another round. We became quite relaxed after our second drink and that was the first time I had ever had a conversation with Mom when we didn't talk about anything bad. It was strange trying to act like everything was normal. But overall, the lunch was a success.

When we walked out of the restaurant, we still had a couple of hours before I had to be back at the hospital. By then I was feeling a little giddy and daring. Mom must have been feeling the same way because she suggested that we go to River Street, a long road on the riverfront with nothing but bars, restaurants, and shops. I was excited and felt like a mischievous teenager who was getting ready to party with her best friend. I was so excited that my best friend was finally going to be my mother that I happily complied with the plan. I silently hoped that maybe this would make her love me.

We were cackling and laughing like two high school girls getting ready for a big night on the town when Mom parked the car and we slowly walked down to a place called The Outer Banks. I couldn't believe she chose that place because it had been one of my favorite partying places. At first, I was a little nervous about being there because I remembered my friends at Turning Point who were trying to help me, and I didn't want to mess up again. But, those thoughts were quickly pushed aside by my desire to connect with my mother. We played pool, drank tequila sunrises, and laughed with each other like we didn't have a care in the world and there was no tomorrow. I was enjoying my time with Mom so much that I didn't care what it cost me. I wanted that feeling to last forever.

When we finally staggered out of the bar, I was surprised that it was dark outside. It was then that I realized that we hadn't made it back to the hospital within the designated four hours, and we were drunk! We wandered up and down the streets of downtown Savannah for almost an hour looking for Mom's car before we found it. Because Mom was completely drunk, she carefully drove to a nearby convenience store to get some coffee so she could appear sober when she escorted me back into the hospital. I tried to help by pouring her coffee for her, but I was so drunk I poured it into her purse which was sitting right next to the coffee cup. We both laughed at my silly mistake. It felt so good to laugh with Mom.

I woke up the next morning alternating between throwing up and choking with dry heaves. I hung my head over the toilet and was afraid because I couldn't remember what happened after the convenience store. I tried to remember if I had gotten into trouble, if I cussed anyone out, or if anyone figured out I was drunk. I shuffled out of my room with an overpowering hangover, and knew I was in trouble by the way everyone was looking at me. A special group therapy session was called so the group could deal with me and what happened with Mom. Since I didn't remember getting back to the hospital, Valerie and Judy confronted me with the fact that I had been hostile, aggressive, and belligerent with them to the point of almost having to be restrained in the Maximum Care Unit. They said Mom was defiant and uncooperative to the staff.

Feeling guilty, I stared at the floor. I knew I had made a grave mistake and had compromised everyone's trust. I was made to tell the group what happened with Mom and how we got drunk. I was completely humiliated and embarrassed for what I had done. I was so sorry, but I knew my words meant nothing to anyone. So I sat silently in my chair awaiting the group's feedback and my punishment.

I was frightened until I realized that the strong messages about how I messed up were also accompanied with an understanding that Mom was the adult who should have been more responsible. For the first time, I felt like everyone understood what I had been trying to tell them about home and I was overwhelmingly relieved. I was punished, and forbidden to go back out on any passes with Mom again. But that was all right because I had finally found some of the understanding I had been looking for.

I worked really hard at school and finished all my classes with A's and was ready to graduate. Unfortunately, I couldn't graduate with my high school class, walk down the isle to get my diploma, have pictures taken of my special day or anything like that. I was very disappointed when graduation day came and went, and I sat in the hospital. But even though I didn't have any family to celebrate my graduation with, no friends at my high school to bask in my accomplishment or make future plans with, I took it very well. The important thing was that I had graduated.

Later that day, everyone in the adolescent program went out into the community with Valerie to pick up various things for the hospital, and to get a cake for a surprise birthday party for one of the staff. It felt great to be out of the hospital and in the real world doing things with other people, even if we were only running errands. I felt like I was a part of something. The thing I enjoyed the most was riding in the back of Valerie's pick-up truck under her low-budget camper top.

When we got back to the hospital, I was amazed at the multitude of decorations in every nook and cranny of the building. There were streamers, balloons, and party favors everywhere. I thought that the staff person we were throwing the surprise birthday party for must be one important individual, as we were giving her the party of a lifetime. How I wished it had been for me.

After I sat the cake down on the table, everyone yelled, "Congratulations!" Excitement filled the air as I looked around to see who was being congratulated, but I couldn't figure out who it was. I anxiously stood there looking for the birthday person, when Valerie walked up to me with a huge smile on her face and told me the party was for me. I was the one being congratulated—it was my graduation party!

I was filled with such warmth and love for everybody in the room. I wanted to cry and hug everyone for doing something special for me, of all people. Even though I didn't feel worthy, I stood there trying to absorb every precious moment of my special day. Valerie put one arm around me and raised the other to silence everyone in the room. When everyone was perfectly still, I could feel their eyes upon me. She then looked proudly at me and handed me my high school diploma. My weary spirit was now filled with my first sense of accomplishment and joy. That was the happiest day of my life.

After my party, I glowed all day long with the wonderful feeling of belonging and basking in my success. I didn't want my special day to ever end. As I floated around the hospital with my new sense of purpose, I was told I had a visitor. When I rounded the corner from the elevator, I saw Mom sitting in the waiting room! For a few moments, I stared at her through the glass window. I felt all my happy feelings drift away and become replaced with fear and anxiety. Panicked, I ran down the hall as quickly as I could to tell Judy that Mom was here, and I didn't know what to do.

A strange sadness covered Judy's eyes as she said, "I knew your Mom was coming—it was supposed to have been a surprise—she was supposed to have been at your party."

My heart grew heavy as I realized that Mom missed my special party and, one more time, she hadn't been there for me. I didn't know what to do, so Judy suggested, "Put your feelings aside and at least talk with her. She did drive almost an hour to see you."

I nodded to the secretary to buzz Mom into the hospital. I stood nervously in front of her while Judy suggested that we visit in the occupational therapy area. Mom and I quietly walked over to some chairs and sat down looking as if we were both waiting to be executed. Mom was the first one to break the silence, "I want to talk to you, and I've brought you a high school ring as a graduation present."

My face brightened with excitement at her words, and I thought that maybe she had done something special just for me. I quickly tore the paper off the small silver colored box only to be disappointed at what I saw. It wasn't the ring I had told Mom about prior to my hospitalization, or one like any of the other kids had. It was just like everything else I had ever gotten from her—it was what she wanted, not what I wanted. Even though I graciously accepted the ring and thanked Mom for it, I felt cheated.

She then told me she needed to talk with me, but not until we had gone for a walk. I was confused, but I did as she asked. Since Judy didn't know what was about to happen, she agreed to let me and Mom walk over to the medical center gardens so we could sit on the grass in front of the gorgeous rose garden. We sat down in the midst of the roses and basked in the warmth of the summer day. She looked at me like she was getting ready to lay something big on me, so I prepared myself for the blow by taking a deep breath.

She spat out, "I won't be having anything to do with you anymore. I hope that you have a good life."

My mouth fell open in complete disbelief and my heart felt like it was being pierced with a sharp knife. I truly couldn't believe the words I was hearing and I wished that she would have just gone ahead and killed me at that very moment. I couldn't believe the only person I needed to love me was telling me that she was leaving, never to return. Was that why she had given me the ugly ring? I was so angry and devastated that my mother, who I wished would love me, was sitting in front of me offering me a graduation present while simultaneously abandoning me again. I was so confused. I wondered what I had done that was so terribly wrong that my mother would have to leave me, especially on the happiest day of my life.

Mom left, and I fell apart. Judy tried to talk me through it, but nothing seemed to really help. I was consumed with a whole new level of despair I had never experienced before. There were no words that could possibly change the fact that I was completely alone and that my mother had abandoned me again. I knew I had been emotionally alone all my life, but now I was left with the understanding that I was once again physically alone with no family.

Judy then confessed that I hadn't been discharged from the hospital because everyone knew Mom was unstable and that I had been abused, even though I didn't come out and tell them. She admitted that they had made arrangements with the insurance company to let me stay so I could graduate from high school and, hopefully, go to college. It felt good to know that they loved me, even though it couldn't erase what Mom had just done.

My stint with drinking, drugging, and starving resurfaced and worsened after my brief interlude with Mom—it remained with me throughout my stay at Turning Point. I still tried to participate in all the activities so I could get everything I could out of the program. I just couldn't put down the alcohol, drugs, or starving, because I didn't know how to fill the hole inside me.

I went out alone on weekend passes and I spent a great deal of time going to Tybee Island, and hanging out at the isolated north end of the beach. Because Valerie had introduced me to this place, I believed I could feel connected to her and my friends at the hospital if I went there. I would sit in my car, staring at the waves and sand dunes, smoking pot and getting drunk all day long while listening to Heart tapes. In my stoned and debilitated state I tried to figure out what I was going to do with my life and the feelings that made me want to hurt myself. No matter how much dope I smoked, and how hard I tried to figure things out, nothing ever changed because I was still me.

Eventually I got tired of getting stoned by myself and needed to find a new place to score some dope. So I started hanging out at the south end of the beach in abandoned houses where the junkies hung out and where private parties were held with free drugs. It was really scary in those houses because they were like mazes. There were a lot of different rooms in them and somehow the houses were confusingly connected to each other. Like a typical shooting gallery, each room contained a different breed of people doing different things—except people were doing more than just shooting drugs. There were people drinking, shooting smack, chasing the heroine dragon, smoking pot, dropping acid, popping pills, and so forth. I couldn't believe that I had stooped to such a level, so out of embarrassment, I went to the shooting galleries only long enough to get what drugs I needed and then headed off to use in isolation. I was also wise enough to realize that I didn't trust myself to be around other people when I was using, especially strangers, because there was no way to know what could happen to me if I blacked out.

After getting my diploma, the hospital helped me to apply to several undergraduate schools. To everyone's surprise, including mine, I was accepted at Georgia Southern College in Statesboro, a small town about 45 minutes outside of Savannah. I was accepted for the fall quarter of 1981, but I didn't have any money to live on. Thus, the hospital let me get a job in the evenings after I finished all my groups.

I got a job at a fast food Mexican restaurant doing food preparation for minimum wage. It was hard keeping up with my responsibilities at work and at the hospital, but I did it anyway. I really liked my job, even though I got stoned every night on the way back to the hospital. Aside from getting high, I was doing pretty well with my new job and handling the idea that I was getting ready to go off to college.

Then, one night, Mom showed up where I worked. She apparently went to the hospital and someone on the evening shift told her where I was working. I didn't understand why anyone would do that but they did. As I was leaving work, Mom and my brother Pat, startled me on the way out the front door of the restaurant. She was obviously in trouble again.

She blurted out, "I divorced Gene and married Jackie (the ugly guy in Felicity with the handle-bar mustache), got pregnant, and had an abortion. After the abortion, I got rid of Jackie and remarried Gene."

I stood there astounded at her confession. She had a lot of explaining to do because I didn't understand how all of this could have happened. It was all too much and by the time she had finished babbling, I was again amazed at the drama that remained in my mother's life. I still didn't know why she felt the need to show up and tell me those things—especially after she had abandoned me—but she did. I guess she thought I could fix whatever she had gotten herself into, but I couldn't, and I no longer wanted to.

After Mom unloaded her burdens and realized I couldn't help her, she turned around and left as quickly as she had come.

I worked all summer, saved my paychecks and prayed that school would be a fresh start for me—the ticket I needed to stop drinking and drugging. I hoped that my focusing on something new would allow me to stop feeling the constant pain of my childhood. On the other hand, I was afraid I was doing the same thing my mother had always done with needing a new place to start over, a geographical cure.

It was now time to leave Turning Point and begin my new journey at Georgia Southern College. I was scared to death. I hadn't been in the real world for nine months and I was used to the protection and comfort of the hospital staff. I wasn't sure I was going to be able to successfully make that move without my family or friends to fall back on. The staff must have been just as nervous as I was because they convinced Dr. Simmons to see me once a week for therapy. They also sent Valerie to escort me to Statesboro and to make sure I got settled.

As I walked out of Turning Point and looked at my family one last time, I was sad at our parting and was reminded of how afraid I was of being on my own. I didn't want to leave them, but I knew it was time. It was all I could do to put myself in my car. I waved good-bye to them as I slowly drove out of the parking lot with Valerie trailing behind me.

The journey to Statesboro seemed endless even though it was less than an hour away. As we pulled into the parking lot of my dorm I cried but dared not shed a tear in front of Valerie. I was too embarrassed. She helped me get settled into my dorm room and I cherished every moment with her. I tried to get a solid mental image of her so I would never forget what she looked like.

My nervous stomach told me it was almost time for her to leave, so I hugged her as hard as I could hoping I would never have to let go. Compassion shone through her eyes as she told me I was going to be all right and that I could write her. She then said good-bye and got into her van. When she drove away I was overwhelmed with fear and feelings of isolation because I was letting go of my only healthy safety net in life and there was no one to catch me if I failed. I felt so completely empty, and I cried until I had no tears left.

PART II

THE AGONY OF EXISTENCE

Chapter 11

Away at School

Hours passed as I sat in my dorm room without the energy to unpack my few belongings or decorate the barren cubicle. Loneliness overwhelmed me and I wondered how I would survive without anyone to talk to about my feelings. Dark despair enveloped me; I wanted to get high. But I had promised myself that this was my new beginning and my way of quitting the alcohol and drugs.

I walked around the dorm and watched the other new arrivals. I was amazed at the number of freshmen whose parents escorted them to their first day of independence. As I watched them, I was both sad and angry because I never had anything like that with my family and I never would.

As I walked up and down the halls, fluctuating between sadness and animosity, a girl stopped me and introduced herself as Dana. "They're getting to you too, aren't they?" she said. Surprised, I looked at the small, thin girl with short, blonde hair standing in front of me and said, "You're right." She, too, was a freshman without any family.

While talking with her, I was relieved that I wasn't the only one having to deal with this new world alone. Since we were both uncomfortable in the distasteful family-filled environment, we left the building and jumped into Dana's old Toyota Corolla hatchback, taking off for nowhere in particular.

"Want to smoke a joint?" she asked as we drove down the streets of Statesboro. Caught off guard by her question, I sat there for a moment in silence. My mind raced back and forth between the promise I had made to myself, and the feelings I wanted to run from. The latter won.

Dana lit the joint and in a matter of seconds the aroma of marijuana filled the car. I inhaled every bit of smoke my lungs could hold, and prayed that God would understand and forgive me for breaking my promise. My brief moment of ecstasy was short-lived. I realized my dream of being clean and sober was again only a fantasy. I was back to my old, self-destructive ways, overwhelmed with guilt and despair.

After school began, I met Teresa, a local who knew the area well. We did everything together, especially partying. She introduced me to the people she hung out with, and for the most part, I really liked them. We had some outrageous parties and I was definitely set up to stay high. Consequently, every time I went out partying, I ended up completely smashed and blacked out—but that didn't stop me.

Going to school at Georgia Southern College wasn't easy, and the partying was my only emotional outlet. I lived in a dorm, and had to apply for financial aid in order to pay for school and basic necessities. I also got a job at a pizza place across the street from the campus, attended classes in the morning and worked in the afternoons. I hated the job. It was hard work for just a few dollars a day. I was barely making ends meet, especially with my expensive alcohol and drug problem.

Despite my substance abuse, I continued to run every day, hoping it would make me feel better emotionally, keep me from getting fat, and help my body process everything I was putting in it. But, most importantly, I ran because it reminded me of my family at Turning Point and the precious moments Valerie and I had spent together. It was my way of holding on to the people I loved and longed to be close to. I frequently wrote to everyone at the hospital. At first they wrote back, but as time passed, the number of letters drastically decreased. Ultimately, the only person I really kept in touch with was Valerie.

I barely functioned in school because I was either hung over or still stoned from the night before. With all the alcohol and drugs polluting my system I could hardly think, much less learn anything.

The hardest part about being in school was trying to get through the holidays and the school breaks. While the other kids went home, I was left with nowhere to go. I stayed on in the dorms alone, dreading the isolation. No matter how many times I walked up and down the hallways, there was never another soul to be found. There was never the smell of turkey cooking in the oven, a Christmas tree to decorate, or presents to wrap. To escape the isolation and feelings of abandonment, I worked extra hours at my dreaded job. Each evening, after work, I went back to my room, sat quietly drinking and drugging myself into oblivion, skirting the fine line between life and death as I contemplated suicide.

Despite the extra hours at work, my financial problems were severe. Then one day I remembered something that could alleviate my financial difficulty. Years after my eye injury at Riley's home, Mom and Gene sued his parents for negligence. The horrible memories and fear of the court proceedings suddenly resurfaced.

I was about ten years old when my family walked into the courtroom in Jacksonville and I saw Riley's parents looking at us with disbelief because Mom and Gene were suing them for something that had happened so many years before.

When I was called to the witness stand, I was so nervous I had to force my shaking legs to carry me to the wooden chair beside the judge. I was afraid of the trouble I would get into with the attorneys and that my testimony might earn me another beating, especially if I didn't say just the right thing. The attorney asked me about that terrible day in the garage. Memories flooded my mind and tears rolled down my face. My voice trembled as I tried to answer his questions. When both of the attorneys had finished questioning me and the trial was over, we went back to our hotel room to await the verdict.

The next morning we were all awakened when the telephone rang. Gene's face lit up with excitement as he was told that we had won the case. Celebrations began, but a few minutes later, our attorney called again, stating there had been a mistake. Apparently, Riley's dad, who was someone of importance in the community, had spoken with the judge and convinced him to reverse his ruling!

Mom and Gene were livid, and Gene barked into the telephone, "You're our lawyer—talk to the judge again!" Once again we anxiously waited for the phone to ring. When it did, we learned the judge reluctantly awarded me a pitiful $5,000 for the loss of my sight! Our lawyer got more than half of the settlement, and the balance was put in a bank account for me to use when I turned eighteen.

Now that I was eighteen, I desperately needed the money to help pay for school. Unfortunately, the only way I could get it was by trying to gather enough courage to call Mom. Just thinking about it filled me with fear, but I finally picked up the phone.

"Mom, I need to get my settlement money so I can pay for school," I told her. There was silence on the line. Then she said, "We need to meet; I'll bring the money with me."

I didn't understand why we had to meet, or why she couldn't just put a check in the mail, but I agreed to meet her at a restaurant in Statesboro. I was so nervous about seeing her again, especially since our last conversation regarding her abortion.

I arrived at the restaurant early to rehearse what I wanted to say, hoping to alleviate my anxiety. This was necessary since everything always went wrong when she was around. But the moment Mom walked into the restaurant, everything I had rehearsed immediately escaped me, crowded out by old childhood fears of being beaten if she didn't like what I was about to say.

She sat down and filled the air with idle chit-chat. Finally, she got to the point. "I don't have the money; I spent it years ago."

My disappointment quickly gave way to anger, as I gasped, "How could you do that to me? How could you spend my money? Take what was awarded to me for the loss of my sight? How?"

"I just spent it," she blandly replied.

I was so hurt and angry that I ran out of the restaurant, got in my car and sped out of the parking lot. As I raced through the streets of Statesboro vacillating between crying and screaming, I tried to figure out what I was going to do. I was devastated. My mother had let me down again.

The anger boiled for hours, and the madder I got, the more I uncovered my hidden courage. The next day I went to a lawyer to fight for what was mine. I was tired of Mom's incessant need to take advantage of me even as an adult. I couldn't let her keep doing it and getting away with it.

My attorney wrote Mom a letter advising her that if she didn't come up with the money, we would sue. Several weeks later, my lawyer received a check on my behalf. After I paid him, I only had $1,800 left, and a mother who had disappeared again.

I continued to see Dr. Simmons while I was at Georgia Southern. My weekly visits helped get me through school, even though I was high every time I saw him because I couldn't make the 45 minute drive to Savannah without lighting up a joint. Although therapy wasn't much help, because of my need to remain anesthetized, I stuck with it. It was comforting to know he was there in case I needed him.

I barely made it through the first two quarters of school. I was using more alcohol and drugs than ever, as I began the third quarter. I was blacked out most of the time, and rarely sobered up long enough to string a few hours together. I wrecked my car, was almost raped, woke up in strange places, and most nights couldn't remember how I got back to my dorm.

During one of my partying excursions I met a guy named Jonathan. He was real cute with his wavy, jet-black hair, big, beautiful brown eyes, and olive skin. I was also impressed with his very cool, forest green, 1965 Mustang. I liked Jonathan because he seemed to like me for who I was, instead of what I could do for him sexually. It was nice to have someone to talk to, and someone who didn't care if I got drunk or stoned.

Unfortunately, our platonic relationship didn't last. Before long,

Jonathan wanted me to have sex with him. Even though I really liked him, I couldn't be with a man sexually after what had happened to me. I just couldn't handle it. As time went on, I could sense his frustration with me, and I was tired of being a prisoner trapped in an isolation cell created by what someone else had done to me.

Even though Jonathan didn't understand why I couldn't have sex with him, he still treated me like I was his girlfriend and didn't force the sex issue. We just partied like there was no tomorrow. I remember one night, after getting plastered at a concert, I woke up in Jonathon's car in the middle of a cornfield. I looked around in complete dismay and silently promised God that if he would help me get out of this mess I would straighten up. Moments later, Jonathan came to and mumbled, "What happened? Where are we?"

"You must've passed out and swerved off the road into this cornfield," I said as I helped him out of the car. "We need help. There must be a house somewhere nearby."

We started walking away from the car, and stumbled upon an old farmhouse in the field off the main road. As we approached the house, an older couple opened the door and yelled, "We're calling the police!"

We knew we would be in trouble if the police found us in their field, so we ran back to the car and took off. The next day Jonathan told me he was concerned about how much I was using and how often I was blacking out. Somewhere inside I knew he was right, but I got defensive and insisted, "I don't have a problem—I can slow down or quit anytime." But Jonathan only looked back at me with hurt in his eyes; I knew I was about to lose him. "I'll slow down!" I promised, though I doubted I could.

The next weekend Jonathan, Teresa, and I went to a new bar in town. Trying to keep my promise to Jonathan, I only drank a few beers and smoked a little pot. He seemed happy with me. But as the hours wore on, the old feelings that reminded me of the abuse, the abandonment and total lack of love from my mother resurfaced, and I couldn't stand it. I needed to get wasted to make those feelings disappear, but I tried to hold on so I wouldn't lose Jonathan.

Moments later I was standing at the bar trying to fight my inner demons when a guy offered to sell me some Quaaludes. They weren't the regular street bootlegged ones, but fresh pharmaceutical ones guaranteed to make me forget everything. I couldn't resist buying some for emergency purposes. I hid them in my pocket for safekeeping, hoping it would be like out-of-sight-out-of-mind. I couldn't ignore them though—the longer they were in my pocket, the more I thought about them. In desperation, I finally gave in to my desires and took a couple of the magical white pills.

I woke up the next morning, slumped over in my car in the dorm parking lot without a clue as to what had happened to me that night, or how I ended up sleeping in my car. I staggered into the dorm and went to Teresa's room for some answers. She explained, "Jonathan got pissed off when he discovered you had taken the pills, so he left you at the bar. You and I kept on partying like there was no tomorrow. Then you tried to drive us home, but on the way back to the dorm, you passed out and drove up under the back end of an 18-wheel semi-truck! Somehow we managed to squeeze out from under the truck and got back to the dorm parking lot where you passed out." Teresa's story was confirmed by the missing chunks of metal near the roof of my car.

My many brushes with death should have scared me into quitting my drinking and drugging, but they didn't.

During the final exams of my third quarter, I fell apart. I was completely toxic, and I wanted to die. In a fit of despair, I drank as much alcohol as I could, smoked a bunch of pot, popped several pills, and dropped several hits of acid. I woke up at Hope Hospital in Savannah. This time my stomach wasn't pumped out, nor was I discharged. Instead, I was admitted to the psychiatric unit because the doctors thought I was a teenager whose brain had been fried from a long history of substance abuse. They had no idea I had overdosed and I dared not say a word, for fear I would be in trouble. But when I started sweating profusely and became disoriented, I realized I was afraid to die. I called out, "Someone please help me, I think I've overdosed!"

I was given several anti-narcotic drugs, pumped full of IV fluids and placed on an intensive medical watch.

I was in the hospital for about a month, sobering up and trying to figure out how I had ended up in another hospital. I had so many questions running around in my head: What was causing me to stay drunk and stoned? Why did I want to die every day of my life? How could I make this crazy stuff stop so I could be happy? As usual, there were no answers and it was a very long month.

While I was in the hospital, only Jonathan came to visit me. He drove all the way from Statesboro to Savannah every weekend, even though he knew I only saw him as a friend.

It was here that I also met Lydia, a psychiatric nurse in the adolescent unit. I remember her because she was the most vivacious person I had ever met. She was in her thirties, was always happy, and made everyone around her feel good. I wanted what she had, but wasn't in the hospital long enough to learn her secret. I never forgot her though because she became an important part of my life in the years to come.

Chapter 12

Vicious Cycles

I COULDN'T GO BACK to Georgia Southern after I was discharged; I knew I'd start using again. My only other option was to stay in Savannah where I had no connections to any drug dealers, and where I could get a job and go to school at Armstrong State College. I was truly afraid of leaving the people who had helped me stay anesthetized to myself and my problems, but somewhere inside I knew I would end up dead if I went back.

I rented a little apartment on Tybee Island where Valerie used to spend time with me. That way I could remain close to her and my family at Turning Point, even if only in my mind. I still yearned to be connected to them even though my time with them had now passed. I still longed for someone to be my family, to take care of me and to love me.

The only place I could afford was in a house that had been converted into apartments. It was on the south end of the beach near the shooting galleries where I used to buy drugs. My place was a tiny, furnished, one-bedroom cubicle on the second floor that I was proud to call my own. I had my very own kitchen, living room, bathroom, and bedroom that I could decorate in any fashion I chose. Decorating my new home filled me with the same feelings of sacredness and comfort I had in Santa Monica when I decorated the safe haven of my closet. There was a refreshing life-affirming feeling associated with it, and relief that I had found a safe place once again.

About a week later, I was filled with a sense of pride when I got a job as an aide at a nursing home in Savannah. I was amazed that anyone outside of the food service industry would hire someone like me, but I was thankful they did. Even though I still struggled with bad feelings about myself, I believed that my new apartment and new job were my ticket to getting myself together. I needed to be free from my past, and away from the drinking and drugging that had enslaved me.

I was so thankful for my new beginning, and I spent a lot of time in my new apartment—just sitting there looking at it, and basking in the warmth and safety that emanated from every room. Pride filled my heart.

Every night I got off work at eleven o'clock, drove to my little beachside apartment, and went running in the brisk midnight ocean air. What freedom I felt as I breezed through the dark streets of Tybee Island with a new sense of accomplishment. It didn't matter that my neighbors thought I was crazy for running at night—I was now free to do whatever I wanted. Running was my saving grace as I still had difficulty sleeping because of the nightmares. Exhausting myself was better than anesthetizing myself.

I managed to hold onto my new job, ran each evening, and stayed fairly productive for about a month. Then, one hot summer day everything changed.

I was cleaning my apartment that afternoon when there was an unexpected knock at the door. I was startled since I didn't have any friends who came to visit. I opened the door, and my world came to a halt. My mouth dropped open. I was unable to speak. It was my mother!

Fear and dread rumbled inside me. How did she find me? What did she want?

Instinctively, I let her into my sacred place and offered her a seat. I yearned for her to ask about my wonderful place, my new job, and how I was doing. I wanted her to be proud of me.

My yearning was quickly put to rest when Mom started complaining about her life with Gene. She wanted me to rescue her as I had always done. Frustrated, I sat there listening to her ramble on about her "awful life." I wanted her to be there as a loving mother who would take pride in her daughter's accomplishments. I didn't want to take part in her misery anymore, or for us to end up fighting again. I didn't want to long for her to love me, or for her to remind me of the things that had happened in the past.

But, ever the good and obedient daughter, I sat there and listened to her complain while my insides tensed with fear and anger because nothing at home had changed and I remembered what living at home had been like. I tried to ease the tension by saying, "Well at least my life is improving. I'm doing well in my new job, and I love my new apartment. Don't you think it's great?"

Mom just sat there with a blank look on her face. She wasn't proud of my accomplishments at all. Instead, she declared, "I can't believe you're renting an apartment; you're just throwing away your money! I know what's best—you'll borrow a travel trailer from me, and rent a small trailer lot. This will reduce your expenses when you go back to school."

Despite how wonderfully happy I was with my apartment, I was so elated that she had offered to do something for me that I was willing to give up my sacred place in the hope that I might finally have a relationship with her. My hopes soared as I fantasized about how she was actually going to be a real mom to me—a mom who would love and help her daughter. I relished my new-found connection with her, and was filled with joy and contentment at the thought of our bright future together.

A week later, Mom showed up again at my apartment. I knew something was wrong by the stern look on her face. She stood in my kitchen looking at me sarcastically and sneered, "You can't use the travel trailer; I'm not going to help you."

"Why not?" I implored.

"I'm just not going to!" she repeated, giving no further explanation.

As the tears rolled down my face, I exploded with feelings of hurt, abandonment, and utter defeat. I yelled at her, "Why are you doing this to me again…why can't you just love me?"

Enraged, she spewed, "I don't have to explain myself to you—I don't owe you anything—you're not special. I just don't think I should help you!" She then stormed out of my apartment.

I paced back and forth in my living room overwrought with conflicting needs. I wanted to strike out at someone in anger, but I also wanted someone to love and hold me. I screamed, "God, I can't take it anymore! Why do you keep letting this happen to me? Why did you curse me with a mother and a life like this?"

My heart was broken. I had reached my limit and lost all control. Not knowing what to do with the hurt and abandonment I felt, I stormed into the kitchen and swallowed a whole bottle of anti-depressants. While I awaited my permanent escape from life, I begged God to forgive me for whatever it was I had done wrong as a child that had caused my mother to hate me so.

Several days later, I woke up in the intensive care unit with a respirator breathing for me and IVs hanging from my arms. I lay there saddened and confused as to why I wasn't dead. A nurse explained, "Your friend Jonathan went to your apartment for a surprise visit and found you unconscious on the floor. He called the ambulance. You had three grand mal seizures and three cardiac arrests on the way to the hospital. When you reached the emergency room you slipped into a coma and no one expected you to survive. That was several days ago."

Tears began rolling down my face, as I understood I was lying in the intensive care unit, still alive and dreading the consequences that would ensue for trying to kill myself again. As the tube was taken out of my throat and the IVs removed from my arms, two medical technicians arrived.

"We're here to escort you to the observation unit at Georgia Regional Hospital." Their words pierced my ears, filling me with panic. Why was this happening again? Despair washed over me when I realized I was going to yet another psychiatric hospital. I wondered when I would figure out how not to give my mother and my childhood this power over me. When would I stop punishing myself for what happened to me so many years ago? I had no answers.

The purpose of my stay in the observation unit was to make sure I was no longer a threat to myself, and to determine if Dr. Simmons was going to remain my psychiatrist. He was so angry about my suicide attempt that he refused to see me. I begged the nurses to convince him not to give up on me, but they ignored me.

Desperate that I would lose the only person I believed could help me, I called Dr. Simmons' office from the hospital pay phone. "Please make him talk to me. Please don't let him leave me," I pleaded with his secretary. Seconds later, Dr. Simmons' angry voice came through the receiver, "I'm so disappointed in you—you are past all of this self-destructive stuff. I can't help you if you keep trying to kill yourself!"

"Dr. Simmons, I'm sorry—please keep seeing me—I promise I'll never try—"

"I'll have to think it over," he interrupted, "Call me tomorrow afternoon."

The next day I anxiously paced back and forth, playing over and over in my head the various scenarios of what Dr. Simmons might say. Finally, it was time. My hands shook violently as I picked up the receiver of the pay phone. His voice was still stern and hard, but he agreed to continue working with me. I thanked God.

After settling this issue with Dr. Simmons, my usual feelings of being useless, unlovable, and burdensome to everyone resurfaced. I isolated myself in my small concrete room, sitting on the floor staring out a window covered with the same black wire mesh the Maximum Care Unit had at Turning Point.

After several days of contemplating my life and what I was going to do, a nurse walked into my room and said, "You're free to go." Relief rushed through me until I realized that I couldn't go back to the place where Mom had abandoned me again and where I had tried to take my life. My safe haven was no longer safe. It was now tainted with darkness—much like my past.

Not knowing what else to do, I followed Mom's advice and bought a tiny travel trailer and rented a lot on Highway 17 for about $100 a month. I was now living on the poor side of town, a huge decline from my wonderful home at the beach with the brisk ocean air and the invigorating midnight runs by the water. However, I tried my hardest to ignore my discontentment and humiliation.

The suicide attempt had also resulted in the loss of my wonderful job at the nursing home. Thus, I had to find another way to pay my bills and my school expenses. The only job I could find was in a day care center. I had no idea how to take care of kids, but I did it because I needed the money. I also enrolled at Armstrong State College for the fall of 1983, majoring in Psychology.

Everything felt different in the tiny travel trailer. I no longer cared about staying clean and sober, or starting my life over. I had no pride, no hope, no help, and I had no fight left in me. I was desperate, lonely, and felt completely unworthy. There was nothing for me to do but return to medicating myself with alcohol and drugs.

On this side of town it was easy to find what I needed. And depending on how messed up I had gotten the night before, I still tried to run three to six miles a day. Somewhere inside, I thought I was okay if I could keep running, and somehow it kept me close to Valerie and my memories of Turning Point.

After working at the day care center a couple of months Carol, a mother of twin boys, asked me if I would watch her boys in the evenings until she got home from work. Because the twins were my favorites at the daycare center, and I needed the extra money, I happily accepted the job.

I don't know what it was about the twins, but I loved them and how wonderful they made me feel about myself. They called me "Miss Sandy" and liked doing things with me. I basked in their attention, free spirits, hugs, and unconditional love. They were my best friends.

After I started babysitting the boys I saw something in myself that concerned me—it was how out of control I felt when they didn't behave. At times I would become consumed with the same anger and rage I had felt as a child. I could literally feel the uncontrollable need to physically hurt them. I would stand over them with fists clenched, barely able to contain myself. But then I would look into their innocent eyes and would be reminded of how much I loved them.

Why was I so explosive? Why did I want to hurt them? Each night I tried to put aside my feelings of rage long enough to get them quickly into bed so I wouldn't hurt them. But even though I made it through the night without injuring them, I wasn't able to control the unnecessary forcefulness with which I threw them into bed. I began to believe I was a horrible and vicious monster who should never have kids. After putting them to bed I would sit on the couch, hating myself and getting stoned until I passed out.

As timed passed, Carol and I became friends, and she introduced me to her best friend, Brittany. Brittany was married and had a beautiful and talented four-year-old daughter. She wasn't a "typical" mother though because she loved to party just as much as I did. We began to hang out together, which usually resulted in us getting into trouble.

My drinking and drugging quickly spun out of control again. I would show up to take care of the boys, drunk, stoned, and occasionally in a black out. After I put them to bed, I kept on drinking and drugging until I literally passed out. That went on night after night until Carol became concerned about whether the twins were safe with me.

She sat me down and talked at length about my habits, and her words of concern and frustration panicked me. I begged her, "Please don't fire me—please give me one more chance. I can't lose the boys. I promise I'll do better."

"Okay. I know you love the boys, so I'll give you just one more chance," she said, looking at me with pity.

My close brush with getting fired scared me, but not enough to make me change. I didn't believe I had a serious problem with the alcohol, drugs, or starving myself because I could still force my weary, worn out, and toxic body to run down the paved road each afternoon, sweating out the poisons I had ingested the day before. In some strange way, I was proud of myself every time I made it home from running. Somehow it made me feel that I was in control, that I was a healthy person.

The thing I liked most about running was going to the 5K and 10K road races because I usually won them. Each time I breezed across the finish line, I was filled with a sense of accomplishment and pride that I couldn't get anywhere else in my life. I was hooked on the feeling I got when other people saw me winning trophies and thought I was good at something.

Meanwhile, Brittany and I continued partying almost non-stop, spiraling down a dark and ugly tunnel, totally out of control. One day, after I had won a major road race I thought was impossible to win, Brittany and I decided to celebrate my miraculous victory by going to the beach to party. Because it was my special day, I chose the north end of Tybee Island, not only for its isolation from the world, but because of the powerful memories and feelings it still evoked about Valerie and my family at Turning Point.

We sat on the sandy shore smoking dope and drinking liquor. As I sat there staring at the ocean, my sense of victory dissipated and was soon replaced by immense sadness and loneliness as I pondered my life. I still didn't understand why I was lost to myself and everyone around me. Those unbearable feelings chased me until I blacked out.

Immense physical pain brought me out of my blackout into a semi-conscious state. I was in the cabin of a boat with a man lying on top me, penetrating me! I didn't know where I was, who he was, or why he was doing that to me. Terrified, I screamed, "Please don't hurt me. Please get off me!"

But he held me down and continued thrusting his penis inside me while yelling, "Just lie there and take it, bitch!"

My mind and body flashed back to what Gene and Miguel had done to me. I couldn't breathe and was having difficulty swallowing. I tried moving and cried out, "Please let me go!"

Drawing his hand back, he slapped me across the face and threw me aside like a worthless whore. He spun around and stomped up the cabin steps to the main deck while I remained below. My hands trembled and my legs shook as I put my clothes back on. I sobbed uncontrollably and wondered where Brittany was.

I climbed to the deck of the boat and saw that we were the only vessel floating in the middle of the vast intra-coastal waterway. I then saw Brittany with another man who was screaming, "Why won't you bitches put out?"

The argument quickly escalated and I feared the men were going to kill us and throw us over the side of the boat. Instead, they pulled over at the next dock and shoved us off their boat.

Looking around I suddenly noticed it was the middle of the night. Brittany and I just stood on the dock, looking at each other. We didn't know where we were. We walked down the dark, deserted streets for what seemed like forever. We finally found a pay phone where we discovered we were in South Carolina. We were hours away from Georgia, so Brittany called a cab to take us back to my car on Tybee Island. We were silent on the long ride back to the beach, humiliated at what had just happened to us, and yet grateful that we were still alive.

I was scheduled to work the next afternoon with the boys, but I was so shaken up about what had happened on the boat that I could barely function. I was anxious and my hands trembled; I was hung over. Brittany called and mumbled, "I'm still shaking, let's get together and party until we forget what happened last night."

Sometime during our escape party, I blacked out again. Then, late in the afternoon, I came out of my blackout, looked at the time and panicked. "Brittany, take me to Carol's, I'm late."

When we arrived at Carol's, she yelled, "You and Brittany are messed up." I just stood in her living room, ashamed and fearful. I didn't want to lose my job so I tried my best to act sober. To prove my worth, I said, "I'm so sorry," and ran into the kitchen to fix the boys something to eat, believing this would prevent me from getting fired. I must have blacked out again though because moments later I came to from the smell of smoke and saw that the stove was on fire.

Carol screamed, "Get out of here! Just go home."

As I walked out the door, I looked at her, and with all the honesty and sincerity I could muster, I said, "I'm sorry... nothing like this will ever happen again."

She must have heard the desperation in my voice because amazingly, she gave me yet another chance to prove myself. So now, my new task was to figure out how much I could use without getting into trouble and still keep myself reasonably self-medicated.

To accomplish this daunting task, I threw myself into running more than ever. I started running on the dirt roads behind Carol's apartment so I wouldn't show up at her place drunk or stoned. I loved that area because it was surrounded by beautiful trees and was isolated from the heavy Savannah traffic. That serene environment allowed me to run in peace and to force my problems out of my mind. I was proud of myself for following my new regime, and Carol was pleased with the new me.

One day, while I was running, a man named Jerrell introduced himself. He began tagging along on my daily runs, and surprisingly, I didn't mind his company. Weeks later, he asked with a smirk, "Want to snort some cocaine before we run?"

I was shocked because he didn't look like the partying type. Although I tried to weigh my decision carefully, my need to escape my feelings far outweighed everything else. Within minutes, I was snorting the white powder up my nose and feeling a new sense of empowerment—like I could do anything. It didn't make me sleepy or physically impaired like the alcohol and other drugs did. Instead, I felt like I could run forever. Cocaine now became my new best friend because I could snort it and appear sober around Carol and everyone else.

I got hooked on the white powder that allowed me to stay in an altered state of consciousness without obvious side effects. But problems began when Jerrell started rationing out the cocaine in very small and unsatisfying amounts. Pretty soon, he started leaving it at his home while we ran so I would have to go over to his house for my fix. Like a naïve child, I believed going to his house was just a friendly thing and nothing to be feared.

One day after a run, he sensed my fragility and, as usual said, "Come over to my place." Desperately anticipating what I needed to get me through the day, I followed him home. We walked into his run-down bachelor pad where my excitement gave way to tension and uneasiness as I realized that he had that all-too-familiar look on his face. He then sneered, "The only way you're getting any cocaine is if you go down on me."

I stood there in complete disbelief. He was just like many of the men I had known. I was absolutely sick to my stomach at his request and at my need to have the drug in my system. I was in a no-win situation.

My body shook with fear and my throat became thick as I tried to convince myself to do what he wanted. But, no matter how much I craved the cocaine, I couldn't force myself into another situation where I was on my knees and feeling as if I were going to die because some man was shoving his penis down my throat. I couldn't subject myself to the edge of insanity again.

Instead, I bolted out of his house, knowing I would never be able to return. That left me with returning to alcohol and other drugs to ward off any potential withdrawals and to help me remain anesthetized.

Then, about a month later, Carol decided to work things out with her estranged husband and took a job in the state where he lived. Devastated by the news, I hugged the twins one last time and wondered how I could survive without my little friends whom I loved so much. I waved goodbye to them while choking back the tears, and returned to my tiny trailer where I drank and drugged myself into oblivion.

Despite my voracious alcohol and drug problem, I attended all my classes and remained conscientious about my grades. Because they defined me as a person, I had to be on the dean's list every quarter or suffer the consequences of self-hatred.

It took me awhile to find another job, but I finally got one at a private school in the afternoons tutoring kids in a new after school program. The building was new, and everything in it was chosen with great care and consideration.

I was now a sophomore at Armstrong State and had made a new friend, Krista. I was attracted to her confidence and aura of inner peacefulness. In many ways, I wanted to be like her. I didn't want to keep being a person who always felt the need to apologize for who I was— a lost and wandering soul "looking for love in all the wrong places."

When we met, it was as if opposite energies pulled together and formed a whole. In mere seconds, Krista figured out I was a fellow partier, and pulled me aside during our class break to invite me to the ladies restroom for a treat. My curiosity peaked, so I eagerly followed her. She introduced me to a new drug, methamphetamine, and one that gave me a magical rush and burst of energy. I loved the fact that I could go to classes, study hard, make good grades, and party all at the same time. But the daunting problem of needing it in order to function remained. When we ran out, I fell apart and went madly searching for something else to take its place. For a while I went back to my old friend, cocaine. But I had to do a lot more of it to get the same effect, and it quickly got out of hand.

Once again, I started having problems functioning at school. I could hardly make it through a quarter without dropping out of half of my classes. Although I managed to show up to class each day, I was in such a fog that I couldn't comprehend anything. This went on for about six months while my life spun completely out of control. Every day I just went through the motions and dug myself deeper and deeper into a pit of despair. I often called in sick to work because I was hung over from the night before, and was having regular nosebleeds from the cocaine. I was constantly drunk and high.

"Sandy, you look bad; I think you need some help," a co-worker said one day when I was having a hard time physically managing my job. "You need to go to AA--Alcoholics Anonymous."

Her daunting words left me silent and afraid that she was right.

After several more days of uncontrolled using, I realized I didn't know how to get off the roller coaster I was on. In desperation, I called AA to see if anyone could help me. I spoke with Candice, a recovering alcoholic.

"Of course we can help you—can you meet me so we can talk?"

"Yes," I replied, even though I was afraid of what she would tell me.

Despite my fear, I got into my car and went to the restaurant where we had agreed to meet. I sat on the trunk of my car in deep thought, my stomach tied in knots and my hands shaking, needing a drink. My thoughts were quickly interrupted when I heard someone say, "Hi, I'm Candice." I looked up and was amazed when I realized she wasn't much older than me. I then looked sheepishly over at her car where I was surprised to see Lydia, the psychiatric nurse from Hope Hospital's adolescent program!

Lydia ran over and embraced me. "I'm here to help because I'm also a recovering alcoholic and I'm doing great."

Her words hit me like a ton of bricks. I couldn't believe a person like Lydia, who seemed so together, could have once been messed up like me. I sat on the trunk of my car and listened to their stories of recovery and wondered if either one of them had the magic key.

They both looked at me with sincerity in their eyes and told me, "There is a way to stop, if you want it." Their words left me excited, yet fearful. They talked about being an alcoholic and drug addict and followed it up with, "Your only way to recovery is going to be through the programs of Alcoholics Anonymous and Narcotics Anonymous."

Their words ran around inside of me like a whirlwind. I couldn't believe what they were saying. I wasn't an alcoholic or a drug addict. My only problem was that I didn't know how to make my horrible childhood feelings and self-hatred stop so I didn't have to party so much.

"I'm not really an addict—I just need relief," I said.

"That's what we've all said in the past. We can get you into a treatment program," they continued.

I stood there in amazement at their offer and wondered why they thought I needed a treatment program. All I needed was for someone to listen to me and to love me so I could stop hurting myself.

I jumped off the trunk of my car, frustrated and confused. I couldn't face the truth. I climbed back into my car and shouted, "I don't need a treatment program—I can quit on my own!" As I heard my own words, I remembered how long I had been trying to control my using and how long I had been trying to quit. Who was I kidding?

Before I drove off, Lydia and Candice gave me their phone numbers so I could call them if I needed to talk or if I wanted to go to a meeting. On my way home, I started to fear that they might be right; I would end up dead if I continued down this same path. I wasn't sure if I could quit using, but I wasn't convinced I was an alcoholic and an addict either. I didn't know what to do.

Even though I couldn't bring myself to go to treatment, I went to a Narcotics Anonymous meeting. I nervously walked into the smoke-filled room where the smell of coffee permeated the air. I saw people sitting around drinking coffee, smoking cigarettes, laughing, and talking. I wondered if I was in the wrong place because these people were too happy to be alcoholics and addicts. I felt completely out of place and afraid of the unknown, but I sat down and listened to each person talk about what was happening in their daily lives and how they were doing with their program of recovery. With each word that filled the room, I was consumed with an almost uncontrollable need to scream out for help, but I couldn't find the courage to speak. I prayed the meeting would soon be over, and when it was, I quickly slipped out, carrying my quagmire of despair and hopelessness with me.

For the next couple weeks, I went to several AA and NA meetings and tried to find the courage to ask for help. But with each meeting the unbearable and self-destructive feelings that lived inside me would resurface. Thus I found it impossible to go to the meetings sober, so I quit going. Instead, I slipped back into my denial, and set out to prove that I could control how much I used.

My failure with the AA and NA meetings left me partying again like there was no tomorrow. I drank to the point of blacking out; put so much cocaine up my nose that I was consumed with paranoia; smoked so much pot I couldn't get high off it anymore; and did anything and everything I could get my hands on. I couldn't work, and was barely able to function physically.

In a moment of extreme hopelessness, I made the phone call: "Lydia, I'm in trouble and I don't know what to do. Please tell me about the treatment program. Am I the kind of person they can help?"

Lydia asked, "Sandy, are you willing to do anything to get clean and sober?"

Filled with the same fear I felt as I sat on the trunk of my car in that parking lot, I whispered, "I'm willing to try."

A sigh of relief resonated through the phone, as Lydia excitedly told me about the program and her belief that it could help me because it had helped her just a few months earlier. She explained, "If you decide to go, you will be in treatment at least six weeks. I'll see if I can get you into the program as soon as possible."

I didn't know what to do. One part of me was excited that there was help, but I was also terrified of giving up my only means of coping and surviving. I wondered how I would be able to make it through the detox part of the program and if I would be able to cope with the feelings that would surface without the alcohol and drugs.

"Sandy, I know you're scared. Think about it; ask your boss for some time off, and get back to me. But do get back to me; you need help."

The next day I asked my boss, "May I talk to you about something important?"

"Certainly, Sandy, come into my office." For several minutes, I just sat there because I didn't know how to admit what was wrong with me and I was afraid she would think badly of me. For several minutes she stared at me in silence, waiting for me to say something.

"I have an alcohol and drug problem and I need time off to go into a treatment program," I finally blurted out. I hung my head in shame, until I realized that she was smiling.

"I'm relieved, Sandy, because I thought you were going to tell me you were gay!"

I sat there for a moment in disbelief and wondered where she would have gotten an idea like that, unless she knew something I didn't. In some small way, her concern about me being gay lightened the tension in the room. I was then granted a leave of absence.

I quickly called Lydia so she could arrange for me to be admitted the next day, July 25, 1984.

Chapter 13

First Glimpse of Recovery

THE NEXT MORNING I woke up completely terrified about going to Castwick Recovery Center. I had to get wasted, so I drank a couple of fifths of liquor, took every pill in my possession, and smoked every joint I had stashed in my tiny trailer.

By the time Lydia got to my place, I was floating in and out of consciousness and was barely able to walk. Somehow, she piled me into the car. When we got to Castwick, the nurses couldn't wake me up, so I was sent directly to the detox unit.

I woke up the next day feeling like road kill. I looked around the room for several minutes, thinking I was in the emergency room at Hope Hospital again. Then I remembered that Lydia was supposed to take me to Castwick, but I couldn't remember how I got there or what had happened during the trip. I lay there worrying about what I had done, afraid of what it would be like when the withdrawals began. I soon found out.

My body was plagued with bouts of throwing up, profuse sweating mixed with chills, dry heaves, uncontrollable shaking, and wanting to use so badly I could hardly stand it. I was so frightened and sick that I didn't think I would survive. Each time the withdrawal cycle began, the nurses gently offered me medication to ease the symptoms. It made me sleep and took the edge off my need to use. I was grateful.

While in detox, I met Dr. Russ Tanner. As soon as I shook his hand, I could sense the gentleness of his spirit and the kindness of his heart. He was an old guy with thinning white hair who dressed each day in a suit and bow tie. He was always in a good mood and seemed to have an inner peace about him. When I was around Dr. Russ, I felt as if I could do anything, that it didn't matter what I had done, because he always understood that I was an alcoholic and drug addict trying to get well, not a bad person trying to get good. I later learned that Dr. Russ knew what it was like to walk in an addict's shoes because he, too, was a recovering alcoholic and addict.

I finally got out of detox two weeks later. It was the first time in seven years I didn't have an ounce of alcohol or drugs in my system. I was moved into the group therapy part of the program, but floundered in it for several weeks because I didn't know how to interact with other people without my precious chemicals to make me feel safe and whole. So I remained silent for fear that everyone would be able to see through to the core of my vulnerability. My emotions were so close to the surface that I wanted to cry at every little thing.

Because I couldn't get down on a feeling level like everyone else, I did a lot of acting out in self-defense. At the same time, the bad thoughts and feelings about my past began resurfacing once again. I didn't know how to make them go away. The more those feelings ran around inside me, the more frightened I became.

Everyone around me seemed to be getting better, while I continued to struggle with the same demons. I became concerned there was something psychologically wrong with me; maybe I was mentally ill with something like manic-depression, schizophrenia, or multiple personality disorder. Desperate to learn the truth, I talked with Dr. Russ. Much to my surprise, he looked at me compassionately and said, "You're not mentally ill."

In my eagerness to convince him of my insanity, I confessed my problems with the nightmares, fitful sleeping habits, and the explosive and dangerous feelings I had. I also expressed my constant desire to kill myself, and my unrelenting depression. But no matter what I said, Dr. Russ didn't think I was mentally ill—just an alcoholic and addict.

"When will the nightmares and difficulty sleeping go away? And the horrible, taunting feelings—will they ever go away?" I asked.

"Once all the alcohol and drugs are out of your system, the sleeping will get better and the nightmares will dissipate," his confident voice assured me.

"I'm not so sure, Dr. Russ. I need you to prove to me that I'm not crazy. I know from school that there is a blood test you can give me to prove that I am not bi-polar or mentally ill. Please give me the blood test so I'll know for sure."

He gave in to my request, and as he predicted, the blood work came back negative. I was relieved even though I still believed there was something wrong with me other than my alcoholism and drug addiction.

For about a month, I made no progress, and only acted out my feelings of abandonment, worthlessness, and disgust with life. In frustration, one of my counselors insisted that I needed help not only with my addictions, but also with whatever was bothering me emotionally. He sensed I was struggling because of a difficult childhood, so he handed me a thin, blue book called The Greatest Miracle in the World by Og Mandino and suggested I read it. I hoped that maybe his precious book contained the answers to my questions and the solutions to my pain.

I was so moved by the little book that I didn't put it down for two whole days. I lay on my bed with my eyes and heart glued to every page and felt every word. While I read the most wonderful truths I had never known, I sobbed tears of pain and wonderment. I felt the character's pain when his friend left him and it tapped into the torturous feelings I had about my mother and her inability to love me. Eventually the tears subsided, and I was left wondering why people always went away.

Then the day came when I was called out of group therapy and escorted to a large conference room where Dr. Russ, the staff, the nurses and my main counselor were seated. Dr. Russ insisted that I sit down. Terrified, I stared at my folded hands with the same fear I had about my mother, anticipating the first blow across my face. When Dr. Russ started speaking, I could hear the seriousness in his voice.

"Everyone sees you as a defeated child, but you are an adult. You are not going to get the benefits of the program if you don't get serious; your attitude about life and recovery needs a major adjustment. You either get off your butt and work on yourself and your recovery program, or go home!"

I was ashamed of my silence in the groups, my acting out, and who I was as a person. Then I remembered hearing the other patients talking about tough love meetings for patients who needed help transitioning from their life of self-destruction to one of recovery. When I understood that this was one of those meetings, my spirit soared because I believed it meant that these people cared about me.

I felt a glimmer of what being loved means, and humbly conceded, "I want to stay because I don't want to be who I am and don't want to go back to drinking and drugging. I want help to get clean and sober and stay that way."

They finally agreed to give me another chance, and for the first time I felt the new energy that only came from emotionally connecting with someone who wanted to help me. I started working on the steps of the program and opening up a little bit. I even found the courage to break my family's code of silence as I wrote about a family secret to read in group therapy.

On the day I was to tell the story, I was afraid. I was getting ready to tell people things I wasn't even allowed to think about as a child, much less discuss. I knew if I didn't do this, I would never be able to let go of my past. So I took a deep breath and read aloud in a trembling voice. I told about Mom physically abusing me in Lexington and about hiding in the corner as she beat me into submission and robbed me of my sense of self.

When I was finished, I closed my notebook and stared at the floor. After several long moments of deafening silence, one of the women spoke to me with tears streaming down her face.

"I'm so proud of you. I had no idea those bad things had happened to you. You come across in a way that makes people think you had things handed to you on a silver platter—like a spoiled, rotten brat who is bound and determined to get her way."

I was stunned by her observation. I had no idea that was how other people perceived me. I soaked up each word, and felt relieved that she had truly heard me. She understood that I wasn't a spoiled brat, but a hurt and wounded child.

My counselor then convinced me to do my fourth and fifth steps— writing my life story and reading it to her. I slaved over the story before I mustered up the courage to read it in front of her. My hands shook and my mouth became dry as I tried my best to reveal the secrets of my past. I had to pause several times frustrated because I couldn't feel any of my words. I was too afraid and was too vulnerable to feel those things in front of anyone. Despite the separation of my feelings from my words, I managed to tell my story and then burned it as a sign that it was all over. As I saw the small manuscript go up in flames I was worried because I didn't feel any different. Instead, I was scared that I would relapse back into my addictions because I couldn't feel and tell my story from my heart. I wanted to know why I was different and why I couldn't feel things around other people. Why I was still so afraid of getting in trouble because of the truths I still held on to.

The better I became with getting clean and sober, the more out of control my eating disorder became. I was getting thinner and thinner and was far below my ideal body weight, but the rehab center wasn't equipped to deal with anything like that.

I also continued running because it was the only thing I felt I could do well. It gave me a sense of purpose, and helped keep the weight off.

During my stay at Castwick, Lydia became a good friend. One day when she was visiting, a mischievous look came over her face as she confessed, "I have a secret to share, but you have to swear you will keep it to yourself."

"Of course I will; you can trust me," I assured her.

Lydia giggled like a schoolgirl and said, "I'm seeing someone who works at the treatment center—more specifically—in your program!"

After several minutes of guessing who it was, she finally told me it was Dr. Russ. I was shocked! He was my doctor, and he was a lot older than she was. I listened to her talk about him and soon realized that she loved him. I was happy for her.

Second to Turning Point, my stay at Castwick was the best thing that had ever happened to me. Everyone who worked there was great, and they really had a good grasp on recovery. I learned how the 12-step program of AA and NA worked, picked up my white chips, did the first seven steps of the program, and tried to do what I was told in order to be successful at my recovery. I wanted to be the "one out of thirty-five people" who got out of a treatment program and remained clean and sober for the first year after treatment.

My six weeks turned into three months, and it was time for me to go back to the real world, even though I didn't have anywhere to go or anyone to go back to. I was essentially homeless. Fortunately, Lydia allowed me to move in with her and her two children until I could find my own place.

As I walked out the front doors of Castwick, I feared leaving my place of safety. I was terrified I would mess up because I was still having difficulty controlling my feelings. I wondered if I would be strong enough to resist using when things got tough. Would I make it, or would I become a statistic?

Lydia was a nurse at a convalescent home and worked the three-to-eleven shift, so I didn't get to see her much. On the weekends, she burned up the roads going back and forth from Savannah to St. Simons Island to see the love of her life, Dr. Russ. Despite her happiness, it bothered me that I didn't see her much anymore, especially since she was my only link to the recovery center.

My release back into the uncaring world, together with the ongoing loneliness, triggered painful feelings about Mom and the things that happened to me growing up. They were sitting right under the surface waiting to consume me. Finally, fear and desperation landed me at Lydia's job, tearfully begging, "Please help me—I can't stand the emotional torment and overwhelming need to kill myself anymore."

Lydia replied in a stern parental voice, "You need to go to a meeting!" At that moment, I knew she didn't hear any of my words because it was parental consternation I received, rather than the motherly comfort and reassurance I was looking for.

Afraid of relapsing and ending up a statistic, I resumed my sessions with Dr. Simmons on a limited basis. Even though seeing him wasn't helping much, I continued my sessions with him because in my mind he represented my family at Turning Point. There were many days when I wanted to tell him that the bad feelings were still running around inside me, and explain that being clean and sober didn't resolve what had happened to me growing up. But, I just followed his lead and didn't discuss anything of emotional importance. I merely provided updates on my progress.

Because my living arrangements with Lydia were temporary, I had to find another place to live. Even though I could only afford a trailer, I was filled with the same excitement I had with my apartment at the beach. That wonderful familiar feeling catapulted me into looking through the newspaper and going to every mobile home dealer in Savannah until I finally found her: an old sixty-foot, 1972 mobile home for $1500. She wasn't much to look at, but I loved her, and I knew she was the one I was supposed to buy. I just had to figure out how to pay for her.

I had always consulted with Dr. Simmons about my major life decisions to ensure I didn't make any mistakes. So with a marvelous taste of excitement and freedom, I described the old mobile home to him and prayed for his seal of approval. He smiled and said, "It would be a good idea to buy the mobile home and put it on a nice lot in town. I know you can't rely on your family and you're really trying hard to do the right thing, so I'll give you the $1500 you need!"

His extremely kind and unsolicited gesture warmed my heart in a way I had never known. Tears of joy ran down my face as I explained, "Dr. Simmons, I don't want to take your money; I'm embarrassed for even considering your offer."

After much discussion and persistence from him, I took the money and said, "Thank you so much, I promise I'll repay every last penny!" I was true to my word; I eventually repaid every cent he had given me.

I moved my mobile home to White Oak Mobile Estates onto one of the prettiest lots that sat right on the marsh. I only had neighbors on two sides of me and my lot rent was just $110 a month.

I returned to work in the after school program, but as I walked in the front door, I could sense that everyone knew where I had been. Embarrassed, I went back to my old practice of pasting on a face that said, "I'm okay." Each person I met in the hall stopped for a brief moment, politely nodded their head and said I looked great. But I could tell they were a little leery about my having been in rehab for the last three months.

I tried to live up to my role as the token recovering alcoholic and drug addict of the facility who was always on display. The constant surveillance left me fearful I would do or say something wrong. It was like being at home again waiting for Mom to catch me messing up and fearing the wrath of her punishment. The stress that came from the expectations at work and not being able to drown those unpleasant feelings began to take a toll on me.

Before I knew it, the painful feelings of my past came back, telling me, "You'll never be all right; you don't fit in anywhere; and you'll always be in trouble for something." They grew stronger with each passing day. I tried to hold on and prayed that I would be okay. Like a desperate religious fanatic, I attended every possible AA and NA meeting so I wouldn't have to be alone with myself or my feelings.

The most difficult thing about my return to the real world, and especially to work, was that everyone saw me as a 20 year-old adult, and expected me to cope with life like a normal well-adjusted adult. The problem was that I barely possessed the coping skills of a teenager, and I had the needs of a very young child. This became evident one day when I naively let one of the kids choose a video for their video party and allowed them to watch it unsupervised while I caught up on some paperwork. I wanted the kids to be my friends (a friend of any age was important to me), so I believed them when they told me it was a good movie for kids. I didn't discover until it was over that it had been a totally inappropriate choice but I didn't say anything to them because I so desperately wanted them to like me.

Then driving home from work that day, I totaled my car and lied to the police about the accident for fear of getting in trouble. I was now hanging on by a thread and wondering how much more I could take. I didn't understand why bad things kept happening to me or why God wouldn't give me a break, just once in my life. My depression made me a prisoner in my own home that night, and I decided not to go to an AA meeting. Instead, I barricaded myself inside and tried to keep a lid on my feelings.

I woke up the next day hating myself because I knew I was still a needy and fearful person inside. But I mustered up the energy to go to work because I hoped it would take my mind off things. Instead, I was greeted with, "I have to fire you because you let the kids watch that inappropriate movie!" my boss said. I couldn't talk my way out of the problem because a parent had insisted that I be terminated. With only a letter of recommendation in my hand, I walked out the door.

I was an emotional wreck. I had lost my car and my job in less than 24 hours! I didn't know what I was going to do. I thought about using and killing myself, but I was too afraid to do either. So I forced myself to go a meeting to see if I could find some relief, and it helped me get through the night.

To complicate things further, the next day, Lydia told me she was leaving Savannah and moving to St. Simon's Island to live with Dr. Russ.

Even though I knew that would be a wonderful thing for her, the idea of losing another person I loved and the closest thing I had to a family brought me to the brink of despair.

Seeing the look of desperation on my face she said, "I'm not leaving you—just going to live on St. Simon's Island in a place where you can visit."

I heard her words, but I wondered if they were true, or if she was just trying to make me feel better.

Lydia and Dr. Russ were married and moved into a huge house. As promised, I went up to see them and spent a lot of time with my surrogate parents. It was strange though, seeing Dr. Russ outside the hospital. I loved them both and worshipped the ground they walked on. I thought that between the two of them they knew everything there was to know about life. They were unconditional with their love and took really good care of me. I really missed Lydia being in Savannah, but I knew she was extremely happy with Dr. Russ. Her happiness, and my being allowed to visit, made everything all right.

My first year in AA and NA was difficult, and was fraught with struggles that I tried to hide. Everyone thought that I was doing great and that I had the AA and NA program down to a science because I did a lot of service work. I chaired meetings, helped clean up, held offices in my home group, and told my story a couple of times. I also followed the advice of the program and had a couple of sponsors. I did a lot of talking in the meetings and said all the right things. In my head, I believed everything the program told me, everything I heard and read, and everything I said. But I just couldn't get it down inside the core of me, and even as I worked toward recovery, I felt myself slowly falling apart. I never felt as if I fit in; I didn't know who I was; and my painful secrets still tortured me. Anything and everything I tried to do was stained with sadness, depression, anger, and self-destructive feelings. I didn't understand why I still felt that way—especially since I was doing what the program told me to do. I was faking it until I could make it, but that didn't seem to be enough.

I tried to hang on to the program as long as I could because I desperately wanted to pick up my one-year chips. I wanted to show myself and everyone else that I could do it and to prove I wasn't a loser or a statistic. I wanted Lydia and Dr. Russ to be proud of me and to feel like I was somebody. I believed that if I held on for one year, everything bad would magically disappear and I would be healed—at least I hoped so.

It was a struggle but I got through a whole year without drinking and drugging! I could hardly believe I'd made it, especially with all the obstacles I had to deal with. My enormous accomplishment was celebrated at both AA and NA with birthday parties. Dr. Russ gave me a gift by telling his story at my AA birthday, while a special counselor from Castwick honored me by speaking at my NA birthday.

As I watched and listened as Dr. Russ told his story, I somehow felt special and believed that his appearance made everyone else think I was somebody special. When he finished his tale of recovery, I anxiously sat in my seat waiting to receive the coveted blue chip. The room fell quiet as Dr. Russ spoke about my year of progress. "Sandy has truly earned her chip with sweat, hard work, and tears," he said. His words reverberated in my heart, and reminded me how relieved and thankful I was that I had finally made it.

I walked down the aisle to the podium to receive the chip, which designated my status among a few elite survivors of alcoholism and drug addiction. With the blue chip clutched in my hand, I thanked everyone for being patient with me and prayed that God would help me stay clean and sober despite the ongoing battle that continued to rage inside me.

Chapter 14

The Downward Spiral

JUST WEEKS after I picked up my one-year chip, I ran into Valerie in downtown Savannah on my way home from a NA meeting.

"I've beaten my addictions—I've been clean and sober for a year!" I said with pride.

"I'm so excited you're finally on the road to recovery and becoming the person everyone at Turning Point knew you could be," Valerie said, smiling at me.

Her words reminded me of how much I had wanted her approval when I was in the hospital. Before I could stop it, those feelings quickly tapped into my old, desperate feelings of needing someone to love me. I tried not to pay attention to that side of me because it always left me feeling self-destructive. Thus, I focused only on basking in the glow of approval I was receiving from my long-lost friend.

"Sandy, why don't you come over to my apartment for dinner tomorrow night? We can spend time together and catch up on each other's lives." I wondered how I had managed to get invited to my hero's home, but I quickly accepted her offer.

I was so excited I could hardly wait for the evening to arrive. My stomach was tied in knots as I yearned for more of Valerie's acceptance and friendship. Since I didn't want her to see the nervous and insecure Sandy she had known at the hospital, I rehearsed in my mind what we might talk about and how I should act. I couldn't risk letting her see that I still being chased by the same demons, even though I wasn't drinking or drugging. I didn't want to lose her again.

I headed downtown to Valerie's place in the old section of the city. She lived on the second floor of an old and beautiful Victorian home that had been converted into apartments. My heart pounded as I pasted on my I'm okay face and knocked quietly on the door. When Valerie opened the door, she hugged me and invited me in with a smile.

Her apartment was earthy and natural, a true reflection of her holistic lifestyle. I remembered how much I had wanted to be like her. I also remembered something I had buried for years. While at Turning Point, I had developed a crush on Valerie and then learned that she was gay. I had fantasized and dreamed about being with someone like her—pretty, loving, centered, and with the kindest heart of anyone I'd ever met. I had fallen in love with her. I wasn't sure what that meant, or what I was supposed to do with my feelings, so I buried them, chalking them up to neediness rather than homosexuality.

I quickly dismissed my memories and tried to relax so I could enjoy our precious time together. The night progressed pleasantly and I was glad that Valerie appeared to enjoy our time as much as I did. As we sat on the couch talking and laughing, I looked at her, soaking up every ounce of wonderfulness that filled our conversations. Our eyes briefly met and I sensed something in the atmosphere change. The room became filled with a forbidden closeness and tension, as if we were a couple wanting to explore each other for the first time. One part of me was filled with nervous excitement. I wanted to feel Valerie's arms around me and to be with her in that special way. To have her hug and touch me and to experience her love and compassion. I wanted the comfort of knowing that I belonged with someone like her.

But, I was also afraid because I had never explored that part of myself, and I never saw myself as gay. Then the desires and lusts that ran through my mind and my body quickly changed into terror and shame as I was reminded of Gene and Miguel, and that being sexual made me feel bad about myself. I didn't know how to be with anyone in a sexual way without feeling shame and guilt, and that saddened me.

As I yearned for Valerie's love, I also remembered the part of me that longed for my mother to love me—and the same feelings of abandonment, hurt, and abuse I felt as a child.

I was also confused because I had heard bad things about gay people and Valerie wasn't anything like that.

Overcome by fear, I ran out of her apartment. I was disgusted with myself for being so utterly weak—for allowing Gene, Miguel and my mother to continue ruining my life. I felt stupid for running out on someone as wonderful as Valerie. How could I have been in love with her for years and have left her just because I was afraid? What was my problem?

The experience with Valerie set my old feelings of desperation into motion. I was consumed with the overwhelming need for someone to love me. I was ashamed and desperate. I needed to escape and punish myself for having these feelings. I needed to use. At the same time, I knew I needed to call someone for help, but I didn't know who. I couldn't call anyone in the program since I had never opened up to anyone in a real way. So I went to a local outpatient treatment facility to see if they could counsel me or do something to keep me from relapsing or killing myself.

"Please help me make the bad feelings go away—help me stay clean and sober," I said with a trembling voice.

In a clinical tone, the counselor said, "I agree you need help. But you can only participate in this program and be provided with counseling if you agree to pay us $6,000 for our services."

Her harsh words left me drowning, without hope. I was stunned that I could only be helped if I could afford it, especially since I had been to weekly AA meetings at their facility. I wondered what made them think I had that kind of money when I was living in a trailer, barely paying my bills, and trying to put myself through school?

I stormed out of the building, recklessly driving home, while trying to contain my explosive feelings. I sat alone in my trailer, afraid I was going to use again. I called the recovery center again and said, "I'm begging you—please help me not to relapse."

"I'm sure you'll be fine; you've been in the program for a year now—just hang on." Her nonchalant tone of voice told me that no one there was taking me seriously. Their limited thinking only infuriated me and left me feeling more desperate. Out of control, I slammed the phone down and ran out of my trailer to buy the biggest bag of dope I could find.

As soon as I had gotten high and realized what I had done, I was immersed in a sea of overwhelming guilt I had never experienced before. I was devastated that I had thrown away everything I had worked so hard for. And that in a moment I had thrown away my only year of being clean and sober since I was thirteen years old.

"I won't go back to AA or NA." I vowed to myself. I couldn't face the people there, especially since I couldn't face myself.

With no hope left, I consumed as much alcohol and drugs as I could to deaden any loose feelings running around inside.

Since I had been out of the drug world for over a year, I had to find a new dealer who could meet my needs and keep up with my level of consumption. The next day as I walked out the front door of my trailer to head downtown in search of a new drug depot, I looked across the trailer park to see a face I hadn't seen in years. It was Tucker, my old drug dealer when I lived in the little travel trailer on Highway 17. I was filled with a strange sense of relief, and ran over and hugged him, even though it seemed a little awkward.

"What are you doing here?" I asked.

"Meet the missus, we're moving in over there," Tucker said, pointing to the trailer directly opposite mine.

A huge smile crossed my face at my good fortune that my old drug dealer was so close. From that moment on, Tucker and I picked up where we had left off on Highway 17, partying non-stop.

The drinking and drugging quickly spiraled out of control, and I remembered what the program had taught me. If a person starts using after they have been clean for a while, they pick up where they left off with their last drink or drug. Physiologically, the body doesn't acknowledge that there was any sober or clean time; it just resumes its course. And the progressiveness of the alcoholism and addiction speeds up with each relapse.

I now understood that I was a slave to my addictions, and felt useless as a human being. I believed I was unlovable, beaten down, and lost.

My search for bigger and better highs sent me farther and farther out of touch with reality and connected me with other non-stop partiers like myself. The only difference between us was that I was employed and educated, and they were neither. They didn't care about their appearance or their run-down apartments. Their places were always dirty, with clothes and personal items strewn about.

In these unimaginable living conditions my new partying friends introduced me to mushrooms. When they didn't have money to buy real drugs they went to cow pastures early in the morning to pick fresh mushrooms out of cow manure.

We would brew up the mushrooms into shroom juice, and gleefully sit around drinking the juice and hallucinating. I quickly figured out that the trick to doing mushrooms was trying to maintain the buzz without skipping off into insanity. So I kept a constant flow of the shroom juice circulating in my body to ensure obliteration instead of annihilation.

Then one morning the shroom juice was much stronger than usual, and I began experiencing a very different trip than I was used to. I was inundated with paranoia: everything around me took on a different shape—looking like it was turned inside out—the furniture appeared to be breathing. I knew I had to get out of the apartment before I freaked out and was unable to drive home. So I grabbed some shroom juice and fell over several pieces of furniture as I made my way to the door. Once outside, I stashed the juice in my car and tried to drive home without hurting myself or killing anyone.

The further I got down the road, the more everything looked backwards and turned inside out. I wasn't sure I was even driving on the right side of the road, or on the street that would lead me home. My heart pounded; my mind was confused; I couldn't differentiate between what was real and what was a hallucination. I begged God to please get me home and to guide me safely through the traffic without me getting in trouble or going crazy. Before I knew it, I was parked in front of my trailer, not knowing how I had gotten there.

Grabbing the shroom juice, I ran into my trailer for safety, shut all the curtains and locked all the doors. I was afraid someone was watching me. I thought I was losing my mind, so I paced the floors with my hands on my head saying over and over, "My name is Sandy…My name is Sandy…"

I was afraid I had ingested too much of the shroom juice and that I wasn't coming back from this trip. It was getting harder and harder to stay lucid, so I picked up the phone and called Lydia. I didn't want her to know I had relapsed, but I didn't know what else to do.

"Lydia, I'm losing my identity…I don't know who I am," was all I could say before I blacked out and dropped the phone.

I came out of my black-out, knocking on my neighbor's door. My mind raced trying to figure out how I had gotten there. Before I could figure out how to get away without being noticed, he opened the door and snarled, "What do you want?" I said, "Please help me find myself because I've lost my identity and I can't find it."

My neighbor stood there looking at me as if I were crazy.

"Please help me find myself," I repeated, but he just stood there saying nothing. Since he wasn't going to help me, I staggered off his porch, and back to my trailer.

In desperation, I picked up the phone again, but this time I dialed Valerie's number. I don't remember what she said, only that she hung up on me. Helplessness surrounded my heart, so I went to the refrigerator and drank the rest of the shroom juice, hoping I would die. Part of me was thankful that the end was near.

A short time later, I looked up to see Valerie standing in my living room, staring at me with disbelief and disgust in her eyes. Tears streamed down my face as I begged her, "Please forgive me—I never meant for this to happen."

"Sandy, you have to go to the hospital."

"I can't do that—they'll think I'm crazy and lock me up again," I cried, as I bowed my head. I couldn't bear the thought of being locked up again, even if I had to die.

"I'm very disappointed in you," Valerie shouted as she walked out. Seeing her walk out of my door, and out of my life, broke my spirit. My pain grew more intense and more unbearable by the second. It was at that moment that I believed I was doomed to be like this the rest of my life. After crying and praying that God would let me die, I passed out.

I awoke the next morning and was neither insane nor permanently impaired. I didn't know why God had chosen to give me another chance, but I was grateful, at least for the moment.

That awful, horrifying experience didn't slow me down, it only caused me to swear off mushrooms. As it was I still couldn't get enough alcohol or drugs in my system to keep me anesthetized. I was merely bouncing in and out of reality, instead of remaining oblivious to it. My feelings and the need to kill myself were seeping through once again.

Needing a more complete barrier against reality, I remembered a woman I had gone through treatment with whose husband was a big time cocaine dealer in Savannah. I frantically found and called her phone number. To my relief, her husband Darrell, answered the phone. When he realized who I was, he dropped the Mr. Nice Guy act and allowed his true identity to shine through.

"I'll meet you at your trailer and bring some cocaine so we can party," he said enthusiastically. One part of me was excited about how wonderful it was going to be while the other part was afraid I would end up blacking out, would be forced to have sex with him, and would end up feeling awful about myself.

Darrell brought over more cocaine than I had ever seen in all my years of using. It was obvious that he came over to party without caution or care. He instructed me to follow him into the bathroom where I carefully watched him arrange his drug equipment on the basin. Watching him, I realized that I had never been able to get stoned properly while shooting up because I had been using the wrong equipment.

"Are you ready for the ride of your life?" Darrell asked, gleefully staring at me. I was afraid of overdosing, but simultaneously excited at what I hoped awaited me on the other side of the needle. I stretched out my arm to be tied off with a tourniquet. I stood as still as a statue while Darrell inserted the needle through my flesh. He then pushed a small amount of the cocaine mixture into my vein. My body instantly cried out for him to push the rest of the magic solution into me. Instead, he drew back ever so gently on the syringe to mix my blood with the cocaine, and then pushed the bloody mixture back into my arm. My body exploded with a rush of ecstasy I had never experienced before. I felt like I was in heaven. I wanted to remain forever in this forbidden paradise of warmth and wholeness. I yearned to feel like this every second of my life.

Moments later, my legs buckled. I reached behind me and shut the lid of the toilet, so I could fall back on it. Nervousness and paranoia replaced my brief moment of delight. My whole body shook. I couldn't sit still. My heart was pounding in my chest. I paced the floor rubbing my hands together, wondering who was watching me.

Panicked and tearful, I turned to Darrell, "Do me again so I can get the good feelings back."

I then understood that I had to keep shooting up to keep the feelings of bliss flowing, and to prevent the horrible, nervous aftermath. That technique eventually failed too, as there was only so much cocaine I could put into my body without having a heart attack. That left me drinking alcohol, smoking pot, and taking downers until I passed out.

I was on a very unstable roller coaster ride that I didn't know how to get off. Every day was spent trying to hit that magical state of ecstasy as many times as I could without doing myself serious harm.

Then one night Darrell and I sat up all night shooting cocaine for the rush, and then smoking dope and drinking liquor to ward off the shakes and paranoia. I had so much cocaine in my system I thought I was going crazy, and my heart raced so fast I believed I was going to have a heart attack. But I was too paranoid to call anyone for help for fear of being hospitalized and arrested. Amazingly, it only took a month for me to start putting needles in my arms and to get to the point where I would rather die than call someone for help. It only took a month for my addiction to spin out of control...again.

By the time the morning sun crested the marsh, I had arrived at yet another crossroad. I stared at Darrell, who was still passed out in my bed. I quickly realized the pain that came from the realization that I was a junkie. Drowning in self-hatred and disappointment in myself, I threw open the door of my trailer, ran out of it with nothing but the clothes on my back, jumped into my car, and headed back to Castwick, praying they could help me.

Days later my eyes opened to find a counselor staring down at me and asking, "What happened? How did you lose a year of recovery and end up in another detox bed?"

I looked around, trying to remember where I was and how I had gotten there. Sadness, desperation, and embarrassment hit me as I remembered the last all-night stint on the roller coaster of cocaine.

Tears flowed as I cried, "Forgive me—I need help. I tried to get help at Plantation Recovery, but no one would take me seriously. They wouldn't help me because I didn't have a bunch of money to give them. I needed someone to talk to—but I couldn't get anyone to listen. I'm so embarrassed and ashamed about losing my year of recovery, and letting the alcohol and drugs get me again. I hate myself all the time now."

I stared at the floor, humiliated that everyone at Castwick was seeing me this way again. I felt like a complete failure. But, the counselor looked at me with compassion, placed his warm hands on my shaking arms and explained, "You didn't lose a year of recovery. You keep everything you learned during that year inside your heart, and no relapse or anything else can ever take it away from you. But you are an alcoholic and drug addict—that's why the alcohol and drugs took control again."

His words warmed my heart and recharged my internal batteries. I was now ready to go another round with trying to be clean and sober—to face the world again and to get the help I so desperately needed.

Chapter 15

A Second Chance

AFTER SPENDING A WEEK in detox, I was discharged to my trailer on the beautiful marsh in Savannah. As I walked out of Castwick one last time, I knew I needed to get help because my next relapse would kill me. On the drive back to Savannah I thought about why I couldn't stand to feel my own feelings without wanting to self-destruct. Surely there had to be a reason (besides being an alcoholic and addict) as to why I drank and drugged myself into oblivion, and why I constantly wanted to die. I honestly didn't know what it was. I wished someone could understand the feelings and confusion that made me a prisoner in my own life and explain them to me.

As soon as I made it back to Savannah, I stopped at a phone booth to investigate facilities that could help me. The only place available was the local mental health center, and the same place I went to my first NA meeting over a year ago. When I walked into the old brick building, I was nervous about asking for help and worried that someone from the program would see me there. I stood at the information window blurting out to the secretary, "I was in the program for a year, relapsed, went to detox, and now need help understanding what is wrong with me."

Void of any emotion, the stone-faced secretary nodded for me to go upstairs to the alcohol and drug rehabilitation unit. There I stood at another window where I was more cautious and conservative with my confession. With the same lack of concern and empathy, the clerk informed me that I was being placed on a sliding-scale fee list because of my unemployment, and I needed to sit down and wait for my name to be called.

A few moments later, someone called my name, and I stood up to see a large woman with a friendly look on her face standing in the doorway with my file in her hand.

"My name is Darlene," she said. "I'm your counselor." She shook my hand with such enthusiasm that I immediately liked her and felt I was in the right place.

I followed Darlene down the long hallway, noting the poor condition of the building, furniture, and equipment. It was obvious this state-run facility operated on virtually no money. I was ashamed I had sunk so low that I had to rely on a place like this for help.

I walked into Darlene's cubbyhole of an office, and immediately liked it because it's coziness reminded me of my sacred closet in Santa Monica. Her demeanor, and the homey appearance of her office, showed me that she was a good person at heart and one who really believed in what she was doing. It seemed as if she derived her life's meaning from helping people, especially those who suffered the terrible fate of alcoholism and drug addiction.

In my sessions with Darlene, we talked about my addictions. I learned from her that I was truly an alcoholic and addict, and more so that I would never be free until I figured out what was making me drink and drug. She made me realize that I had to find the root cause of what was making me self-destruct. I knew she was right because I, too, had those same thoughts.

To free myself I tried to tell Darlene, to the best of my ability, some of the things that had happened to me. Even though I didn't say it, she quickly figured out that someone had sexually abused me. I only nodded that she was right and mumbled, "Gene hurt me."

But fear and embarrassment stopped me from providing her with any details. I also found that I couldn't offer up any confessions about what the other men had done to me because I didn't know how to talk about it without becoming overwhelmed with shame and self-hatred. I was so desperate for her approval that I hid behind the truth so she wouldn't think badly of me.

Again, I could only talk about what happened from my head, not from my heart. I was too afraid of being hurt again. I was terrified that the old memories would consume me—take me to the bad place within myself and I would never be able to return. Still, I worked hard with Darlene to figure out what was wrong so I could stay clean and sober, even if I didn't discuss the details.

Meanwhile, I went back to my AA and NA meetings. I was embarrassed and ashamed about my relapse, but I reminded myself of the magical words I'd heard at Castwick: "No matter what you do, no one can ever take away your year of recovery."

I picked up new white poker chips that designated my new dedication to recovery and emotional freedom. I made sure that I always carried them around in my pocket as a reminder of who I was. My mind was determined to stay clean and sober, even though my heart was still afraid that I would always be a slave to my addictions and self-destructive behaviors.

It seemed that things were looking up once again. I got a job a couple of miles from the college, at a small, private school with classes for Pre-Kindergarten through ninth grade. I went to classes until noon each day, and then directly to work until about 6:00 p.m. My job was to tutor children with Attention Deficit Disorders and learning disabilities. I also monitored study hall after school. It was a very demanding position and my experience was limited, but I was proud because my kids always knew how to read and function by the time I had finished tutoring them.

I also decided to rent out the extra bedroom in my trailer to help with finances. Although I wasn't thrilled about having someone living in my personal space, it was necessary to pay my bills. That was how Leroy came to move in with me. He was a fairly large, overweight, balding man in his thirties who worked nights.   I was elated that I could earn extra money and still have the place to myself when I got home in the evening.

On the days Leroy didn't work, he hung out at the trailer trying to make his small room his home, and me his friend. He wasn't anything like I expected. He would invite me to grill steaks with him in the backyard and then we'd eat them while watching movies on his VCR. During these normal experiences I realized that Leroy, with his large body and meek personality, was the sweetest and most humble guy I had ever met. He reminded me of a big teddy bear who needed cuddling. He became the first male I wasn't afraid to be around, and one I actually enjoyed talking to. I learned that he, too, was lonely and was looking for someone to love him. His struggle was different from mine. His difficulty with finding his soul mate was due to his appearance.

As we got to know each other we became best buddies and hung out together all the time. Then, several months later, my relationship with Leroy became strained when he began having feelings for me that weren't solely about friendship. When I figured it out, I felt that I couldn't be myself around him anymore. I nervously hinted that I wasn't interested in a relationship with anyone. Leroy, unlike all of the other men I'd known, sensed my fear and didn't press the issue any further. I was grateful because that allowed us to continue to hang out together and confide in each other about all sorts of things.

My life appeared to be going well until one day my phone rang and the now unfamiliar voice of my mother came through the receiver. I stood there for a brief moment in shock since she hadn't spoken to me since our excursion at my apartment on Tybee Island two years ago. I was amazed at how she rambled on as if nothing bad had ever happened between us.

"There's an eye specialist at Emory University in Atlanta who's doing experimental reconstructive eye surgery. He's supposed to be the best in the country, and he can help you see again out of your bad eye." Mom said, finally getting to the purpose of her call.

I was confused over her concern about my eye since it had always made me less than perfect to her. But I eagerly listened to her words and was excited at the possibility of being able to see normally again.

"My eye doctor knows about the surgery, so you should make an appointment with him," she continued.

My excitement continued to grow until she added, "I want to go to the appointment with you."

Experience should have told me to decline her offer, but I accepted it because I thought that maybe this combined effort would bring us together as mother and daughter.

One week later I sat nervously in the doctor's waiting room trying to keep my hopes at bay while dreaming about how it would be to see like everyone else. I was called into an examination and was instructed, "Look into the machine and tell me what you see."

My heart raced with fear as I leaned toward the eyepiece, but I was immediately filled with joy because I could see clearly for first time since my accident! Tears of gratitude ran down my face. I knew I had to find a way to have this surgery so I could be normal again. So no one would ever tease me again. So I would no longer be ugly. Everyone was excited by my miraculous ability to see and an appointment was set up with Dr. Wirth at Emory University.

Mom insisted on going with me on the ten-hour round trip drive to Atlanta. Even though I was anxious about being around her for that length of time, I agreed to let her go. Surely she couldn't cause any problems just by going to a doctor's appointment.

The morning I was to see Dr. Wirth finally arrived. Mom dropped her car off at my place so she could ride with me. Once she was securely buckled into my little car, a thick cloud of tension filled the air. It was only broken by my mother's uncanny ability to act as if there had never been any problems in our family or between us. I quickly let down my defenses, once again wanting my mother to love and be proud of me. I also put up a façade and said, "I'm doing really well with my life now. And Mom, I want you to know that I love you, no matter what you've done in the past. And I want you to love me." There was no response. Consequently, the drive to Emory was a strained and uncomfortable one.

Emory Eye Clinic was amazing. It was a large modern building decorated with contemporary art, fancy furniture, transparent walls, and talking elevators. Once in Dr. Wirth's office we waited for hours. An assistant finally called my name and took us to an examination room.

After Dr. Wirth completed his examination, he said, "I can do the surgery, but you must realize that it is still only experimental. I'm also concerned because I've never done this procedure on anyone younger than 40, therefore I don't know how long the transplants or surgery will last."

I considered every word he said until I realized that I didn't care what the risks were as long as I could see and look like everyone else. I begged Dr. Wirth to give me a chance and he agreed. But my hope was short-lived because the surgery was thousands of dollars and far too expensive for me. Another dream had disappeared in a flash, causing me to always be different from everyone else.

Disappointed and defeated, I headed back to Savannah with Mom. I drove without saying a word because one part of me was angry, while the other part was afraid of breaking down and crying. I tried as hard as I could to hold back the tears, remembering Mom's words from the past: "You're ugly when you cry."

I also tried to think through my feelings because it was at times like these that I wanted to act out my anger, anesthetize my pain, and kill myself. I wanted to yell at someone for the unfairness of my life, and the disappointment I felt now that I was trying as hard as I could to stay clean and sober.

Mom, however, wouldn't leave me alone so I could put what had just happened in its proper place. She yelled at me about my silence, as if my thoughts and feelings were unwarranted. I couldn't comprehend why she wouldn't try to be understanding, hold me, and just tell me that everything was going to be all right. Instead, she degraded my character, just like she used to do when I was a teenager standing in the kitchen in Felicity, begging her not to hit me.

After an hour of listening to her accusations, I became infuriated, but still sat there and said nothing. She knew she was pushing my buttons yet she continued to hound me. To prevent a fight, I looked at her, and said, "I don't want to argue—it would be best if you leave me alone before I lose control."

My words fell upon deaf ears; she pushed and pushed me until I gave in to uncontrollable rage. Fiery words flew out of my mouth as I stooped to my mother's level. At this point, I wasn't only angry about the surgery, but about everything in my past. When I realized how out of control I was, I begged, "Mom, just leave me alone!" But she continued with her deliberate attacks until I finally screamed, "If you don't shut up, I'm going to put you out on the highway and you can walk home!"

She looked at me in disbelief and continued nagging and picking on me. Finally, I got so angry that I was either going to hurt her or put her out on the highway. So I slammed on my brakes, not too far from an exit, and screamed, "Get out of my car and never call me again!"

With sarcasm and hate written all over her face, she threw open the car door, got out and screamed, "You're a shitty daughter!" She slammed the door shut, and I sped off like an angry teenager.

About a mile down the road I realized what I had done: I had put my own mother out on the highway at night with no one around! My heart was so broken and filled with such guilt that I threw the car into reverse and backed down the road to find her.

I was startled by a cop pulling up behind me with his bright, blue lights flashing. When the officer questioned me about my unusual behavior, I grew panicky. I shamefully confessed what had happened and that I was trying to find my mom. Together we looked, but were unable to find her anywhere. He told me there was a pay phone at the end of the exit and he was sure that Mom must have used it to call someone.

I had no choice but to drive on home. The next morning I awoke feeling awful about the trip and wondered why Mom would suggest that I see Dr. Wirth when she knew I didn't have any health insurance and no money for something as expensive as an operation. But I forced myself out of bed and peered out the window. I was relieved to see that Mom's car was gone from my driveway because it meant that she had made it home safely. I was also saddened because I knew my punishment would be her silence for some unspecified period of time.

A couple of weeks after the painful incident with Mom, Dr. Wirth contacted me with the wonderful news that I was still covered by Gene's insurance policy. He also said that his office had gotten approval from the Lion's Club to pay whatever the insurance didn't cover. I was elated that I finally had a chance to be normal. Without a moment's hesitation, I scheduled my surgery. The sad thing about it all was that I couldn't share this joy with my mother. I was about to get the chance of a lifetime and, once again, there was no one in my family to be there for me.

Unfortunately the surgery wasn't successful. Dr. Wirth believed it was because the accident happened at an age before my brain learned how to see binocularly and it was too late to teach it now.

I was disappointed, but determined to stay clean, so I continued going to my meetings. It was frustrating though because I still couldn't get a handle on what was making me want to self-destruct. No matter how many meetings and how many counseling sessions I went to, I still felt as if I was an outcast, unworthy of anyone's compassion or friendship. I was convinced that I was the ugly "disturbed young girl" whose childhood traumas were her own fault. But, I forced myself to maintain the pasted face that said I'm okay so I wouldn't disappoint anyone with my lack of progress.

The negative feelings motivated me to keep seeing Darlene. I tried my hardest to get rid of the demons of my past, while trying to ignore my need to kill myself or to use again. But the more I tried to ignore the knowledge that everything would change with a syringe of cocaine hanging out of my arm, the more I yearned for that experience—that feeling of wholeness and ecstasy. No matter what I did, I couldn't get that overwhelming need out of my mind. As the daily battle between the feelings of my past and the need for wholeness raged on, I tried my best to focus on recovery and managed to do so for about six more months.

Then the day finally came when I couldn't fight the battle any longer, and I gave in to my cravings.

I tried to hide from Darlene the fact that I was using again by keeping my appointments with her. I didn't want to lose her because I was afraid I would completely lose myself or end up killing myself if I did. However, I knew one day by the disappointed look on her face that she had figured it out.

In her usual compassionate way, she sat me down and told me, "I understand how hard you have been trying, but you're losing the battle of addiction and the war to save your own life."

Faced with the truth of her words, I became sad. I wanted to crawl into her lap so she could hold me, help me, and make everything bad disappear. But, I knew it was too late and there was nothing she could do to help me. Desperation swept over me as Darlene said, "There is only one thing I can offer you, and that is to admit you to the clinic's detox unit so you can start over."

The thought of battling detox again or picking up yet another white chip was too much to bear. So I stood up, looked at my friend and said, "I'm sorry." I walked out of her office to return to my world of isolation and misery and, I thought then, imminent death.

With my return to the world of addiction, I was buying cocaine by the ounces and insulin syringes by the boxes. The dirty remnants of my "junkie" life where scattered all around my room—my personal shooting gallery. I locked myself in it and did nothing but shoot up, and then smoked pot and drank liquor to take the edge off of the shakes and paranoia. I was pumping so much cocaine into my arms it was almost certain I would die.

My new life of isolation and continuous using, made it certain that I rarely saw anyone, including Leroy. I knew he had to be curious about my disappearance and had to know that I was using again, yet he never said a word. He remained my silent friend and the sweetest person I knew. Our paths would occasionally cross going to the bathroom, and Leroy would look at me with concern in his eyes and ask, "Are you okay?" I would stare at the floor and politely utter, "Yes."

I was also trying to work during all of this, even though it was becoming impossible. I was shooting up at work and calling in sick a lot. I couldn't put the needle down long enough to make it through any of the classes I taught. Every 15 or so minutes I would excuse myself to go to the bathroom so I could load my veins. The longer this went on, the more frustrated and alone I felt. I didn't know what to do with myself.

One day, while I was shooting up I felt an overwhelming sense of desperation—a need for help. I was afraid I was never going to be all right and that everything I had learned in the program would be lost forever. Once again I jumped into my car and drove as fast as I could to the mental health center to see if Darlene would help me. Strung-out, I paced back and forth in her office. Tears rolled down my face as I confessed, "I'm shooting up all the time and I can't put the needle down. Darlene, please help me make all of the horrible memories and feelings go away—teach me how to like myself."

She looked at me as if she understood that I was at the end of my rope. "I'll help you if you go through detox at the clinic."

Because I knew I would be dead within a day or so if I didn't, I agreed to go through detox one more time and to be admitted that same day. As we walked downstairs to the detox unit, I started hallucinating. My memory of being admitted was blurred. I didn't fully comprehend that I was there until I woke up during the night to find myself in a room with a large, overweight woman who was lying in a bed next to me talking to herself. Then the withdrawals began. Paranoia set in and beads of sweat poured off my forehead. I couldn't stop myself from shaking. I was exhausted and needed to sleep. But, sleep was impossible because my crazy roommate talked incessantly.

I pleaded with the nurses, "Please move me or make her shut up!"

But they knew they were looking at a junkie so they ignored me. I then realized I had stooped to my lowest level yet. I was now considered a burden to society, and nothing more than a parasite living off the system.

Morning finally arrived and I had taken all I could with not being able to get any sleep. I crawled out of bed one last time and begged the nurses, "Please, please, either silence that crazy woman, or move me into another room where I can go through withdrawals in peace."

They looked at me as if I were an insect, deserving only to be crushed and put out of its misery. When I realized they weren't going to help me, and that they loathed me because of my addiction, I became frustrated and then infuriated. I was immediately overwhelmed with the need to kill myself, so I marched out of the detox unit without saying a word.

When the fresh morning air hit my face, I knew I shouldn't have walked out because Darlene would be angry with me. I had to find a way to tell her what had happened, so I hunched down in a corner of the building to stay warm while I waited for her to arrive at work.

When Darlene pulled into the parking deck I became so scared I froze. I couldn't face her and tell her all the things I needed to say. I was afraid she wouldn't believe me and that she would throw me away, just like my mother had done. I remained hidden in the corner until she was safely inside the building. Once the threat of rejection was gone, I pulled my shaking body upright and hitched a ride home.

By the time I got home, I was angry with myself about everything that happened since the night before. I declared I was now finished with all of this bullshit recovery stuff since no one was going to believe me anyway. I returned to shooting up all day long and praying I would kill myself in the process. But, despite my anger, I held on to the hope that Darlene would call to ask my side of the story and to see if I was all right, but the call never did come.

By nightfall there was still no call from Darlene and I was still just as empty and alone on the inside, as I was when I left detox. Moments later I shot up my last little bit of cocaine. My heart started fluttering, my breathing became difficult, and any strength I had left in my body slipped away. I knew I had overdosed again, but as the blackness grew nearer, I found that I didn't want to die—I just wanted someone to love me and to help me. I crawled to the phone and called Darlene. I explained what was happening, and begged her to help me.

"I don't believe you Sandy, and I'm really angry you walked out of detox."

"No, really Darlene, I couldn't take that woman babbling all night and keeping me awake while I was trying to deal with withdrawals. Please believe me! I really need and want help, but I need to be somewhere where I can detox in a good way."

"Are you really serious about getting clean and sober?"

"Yes, yes, I can't keep doing this—and I can't get clean and sober without help."

"OK, if you're serious, then call the sheriff and have them escort you to Georgia Regional Hospital to their detox unit," Darlene challenged.

I was immediately filled with apprehension at calling the police. I was afraid of going to jail. But I soon realized I was more afraid of losing Darlene and dying as a junkie than I was of being incarcerated. So I made the call.

Moments later, a couple of deputies came to my trailer thinking it was prank that someone called them for a ride to Georgia Regional Hospital. They thought it was a joke until they saw me and realized I was a junkie. They helped me into the back of the squad car and escorted me to the detox unit. Once there I became lethargic, slumped over in my chair, and began gasping for air. I heard someone scream, "Call an ambulance—she's overdosed."

I woke up several hours later with IVs coming out of everywhere, and a disgruntled doctor standing over me, "You've overdosed and have cocaine toxicity again."

Because of my frequent admissions, the doctor committed me to the alcohol and drug ward at Georgia Regional Hospital. The police escorted me, along with several other people, to a paddy wagon and carted us all off to the detox unit.

I woke up the next morning filled with disbelief that I was back in the hospital again. I was so disheartened and discouraged I could hardly find the energy to breathe. I wanted to die. I now believed that I was truly hopeless. I had hit my all-time low. However, I didn't know how not to be an alcoholic and drug addict and live with my painful feelings all at the same time. I wondered how I would ever be able to recover from this relapse because there was no one left to help me except the AA and NA programs. How would I be able to go back and face all the people who used to think I had my act together? Could I start my recovery over again, and pick up yet another white chip? Where would I get the strength to do what had to be done and endure it?

"You have a visitor," a nurse announced, interrupting my thoughts.

"There is no one who would want to see me," I told her.

"You have a visitor!" she repeated in an angry tone.

As I entered the visiting area, I saw that it was Leroy. I stared at him, and feeling worthless I whispered, "I'm so sorry. Please forgive me—I don't mean to be this way. I need help, but I don't know if I've got enough left inside me to try again."

Leroy touched my hands and said, "I've been worried about you for some time, but don't you worry, I'll always be your friend and help you."

His sincerity sparked a tiny flame of hope. Because someone cared, it gave me a reason to walk into the AA meeting in the next room; even though I was ashamed of who I was as a person and humiliated by my inability to abide by the simple concepts of the program. I looked around the room at the people I knew so well, listening to the words I had heard so many times before. However, this time they sounded different and were filled with new meaning. A sense of rejuvenation touched my soul and a small voice inside said, "It's alright to come back to the program and try again."

It was as if someone turned the light switch on in my head and I now understood what had been said to me all those years. With this strange refreshing view of the program, I braved my embarrassment and walked to the front of the room to pick up my white chip, affirming my new vow of sobriety.

Several days after my admission, I was called into an office to see my psychiatrist. I sat nervously in the chair clutching my new white chip. Before he could say a word, I implored, "Please let me go home because I'll lose my job if I don't go back to work this afternoon."

I knew it was too soon to leave the detox unit because I was still withdrawing, but I had no choice if I wanted to keep my job. During the entire time that I sat in his office, the psychiatrist didn't look at me once. He only stated, "I don't care if you leave because you're an addict and it's your choice whether you want to live or die." So I chose to be discharged.

I walked out the doors of the detox unit back into the big, scary world. I was afraid and unsure of how I was going to make it this time. But, as I drove home to my trailer on the marsh, I was grateful to be alive and filled with determination that everything was going to be different this time.

Chapter 16

Desperate Stab at Recovery
and a New Life

I WAS CONCERNED about going back home, and walking into my room where I would find scores of drugs, paraphernalia, and liquor. But, to my surprise, Leroy proved to be a good friend once again as he made sure my room was sterile of anything that was remotely connected to the drug world. I changed my clothes, pasted on my infamous I'm okay face, jumped into my car and headed to work so I wouldn't get fired.

Driving down the familiar streets of Savannah I realized how worried I was about getting past everyone at work. But after I'd made it to the classroom without incident, I was relieved to find that no one had noticed my absence.

I knew that starting over was going to be the hardest thing I'd ever had to do in my entire life, but there wasn't anything else I could do short of quitting or killing myself. So I forced myself to get up each morning and put one foot in front of the other, whether I wanted to or not. I went back to my AA and NA meetings every night and worked the program to the best of my ability.

I also humbled myself and went back to the mental health center to resume my weekly visits with Darlene. I also started running again, hoping I could find the peace I used to have when Valerie took me running each morning at Turning Point. Each day that passed, I fought to hang on until I could get to a meeting or to see Darlene.

In my determination to stay clean and sober, I asked Kendra, a nurse and an avid runner, to be my sponsor. She had many years of experience with the recovery program. I realized that my biggest problem with her would be disclosing things about myself. I was afraid of what she might think, and terrified that I would eventually be forced to betray the forbidden family secrets. Thus, I was surprised when she said, "It's obvious that you have an eating disorder because you look emaciated and you run too much."

She went on to explain that she knew those things because she, too, had an eating disorder. She continued, "My biggest problem is my anorexia and bulimia…I'm still caught up in its vicious cycle even though I appear to have recovered from my alcoholism and addictions. I control my weight and emotions by compulsive running just like you do."

Her openness and honesty provided relief because I now knew there was someone else like me. I was still too afraid to let her in, so I said, "I don't have an eating disorder. I just don't like to eat because I want to be thin, and I run to maintain my weight and keep my feelings under control."

We went to meetings, ran together almost every day and were practically inseparable. As we worked the steps of the program with each other, we became best friends. As I had always done, I began forcing my need for someone to love me and take care of me onto her. My feelings became easily hurt, especially when she arrived late to run, when she didn't call me as planned, or whenever I perceived her as being distant. My old patterns of depression, sadness, and suicidal thoughts resurfaced frequently. But no matter how often I fell back into that pit, she hung in there with me.

Kendra was my sponsor for quite some time before she told me that she and her family were moving to Athens, Georgia. The day she was to leave, we stood in her driveway crying and telling each other how hard it would be for us to part ways. After we hugged and told each other good-bye, she placed her gold crucifix necklace in my hand and told me to keep it as a reminder of her. Then she drove away, leaving me terribly saddened that someone else I loved had left me. But, I also knew, as my fingers caressed the tangible evidence of her love, that somehow it was different this time.

Because it was imperative that I find a way to fill my time, and in a way that would keep my feelings silent, I threw myself into compulsively working out and running. My mornings were spent working out in the gym with free weights and swimming, while my nights were filled with running great distances and then to my meetings. On the weekends I ran as many road races as my pencil-thin legs could withstand because my beautiful, shiny trophies made other people think I was good at something. Running was the only thing I loved. It temporarily filled the gaping hole inside my heart.

I soon began equating my self-esteem with how many races I won, and my identity with my ability to perform. My driving need to feel good about myself escalated with each race I won, so I trained harder and harder while putting fewer and fewer calories into my body. It quickly became more difficult to run without any food and nutrients to operate on. But, despite that, I continued starving myself and trying to win as many races as possible.

Before I knew it, I had been in the program a whole year, but the milestone lacked the flare and glamour it used to possess. It was just another day that came and went because I didn't trust that I would be able to maintain my sobriety for more than a year at a time. One part of me was proud that I was able to abstain, but I also remembered what had happened after my last birthday. I was afraid of relapsing again if I celebrated my accomplishment or got too comfortable with myself or my sobriety. So I tried to remain focused on work, attending classes at Armstrong State, going to my meetings, running, and seeing Darlene for counseling.

However, fate soon decided to shake my life up a little bit and to force me to remember where I came from and where I needed to go.

One day at work, I saw an absolutely gorgeous guy park his motorcycle and confidently walk into the front office to pick up one of the kids, Jessie. I was absolutely smitten and knew I had to find out who he was. I was mesmerized by his slender build, shoulder length, dark brown hair and the prettiest blue eyes I had ever seen. He reminded me of the movie star, Kevin Costner. For a few moments, everything seemed to escape me as I tried to figure how I could find out who this mystery man was, and how I could make myself known to him. Unfortunately, I would have to wait until the next day to pump Jessie for the needed information about his cute friend.

By the next day, I could hardly wait for school to let out so I could see if the gorgeous man would show up again. Through Jessie, I learned that his friend's name was Randy Riggin, and was a friend of his father's from a long time ago. He was living with them until he could find his own place and Jessie insinuated that he was single. I prayed that God would let Randy notice me.

I saw Randy again that afternoon and for a brief moment, our eyes met. I was excited when he nodded and smiled at me, but I quickly looked away like a shy, embarrassed teenager. When I looked back up, he had already walked out the door again. I was disgusted with myself for not talking to him. As I remembered the things that had happened to me as a child, I knew I would never be able to make that kind of move toward a man. So I completely abandoned any hope I had about Randy, or anyone else for that matter.

The next day I returned to my usual routine at work. School let out and I was preparing for my daily stint with study hall when the intercom announced I had a visitor at the front desk. I was afraid that Jessie had told Randy about my questions, but I quickly dismissed that foolish idea. I rounded the corner to the front office and saw Randy standing there, looking nervous. Even though I found it difficult to look into his beautiful blue eyes, I walked over to him and introduced myself. I immediately stared at the floor to hide my fears and insecurities. I felt like a teenager full of confusing and unfamiliar emotions.

Randy invited me outside to see his beautiful, maroon motorcycle and awkwardly ask me out on a date. I was afraid of being hurt again, but something inside me prompted me to accept his offer.

The night of our first date finally arrived. I could hardly wait for my knight in shining armor to pick me up. In one sense, I was excited because I'd never been on a real date before and I'd always wondered what it felt like to be at dinner or a movie with a nice looking guy. On the other hand, I was afraid of what he would do to me.

Randy picked me up and I felt like a real woman when he opened the door for me. I wondered why I had never had this kind of experience with a man before now. Thinking of what happened with Gene and Miguel, I intuitively knew the answer.

I was quickly brought back to the moment when Randy pulled into a bar-type restaurant. As we walked inside, I was immediately uncomfortable with the smell of booze and cigarettes. My hands began to shake and my thoughts raced. I quickly asked the hostess for seats in a non-smoking area as far away from the bar as possible. When I realized how anxiously I spoke, I was embarrassed and hoped that Randy didn't pick up on my discomfort.

In our isolated booth we talked and enjoyed each other's company without a care or consideration for dinner. The conversation was filled with typical first date questions about who we were and what we liked to do. Just when we began feeling comfortable with one another and our numerous commonalties, a waitress interrupted us to inquire if we wanted a drink from the bar.

For a moment I felt scared and was only able to squeak out, "I only want water, thank you." I was embarrassed, but looked directly at Randy and said, "I don't drink or use drugs because I am a recovering addict and alcoholic." I dropped my eyes and continued, "I want to be honest with you from the very beginning because I don't want to end up using again."

I wanted to give him the option of never seeing me again if he couldn't handle this aspect of me. A moment of silence filled the air before Randy smiled and explained, "I only drink socially, smoke a little pot, and don't have a problem with either of them." He then reached across the table and placed his hand on mine. In a gentle voice he promised, "This won't be a problem for me or us—I want to continue seeing you, in spite of your alcoholism and addiction." I was immediately filled with warmth and happiness, because I really liked him.

Randy and I began spending a lot of time with each other. I was so excited about my relationship I could hardly think about anything else. I thought about him all day and how much I liked him and how I wanted to spend time with him. It was so easy being around him because we had so much in common. We both loved music and played the guitar, though my passion was strumming out funky rhythms on an acoustic or electric guitar, while he enjoyed banging out the heartbeat of a song on the bass. Not only that, but we both loved the thrill and freedom that came from riding his motorcycle. There were many days we jumped on his bike and cruised to Tybee Island just to feel the wind blow in our hair and take in the beauty of the marsh and beach. We also spent many days camping and backpacking, enjoying the splendor of each other and nature around us.

We were so much alike it was almost unnerving. It was as if Randy was the long lost twin I never knew at birth and who finally wandered into my life to make things complete. When I was with him I felt whole.

Even though we were dating, I still maintained my independence and emotional separation, especially since he didn't know about my past. I was afraid I'd lose him if I told him about the caustic emotions that made me want to kill myself. I didn't know how to confess that I grew up in a terribly poor, abusive family where I was beaten, sexually assaulted, and emotionally battered by extremely troubled parents. I didn't want him to know the self-destructive, lonely, and desperate Sandy who yearned for her mother's love and who needed to escape her vicious past. I was afraid he would leave me if he knew the truth…if he knew the real me.

To keep my feelings under control, I had to schedule time to spend by myself so I could deal with my inner demons, regroup and reinforce my protective defenses. In some ways, I had become too used to the private and lonely space and liked it. However, Randy wasn't particularly thrilled with that part of me, and it began to show.

One of my most cherished activities was backpacking and camping at Cumberland Island. Before I met Randy, I had put in for a two-week summer vacation from work to go to there and then on to Jacksonville to see the house where I grew up. I hoped that seeing the old home would settle some of the issues Darlene and I had been working on about my dad.

"I need some time alone, so I'll be gone for a couple of weeks," I tried to explain to Randy.

He smiled and said, "I want to go with you."

I yearned to explain why I couldn't let him go, but I couldn't bring myself to let him know my secrets just yet. So I said, "There are some things that I need to do alone." He seemed hurt and disappointed, so I took his hand and said, "I love you, but I just need this time to myself to work some things out. I've got to go."

I drove through St. Mary's and directly to the ferry hoping it would have some space to take me to Cumberland Island. I got out of my car and was mesmerized by the scent of salt in the air and the beautiful blue-green ocean water. My spirit was at peace because I knew I would soon be on that island with its mystical beauty and wondrous sounds of nature. I made my way into the reservation office to discover that there was no more room on the ferry. So I jumped back into my car and headed toward Jacksonville, Florida. Driving across the magnificent bridge of the city, I was amazed at the sheer size of the urbanized area and how unfamiliar everything seemed after all those years. Having been absent from Jacksonville since I was eight years old, I had no idea how to get around the city, much less to the old house.

I eventually tracked down the address and headed for the street where my childhood began. Suddenly I recognized that I was passing my old school and had to stop to take a look. Almost immediately, my soul was filled with a strange sense of sadness that I didn't understand. I got out of the car and began walking around the empty school grounds. I suddenly wanted to cry for the child who used to attend school here. I was overwhelmed with a need to reach inside myself and to hold my scared and hurt child, but I didn't know how. My insides screamed for someone to hold me and to tell me that they loved me, but, as usual, there was no one. I just walked around the old grounds and ancient buildings, trying to imagine who I was as a young girl, to remember what happened to me and to connect myself with the pictures I held in my heart.

The most disturbing part of my visit occurred when I walked into the cafeteria that had been left unlocked. It still had the smell of old milk. My mind quickly flashed back to the little milk cartons we drank from. It stirred up a sense of sadness and disappointment I didn't understand. The feelings became so overwhelming that I ran out of the cafeteria, back out into the open, grassy area between the buildings. I stood there for a moment with the sun on my face, hoping it would bring me back to the present.

I got back into the car and was heading for the house when I drove by a park I remembered seeing in baby pictures. I stopped and my mind flashed back to that photo where I must have been about two years old. I was standing in front of a pond where several ducks were floating. I could now see the same pond in front of me. In the photo I was wearing a pretty little white dress and my diapers hung ever so slightly out from underneath. I remembered the look on my face. It was one of immense sadness and hurt. My left knee and right cheek also had Band-Aids covering mysterious injuries. It was all too evident by the look on my face that life was already terribly painful—that I felt alone and afraid.

I tried to remember what had happened to me at that young age that caused me such pain, but I couldn't. So I continued my search for the house.

When I finally found it I was amazed at how different it looked. It was built out of light red brick in a rigidly square shape that made it appear extremely small. The honeysuckle bushes, which once draped across a fence in the front and side of the house, had been cut down, leaving the yard looking barren.

I sat in the car for a moment afraid to get out. My body grew tense and trembled at the thought of entering the house that held so much pain. My stomach burned with nervous anticipation as I told myself, I must get out of the car. I had to follow through with this or my childhood would never be over.

I finally gathered the courage to go up to the small front door and gently rang the doorbell. In an instant the door opened ever so slightly. An older lady with white hair stood before me with a confused look on her face, and asked, "What do you want?"

Staring at the ground, I confided, "I used to live here and I came back to see the place where I spent the first eight years of my life. Would it be all right for me to come in and see the house? I promise I won't stay long." Silence fell. I glanced up to see that the woman had turned pale and had a really strange look of fear on her face. "Why was she looking at me that way?" I wondered.

"Wait there for a minute," the old lady said as she closed the door. I dared not move an inch for fear of being in trouble—for what—I didn't know. I just knew that I had to see the house and I wasn't going to do anything to jeopardize my chance of doing so.

Moments later, an older gentleman with thin white hair came to the door with a smile on his face and said, "Come in."

I took one last, long, deep breath and gently opened the glass door to fearfully, yet excitedly, take a step back in time.

As I stood in the middle of the living room, a feeling of uneasiness surrounded me.

"How different and small everything is," I muttered.

The lady smiled at me and said, "You were a small child when you lived here, so everything back then looked big to you."

Even though her words made perfect sense, I was still flabbergasted with the claustrophobic feel. In a kind, gentle voice, the older lady offered to show me around and escorted me to each room. When we came to my old room, I flashed back the violent fights and how it was my job to protect Mom. I remembered feeling desperate and hurt; the lack of family cohesiveness; the indescribable need for Mom to love me; dad constantly terrorizing me; and my mother distancing herself after my eye accident. Pain and sadness welled up inside me. My mind quickly flashed back to the pink wallpaper that once lined my walls, and the small twin bed that sat next to a night table. This was the room pink kitty and I called our safe place.

I looked across the hall to Mom and Dad's old room where I remembered Mom standing on the bed screaming and crying, and Dad throwing dresser drawers at her. I could see Mom standing in the hall between our rooms with blood trickling out of her mouth as Dad repeatedly punched her in the face. The old woman must have noticed my momentary absence because she touched my arm and offered to take me outside for a tour of the backyard. I followed her into the bright and refreshing sunshine where we met her husband.

I stood in the grassy backyard marveling at how it looked exactly the same, even though, it too, appeared smaller. I was amazed that the old barbecue pit, bird feeder, and fountain my dad had built were still standing firm. When I looked closer I could see that the bird feeder still had my, and my brothers', handprints cemented into it. I gently knelt down and placed my hands on top of my little girl prints. Immediately my child's pain came rushing back and it reminded me just how bad things were and how much she hurt. It was all I could do not to cry.

I quickly turned away so I could find something to distract me, but my eyes fell upon the old cinder block garage. I went into the old musty building where I was taken back to the terrorizing showers with the spiders and the unforgivable beatings from my dad. The unpleasant memories were too much, and I ran as fast as I could out of the garage and back into the sunshine. I prayed for a reprieve and that God would magically take those memories away from me. I wanted to cry giant tears of sorrow, but I forced myself to hold them back.

With a look of immense sorrow on their faces, the old couple admitted,

"We know who you are—we know about your past and have been expecting you for years. The stories are still being told about how abusive and mean your dad was to your mother and you kids. The whole neighborhood felt sorry for you children because you were forced to grow up feeling like no one loved you. We feel so guilty because there was nothing we could do to help you."

The old man then looked at me with pain in his eyes and continued, "I know you are the one who had the terrible eye accident."

I was astounded that someone, other than myself, acknowledged the truth and the terrible things that happened here. I almost found it impossible to hold the tears back any longer. I thought, I have to get out of here before I start crying again. I thanked the old couple for showing me the house with the most sincere and heart-felt appreciation I could find. They smiled at me and said, "You can come back anytime you want because there will be a day when you'll have to bury your past, once and for all." I then turned and left.

Because I didn't have enough sobriety or counseling under my belt to survive this emotional revelation alone, I cut my vacation short and went back to Georgia.

After my return home, Randy and I spent a lot of time together. There was definitely a connection between us, one that neither one of us could deny. The relationship progressed quickly, and, in some ways, a little too quickly for me because Randy wanted to pursue the sexual aspect of our relationship. The problem was that I had never had sex with a man that wasn't abusive, or when I wasn't drunk. And, I was afraid to tell him how I had been hurt.

One sunny day, when Leroy was at work, Randy and I took a long ride on his motorcycle. It was exhilarating with the warm summer wind brushing against my body and my arms wrapped around my best friend and companion's waist. We rode around the islands and beaches most of the afternoon before going back to my trailer to hang out and enjoy the beautiful view of the marsh. After cooling off, Randy smiled at me in a mischievous way, gently took hold of my hand and said, "Follow me."

When I realized he was taking me toward my bedroom, my body became rigid and my breath shallow. My vision became distorted—everything looked small and far away. The distortion made it seem like it took forever to get from the living room to the bedroom, even though it was only a few feet away. My mind raced with thoughts of possible routes of escape. But in a loving and kind way, Randy laid me down on the waterbed and placed his body on top of mine.

He looked at me with passion in his eyes as he began kissing me and then slowly undressing me. Inside, I cried out for him to stop, but I didn't know how to say, "No." I was too afraid that he would hurt me or get angry just like everyone else had always done.

I wanted to jump out of my skin every time he touched my body. I was terrified when I felt his penis growing hard between my tightly clinched legs. My mind raced back to the day when Gene penetrated me, and I unknowingly slipped off into another reality.

My thoughts quickly returned to the present moment when Randy delicately spread my legs and inched his way inside me. I was instantly filled with body memories of that helpless child who couldn't make the grown-ups stop; the child who was doing something wrong. The panic and fear continued until I was unable to breathe and was about to go away in my mind. As Randy thrust his body up and down, shame, guilt, and helplessness crushed me. I couldn't hold back the tears any longer. He stared at me with a look of confusion. His body stopped moving and he asked, "What's wrong?"

All I could do was jump out of bed and run down the hall to the living room where I crawled into a corner, curled up into a fetal position and cried hysterically. Randy stood over me with a look of regret and sorrow covering his face. He pleaded with me to tell him what had just happened. I kept my face hidden as I reluctantly told him about the sexual abuse with Gene, without divulging specific details, and without telling him about the other men who had abused me.

When my secret was out in the open, I felt as if I was about to dissociate to the point of never being able to come back. He knelt down to hold me, but I shied away as I couldn't stand him touching me. So, he called my AA sponsor to come over and talk to me.

Despite the terrible outcome of our first sexual encounter, Randy didn't break off the relationship. Instead, he continued dating me as if nothing had ever happened. That was my first clue that he didn't understand the magnitude of the problem. So I sat him down to explain in a more detailed fashion what happened with Gene, and eventually Miguel.

The humiliation and shame I felt were intense, but Randy was so enraged that he spat out, "I want to find those people and hurt them real bad!"

It was then that I also admitted, "I'm in counseling with Darlene to work on these issues. I hope you can be patient with me and allow me the space I need to resolve this, so I can eventually have a sexual relationship with you." He put his wonderful arms around me and gave me a huge, yet gentle, hug. He whispered, "I'll give you all the room you need so you can heal." I rested comfortably in his arms, feeling relieved.

I continued counseling with Darlene, but it was now clearer that I didn't know how to feel the hurtful things that happened to me when I tried to talk about them. I didn't know how to open up for fear of getting hurt again. Darlene looked at me and said, "The key to resolving your addiction problem lies in the sexual abuse—it is imperative that you feel it and face it."

Since I couldn't freely and openly discuss what happened, and I knew Mom didn't believe my accusations surrounding the sexual abuse, very little progress was made. So Darlene suggested that we bring Mom, Gene and Randy in for a counseling session with the goal of getting the truth out in the open so it could be dealt with. I was horrified. I wasn't sure I could be in the same room with Mom or Gene, or confront them about anything, because I was still the small and helpless child who was afraid of them.

The day finally arrived for the counseling session that I hoped would resolve all my problems and set me free from my addictions. While Randy and I drove to the appointment, it was obvious that he was apprehensive about seeing my folks and a counselor all in the same day. So I placed my hand on top of his and reassured him, "Everything is going to be alright."

When we got to the counseling center, we parked the car and walked upstairs to the waiting area without saying a word to each other. Neither one of us really knew what to expect. I was also afraid because Mom's help had always ended in catastrophe and with her not talking to me for some unspecified period of time.

Moments later, Darlene called me into her office so she could prepare me for the meeting. I sat in my usual place trying to concentrate on her words of advice, but was so constricted with fear that I could hardly breathe. She opened the door and politely invited Mom and Gene to come in. They sat in the two vacant chairs directly across from me. Darlene explained the purpose of the meeting to everyone, while I fearfully stared at the floor. Mom didn't waste any time before she jumped right into playing the role of, I'm the perfect mother with a disturbed child role, while Gene maintained his silence.

Darlene looked directly at Gene and asked, "Is it true that you molested Sandy and had sex with her?"

The room fell silent at her blunt approach. I looked at Gene and watched his face drain of color, as if he were an animal caught in a hunter's trap. Under obligation to answer her question, he sat there spewing empty words. He made innuendoes and said, "There is no need to confess anything, it's a moot point now."

No matter how much Darlene pressed Gene to confess the truth, he remained silent.

Then he boldly stated, "Sandy was the only person in the family who appeared to like me and who was nice to me. She was the only one I could talk to and I confused my love for a child with what I should have been showing her mother."

I ached to hear him tell the truth about how he touched me and made me have sex with him, not mask it in ramblings of evasive recollections. As I heard him talk, I felt defeated because I knew he was never going to admit what he did.

Mom became hysterical and began crying, acting as if this meeting was about her, instead of to help me. She acted as if she were the one who had been wounded. She continued to act as if she had no idea that Gene had ever sexually abused me, despite my confession at Gloria and Ronnie's home, which landed me in Turning Point Hospital for nine months.

Since it was obvious that Gene was going to remain forever silent, Randy was asked to come in to the office. He refused to sit down. Instead, he stood there looking apprehensive as Darlene explained what had transpired and asked, "How do you feel about this, Randy? What do you think needs to be done?"

His face turned bright red. He looked directly at Gene and said, "You don't deserve to live!"

Gene did nothing but stare silently at the floor, while Mom continued with her hysterical antics.

There was no purpose in continuing the session because everyone was too caught up in their own agendas. After everyone left the room, I felt shattered and wondered how I was ever going to be able to get over my past when no one was willing to speak the truth. As I got up to walk out, Darlene just looked at me sorrowfully because I wasn't able to obtain the resolution I needed.

On the way home, Randy vowed, "I'll never go back to another counseling session with you again—even if our future depends on it."

His words stung my heart, and I was left without any hope of ever being normal. I was only left with fear and the feeling that I was to blame for what happened with Gene; Mom getting upset and hysterical; and Randy refusing to help me anymore. I also wondered how I would be able to handle the revived feelings until my next session with Darlene without resorting to my old self-destructive behaviors.

In order not to lose Randy, I tried to bury my disappointment at the failed meeting, and his vow of never going to therapy with me again. I attempted to become the person he wanted me to be. That meant I had sex with him whenever he wanted me to, even though I could hardly handle it.

As I endured each sexual encounter, Randy would ask, "What's wrong? How can I make things better?"

I would say, "If you'll just leave me alone for a little while, and give me time to work through what happened to me as a child, then everything will be okay."

I tried to help him understand that I needed to feel that he wanted to be with me in a romantic way because he loved me, and not for what I could do for him sexually. However, Randy being a typical young male, with a continuous influx of testosterone, didn't know how to leave the sexual part of the relationship alone. As a result, the problem got worse and left both of us constantly upset and confused.

His sexual pursuit only confused me because I had truly believed his promise of giving me the space I needed so I could heal. And because I was too afraid to speak my mind, I remained silent. I tried to focus only on the hope that if I could make it through one sexual act with him normally, then maybe I would be okay.

However, the more he wanted to have sex, the more upset and confused I became. I wanted him to be with me because he loved me, not because of what I could do for him sexually. I wanted to know that he loved me, and that we were connected in a special way. I needed to know that his wanting to have sex was out of love, and not because of some dysfunctional reason that would result in me being hurt again. I wanted a relationship first, then slowly work through the abuse so I would be able to have sex like a normal woman. Was that too much to ask?

Time and support were apparently too much to ask for because my having to meet Randy's sexual needs continued. I made every attempt to do what he wanted and tried to get through it the best way I could. I tried to make myself not feel and not cry in front of him. I wanted us to be okay; I didn't want him to leave me.

Meanwhile, I continued going to my AA and NA meetings. What surprised me the most was Randy's support and understanding about them, and that he attended several of them with me. I loved it when he drove me to the meetings, proudly perched on the back of his motorcycle, so I could show him off.

With each meeting that passed, Randy appeared more uncomfortable. Then three months later he told me that he thought he might have a problem with alcohol and drugs, picked up a white chip and started attending as many meetings as I did. I was so proud of him, but also thankful that we could now work our programs together without fear of alcohol and drugs interfering in our relationship.

Randy did all the right things. He got a sponsor and worked the program just like everyone else. Our bond together became stronger as we both understood that our recovery came first because without it, nothing else would work. It also seemed as if there wasn't a day that passed where we didn't see each other. I was happy and believed that I loved him, despite my fear of the sex.

Leroy continued renting a room from me and we continued our periodic cookouts and spent time together as friends. I really enjoyed the time I spent with him and his wonderful sense of humor, but it became apparent that he was uncomfortable when Randy came over. My heart ached for him, but I didn't know what else to do or how to make the situation any different. The day finally arrived when Leroy looked at me with hurt in his eyes and said that he had to move out. I was terribly saddened that I was losing my friend.

I lay in bed that night replaying Leroy's words in my mind and realizing how much I was going to miss him. I had become so use to his presence and on-going support that I was afraid I would be lonely and relapse without him. So many thoughts and worries ran through my mind that I couldn't drift off to sleep until the early morning hours. I woke up in a fog, but forced myself out of bed to meet Randy at the local waffle place for breakfast.

"Leroy is moving out because of our relationship," I said with a heavy voice.

Randy held my hand and said, "I'm in a dilemma too—my roommate is moving and I have to find another place to live, even though I can't afford it." Randy then smiled at me with excitement and said, "This is all too perfect—I can just move in with you."

I became anxious because that would mean that I would have to have sex with him more often, but I dared not tell him how I felt. I knew I needed the extra income in order to keep myself financially above water, but I wasn't ready to live with him, nor was I ready to lose him as my significant other.

I stared at the table while silence hung between us. Randy asked, "What's the problem?" I tried to open my mouth to get the simple, yet honest words out, but nothing happened. "Oh come on, Sandy, let me move in," he continued pushing.

"Randy, I don't believe, from a moral standpoint, that a couple should live together if they aren't married," I finally said. The strange look of confusion on his face left me embarrassed and staring at the floor.

He finally shrugged his shoulders, let the issue go, and we ate breakfast in silence. When the meal ended, we hugged each other and went our separate ways to try and figure out how to resolve our individual problems.

I went home and stared out my dining room window into the vast open marsh where the beautiful white egrets flocked. I was occupied with thoughts of my childhood, and how it had ruined my life and was now affecting my relationship with Randy, when there was a knock on the door. I opened the door to see Randy standing there with a strange look on his face as if something terrible had happened. I invited him in, but he remained stationary on the concrete patio. I became scared and asked what was wrong. There was no reply.

My mind raced with the thought that he was there to break up with me because I wouldn't allow him to move in.

"I need to ask you something, and I need to do it outside," he said, pacing back and forth on the concrete landing, like a caged animal.

Without warning, he stopped, took a deep breath, bent down on one knee and stared up at me like a scared child. I thought he had lost his mind until I heard his words, "Sandy, will you marry me? Will you be my wife?"

He caught me totally off guard. I just stood there not knowing what to say. Everything about me wanted to say, "Yes" because I desperately needed to feel that someone loved me and I believed his proposal signified that. I also believed that it meant all my problems and my past would magically disappear. But I was also afraid because I still couldn't be with him sexually and that bothered me greatly. I had no idea what I was going to do. I was afraid to say, "No" for fear of losing my only chance at being loved. So I forced myself to focus only on the idea that Randy loved me, that he was my best friend, and that I didn't want to lose him.

I pushed the sexual conflict aside long enough to say, "Yes!" Randy's face lit up with happiness while I wondered if I was making a terrible mistake. I'd always told myself that I would never get married. But the thought of someone loving me really made me happy, so I tried to make the most of it.

I buried my insecurities about the marriage and focused only on the thoughts of being accepted and loved. I grew excited about my future with Randy and I couldn't wait to share my special news with Darlene. In her office, I sat in the same vinyl chair in front of her cluttered desk with my eyes gleaming like a mischievous child. I smiled and told her,

"Someone finally loves me and I'm getting married!"

Darlene turned ghostly pale, her mouth dropped open and she fell silent. My stomach became tied in knots because I was afraid I was in trouble. She looked at me with grave concern, and told me in a stern voice, "You're making the biggest mistake of your life — you're not ready for anything like marriage."

Her words deeply saddened me because I needed her to reassure me that I wasn't making a mistake. I needed her to be happy for me and to understand that I had to marry Randy because I believed it would free me from my past and fill the hole deep within me. Somewhere inside I knew she was right, but my weary heart couldn't bear the truth or the idea of remaining alone another minute. So I put aside my common sense and maintained my desperate decision to marry Randy.

Chapter 17

A Different Kind of Pain

THE MONTHS PASSED BY QUICKLY as I focused only on the wedding and how marrying my best friend would miraculously heal me. I ordered a beautiful tiered cake and found the most perfect chapel. I chose the prettiest wedding gown I could find so everyone would think I was beautiful, especially Randy. I wanted so badly to be normal just once in my life, and that meant having a big wedding with a beautiful white dress and a large crowd of people who thought I was important because someone wanted to marry me. I wanted that day to be perfect and for us to live happily ever after.

I even developed a temporary relationship with Mom as she joined in on the fantasy of her daughter marrying a handsome man and riding off into the sunset, just as she had fantasized about doing with Gene. I prayed that she and Gene could force themselves to make it through the most important day of my life without fighting and embarrassing me in front of everyone.

As our wedding day drew near, my excitement gave way to fear. I worried that everything would change for the worse after we exchanged our vows. Would Randy become like all the men my mother had married and become abusive to me? Would he hurt me so much that I would feel trapped like my mother did? And most of all, would I be able to change enough so Randy and I could have a normal sexual relationship? Could I let go of my past long enough to have a normal life with the man I loved? Was I about to get myself into something that I wouldn't be able to get out of? Those huge questions plagued me, but my need for someone to love me outweighed my fears.

The warm July day finally arrived. I stood in the dressing room looking at myself in the mirror. At first, I didn't recognize myself because the person staring back at me was so beautiful. At the same time, I was bothered because I could see immense fear hidden deep in my eyes at what I was about to do.

One part of me wanted to call off the wedding. I wasn't sure I was ready to be everything a wife should be to her husband, but I was afraid of getting in trouble if I backed out now. So I tried to focus on how much I loved Randy and reminded myself that I was going to be magically transformed into a self-confident woman who could have wonderful, enjoyable sex with her husband once she was married. Focusing only on those thoughts, I forced myself to slowly walk out to meet the only person available to give me away, Gene. I nervously slid my small arm through his so he could escort me down the aisle. When I touched him, thoughts of how he abused me rose to the surface. The music started playing as I walked toward my knight in shining armor, who was waiting to carry me away from myself on his beautiful white horse.

After the ceremony, there were the usual wedding traditions. I threw my bouquet and then Randy removed my garter and slung it into the crowd of eligible bachelors. We smiled at each other and held hands as we happily ran out to the decorated get-away car to head off on our honeymoon to Disney World. Mom and Gene had given us money as a wedding gift, and since I was still a deprived child at heart, I chose that magical place.

As we drove to Florida, silence filled the air. I just stared out the window, watching things pass quickly by. I was sad because I still felt like the same person and because no magical metamorphosis had taken place. I felt alone. I wondered how long it would be before Randy would hurt me. And scared because now that I was married, there wouldn't be anyone to help me. I was especially afraid of the honeymoon because my mysterious change never came. I still didn't know how I would be able to have sex with him. I wanted to cry out for someone to rescue me from my tragic mistake.

The only thing I can say about the honeymoon was that I was smart enough to know that I didn't have any business having children, so I started taking birth control pills about a week before I got married. The pills made me violently ill and caused the honeymoon to get cut short. We left sunny Orlando and drove back to Savannah where we started our marriage off in my trailer.

As we walked into the place we now called home as a couple, I instinctively understood what it meant when people said, "Everything changes once the ring goes on the finger." Randy appeared nervous about being alone with me, and neither one of us knew what to do or how to act. I was definitely afraid of the sexual responsibility I now had. I felt as if I were drowning in a bottomless well.

Things went downhill quickly because we were dealing with the same issues we had before we married. The primary issue was centered around my inability to have sex with my husband without getting upset and crying. Every time we had sex, I would lie in bed with tears running down my face and the past flashing through my mind.

Things were also further complicated by the fact that I didn't go back to see Darlene because of her disapproval of my marriage.

As the battled raged on with Randy's insatiable need for sex, my eating disorder flared up, though I didn't recognize it at first. The only thing I ate was fruit, and, some days, it was even difficult eating just a few pieces of it. I was 5'4" and had lost 19 pounds since I had gotten married, bringing me down to 105 pounds. I was still going to school, working out, running, and attending meetings every night on less than 300 calories a day. Despite my very limited food intake, I saw myself as a gross and horrible person. I hated the way my body looked and felt. I wanted to crawl out of my skin and begged God to let me be someone else. I hated how I felt on the inside and how I looked on the outside. Those feelings, coupled with Randy's overwhelming need for sex, made me wonder how I was going to survive without going crazy.

In a matter of weeks, I was weighing myself every day and had dropped to ninety-six pounds. Everyone began asking what was wrong. Since I had no idea what was happening to me or why, I had no answers. The only thing I knew for sure was that I wasn't able to eat much of anything—I felt fat and hated myself. I needed to talk with someone about my feelings, but I had turned my back on Darlene and there was no one else around.

Everyone started pressuring me to put on weight, so I began isolating myself. I worked out at the gym before daylight, went to aerobics classes, ran on a cross country team in the afternoon, and ran six to fifteen miles a day after work.

With each day that passed, I got thinner and thinner. I was having trouble concentrating in school and at work. My body became so wafer thin that my bony skeleton began protruding through my clothes. Randy was confused and tried to force me to eat. Night after night, we sat on the couch where he pushed a plate of food in front of me and stared at me with concern. That routine only exacerbated the problem. I silently cried and felt guilty because I wasn't able to please Randy and I couldn't force the food down. I wanted so badly to be able to eat, to be happy with my life and the one person I loved, but the center of my being was drowning and I didn't know how to make it stop.

As the thinness and silence prevailed, people at school began treating me differently. They acted as if I had a contagious disease and they didn't want to be around me. One student finally asked me if I needed help with my eating disorder. Despite my denials, she gave me a phone number of an eating disorder specialist. I folded the paper with the information on it and tucked it into my pocket for quick disposal as soon as I reached home.

Nothing in my life appeared to be going in the right direction. I couldn't have sex with my husband, we were constantly arguing about the lack of intimacy, and I felt isolated and alone with no one to talk to. My grades were plummeting, it was becoming harder and harder to exercise, and I hated myself. My desperation grew by the day.

I realized that my life was deteriorating faster than I could keep up, so I called the eating disorders counselor, Ann Davis. Our first meeting was under false pretenses as I told her I needed information for a school project. She really impressed me with her understanding of eating disorders. A few days later, when I fell into a pit of despair, I went back to her office crying and trying to explain my problem.

I sat in my chair shaking and ashamed. Ann looked at me with compassion and said, "I can help you, but there's one stipulation, you have to bring Randy to your next session."

I was relieved that she believed she could help, but angry that I had to get Randy involved so I could receive that help. But I went home anyway, and humbly asked Randy to go to my next counseling session with me. When he agreed to go, I felt scared but lighter than I had in months.

In Ann's office, I sat nervously as she explained to Randy that I was anorexic. I sank deep into my chair, hiding my face from both of them, as I awaited his response. I wanted to run out of the room.

"I know about Sandy's eating disorder, but I don't know why she is starving herself," Randy said, with tears welling up in his eyes. "Why can't she just pick up a fork and start eating again?"

"The issue isn't that Sandy has stopped eating, but why she is starving herself," Ann said. Looking sternly at me, she continued, "I'll try to help you, but there is one last stipulation you have to meet. You have to sign a contract specifically outlining that you will eat, won't starve yourself anymore, will stop exercising, and will see me for counseling."

Her one last stipulation shocked me and reinforced that I couldn't trust anyone, including her. I knew there was no way I could commit to something that rigid. Surely she understood that she couldn't ask me to give up all my coping mechanisms in one day, without first helping me to resolve some of my issues or giving me something to put in their place. I didn't know how I could do it.

"If you don't sign the contract we'll put you in the hospital and tube feed you," she continued.

I was in a no-win situation. After many hours of debate, I knew there was only one way out of Ann's office, and one way to stay out of the hospital, so I agreed to sign the stupid contract. Begrudgingly, I picked up the pen from Ann's desk, glared at both of them with distrust and hatred and screeched, "It doesn't mean I'm making any promises." Ann had no idea that she had ruined the trust I had in her, and that she had lost the battle before we ever got started.

Because I didn't abide by the rules of the contract, my eating disorder started quickly catching up with me. Ann pointed out that I had lost two inches in my height from the lack of calcium in my fruit diet. I was having difficulty just getting around. I was weak, and couldn't think clearly. I was barely functioning at school and at work, and was having a lot of difficulty exercising.

She explained, "You're in the advanced stages of your eating disorder— it's serious." But my weight continued slipping in the wrong direction because I didn't know how to stop the vicious cycle I had gotten myself into.

Ann spent most of our counseling time focusing on the fact that I wasn't eating and threatening to put me in the hospital. We never got beyond that to talk about what was behind my need to starve. We just talked about the mechanics of the disorder and how it would eventually affect my body. I felt hopeless and destined to always starve and hurt myself. I wondered how much worse I could feel about myself and how much more I could manage to screw things up, but I was thankful to God that I was at least clean and sober.

I really tried to do things the way Ann wanted me to do them, but I just couldn't get past my self-hatred. So I ate like a bird, eating fruit for my main meals and gum in between to stave off any hunger pangs. After a while, I wasn't hungry anymore, and it was easier to starve myself. Little did I know that when the hunger went away it meant that my body was feeding on itself in order to survive. My body fat dropped below ten percent, and it was now consuming my muscles as a source of food. I stopped having menstrual cycles, and strangely enough, was proud of it. That kind of control gave me a distorted sense of accomplishment that felt extremely good.

I quickly dropped to eighty-six pounds. My complexion turned morbidly pale. My face was gaunt and lifeless. My bones protruded through my dry and scaly skin. My arms and legs resembled someone who had been in a concentration camp. My figure was square and lacked any semblance of a woman's body. It merely resembled that of a small underdeveloped teenage girl. My hair was thin, limp and falling out. My fingernails were short and brittle.

"Your body will start fighting itself and you could very well end up dead," Ann said one day with a fearful look on her face.

Her words scared me, but I couldn't face what she was saying. While sitting there listening to my death sentence, I ached for her to know the truth about my past and the reasons I hurt so badly. I wanted her to love me, take care of me, and make all the bad things on the inside stop, but it was as if she didn't understand what I needed from her or how to help me.

My relationship with Randy continued to deteriorate. We had reached a point where neither one of us knew what to do. There was no hanging out together or enjoying each other's company as we once did. There was a huge emotional precipice between us, filled with a myriad of confusing feelings, running the gamut from love to undeniable anger. The only positive aspect was that the further we drifted apart, the less I had to force myself to participate in the unbearable sexual acts that normal people called making love.

The problem with the anorexia worsened because I didn't think I should need food like everyone else. And my body could only feed off itself for so long. Eventually the hunger pangs broke through, and I hated myself for not being able to control my appetite. I quickly learned that the more I tried to control my hunger, the less control I had over it. But the hunger pains increased until I sank to a whole new level, and a very shameful one.

At work, I sat in my secluded room with my body crying out for food. But I couldn't make the pain go away or let anyone see me eat. My thoughts turned to food that was discarded daily in the trashcan, which sat about ten feet from my desk. I tried to ignore it, but I couldn't. So I slowly got up from my chair and began sifting through the trash for morsels of edible food. As I hovered over the trashcan like a vulture protecting its roadside meal, I kept a watchful eye out for anyone who might walk into the room. With each piece of discarded food I shoveled into my mouth, my body sighed with relief while the core of my being felt shame. Now that I had found a few scraps of food I could eat without anyone seeing me, I couldn't keep my mind off the trashcan. So everyday I found myself sifting through it, hating myself for eating the garbage and being out of control.

As punishment for my new behavior, the leftover food in the trashcan became the only nourishment I allowed into my body, except for the several packs of gum I chewed to make my stomach think it wasn't hungry. I thought I'd hit rock bottom.

When I came to understand that the trash was my only means of survival and my marriage was disintegrating because of the state I was in, my heart broke. Self-hatred and frustration ate away at me until my eating problem took on yet another dimension.

I drove to the nearest fast food drive-thru restaurant, and hid in my car as I ordered scores of various foods. My hands and body shook with anticipation while I dreaded the guilt I would experience if I ate everything I had ordered. Convinced that the cashier knew what I was about to do, I hung my head in shame. I handed her my money and quickly sped off as fast as I could. Driving down the streets of Savannah I voraciously tore open the bags of hamburgers, french fries, apple pies, and milk shakes, and shoved the greasy food into my mouth. My body was momentarily relieved, but then my stomach began to bulge and bloat from the tremendous volume it now contained. I couldn't stand the shame and guilt. I was compelled to undo this horrible thing, so I raced home and ran into the bathroom to hide, much like I did when I was shooting drugs. I sat on the floor with excruciating stomach pain. I suddenly remembered hearing about women who ate anything they wanted, made themselves throw it up, and never gained a pound. So I lifted the lid of the toilet and pulled my hair back into a ponytail. I fearfully knelt down on the floor and placed my head squarely over the toilet, trying not to choke on the residual smell of urine in the toilet bowl. I took one last deep breath and pushed my fingers down my throat to gag up all the forbidden food.

I strained and choked, while tears ran down my cheeks. My face felt as if it were going to explode from the blood rushing to it. My eyes and face began to swell from the exertion. My throat burned from the stomach acid that shot past it. I cried because I knew that I had somehow crossed a magical line that wouldn't allow me to go back to just starving myself. My body now had a mind of its own, as it believed I could binge, throw up, and not get fat.

The bingeing and purging got quickly out of control. It went from being a once a day occurrence to several times a day, every day of the week. I hated the helpless and worthless feelings I had after each bout, but I didn't know how to get off that insane roller coaster. I looked and felt exhausted from the vicious cycle of eating and vomiting. My face appeared swollen and red, while my throat was raw and bleeding from the stomach acid that constantly coated it.

I fell deeper and deeper into the vicious cycle of getting angry, depressed, bingeing on food, then forcing myself to throw up, then adding boxes of laxatives to ensure no food stayed in my body.

I didn't understand it at the time, but my body began literally shutting down. I woke up one morning to find my legs swollen and red. Incredible pain shot through them as I tried to walk. With each step they felt as if they were going to explode. My feet and calves became prickly and numb. As I stood there staring at my horrible elephant-looking legs I knew there was no way I could go to school or work. Tears rolled down my face because I didn't know what to do. I was so afraid that I would permanently lose my legs that I tracked down Ann, who was out of town.

"Please tell me what's happening," I cried hysterically.

Ann's voice took on a sound of panic as she explained, "The protein in your cells is leaking out into the tissues of your legs, causing the pain and swelling. You need to go to the emergency room as soon as possible."

"I'm begging you, please don't make me go to the hospital. Randy will find out and I'm terrified the doctor will lock me up."

Ann's voice became forceful, "You could lose your legs if you don't go!"

I immediately went to the emergency room and sat in the examination room until the doctor finally came in, took one look at me and said, "Just go home and eat like a normal person." His cold and misguided words hurt me deeply. I sat there crying because I didn't know how to do what he had prescribed. It was then that I truly realized for the first time that I didn't know how to eat anymore—I was lost and in serious trouble.

I now believed there was no hope for me, so I continued with my self-destructive eating disorder, despite its consequences. I would stop what I was doing several times during the day to cram myself full of food and then throw it up in various bathrooms all over town.

After a particularly difficult bingeing session on the way to an AA meeting, I nearly passed out in front of everyone. A couple of the women, who witnessed my near collapse, pulled me aside and asked "What's been wrong with you this past year?" As usual, I said nothing and just stared at the floor. I desperately wanted to blurt out how out of control I was and how bad the bingeing and purging had become, but I didn't.

Eventually they convinced me to talk, and believing them to be sincerely concerned, I unveiled my secret truth. One of the women came over and placed her arms around me. My heart melted at her kindness, I sank deep into her arms and then found myself going with her back to

Hope Hospital.

While waiting in the emergency room, I looked up to see Randy walking in. A part of me was glad to see him and wanted to run up to him and hug him. But another part was afraid that someone would convince him to commit me to the hospital.

My records from the last emergency room visit were pulled and I was sent directly to the eating disorders counselor. Janie introduced herself as a recovering anorexic and bulimic. I must admit that I was relieved that there was someone else who had my problem, but I still didn't trust that she wouldn't lock me up. I vaguely listened to her speech about what would happen to me if I continued bingeing and purging, until she hit on the one thing I was afraid of the most—permanently damaging my body.

"You need to check yourself into the eating disorders program because you have definitely physically compromised your body—possibly beyond repair," she said. Her words stuck in my heart like a knife. I began to cry.

I mumbled, "I just can't do it. I'm too afraid." I was frightened that they would weigh me and force me to eat. Even though Janie recognized the familiar excuses and rationalizations, she just wouldn't leave it alone. After listening to her justifications and pleading for hours, I was too tired to argue anymore, so I agreed to stay overnight—but just overnight..

The next morning, a nurse woke me up to take my vital signs. I looked around the room and realized I didn't remember much about the emergency room or being admitted, only that I was to be discharged that day.

After getting up, I saw that I was on a locked ward. My bathroom door was locked so I wouldn't throw up. The scales were locked away in closets so the patients wouldn't weigh themselves every minute of every day. The patients were weighed daily and meals were prescribed. If they didn't eat, they were tube fed. I wondered what I had gotten myself into.

A nurse came in to weigh me and I demanded to be released from the hospital. When she realized the seriousness of my plea and desperation to be discharged, she sent the big guns in to talk to me. Janie and my doctor told me that I would probably die if I didn't get help. Because I was more afraid of the scales and food than my own death, I demand to be discharged. They respected my wishes.

After my discharge from the hospital, I forced myself to go to an eating disorder support group supervised by Ann, even though I continued bingeing, purging, taking laxatives, and exercising.

The overwhelming need to gain even more control over my body and weight led me to join a gym. I would take two or three aerobics classes every day and sit in the sauna until I burned up every calorie I took in. But I was eventually barred from the gym after I passed out in the shower. Even though I weighed only eighty-four pounds, I still didn't believe I was thin enough. I still didn't believe that I could die; I still couldn't talk with Ann about anything of substance; I still didn't believe the group about the seriousness of my disorder; and I still couldn't let anyone in to help me, not Ann, not the group, not even Randy.

My life again spun totally out of control.

Chapter 18

Almost Too Late

I FINALLY GRADUATED from Armstrong State College in June of 1988 with a Bachelor of Arts Degree in Psychology. I was notably humbled since it took me almost seven years to complete the four-year program because of my alcoholism, drug addictions and eating disorder. I thanked God that I was able to walk across the stage and experience what it felt like to accomplish something so big, especially since I had missed my high school graduation. I loved wearing the cap and gown and having my degree handed to me in front of a large audience.

Behind the joy of completing school was the pain of my quickly disintegrating marriage. Randy and I were getting into huge fights and weren't acting like ourselves. Somewhere deep inside, we knew we loved each other, but neither one of us could bear what was happening to us. Randy then made things worse by quitting AA and NA to return to drinking and smoking pot. This was a huge problem since I had been clean and sober this time for almost two and a half years. I wondered how I would be able to maintain my sobriety and my marriage if Randy was drinking and drugging. I felt abandoned by his decision and realized that this was probably the beginning of the end of us.

No matter how much I mulled it over, I didn't know how to help either one of us. We tried to discuss our dilemma, but silence prevailed, as we both knew there was no hope of salvaging our relationship.

My heart sank, and I gave up. There was nothing left to hold on to. The bad feelings resurfaced and took over until I was left with nothing but a desperate need to destroy myself. I wanted to kill myself for all of my shortcomings with my husband and because of who I was as a person. I hated myself for carrying around the pain of my past and for letting it ruin my life. I detested the fact that I had finally found someone who loved me and whom I loved, but that I couldn't have sex with him. And, more so, that he wouldn't put the sexual part of our relationship aside long enough for me to heal. I was furious at myself, Randy, and at the thought of losing my marriage.

That night Randy and I went to band practice, and my goal was to lose myself in the music. It was great to be a part of something and forget my problems if only for a few hours. Then someone lit up a joint and passed it to me. I sat there with the joint in my hand, remembering how wonderful getting high felt and how I missed the feeling of wholeness it gave me. My mouth began to water and my body vibrated with anticipation. I tried to stop myself by remembering how guilty I felt after my last relapse. But my need to anesthetize my feelings about losing Randy and hating myself outweighed the devastating consequences that would surely follow. As I slowly raised the joint to my lips and inhaled the mood altering smoke, I saw Randy doing the same thing. It felt strange getting high with him. One part of me hoped that it would bring us back together and make us happy again, even though, somewhere in the back of my mind, I knew better.

I woke up the next morning disappointed and disgusted with myself that I had relapsed again. I could barely withstand the guilt. I wanted to go ahead and kill myself and get it over with. Then the truth of the program shone through once again as my addiction picked up right where it had left off, just as the program taught me it would. I jumped out of bed and smoked a joint with Randy. When he left for work, all I could think about was finding some cocaine to fill the hole in my soul and make me forget everything. I didn't know what else to do so I got in my car and raced downtown to find some cocaine.

I was back cruising around the dirtiest and poorest sections of the city. After interrogating scores of addicts, I met one poor soul who looked as if he had been on the streets for years. His face had become a molded, leathery mask and his eyes were bloodshot from cheap wine. He carried all of his earthly possessions on his back and sold small vials of crack cocaine in the park. When he saw how desperate I was for a fix, he graciously hooked me up with a guy named Casey.

Minutes later, I was standing at Casey's home, off the main road to the airport. When he answered the door, I was momentarily shocked to see that he was an overweight hippie with long hair. I was frightened, but told him what I was looking for. I got my precious cocaine and was once again thrust into a pain-free world. I thanked God for allowing me to experience that feeling of ecstasy just one more time and asked Him to forgive me for giving in to my addiction.

My need to remain in that altered state was now resurrected, and

Casey, with his endless drug connections, became my new best friend. I spent more time with him than I did with Randy, in a drug-induced haze.

My intravenous drug use rapidly sped out of control. I spiraled down the same familiar dark tunnels as before, but this time I completely isolated myself. I invented deceptive ways of hiding my relapse from Randy, Ann, and everyone else, and no one figured it out until it was too late. I became the master of deception and denial, which left no one knowing or understanding me.

I rarely drew a sober breath and constantly skated that fine line between life, death, and permanent brain damage. My intimate dance with death became a little too apparent in Casey's bathroom one day. We were shooting up and both collapsed from an overdose. Somehow, we survived and in the true junkie fashion, just looked at each other with pasted smiles on our faces and said, "We need to be careful with the new stuff because it's lethal and could kill someone."

I fell deeper and deeper into my addiction, and found it almost impossible to make it through any part of my day without using. I constantly needed a fix in order to survive. I was compelled to use at home and at work—anywhere I could get away with it—it didn't matter.

By now I was also sinking myself into a deep financial abyss. To support my drug habit, I borrowed over seven thousand dollars off my credit cards in just a couple of months. Instead of making purchases, I used my cards to get cash advances until I maxed out all of them. I then crossed a dangerous line and started stealing cash from my job.

With my new source of money, I began buying large quantities of cocaine and shooting up in complete isolation. My alienation from the world grew more intense and severe by the day, and was aggravated by on-going paranoia that was now my constant companion. Every minute of each day I was afraid of getting caught; afraid that the police and other people were watching me. My brain told me it was the cocaine, but my body didn't trust that information. With this, my need to use escalated. I felt I had to get completely away from everyone before I cracked up. I needed to remove myself from civilization so I could once again experience the needed rush without it being cut short by my fear of getting busted.

I headed for an isolated campground to escape in peace. I used so much cocaine that I became paranoid. For hours, I hid in the marshes imagining the police were after me. In my delirious state, I buried my drug supply in the swamp and then got desperate to retrieve it. I crawled around in the muddy swamp water in the dark for hours trying to find my stash, but to no avail. Panicking about withdrawals, I fled to Lydia's to pick up my graduation present. I was somehow able to cover up my relapse and cravings in front of her just long enough to retrieve my $500 present. I quickly sped to Casey's to buy more drugs and got wasted the rest of the day.

I made it back home around midnight to find Randy sitting on the couch with a strange look on his face. I quickly looked away and stared at the floor in my usual state of submission. I was convinced that I was in trouble and that he knew the extent of my relapse. However, silence filled the room until he looked at me with compassion in his eyes and gently asked me to sit down on the couch. I didn't understand the change in his behavior, so I just did as he had asked.

He looked sad and said, "I'm concerned about our marriage and how much you're using."

I realized, for the first time in a long time, that we were talking about what was important and admitting how bad things had become. It was as if it was finally all right to admit that we still loved each other and that we didn't want to lose our marriage. However, the facts still remained: we were both using; I had an eating disorder; I still couldn't have sex with him; and neither one of us knew how to make things better. Desperate to hold onto my husband and the love I felt for him, I thought things might be better if we were at least using together.

"Randy, I know we've both relapsed, but we could be doing it together—maybe it would make us close again." He looked stunned at my request but agreed to party with me that night. We sat there smoking crack cocaine until there was nothing left. We both wanted more, but he didn't seem to possess the same insatiable need that I had. Desperate for something else to put into my system and feeling comfortable with this new connection with my husband I also admitted, "I'm shooting up again—do you want to try that, too?" A look of horror immediately covered his face and he stared at me and said, "No! And I don't know what to think about all this!" I began kicking myself for divulging too much about my drug use, but I didn't let it hamper my need. So I loaded up a syringe right in front of him and I was off to the races again.

About a month after my camping trip and smoking crack with Randy, I became useless to everyone, including myself. My days consisted of trudging through vicious cycles of starving, then bingeing and purging, and eating laxatives by the boxes while shooting drugs all day long.

I had several overdose episodes alone in my trailer and one heart attack. They were terrifying, lonely experiences where I would find myself lying on the floor gasping for air, sure that I was about to die. Somehow, I would survive and then do it all over again.

The arguments with Randy escalated about the lack of sexual activity in our relationship, my eating disorder, and our inability to communicate without yelling and screaming. Finally, after a huge argument, he moved out and went to stay with a friend. We had only been married ten months.

Even though I loved him, one part of me was glad he was gone because I could now use drugs and continue with my eating disorder without anyone stopping me or trying to protect me from myself. After all I had nothing left to live for.

With my new freedom came all kinds of new problems and consequences I hadn't anticipated. One night I woke up to find my left arm swollen and black, and excruciating pain shooting all the way up to my shoulder. Frightened that I would lose my arm, I knew I had to go to the hospital. But, somehow I had to find a way to get a fix into my system so the doctors wouldn't figure out I was a junkie.

Desperate, I tried shooting up in my feet and then my bone thin hands. After getting enough drugs into my body, I got into my car and drove back to Hope Hospital. I leaned on the registration desk and told the nurse about my need to see a doctor about my arm. She took one look at my ghostly pale skin and dark, sunken eyes and immediately escorted me to an examination room. I dared not look at her as I unveiled my grotesque arm that had faithfully served me so well. The room fell silent. I glanced up to see the nurse standing there with a disturbed look on her face. She quickly called for a physician to see me immediately.

The resident examined my arm and said, "I know you're a junkie, but we'll have to cut open your arm to drain the infection out of it, or it will eventually have to be amputated." I realized the seriousness of his words and burst into tears. I had no choice but to let him cut me open.

In less than five minutes, the physician had a "cut-down" tray brought into the room. I held my breath in anticipation of the pain that would soon follow. He injected my arm with several anesthetics and I watched as he cut my arm open and drained the thick, black puss. I watched him dig and scrape out all the remaining black material that wouldn't drain. The doctor shook his head in disbelief at all the infection that had emptied into the tray, and he packed the gaping incision with eight inches of Iodoform gauze. His constant, incredulous look told me he was no different than any other doctor who had ever treated me; disgusted he had to work on a junkie. He then neatly wrapped my arm in pure white strips of gauze.

"Thanks for helping me," I said sincerely. My words must have touched his seemingly judgmental heart as his look of disgust changed to one of compassion and he said, "Call me if you need anything."

A couple of days later, excruciating pain began shooting through my arm and I noticed the nice clean gauze turning a gross shade of green.

I unwrapped the dressing only to find greenish, black stuff oozing out of my red, swollen appendage and a small piece of the Iodoform gauze hanging from the incision. I began wondering how long I was supposed to leave the packing in now that my arm seemed to be infected. I tried to straighten my arm out but couldn't. Panicked, I jumped into my car and raced to an emergency clinic.

Thoughts flashed through my mind that I could permanently lose my arm, so I begged the nurse at the clinic to help me, and prayed for God to spare my arm. I was placed in yet another examination room and, once again, was asked to reveal my disfigured arm. The doctor looked at it and explained, "Your arm is infected, but this time from the gauze. The packing was supposed to have been changed every day to prevent infection."

"But I was never told about that," I said.

I was instructed to lie down on the examination table while the nurse injected me with several powerful antibiotics. The doctor slowly pulled the eight inches of algae-green packing from the depths of my arm. The flap of the incision caved in on itself about an inch when there was no gauze left to support it. I lay there crying silently, enduring the pain and humiliation, because, even now, I had no idea how to get off the drugs. I felt the cold hydrogen peroxide as it was poured into the wound and overflowed onto a protective pad. I held my breath, praying the pain would soon subside.

Now that the incision and gaping hole were sterile, the physician repacked it and gave me a long speech about IV drug use and specific instructions about how to care for my arm. "Change the packing and dressing every day, soak your arm twice a day in hot water, and try to straighten it out before it becomes permanently contracted at the elbow."

The fear of losing my arm and/or having it forever locked at the elbow terrified me, so I called Ann when I got home and told her about my relapse and what had happened the last several months. I also asked her to help me work on straightening my arm.

When she came to help with the physical therapy, I was grateful and, yet amazed, because she treated me like a person rather than a worthless junkie. That was the truest act of forgiveness anyone could have shown me at that point. She assisted me with the painful and arduous process until my arm was finally straight again.

The horror of almost losing my arm terrified me that I was either going to die or permanently dismember or disfigure my body unless I could find a way to stop using drugs. So I tucked my pride deep inside and dragged myself to an AA meeting. I stood in the doorway, staring at the floor. My body shook and my knees felt as if they were about to give way. Everyone went silent and just stared at me. They were amazed that someone who once had over two years of sobriety could look so bad. I was everyone's nightmare because I represented what every person in AA and NA feared the most...relapse and death.

Shame and embarrassment left me wanting to run out of the building and back to my silent world of addiction where no one would judge or fear me. But I put one foot in front of the other and dragged myself into the main meeting room and sat in an isolated row of chairs. The room quickly filled with recovering addicts and alcoholics whose eyes weren't dulled or tired from endless nights of drinking and drugging, but filled with life. I dared not look at anyone. I just sat there and kept my shaking hands close to my chest.

In the meeting, I found it difficult to pay attention to the wonderful words of the speaker. Instead, overwhelming hopelessness and loneliness took control as the old thoughts and feelings I constantly ran from began resurfacing. Bewilderment flooded over me as I realized that I was caught between two worlds: one of sobriety and one of self-destruction.

I desperately wanted someone to help me but I knew that it wasn't my time to return to the program just yet. My body began shaking violently and I knew the withdrawals were coming like demons to take control of me. My mind raced with unanswered questions about what I was going to do. I couldn't let those people see what was happening and I had no place left to detox. Depression and thoughts of suicide set in.

I was convinced no one wanted me, so I ran back to my personal shooting gallery at my small, isolated trailer on the marsh. If I was going to die, it would be by my own hands and with a needle stuck in my arm. I sat in my trailer making a desperate attempt at figuring out what I could do to ease my pain instead of using drugs. The longer I debated it, the more the feelings and memories I was running from crept to the surface.

I had to block out the pain, so I spent about two weeks shooting drugs in a black out. I remembered absolutely nothing except for the times when I woke up on the blood-soaked carpet with needles hanging out of my arm and saliva drooling from the corner of my mouth.

Then one very confusing morning, my black out mysteriously ended at work. I came to standing face to face with my boss, not knowing how I had gotten there or how long I had been there.

"What's going on? Why have you missed almost two weeks of work without anyone knowing why, or where you were? And why do you look like hell?" she demanded.

I stood there confused and trying to concentrate on her words so I could put the pieces of the puzzle together enough to answer her questions. I became uncontrollably angry because I had wanted someone to ask me those same questions a long time ago and to help me. Now the only person who was asking couldn't help me. I was so angry that I began to cry, rolled up my sleeve and screamed, "I'm not perfect—I've relapsed!"

My angry and hateful words reverberated in the room like the echo in a tunnel. I couldn't believe how bold and crass I had been to the person who held my job in her hands. For a moment, she stood there speechless at the sight of my black and blue arms, filled with track marks. She was obviously horrified and leaning toward being sympathetic until she realized that everyone was staring at us. Her face turned to stone as she said in a stern voice, "You're fired!" I was devastated. It was then that I realized it was October,1988, just days before my twenty-fifth birthday, and only four months after my graduation from college.

I had no idea what I was I going to do now. I had lost my husband, was fired from my job, living alone, wanted to kill myself every day, and continued fighting a life-threatening eating disorder and out of control addiction. I was alone and there was no one who knew how to help me. It was then that I gave up on everything, including myself.

I locked myself away in my trailer and journeyed into the depths of hopelessness. The drapes were tightly shut, doors securely locked, and the phone unplugged. I remained steadfastly locked away in my dark, silent bedroom. The days passed slowly as my spirit grew heavier and heavier from the realization that there was truly no hope for me and I was, indeed, going to die with a needle hanging out of my arm.

My next memory was that of coming out of a black out with Ann standing over me with a look of concern on her face. I wasn't in my dark and dingy trailer, but in a bright, sun-filled room. I was freshly bathed and wearing clean clothes. I felt queasy and confused. I glanced around the room trying to figure out where I was and how I had gotten there.

"I was concerned when I hadn't heard from you, so I went by your trailer and found you lying unconscious in the hall with a syringe hanging out of your arm and alcohol and drugs scattered everywhere. I brought you to my house to try and keep you alive, and to help you through the withdrawals. You've been here for several days, floating in and out unconscious. I also took you to several AA and NA meetings, even though all you did was lay your head down on a table in a black out."

As soon as she told me about the meetings, I had a flashback of sitting in a room, feeling as if I were about to fall out of my chair and then being afraid I was going to pass out from nausea. I remembered feeling embarrassed because everyone in the program had seen how bad off I was.

Sitting in Ann's home, I contemplated everything she had told me. My body hurt and it was clear that the withdrawals weren't over. I didn't want to go back to doing drugs. I just wanted someone to listen to me, love me and help me. However, Ann still didn't want to talk about what bothered me. She just wanted to do what she did best, and that was to take care of me physically. The problem was that I was dying for someone to hold me and to let me know that everything was going to be all right, but that always seemed to be beyond everyone's comprehension.

Later that day I couldn't stand the withdrawals another minute, so I snuck out of her house, scored some more cocaine and went back to my place. I locked myself back up again in my trailer and used like there was no tomorrow.

I came to the next morning, November 4, 1988 at the age of twenty-five, with tremendous pain shooting through my arms. When I pulled the sheets down I gasped for breath when I saw that both of my arms were swollen, bleeding, and turning black! Tears rolled down my face as I lay in my bed disappointed and hating myself for leaving Ann's house to use again.

"Why can't I stop shooting drugs long enough to get my act together?" I wailed. The memories and feelings I had been running from suddenly washed over me like a tidal wave and it was at that moment that I realized I couldn't get clean by myself.

I drove back to the hospital where the medical staff shook their heads at my insidious addiction, cut both of my arms open, drained them and packed them with the same Iodoform gauze. After being released, I went back to my trailer and wondered how I would be able to put down the alcohol and drugs for good this time. My body then reminded me of who I truly was as I doubled over in pain, desperate for a fix. Beads of sweat began pouring off my brow. I needed help.

Not knowing what else to do, I called Ann and begged her to help me one last time. Sternly, she said, "You have to commit to being clean or I won't help!" Surrendering to everything I thought to be true, I promised, "This is the last time. I am at the bottom with nowhere else to go and I don't want to die a junkie. But if we're going to do this, then I need to go ahead and do it now before the cravings and withdrawals take over."

"OK, gather your things and get over here now!"

As I packed a few of my personal belongings, I began to grow desperate and wondered how I would survive this. I hid some cocaine in my jeans—just in case the withdrawals became too much for me to handle.

Thirty minutes later, I arrived at Ann's home, on the beautiful waterfront section of Wilmington Island. My arms were bandaged in white gauze and my pride was securely tucked away, fearing what was to come. I bowed my head in shame, as I knocked on the only door available to me for help. My heart was bursting with the need for Ann to hug me and to tell me that everything was going to be all right. But when she opened the door she just invited me in and bypassed my need for comforting. She took me directly to her room and put me to bed in preparation for the long night ahead. In a matter of a few short hours, the withdrawals were so severe that I didn't think I was going to survive, but I remained silent.

Night eventually set in, and I was lying in a fetal position in my own sweat, with my entire body shaking with pain. Waves of nausea and vomiting pounded me. Then, I remembered there was a remedy in my jeans pocket. I got up and snorted the cocaine up my nose. I lay on the floor trying to bask in what was supposed to be ecstasy, but, instead, only found guilt and shame. I couldn't believe I was doing this again!

I saw my reflection glaring back at me in the sliding glass doors and knew I was at a crossroads. For the first time, I truly understood that I was going to end up being a junkie the rest of my life if I didn't stop that night—November 5, 1988. That thought hurt so much that tears began flowing down my face and I flushed the remaining cocaine down the toilet.

I didn't admit to Ann what I had done, or explain why the withdrawal was so drawn out. Several days later, I got out of bed, frustrated and irritable because there was nothing left in my system—nothing to help me cope with my feelings or to protect me from myself. I sat on the floor in Ann's living room and found it immensely difficult to be polite because the same feelings I always tried to run from began resurfacing. I needed someone to hold me, to love me. And, I became angry because Ann only seemed to care about my physical needs and not my emotional ones.

Overwhelmed, I ran out of her house, not to use, but to go back to my lonely trailer to kill myself. I wanted to put myself out of my own misery once and for all. I drove as fast and as recklessly as I could down the road, crying and praying that I would wreck my car and die so no one would ever find out about my silent need to kill myself.

Instead, I ended up standing at a pay phone with the receiver in my hand. I had to call Ann and beg her, one more time, to please forgive me and not give up on me. To please help me not be an addict or self-destructive anymore. Even though I was scared, I dialed her number.

When I heard Ann's voice, I cried like I had never cried before. "I'm so sorry, and I'm angry at who I am."

"Look Sandy, I can't give you what you need because I'm having problems of my own. I can't help you. Please don't come back to my house. I suggest you go to a meeting tonight so you won't relapse."

Desperate, I proclaimed over and over again that I was sorry, but Ann hung up the phone. I finally understood her limitations, and those of everyone else who had ever been in my life. But that didn't make me feel better—it only exacerbated my need to end my disparaging life. So I went home to my lonely trailer and threw myself down on the couch in sheer exhaustion. Vacillating between wanting to use and wanting to kill myself, I prayed one last time that God would help me.

At that very moment I discovered, at a deep level, what complete isolation was all about. I cried like I did when I lost my pink kitty. But now I understood that it was my responsibility to choose whether I was going to get clean and sober, or whether I was going to go back to shooting drugs and die. It was entirely up to me because the only person who could ensure my survival was ME.

I made it to a meeting, and despite my previous failed attempts at recovery, there was a woman who was kind to me. She took my shaking hand and escorted me to a safe place to sit; one that was next to her where I would feel comfortable and accepted. I sat in the meeting trembling, but listening intently to every word that was spoken. Somehow the same words I had heard many times before resonated with a new meaning.

That unsettling thought sent me staggering to the front of the room to receive what was to be my last white chip. By the end of the meeting, I understood that I still had a very long way to go, but it didn't seem nearly as impossible. I went to two and sometimes three meetings a day to get help with the withdrawals, so I wouldn't think about using, or about my problems. I got several sponsors and talked with them daily. I started looking for a job and threw myself into the program.

The first several months were a living hell, but my determination, the grace of God, and the program kept me clean and sober from that day on.

Chapter 19

Substitutions

My new dedication to recovery brought with it the desire to work the steps of the program perfectly. I believed it would keep me from relapsing. I tried to convince everyone that I was all right by pasting on my patented I'm okay face. It was the only protection I had left from the world. It was my only way of ensuring that no one would ever hurt me again. It still felt too risky to admit to anyone that even though I had quit drinking and drugging, my past still haunted me. The tragic memories were still sitting just below the surface. I knew I couldn't make the pain go away with alcohol or drugs, so I tried to ignore my feelings and went to every meeting I could.

After several months, the craving for a drink and a fix slowly began to subside. My body grew stronger and I began to heal. But the problem of tolerating those feelings remained. I was restless and agitated, frustrated and angry. My insides cried out to tell someone what had happened to me as a child. I wanted to strike out because there was no one qualified to listen, or who knew how to help. I didn't know what to do. So I threw myself back into my running again. Somehow the long stints of physical exercise always made me feel better about myself. Any time I could slide into a six-to-fifteen mile run, I considered it a perfect day. It filled my emotional needs and gave me the attention I craved. I was especially proud when I ran to my meetings because I got such positive feedback about how physically fit I was, even though I still looked like a person from Auschwitz. Running had replaced my addictions.

It was now the end of December, 1988, just six months after I graduated from school, two months since I lost my job, and almost two months since I got clean and sober. Uncontrollable bingeing and purging were still consuming most of my days. I was shoving larger and larger quantities of laxatives into my body to make sure they got rid of any and all food that might cause me to gain an ounce of weight. My legs were bloated once again from the protein in my cells leaking out into them. My throat was raw and bleeding. I was physically run down almost to the point of collapse, and was setting myself up for osteoporosis from not menstruating in several years.

Then, one day, I hit my bottom with my eating disorder. I woke up and began my relentless daily routine of bingeing and purging, but this time I wasn't able to throw anything back up. Frustrated and panicked, tears rolled down my face. I tried for another hour to shove my fingers down my throat to get the horrible food out of me, but nothing happened. My knees were about to buckle. My face was bright red, and my eyes were almost swollen shut. All I could do was fall to the bathroom floor, crying and exhausted. My tears turned into self-hatred and then determination as I swallowed a box of laxatives and prayed that God would help me. Again, my body refused to cooperate. Pain began shooting through my stomach and chest, but I ate another box of laxatives and then drank a bottle of Epicac Syrup. By nightfall, there was still there was no response. I was terrified that my body had completely shut down. I lay in my bed alone and hating myself. Tears continued to flow and I cried myself to sleep.

The next morning, I was overwhelmed with nausea. Excruciating pain shot through my body so badly that I didn't think I could get out of bed. About to throw up, I tried to get to the bathroom. But when I stood up, I began to shake uncontrollably. My knees buckled and I fell to the floor. I tried again to stand up, and this time braced my body against the wall as I rounded the corner to the bathroom. Overwhelming pain shot through my stomach as my body produced massive amounts of watery diarrhea and I was overcome with dry heaves. I sat there shaking. My heart was beating fast and beads of sweat covered my face. I was scared because I felt like I was going to pass out, and somehow I had to get back to bed before I was unable to walk. Bracing myself again against the wall, I tried to get out of the bathroom. As I slid passed the mirror, I was horrified at reflection: my eyes were black and sunken in, my lips were blue, and my complexion ghostly. For a moment, I didn't recognize my own face, and I could no longer deny that something was terribly wrong.

It took several more bouts of collapsing and waking up on the floor before I made it back to my bed. I lay there staring at the ceiling, crying and afraid I was going to die. When my body became icy cold and I couldn't stay conscious, I knew I had to call someone for help. Calling Ann was out of the question because she would only hospitalize me, so I called my sponsor, Kyla.

As soon as I told her I needed help, my chest began to hurt, my breath grew shallow and I passed out again with Kyla still on the phone. About thirty minutes later I briefly regained consciousness with Kyla and another woman standing over me saying, "She looks like she's going to die." So they bundled me up, threw me into their car and rushed me to the emergency clinic.

I was unconscious when several nurses and orderlies unloaded me out of the car and took me to an examination room. Moments later, I came to long enough to hear the doctor telling Kyla, "You need to get her to the hospital as quickly as possible because her body temperature has dropped to eighty-six degrees, which is generally too low for anything living. And her blood pressure and heart rate are also virtually non-existent." They wrapped several warm blankets around me, threw me back into the car and rushed me to Hope Hospital.

At some point late in the evening, I woke up unsure of where I was. I realized by the tubes that were coming out of my arms and the bags of IV fluids hanging on a pole next to my bed, that I was in the emergency room. I was crushed. Once again, I was alone in the hospital for something I had done to myself. As I had done on similar occasions, I lay there silently crying and wondering why I continued to do this to myself. When a nurse entered my room to check on me, I quickly wiped away the tears and tried to hide my sadness.

"What's happening? How long have I been here?" I mumbled.

"The doctor kept you in the emergency room overnight instead of sending you to a regular bed because he was afraid you were finally going to end up dead this time!" she screeched. "The number of laxatives you ingested has completely wiped out your metabolic system, almost shut down your kidneys, and you were so dehydrated we had to put three bags of IV fluids in you!"

I bowed my head in shame and embarrassment and asked, "What's going to happen to me? Are you going to lock me up?" Her face suggested that she was hiding something, but she said, "I don't know anything" and quickly left the room.

I knew I had to see the doctor so I could talk my way out of trouble one last time. But as I lay there worried about my destiny, I wondered where Randy was and if he knew or cared about what was happening to me.

When the doctor finally arrived, he voiced his concern about my eating disorder, the number of laxatives I had taken, and the reasons why I took them. He also explained that he had spoken with Randy, who was on the way to the hospital to have me committed to the eating disorders program.

Panicked, I begged the doctor, "Please don't do that to me—I promise I'll be a good little girl if you will just let me go home." Even though one part of me wanted help, I knew that locking me up, doing daily weight checks, keeping me out of the bathroom, and forcing me to eat wasn't what I needed. I still just needed someone to love me. For someone to hold me and tell me that everything was going to be all right. For someone to help me get rid of my feelings about the past so I could start eating again.

My pleading fell on unsympathetic ears. So I said the same things to Randy and convinced him not to let them lock me up. In turn, he spoke with the doctor and explained that I wasn't going to be committed to the eating disorders program, but was going home. The physician shook his head and advised Randy to reconsider, but he took me home anyway.

Randy drove me back home, helped me to the couch and momentarily sat on the edge of the cushion. He gently kissed my forehead and stared at me compassionately. Without words, he conveyed his love and then left.

When I heard the door close, my heart broke. The only person I had ever loved was leaving me because I was defective and permanently damaged because of things other people had done to me as a child. I wondered why he wouldn't help me. Why didn't he love me enough to let me work through my problems so we could be together? All I could do was lie there and think about what had just happened, how much I loved Randy, and how much I hated myself.

I was startled back to reality when the phone rang. It was a lady named Hillary telling me that she was responding to resume I had sent her after I lost my job at the school. She said that she wanted me to come in for a job interview and insisted that it had to be done that day. I knew I couldn't say, "I'm sorry I can't come in for an interview today because I just got out of the hospital after almost killing myself with laxatives because of an eating disorder—can we do this tomorrow?" So I did what needed to be done and agreed to meet with her.

I had no idea how I would be able to make it through the interview without everyone being able to see who I truly was—a person who had only been clean and sober a couple of months and who had a very debilitating eating disorder. I was afraid that my ghostly complexion and sunken eyes would reveal that I had just gotten out of the hospital, but I made sure I dressed so no one could see my pencil sized arms or the punctures and bruises from the IV fluids.

I had a group interview with the staff, and then an individual one with the big boss. I found it difficult to focus on the questions at hand, but did the best I could. Embarrassed at being emaciated and sickly looking, I stared at the floor. By the end of the interviews, I had given up any hope of being hired.

"Do you want the job?" Hillary asked, looking at me compassionately, as if she knew my secrets. "You are the most qualified person we've interviewed."

I couldn't hear her compliment because of the internal voice that maintained my self-hatred and told me that she only wanted to hire me out of desperation and pity. Still, I accepted the position because I needed the income and a fresh start. Before leaving, everyone shook my hand and welcomed me as the new assistant program manager. My job was to complete vocational evaluations on people with disabilities and assist the program managers.

Enthusiastic and excited, I started my new job on January 4, 1989. I wanted to do a good job and not let my alcoholism, drug addiction, or eating disorder mess anything up this time. I was determined to do something right for a change.

After almost dying in the emergency room, I gave up the bingeing and purging and resorted to just starving myself again. Fruit and water were the only things allowed past my lips. I dedicated every spare moment I had to running up to fifteen miles a day, biking thirty miles at least three days a week, compulsively exercising in my living room, and running all the road races I could physically manage to run. Since I kept my food consumption down to about three hundred calories a day and maintained my exercise regime, I didn't need to binge or purge. My mastery of the bulimia left me feeling revitalized. I had forgotten how wonderful it felt to be in charge of my weight and food intake. I was eighty-four pounds and excited that I wasn't bingeing, purging or using laxatives anymore.

My new position not only provided me with a new lease on life, but with a boss I really liked. Hillary seemed to really have her life together. She was a beautiful thirty-two year old woman with short brown hair. She had her own home, a new car, and a bubbly personality that commanded everyone's admiration. I was impressed that she was always in a good mood and seemed to enjoy life. She was well respected as a supervisor and seemed to leave her professional and personal touch on everyone's lives. An intelligent woman who read a lot, she was especially well-versed in psychological treatises and books dealing with the human spirit. Conclusively, Hillary was the smartest person I had ever met and I wanted to be just like her.

Even though I enjoyed my job, I didn't feel comfortable at work. There were a few people who immediately picked up on the fact that I was anorexic and found it necessary to humiliate and tease me about it. Also, my sense of desperation and fear of getting into trouble began creeping back to the surface. Every day I would panic and become afraid that I had done something wrong and that Hillary would punish me like my mother used to do. The feeling was so strong I wanted to hide.

I also missed Randy and found myself wanting to reconnect with him.

Since I wanted more than anything to be successful and happy, I called a psychiatrist, Dr. Jamison, to see if he could help me. I hoped that he could help me get myself together enough so I wouldn't lose my husband, and could have sex with the only man I had ever loved, so I wouldn't be afraid at work anymore, and so I could start eating again.

It was extremely difficult to talk to Dr. Jamison or connect with him, especially since his only advice was, "Meditate and everything will be all right." Desperate and not knowing where else to turn, I lay on his couch once, sometimes twice, a week trying to pry open the hatches of my past. As the sessions progressed, I became frustrated because I didn't feel as if we were getting anywhere, especially with his ethereal techniques. I wanted to work on the sexual abuse and my past so I wouldn't lose Randy, but we didn't delve into those topics even though he was aware of my desire to do so.

Dr. Jamison finally glared at me and begrudgingly offered, "If you are compelled to look at the abuse issues, I'll help you with it, but Randy will have to be willing to do couple's counseling." I immediately latched onto his promising words as a sign that Randy and I could get back together again and live happily ever after. For the first time in a long time I felt alive and I wanted to save my marriage.

I ran out of Dr. Jamison's office filled to the brim with hope, jumped into my car and raced over to Randy's home to tell him the wonderful news. All the way there, I rehearsed what I was going to say, until I thought it was perfect in every way. When I arrived, he greeted my request to talk with a strange look on his face but said, "OK, but only for a few moments."

At first, I was so nervous I just stared at the ground. I then reached over and took hold of Randy's hand and babbled, "I've found someone who can help me with the sexual stuff so we can save our relationship. Can you give us a second chance and come to therapy with me?" Nothing but silence filled the air.

I slowly glanced up to see a look of confusion on his face and then heard him say, "No." His defensive tone of voice told me that he would never go back to therapy with me, or anyone else, after what happened in Darlene's office with Mom and Gene. I was crushed.

Desperate, I cried, "Please Randy—I'm begging you—don't throw us away!"

But my husband boldly stood there maintaining his firm stance that therapy was out of the question. That was when I realized that my marriage was over, and, there was nothing left but divorce.

I tried to choke back the tears as I whispered, "I can't file for divorce. If you want to give up on us, then you'll have to do it yourself." Randy just shook his head and walked away.

Broken-down and shattered with sadness and desperation, I didn't know what I was going to do now that I had lost my husband. I believed everything that was bad and wrong about our marriage was my fault. I told myself, "If only you could have slept with him, then none of this bad stuff would be happening and you could stay married."

Randy eventually filed for divorce and I didn't contest it. It would take several months to get the paperwork finalized, so I just waited. In some childish way, I thought if I ignored the whole process, it would go away and he would come back home to me, but I was just fooling myself.

At this point, it looked like there was no hope of things ever getting better for me. I had lost my best friend and husband, and was working in a place where most of the people hated me because of my anorexia. I knew I couldn't go back to drinking and drugging again and that left me with very limited options. So I stopped seeing Dr. Jamison and began fantasizing about killing myself.

Chapter 20

A Different Kind of Relationship

DEPRESSION AND SUICIDAL FANTASIES filled every minute of my day, but I didn't say anything to anyone. Pasting on my I'm okay face became tiring, so I locked myself in my office during the day and in my trailer at night. There were no phone calls to anyone and there were no friends—just suffocating silence and the lingering, taunting feelings that there was no hope left for me.

One day as I sat in my office silently crying and thinking about suicide, Hillary called me into her office. I immediately feared I was about to lose my job, for what I didn't know.

I took a deep breath and walked into her office. I dared not look at her but stared at the floor while I awaited my punishment. After a long pause she invited me to sit down and then asked, "What's going on with you? You haven't been yourself, and the grapevine has it that you're getting a divorce."

My heart broke because someone was finally asking if I was all right. I tried to remain silent so Hillary wouldn't see how weak I was, but I couldn't hold the tears back any longer. They began to fall as I admitted, "The gossip is true, I am struggling." When I heard my own words, I felt the familiar heaviness and realized that I had given up on myself.

Hillary tried to make things better by imparting some of her book-learned wisdom while I just sat there and listened. When the lecture was over, she asked, "Are you thinking about killing yourself?" I was startled that she had the courage to ask such a question, and yet amazed at her keen sense of intuitiveness. One part of me wanted to tell her the truth, but I couldn't. I didn't trust anyone at that stage of my life. So I continued to hide inside my shell to protect myself.

I stood up to leave, and she asked, "Why don't you come over to my house tonight so we can talk." I was confused as to why someone of

Hillary's caliber would invite me, of all people, to her place. Her invitation gave me the hope I needed to hang on a little bit longer—hope that I could admit my suicidal need, so I gratefully accepted her invitation.

When I arrived at Hillary's house that night she acted as if she was glad to see me. I was surprised that she maintained her usual light-hearted and humorous demeanor at home. She grabbed herself a beer and then gave me the nickel tour of her place. I marveled at her cute little house in midtown Savannah. I wanted a place just like hers one day, and it rekindled my desire to be just like her.

As the evening progressed, I found that I was extremely comfortable around her. We sat on her couch, listened to music and talked until about four o'clock in the morning. By that time, we both had shared a great deal about ourselves and Hillary had shown me some private things she had written regarding her life and personal struggles. Reading her memoirs, I felt a wonderful sense of belonging because someone trusted me enough to share their innermost thoughts and feelings with me. But, the pain and loneliness she had put down on paper also troubled me.

Somehow I vicariously lived Hillary's life experiences, which were filled with many emotional wounds and a persisting abyss of extreme loneliness. I could feel her emotional pain just as I could my mother's when I was a child. I was perplexed because what I had read didn't match the outgoing woman I knew at work. The masterfully written works also left me suspicious that my new friend wasn't only lonely, but gay. I was now confused. I didn't know what to think about my new friend, so I tried to push the uncertainty of Hillary's sexual orientation and dysfunctional life out of my mind because there was something about her that absolutely intrigued me.

By the end of the wonderful evening, Hillary was completely inebriated and I was tired from the long day of unpredictable emotions. But I was also thrilled because this was the first time I had ever experienced the wonderful feelings that came from connecting with another person in this way. I found it extremely life-affirming and wanted more encounters like this one.

Morning was only a couple hours away and it was obvious that Hillary's feelings of loneliness were taking control of her. She looked sad and said, "Spend the night with me—it's too late for you to drive the dangerous streets of Savannah."

I hesitated because I didn't know if there was a hidden agenda, especially since I wasn't sure if she was gay. I was afraid I would be getting myself into something that I wouldn't know how to get out of, much like what I had experienced with Gene and Miguel. I was also reminded of the feelings I'd had for Valerie when I was at her apartment for dinner; how I fled from her home and began using again when I thought something sexual was going to happen between us.

Hillary continued, "I just want someone to share my bed with— nothing more." I understood what it was like not to want to be alone, so I gave in to her request.

The new morning arrived and I woke up to find that the night went just as Hillary had promised. I loved the time we had spent together and I didn't want to go back to my lonely existence. The feeling must have been mutual because she hugged me and invited me to come back later that evening for another visit. I marveled at the possibility that I might actually have a friend and it made something inside my soul tingle.

As night quickly approached, I was extremely excited about spending more time with my new friend and having more long talks with her. That was what I had always wanted to experience with another human being and I couldn't believe it was finally happening to me at the age of twenty-five.

I arrived at Hillary's home once again where she greeted me with a smile, a hug and a firm grip on her can of beer. The evening proceeded much in the same manner as the previous one, sharing personal information about ourselves, mostly on Hillary's part. She also got drunk again, but I assumed it was merely a means of unwinding at the end of a very long day from an extremely stressful job.

As I listened to her talk about her past and who she was, her face became contorted with fear, as if she were about to divulge something that could only be shared in the strictest of confidence. So I focused my attention solely on her words. She stared at her beer and then confessed that she was gay. To justify her condition, she provided an endless flow of explanations about how she had figured it out, had tried to kill herself over it, and had been hurt by several of her past lovers.

I was honored that she felt safe enough to divulge her innermost secrets with me. I felt an incredible need to hold and comfort her and tell her that everything was going to be all right, but I refrained. By the time Hillary finished telling her stories, it was too late to drive home. With sadness and loneliness in her eyes, and grief in her voice, she whispered, "Can you spend the night again?"

I didn't know what to say. One part of me wanted to stay so I wouldn't have to be alone in my trailer, but another part was afraid because she was gay.

She took hold of my hand and said, "There's nothing to worry about." Somehow I believed her, so I agreed to stay one more night.

Once in bed I was startled when Hillary's voice emerged from the darkness to ask, "Is it all right if I hold you?"

Even though I craved someone to do that, I ignored her proposal and remained silent because of my fear. Seconds later, I felt her hand touch my shoulder. She pulled her body close to mine, placed her warm arm around me and held me close. My body grew rigid, afraid of getting hurt again, until Hillary whispered in my ear, ever so gently, "We don't have to do anything except lie here."

Despite the fact that my curiosity about homosexuality had peaked over the past couple of days, I wasn't ready for anything like that to take place between us. I only wanted the healing that could come from being held. So I lay there with Hillary's arms wrapped around me, my heart melting and silently crying because I couldn't believe how good it felt to be held. It was remarkable not to feel trapped, but completely safe. I thought I was in heaven.

Each day at work, Hillary and I played the roles of employer and employee even though we spent many nights and weekends hanging out together and enjoying each other's company. No one even suspected we were friends. During the times I wasn't with her, I was sad and felt isolated. I desperately tried to hide the fact that I missed my friend and the place inside me that she filled so well with friendship. I thought about her all the time.

Then something started happening to me that I didn't understand. Thoughts about Hillary being gay kept running through my mind, and I soon found myself wanting to discover what it was all about. Every time I thought about her, I quivered with excitement and dreams of getting closer to her.

Those feelings screamed out to be explored, especially since they were the same ones I'd had about Valerie. My own thoughts scared me, and I wondered what kind of a person it would make me if I were gay. Would I be stereotyped like everyone else? What would my mother and my brothers think? What would everyone else think? I had no idea what to do.

Despite my quandary, something tugged at my heart to try the gay thing and to see if it could explain why I couldn't be with Randy in a sexual way. But each time I wondered what it would be like to have Hillary love me and kiss me, my excitement was overshadowed by the memories of what happened with Gene, Miguel, and the other men who had abused me. So I pushed all thoughts about being with Hillary in a sexual way out of my mind.

I continued to enjoy her company so much that I rarely went home and almost forgot about my small private world on the marsh. Then, one day, I was sitting in Hillary's living room from another long night of talking while she drank her beer. Something inside told me this night was different somehow.

As I lay in her bed, basking in how great it felt to be held, I could sense that she was staring at me. My heart began to beat with excitement. Suddenly Hillary's lips pressed gently against mine. I melted with astonishment at how well a woman could kiss. It was definitely different from Randy. It was charismatic, gentle, and respectful—I really liked it. Inside, I soared with excitement as Hillary's lips fell upon mine once again. She began to touch my body and I shuddered with curiosity. In a matter of seconds, I was momentarily absent from the safe and warm bed I now occupied with Hillary. I was transformed back into a little girl lying in Gene's bed with him penetrating me, ashamed and guilty. Somehow she sensed my nervousness, and spoke the most wonderful words I had ever heard, "If we never had sex, I would still love you."

I began crying because of the warmth and understanding that one human being was giving me after all those years of torment and misunderstanding. I then wondered how a woman could understand those things but not a man. As promised, we spent the night just hugging and cuddling each other, never crossing the sexual boundary.

Hillary maintained her gentleness and patience. In a matter of weeks I felt so comfortable with her that I began exploring and participating in a sexual life with her. I was amazed to discover that it wasn't like being with a man. It wasn't rough, selfish, quick or one-sided. Instead, it was gentle, loving, caring, and involved a lot of time holding and caressing each other. I had truly found bliss. I didn't know that being with someone could feel so good.

It was hard going to work each day and acting as if Hillary and I were just friends. It was difficult not to touch her and talk to her in a warm and loving way, especially since every moment of my waking hours were consumed with how good she made me feel. I was in love and wanted to spend the rest of my life with her.

My relationship with Hillary brought with it the understanding that I was now gay. I was surprised at the ease with which I was able to embrace my new lifestyle and the comfort I found in welcoming my new identity. It was as if I had finally figured out who I was and it made everything fit together so nicely and neatly. But it didn't chase away the horrible things that happened to me as a child. There were several sexual activities that I still wasn't able to do because of the sexual abuse, even with a woman. The most important difference was that Hillary respected my past and my limitations. She didn't force me to do things that made me uncomfortable and her understanding was a great relief.

Even though Hillary and I remained companions and I loved her deeply, I continued starving myself. I didn't know how to make it stop, especially since my perception of how I looked was different from everyone else's. Hillary, Ann, and everyone around me constantly told me that I looked as if I were from Ethiopia because my bones protruded through my skin, my face was ash white, and my eyes were black and sunken in. No matter how much I looked at myself in the mirror or how much I exercised, I always saw myself as disgustingly fat. I hated how it felt to be in my own skin.

The anorexia escalated and so did the on-going physical problems including my passing out at work in front of everyone. But, no matter how much I tried, I couldn't eat, and I was too afraid to put anything but fruit and sugarless gum in my mouth.

Eventually, after passing out at work several times, the executive director called me into his office and said, "I'm going let you go if you continue to faint and don't put some weight on." When I realized that my job was on the line because I didn't know how to eat, my self-loathing returned with a vengeance. I left work that day, hating every thing about myself. I went to Hillary's house with a desperate need to talk to her and to find some answers. I broke down and cried as I told her, "I love you and I'm afraid I'll be fired because I don't know how to stop starving."

Surprisingly, Hillary wasn't sympathetic to my plight. Instead, she agreed with my supervisor and everyone else. When I saw her alliance with my enemies, I was afraid I wasn't only going to lose my job, but the one person I loved. I realized that the only way I was going to keep my job and Hillary was by getting my eating disorder under control.

Hillary saw the desperation in my eyes and assigned herself the role of helping me overcome my eating disorder. She didn't force me to take in mass quantities of calories, didn't weigh me, didn't prevent me from exercising, and let me move at my own pace while she prepared the meals and provided support. It was the beginning of an extremely slow and radically painful process of re-feeding my eighty-four pound body.

The re-feeding process initially consisted of nothing but broth, and went on for months. When my body was able to tolerate the liquids, Hillary started putting a small piece of skinless chicken in my broth. When I tolerated that, I advanced to pureed food and then soups and soft things like eggs and cream of wheat. After a great deal of hard work and many days of wanting to give up, I was finally able to tolerate solid food without excruciating pain.

There were many days I didn't think I would survive. My body cried out in pain while my mind played torturous games that told me I was fat, unlovable and a bad person; that I deserved to suffer. But somehow I managed to scratch and claw my way to survival during the 18 long months that it took me to get enough weight on my body so I could function without any further physical damage or the loss of my job. By the time we were done, I weighed in at ninety-six pounds. Even though that wasn't close to my ideal body weight of 120 pounds, at least I now had a fighting chance.

As my body grew stronger and the fog of the eating disorder began to lift, I became aware of something that I hadn't seen before. I noticed that Hillary was carrying around her own set of demons. I saw that her secret source of self-destruction was alcohol and that it protected her from the tragic memories of her family and a childhood that was void of any affection. I began to see that when she drank she always got drunk. When she got drunk she turned into someone I didn't know. Instead of being the wonderful, intelligent and caring person I had grown to love, she turned into a self-absorbed, unaffectionate, terribly depressed, spiteful and sometimes mean woman. Each time that happened, I felt like I was going to emotionally break because it was during those times that she took her love away from me.

It became progressively more difficult to hide the depth of the hurt and despair I felt when Hillary drank, and it eventually reawakened the small child within me that screamed out for someone to love and hold me. Hillary's drinking problem worsened until both of us were out of control and hopelessly needy.

Despite Hillary's drinking, I managed to stick with the eating regime because I held onto the hope that she would stop drinking one day as a sign that she loved me. My weight became relatively stable, and eventually I celebrated my one-year birthday of being clean and sober. As a present, Hillary said, "Sell your trailer and move in with me."

Even though my divorce wasn't final yet, I didn't see what harm it could do for me to move in with the person I loved. My spirit soared because her invitation meant that she loved me and that we were now life partners. I buried my apprehension and concerns about her drinking, and gladly gave up my sacred place on the marsh so I could be with her.

The trailer eventually sold and I had nothing left to remind me of the painful and lonely days of my addiction or my life with Randy, except for the scars on my arms and the pending divorce. I also stopped relying on AA and NA to help me abstain from my alcoholism and drug addiction, and instead became dependent on my relationship with Hillary to protect me from those self-destructive behaviors.

One day Randy called to say, "I've got the divorce papers and all you have to do is sign them." The finality of his words shook me. My heart remembered how much I loved him and that I knew he was my soul mate, despite the fact he wouldn't allow me the room I needed to change.

Even though I knew I was happy with Hillary, my heart ached. I believed it was my fault and that my inability to be a wife had caused Randy to leave me. I also believed that counseling would have worked for us and, if Randy had agreed to it, we wouldn't be doing this now. But, it was too late—I had lost my husband.

The next day Randy pressed his face against the glass door of my office where I was having a meeting. My breath grew shallow from nervousness when I saw him. Everyone in the room knew about the divorce, so no one dared say a word. I quietly excused myself from the now silent room.

Standing outside my office door, Randy bent down to kiss me. He seemed nervous, like the first time when he kissed me. I just stared at the floor and tried to hold back the tears that came from believing my husband was abandoning me. I took him down to an empty office where we could talk and I could sign the papers without being embarrassed at my defeat and failure as a wife and human being.

My hands shook as I bent over and signed the papers. For a moment I wondered if we were making a mistake. Tears welled up inside of me as I remembered how much I wanted and needed Randy to love me, just as I had needed my mother to do. We looked at each other solemnly as we realized that this meant we were no longer bound together as man and wife. He looked at me with sadness in his eyes and said, "I love you and always will." He bent down one last time and kissed me. As his lips pressed firmly against mine, my heart broke because he was my best friend and the love of my life. I wanted, more than anything, to be a normal heterosexual woman who hadn't been abused as a child and who could have sex with the man she loved. As I realized that I would never be normal and could never be intimate with a man, I felt hopeless and defective. Silence filled the room as Randy slowly turned and walked back down the long hall and out of my life.

Now that my divorce was final and I relied solely on my relationship with Hillary. I found comfort in the fact that I was gay and in love, even though it was with a woman who drank too much. But as usual, as soon as I allowed myself to relax and feel safe, all hell broke lose.

Terrible things started happening that I didn't understand and wasn't equipped to handle. I had always known that Hillary drank a lot, but I never fully understood the depth of the problem until now. She drank a minimum of a six-pack of beer every weeknight, and as much as a whole case of beer on each weekend night.

My days grew darker. I felt that Hillary had stopped loving me and that she no longer wanted to be around me. I watched my lover and companion dive into a precipice of depression, demanding to be left alone. She cut herself off from everyone as she drowned her sorrows in beer, old photographs, and sad songs. The alcoholic who resided inside me understood why she was doing those things because I used to do them myself. But it hurt and made me angry because she wouldn't let me help her like she had helped me. I was convinced that if she would stop drinking everything between us would be all right again. I really tried, but I couldn't understand why she wouldn't stop drinking for me like I had stopped starving for her. Was I not worth changing for?

After a while her uncontrollable drinking caused huge arguments between us. I would stand before her with tears in my eyes, trying to explain, "My heart breaks every time you get drunk. Our relationship is falling apart."

She would just stare back at me with emptiness and apathy in her eyes and say, "I don't care whether I live or die!" I understood that she was hurting herself for the same reasons I had hurt myself—she had never felt loved and it was her way of punishing her parents for their lack of affection. But Hillary didn't see it that way.

Instead, she blamed me for the problems in our relationship, "You're too needy and too angry—I can't always do what you need or want me to do. I'm only catering to your neediness because I don't want to upset you and you start starving again!"

She failed to see that she was drunk ninety percent of the time, leaving me to try to meet her needs so she wouldn't drink. But everything I said fell on deaf ears and Hillary remained in her cocoon of alcoholism and denial.

I, on the other hand, fell apart because I believed that no one would ever love me unconditionally. I felt as if I were being punished for the love I needed from Hillary to recover from my eating disorder. And, once again, my childhood fears and desperation began bleeding their way to the surface.

Even though I intellectually understood that it was Hillary who now had the problem, I struggled with guilt and self-hatred, until I eventually fell back into the same old trap of taking responsibility for everything. I was convinced I was a bad person and that everything, including Hillary's drinking, was my fault. Somehow, I forgot that she drank excessively before we became involved.

Hillary and I had been together almost two years when her drinking climaxed beyond my wildest dreams and produced situations that pushed me back down into the dark pit where my helpless, dissociative child lived.

She began hitting me when she got drunk. With each blow to my body, I stood there looking at her with tears flowing down my face. I wondered how she could have known the innermost secrets of my childhood—that my mother had hit me—and yet think it was all right to follow in her footsteps.

In the beginning, no matter how much Hillary hit me, I couldn't bring myself to fight back. I was merely being transformed back into that little girl who couldn't defend herself. After each strike from Hillary, I would glance under my arms to see the same look of anger and intention on her face that my mother had when she tried to provoke me into fights.

My refusal to fight back had the same effect on Hillary as it did my mother—infuriation. It made her hit me harder and harder while she screamed at me. But all I could do was stand there, crying and wondering why she was hurting me. I cowered like a wounded dog, not knowing what else to do.

"What's your problem?" Hillary screamed at me one night when I tried to ignore her drunken return home from a bar.

"I'm not going to argue with you, especially since you're drunk," I said tearfully, remaining seated. That infuriated her even more and she started yelling, "Everything's your fault—you're a pitiful human being!"

I sat there in silence and told myself that she was just trying to provoke me into a fight so she could say, "I told you so" and make it all my fault. I waited for her to finish verbally battering me so I could go to bed. When Hillary realized that she couldn't make me out to be the bad guy, she stood there confused and silent.

I got up from my chair and went into the kitchen to escape any further attacks, but she was right behind me, yelling and cursing. I turned and looked into her angry and inebriated eyes and begged, "Please leave me alone, or explain what I've done that was so bad that made you stop loving me."

She looked at me and then slapped me across the face, leaving my cheek red and stinging. I bowed my head in submission as she continued hitting me. My hands and arms assumed their usual position over my head, while she screamed at me, "Why don't you get mad and say what's on your mind...why don't you get angry and hit me back?"

"I can't hit you because I love you—I just want you to stop drinking so we can be together," I cried.

Her eyes glazed over with fury as she pushed me against the stove. As my body lay in pain over the old appliance, I flashed back to when Mom used to do the same thing to me. I could feel the anger starting to boil inside me.

Hillary continued shoving and hitting me and demanding, "Hit me back!" Then something happened, *I snapped.* I became filled with so much rage that I turned around, glared at her and then punched her right in the face. As soon as I realized what I had done, I remembered what it felt like to live at home where physical violence was a way of life and where I had always been the victim. I didn't wish that on anyone, including Hillary. I was immediately overcome with shame and guilt because I had fallen into the role of hurting someone I loved. I felt completely out of control.

Despite the obvious look of pain and astonishment in my eyes at what I had just done, Hillary got right back in my face. She pushed and yelled, "Get angry—hit me again!"

I just stood there shaking and stunned. She pushed me again, and then again, and then one time too many. Overwrought with rage and hatred, I hit her over and over again, not caring if I killed her. I was so tired of being unloved and hurt by everyone that I wanted to tear Hillary apart, limb by limb.

When I saw my fists balled up so tightly that my knuckles were white, felt my teeth clinched together and my eyes burning with anger, I realized I was acting on nothing but pure hatred and rage. I now had no control over what was happing to me. *I had become my mother.*

Unnerved and horrified, I ran out of the kitchen into my bedroom where I did nothing but cry with the same feelings I had as a child. That night changed me forever and it eventually became more than Hillary had bargained for.

With the dawn of a new day, came an emotional hangover like never before. I felt embarrassed, sad, and hopeless because the darkest side of my soul had been unleashed. I was once again at a place in my life where I couldn't control what was happening to me. The portal that led back to the physical abuse and emotional neglect from my mother, and all the horrible things that had happened to me had been unlocked. The deep, dark wounds that hadn't seen the light of day in years were ripped open. The hurts that had never been talked about screamed out to be heard. Injuries and memories that I had forgotten were brought back to life. I was no longer reacting only to Hillary's drinking and physical abuse, but to everything that had happened to me as a child.

Each bout of drunkenness now precipitated a hostile confrontation, which resulted in me drifting further and further out of control. In the middle of each argument, my desperate cry for Hillary to love me went ignored. My heart cried out in agony, as if I were dying.

Then, one evening, after Hillary got drunk, my desperate child started coming to the surface. My heart felt so vulnerable and was about to crumble. It reminded me of when I used to crouch in the corner of the kitchen when Mom would hit me, and all I wanted was for her to love and comfort me. The feelings overwhelmed me so much that I ran and hid in the corner of my bedroom between my bed and the wall, where no one could see me. I assumed a fetal position and tried to soothe myself by rocking back and forth. When I reached a trance-like state, I whispered the same phrase over and over to myself, "It's okay. It's okay." I tried to comfort myself so I wouldn't slip off into that dismal world of insanity. Feeling completely abandoned and as if there was no hope of anything ever changing in my life, I begged God to make Hillary—or someone— come to my hiding place, hold me and tell me that they loved me. But no one came. I was left with the terrible belief that there wasn't now, nor would there ever be, any hope for me.

Eventually, my suicidal feelings were glaring like a neon sign. Frustration and hurt ate away at my soul while Hillary got drunk again. This time I blew apart with rage and almost destroyed the whole house.

The next morning I was so emotionally hung over that I could barely function enough to get dressed for work. I just sat on the edge of my bed feeling utterly defeated. I didn't know what to do with the monster Hillary had unleashed. I felt lost in a thicket of emotional turmoil that was so complicated I couldn't understand it and couldn't change it without help.

Not knowing who else to ask, I begged Hillary, "Please tell me what's wrong with me and why I can't control my rage."

Smugness spread across her face as she offered some nonsensical, psychoanalytical reason for my behavior. I knew she was wrong, that I was losing her, and I was falling apart. Spiritually, I was tired and felt I had nothing left to live for. I knew I was about to kill myself because I believed it would make all the bad things disappear. Even though I didn't want to have to resort to that option, I didn't know what else to do or who could help me.

Chapter 21

Emotional Crossroads

I MADE IT TO WORK and sat in my office with the door closed and the lights off. I wondered how much longer I could scrape up enough energy just to breathe and put one foot in front of the other. I hated myself and my life. There still wasn't anyone to love me. Tears rolled down my cheeks—I felt like my best friend has just died.

I was at a crossroad—I was either going to kill myself or find someone who could help me.

A small, fragile voice inside then whispered, "If you can get your rage and depression under control, Hillary will love you again." So I decided to find a psychologist who could help me. After several calls I was referred to Susan Lamb, a psychologist who specialized in my area of need. When I spoke with her on the phone, she explained, "I'm sorry— I have a full caseload."

I couldn't stop myself from sobbing and pleading, "Please, you have to help me—I'm going to kill myself if someone doesn't help me—please, please help me."

"Alright Sandy, I'll see you this afternoon, but only for an evaluation. If it doesn't look like I can help you, then I'll have to refer you to someone else."

I arrived at her office with hope fluttering inside my heart. Moments later, a thin woman in her late forties walked down the stairs. I immediately liked Susan because she reminded me of someone who grew up in the sixties: a flower child with a sense of inner peace.

Nervously sitting in the office, I told her, "I'm gay and in a relationship with a woman who is an alcoholic and physically abuses me. I feel out of control and I'm spiraling back down a familiar path of self-destructiveness that I've been away from for a while. I'm a recovering addict and alcoholic and I don't want to end up using again just because of the feelings Hillary has stirred up in me about my childhood. I'm having violent outbursts when she gets drunk and she takes her love away from me."

I was stunned at the words I spoke so freely, and realized it was the first time I had walked into a therapist's office and revealed important things, rather than superficial stuff that lacked any emotional component. I was truly desperate for help and knew at some level that if I didn't tell her what was happening she wouldn't treat me and I'd end up dead or lost forever.

At the end of my confession, I stared at the floor while Susan finished writing her notes. Tears were dripping onto my lap. I looked up to see Susan take a deep breath and smile, as she said, "I'm willing to work with you, Sandy."

Joy leapt through my heart—I was happy because I believed I was going to be all right and that Hillary would love me again!

This was the beginning of my journey with Susan and I started seeing her twice a month.

I had a picture in my mind of who I wanted to be and how I wanted to act, but, it seemed that I couldn't control the painful feelings long enough to get there. And seeing Susan didn't immediately change those feelings, even though she provided me with the hope and friendship I needed to keep holding on to life and the possibility that I might become emotionally self-sufficient one day. Her positive attitude and vision of who I was gave me a goal to work toward. I wanted to be the person she envisioned because it matched who I had always wanted to be. I wanted to be emotionally healthy and be able to accomplish anything I set my mind to. I wanted to be independent, self-confident and full of life. I was determined to work hard and learn everything I could about recovering. My goal was to be just like my well-adjusted counselor and friend, Susan.

During that time, I also met a new friend: a stray dog who wandered onto the front porch of our house. She was a small brown and white hound with beautiful brown eyes. She looked lost and like she needed a friend as much as I did. One part of me wanted to keep her, but I wasn't sure if I could take on that kind of responsibility just yet. But Hillary encouraged me to keep her. I knew I needed friendship, even if it was only from a dog, so I thought, "Why not?" I called her Chelsey, and she kept me company when Hillary was drinking.

Training Chelsey was difficult; she made me angry when she didn't do what she was told. Several times I hurt and disciplined her more than I should have. I felt guilty and ashamed. I questioned who I was becoming, especially if I couldn't be kind to a dog. I hated the fact that she tapped into the feelings I had as a child, and I couldn't control them. It was then I realized that I should never have children because I would end up physically hurting them, even though I loved them.

I would sit and cry about how I was hurting Chelsey, even though I knew I loved her and that she was my best friend. We ran together and hung out all the time. She was my sidekick and my confidante. She helped me hang in there with Hillary. I couldn't imagine my life without her.

Life with Hillary was getting progressively worse. She continued drinking excessively. With each bout of drunkenness there was a fight. I was still losing control, breaking things and acting out. I still wasn't at a place where I could control the overwhelming feelings that Hillary tapped into when she got drunk and hit me

Eventually, there wasn't any positive communication between us. We were going in different directions. I was focused on therapy and resolving the feelings that were running rampant inside me, while Hillary was drowning herself in booze and frequent job changes because her alcoholism was affecting her work performance. Somewhere deep inside we still loved each other, but neither one of us knew how to break the vicious cycle we were in.

Then, one day, I finished some gardening and wanted to spend some time with Hillary. I went into the dark living room, sat on the arm of her chair and whispered, "Sweetie, come outside with me, it's a beautiful summer day." I thought this might help us recapture some of the love and friendship we had lost. But Hillary didn't respond. She just sat there with a beer in one hand and a book in the other. I asked again, but this time she only slurred, "No."

It was then that I realized it was too late, she was already drunk. I was so hurt and sad.

I screamed, "I'm tired of your drinking and isolating yourself...why can't you just love me?" Hillary ignored me, and walked away to get another beer. At that very moment I thought I would die if she didn't put her arms around me, and help me feel as if everything was going to be all right. My mind raced with fury and feelings of abandonment. I wondered why God was still punishing me.

"Hillary, please just love me and stop drinking so we can be happy!" I wailed.

She stared back at me in a drunken stupor, and screamed, "Everything's your fault!"

That was it—my heart broke and I was back to being the angry teenager. Rage was building inside me. I looked at my hands that were now balled up into tight fists and realized I was about to hurt Hillary. I felt the urge to explode, to break things. I wanted her to hug me and make this stop, but she wouldn't. So I ran back to my corner behind the bed and tried to rock myself so the demons would go away, but it didn't work this time. Instead, my old pal, suicide, began knocking on the door of my heart.

I kept rocking while Hillary kept drinking. I got to the point where I couldn't take it any more, so I grabbed my Last Will and Testament and stash of pills and ran for the car, heading for Tybee Island to kill myself.

As I drove to the island, a veil of tears covered my face. Inside I knew I didn't want to have to resort to killing myself; I just wanted the pain and hurt to go away. My thoughts flashed to Susan and I wondered if she could help me. I knew I trusted her, but I was afraid she would lock me up if she understood how suicidal I was this time. Thinking about it more, I decided that death was still more frightening.

I stopped at the nearest phone booth and called Susan's office only to find that she wasn't in. Desperate for help, I told the on-call psychologist, "I want to hurt myself—please page Susan, she's the only one who can make the bad feelings go away."

I was placed on hold as they tried to find her, but somehow we got disconnected. I didn't know what else to do so I got back into my car, heading to Tybee Island. Terrified of succeeding this time with ending my life, I headed back to the phone booth to try calling Susan one more time. Before I could get there, a police car pulled me over. I was frightened as the two police officers demanded that I get out of the car. They told me that Hillary had called 911 stating I was suicidal, so they were taking me to Georgia Regional Hospital. Panicked and crying, I explained that I needed to see Susan, and convinced them to call her.

Surprisingly, the police were able to track her down. Susan explained that I didn't need to be locked up and she was on her way to get me! Once there, she convinced them to release me into her custody and took me back to her office to talk about what had happened.

Two hours of gut-wrenching and painful discussion took place about Hillary, what happened and what she was triggering from my past. Somehow the session that day made something inside me change. I finally understood that I truly had someone on my side, and that I didn't have to fight my battles by myself anymore. So I went home, determined to handle everything differently.

I started focusing all my energy on my own recovery process, and stopped reacting to Hillary in an angry and suicidal fashion. I worked diligently on my issues with Susan and allowed her to help me.

She explained, "Our goal is to find the parts of you that are calling out from a different time in your life; the child inside you that was hurt and is now destructive to you as an adult. We have to try to integrate her with the new parts of you."

Again, the problem was that I didn't know how to feel what we were talking about and that frustrated me. I wanted to feel the things I was sharing with her. Thus, I was only able to verbalize and revisit some of the critical memories, like when I was hiding in my closet in Santa Monica, feeling violated when Mom invaded my privacy by letting my brothers into my sacred place. We talked about how I took care of my brothers when I was young and how out of control my folks were. I could feel the pain in my heart, but somehow it would get stuck in my throat so I couldn't express the words and feel the feelings at the same time. So I usually just talked from my head in the therapy sessions, and then suffered the emotional consequences when I was alone.

Susan said, "You're a paradoxical individual—you're very fragile, yet you have a lot of strength. It's extremely important for you to live out the vision you hold of yourself which lies buried deep within your soul. You are bright, talented, and have a strong will to overcome everything that has happened to you. And I know you won't rest until you figure out how to rid yourself of the unbearable memories and torturous feelings about your mother and your childhood. You have to survive even though it is periodically complicated by a dire need to hurt and punish yourself for the past." Her words made sense, and I hoped that she was right— that I was a *survivor*.

My life kept changing and demanding my involvement. I still loved and admired Hillary for the person she was when she wasn't drinking and hurting me. And in a small, silent place inside me, I still held onto the hope that one day we would be all right again.

I started graduate school at the University of Georgia in Athens. I went to school one week a month and worked the remaining three weeks to satisfy my practicuum requirements. As long as I worked in the field and maintained my grades, my tuition and some of my book, lodging, and transportation expenses were paid for by the university.

Even though I was back in school, it didn't change the fact that I still hated my job. It didn't matter how much I tried or what I did to make things better, there was always someone lurking around the corner, waiting for me to make a mistake. The workplace revolved around people lying about each other, stabbing each other in the back, and trying to sabotage each other, just to move up the organizational ladder. I hated the games.

I was tired of living in constant fear that I would be in trouble for something I hadn't done. It was becoming more than I could handle.

Each day that went by, I felt more oppressed. I was emotionally exhausted, sick all the time and started missing a lot of work. Afraid there was something wrong with me, I decided to see a doctor. To my surprise the physician said, "The cause of your ailments aren't physiological, but the result of work stress and living with an alcoholic. In short, you're depressed."

At first I didn't believe her, but after much consideration I was afraid that she might be right. And if she was, maybe there was some medication that could permanently take away the suicidal feelings, make me like my job and help me live with an alcoholic who drank herself into oblivion every night.

The physician prescribed an anti-depressant, but I wasn't sure I could follow through with taking it. I felt guilty about it. I also was afraid of being stigmatized, so I voiced my concerns to Susan. I explained that I didn't want to be one of those "emotionally unstable" people who needed to take medication to be normal, or rely on an anti-depressant to change the way I felt. I also admitted that I was afraid I wouldn't be able to resolve my problems if I couldn't feel anything because of the drug.

Susan merely said, "I can't see any harm in taking the medication. Try it for a while, and, if you don't like it, you can always quit." So I agreed to take the medicine even though it didn't make me feel any different.

Because of my relationship with Hillary, Lydia and Dr. Russ became an almost non-existent part of my life. I missed them. But I was too afraid of telling my surrogate parents that I was in a relationship with a woman and that she was an alcoholic. I believed it was best to hide the relationship so there wouldn't be any chance of them meeting and Hillary embarrassing me. I couldn't run the risk of having the people I held in the highest regard thinking badly about me and my new lifestyle.

I finally graduated with my master's degree from the University of Georgia, at the age of twenty-nine. I was ecstatic and relieved that the long and arduous process of school was over, and that I had survived it with a perfect grade point average! Unfortunately though, Hillary and Lydia would now have to meet at my graduation ceremony.

As suspected, Hillary acted so cold and distant towards Lydia that she left the ceremony early without saying good-bye. Hillary's aloofness and inexcusable behavior drove away the only person I considered my family. She then finished off the evening by getting uncontrollably drunk at the graduation celebration we had with some friends in Atlanta.

I was astounded that my lover and companion had been so self-centered that she couldn't put herself aside long enough for me to feel good about myself or to receive congratulations from other people. I was now at the place where I wasn't willing to continue dealing with Hillary's drinking and lack of respect for my needs, but I didn't know what to do about it just yet.

The next day I called Lydia and told her, "I need to apologize for Hillary's behavior and I need to tell you something. I'm gay, Hillary is my lover and she's an alcoholic."

She replied, "It's okay, Sandy—I already figured it out. But you have to deal with Hillary's drinking because that's not a safe environment for you or your recovery."

I knew that I should stand up for myself, demand that Hillary either get sober or I would leave. But somewhere inside I was still too afraid of losing her and being alone. So I said, "Lydia, I promise I'll think about what you're saying."

"Good. And Sandy, I fully support your being gay."

Graduating from school opened my life up to new professional and personal experiences that excited me. My co-workers threw me a huge graduation party and then my supervisor promoted me to the position of director and manager of a new program they were opening. My new responsibilities of designing a program from the ground up and establishing a working relationship with other agencies in the community were exciting. One of my responsibilities was to hire a staff. I immediately found two people worthy of the challenge. Karen, a job coach I had worked with in the past, and Deborah, a person who was very earthy, artistic, and believed in approaching life from an alternative perspective.

We worked really well together and relied on each other for moral support and friendship, in and outside the workplace. Karen was the most normal one in our group. She'd had a pretty decent childhood and seemed fairly stable. She had been married for over 25 years and had three kids who appeared to be well adjusted. Deborah, on the other hand, came from a troubled family, much like my own. She, too, was left with a lot of the same feelings that only come from surviving the worst circumstances. Those life experiences left her permanently scarred with the same low self-esteem and depression that I had.

Of the three of us, I had the most unstable home environment because of Hillary's drinking. Both Karen and Deborah witnessed how life with Hillary was when they occasionally came over to visit. I was embarrassed that my friends saw how beaten down I was, and that I didn't have the courage to leave her. But their comments and observations were helpful because they allowed me to understand that I wasn't the only one seeing Hillary's drinking and behavior as a problem.

Not long after my promotion, my brother, Pat, called to say, "I'm in Savannah because Gene is in hospital with lung cancer. They're going to remove a lung to see if they can eradicate the disease. Will you come to visit him tonight? Mom and I will be there."

My mind raced, telling me that I couldn't do it. But I was also torn because I didn't know if it would be wrong not to go. I didn't give him an answer, but merely said I would think about it. I felt ill. I didn't want to see Mom or the man who had abused me. Not knowing what to do, I spent the rest of the afternoon panicked and confused. After Hillary came home from work, I asked her what I should do.

"You should NOT go see him after what he did to you—hold on to your anger and don't give him the satisfaction of seeing you again!" she said with bloodshot eyes.

Her harsh, drunken words were difficult for me to swallow. No matter how much I considered her theory, I couldn't find peace with the idea of letting someone die, thinking I was angry with them. And, I didn't want to make another person feel abandoned like I had felt in the past.

I agonized for hours before I finally decided to go to the hospital to see Gene. But I didn't leave until late in the evening because I didn't want to run into Mom. As I drove to the hospital, the memories of what Gene had done to me came flooding back. I sat in my car for what seemed like forever trying to find the courage to face him. My legs trembled and my heart was heavy as I found my way into the large Catholic hospital, meandering through the halls until I found the small intensive care unit.

I walked into his room and was immediately taken back by how thin and frail he looked, and then by the fact that he appeared glad to see me. He seemed lonely and vulnerable, as though he knew he might die soon. I didn't know what to say, so I tried to fill our time with small talk. The more I talked, the more my feelings began to overwhelm me. Tears welled up in my eyes for the little girl he had hurt so long ago, but also for him because I knew he was facing death. So I took hold of his hand, and said, "I don't harbor any ill-feelings against you because of the things you did to me. I'm not angry anymore; I've forgiven you."

I didn't know how what I was saying could be true, but I didn't know how to feel animosity toward him either. He turned his head, looked at me mournfully and said nothing. In one sense, I was frustrated because

I was still left without validation from him about what he had done. But I was also relieved because he wouldn't die thinking I was angry.

The room was filled with silence once again. There were no words left that could break the stillness of the moment. So I turned and slowly walked out of the room with the pain and hurts of my past welling up inside of me.

I desperately wanted Gene to believe what I had said, even though I wasn't sure I had come to terms with everything he had done to me. I knew that I had forgiven him, but I wasn't sure the issues were resolved.

Surprisingly, Gene survived the hospitalization, started radiation therapy and dropped out of my life again.

As time passed, I became more intolerant of Hillary's drinking and watching her slowly kill herself. Because my old coping mechanisms of starvation, drinking, drugging, and compulsively exercising were extinct, I had to discover different ways of dealing with things. I needed something constructive to hold onto that would let me know everything was okay. Glowing with fresh ideas, I thought that if I went to church and found God then I could persuade Him to help me, and convince Hillary to stop drinking. So I pleaded with her, "Hillary, please come to church with me."

She just glared at me, burning a hole right through my soul. She then said, "You're stupid," turned around and picked up another can of beer.

Since Hillary wouldn't go to church with me, and I was too afraid to go alone, I signed up for martial arts classes. I started taking Tae Kwon Do and found that I loved the forms and rituals. I attended classes every night and began feeling confident and centered. When I was in class wearing my sparkling white uniform, and gracefully moving through the air with purpose, I felt free and capable of anything.

Meanwhile, Hillary stayed at home and slipped deeper and deeper into her alcoholism. We continued fighting, but I maintained control and abstained from getting outwardly violent. However, I still found that I wanted to hurt myself when Hillary was drinking and treating me badly. But I didn't know what else to do or how to help her. In desperation, I went to see a female counselor who was also a chaplain at Hope Hospital. In essence, she confirmed what I knew had to be done.

So I went home and said, "Hillary, we need to talk." She didn't disagree, but chose to sit on the front porch in front of God and everyone in the neighborhood. I whispered, "Hillary, you have to stop drinking or I'm going to move out."

She looked at me with disdain in her eyes and yelled, "I won't stop drinking for you, or anyone."

I cried, but continued, "Then I have no choice but to move out."

She looked at me in disbelief, like I wouldn't follow through with my ultimatum, but I knew I had to.

I spent the next several weeks trying to get used to the idea that I was leaving Hillary as I searched for another place to live. Surprisingly, my sponsor, Kyla, offered to let me move into a small, one-bedroom efficiency apartment that was connected to the side of her home. Excited, I went over to see it. It was tiny, but a great solution to my immediate problem and it was the right price until I could afford to buy my own house. The only problem was that Kyla wouldn't let me bring my dog, Chelsey, with me. So I had to ask Hillary if she could keep her until I found a house. Fortunately, she loved Chelsey as much as I did and agreed to keep her. She promised to keep her safe and treat her kindly until I got my own place.

The day arrived for me to move out of our home. It was very tense and uncomfortable because Hillary watched my every move. Her eyes seem to glare through me, but I kept on going until it was time for me to tell her good-bye.

I walked into the living room where she was standing with a can of beer in her hand. "I'm surprised that you've moved everything out," she sneered.

"I have to move everything out for now, but I love you and I wish things were different so we could stay together."

She put the can of beer to her lips and with a blank, emotionless look on her face said, "I'll see you around sometime."

I tried to hold back the tears as I hugged her one last time. Then I walked out, jumped into the truck I had borrowed and drove to my new place. Sitting alone in the small apartment I felt sad and lonely. My heart still ached for Hillary to love me enough to stop drinking. My thoughts then turned to Mom and the painful experiences I'd had with her. I was alone again, listening to sad music and lying rolled up in a fetal position on the floor, wishing I could kill myself to make the pain go away. But somewhere in the back of my mind, I knew I had to hang on.

Chapter 22

Compromises

Because my relationship with Hillary had ended, it was imperative that I continue seeing Susan for counseling. She was the only one who could help me deal with my suicidal feelings, my child who cried out for love and my feelings of worthlessness. She helped remind me that I wasn't making a mistake by leaving Hillary, but reinforced how much I had to look forward to. Like the good patient, I kept my eyes fixed on her so my feelings wouldn't cause me to do something stupid.

I also began developing a new friendship with one of the women I hired at work. Karen and I started spending a lot of time together because she liked coming to Savannah to get away from her husband. She usually ended up at my place where we would spend most of the day talking about what was happening in our lives, what it was like for her to have sex with men, and silly things that only women talked about. It was great having someone to just hang out with, a buddy.

Then, one day, Karen and I were hanging out having one of our usual "talk about everything days" at my place. The conversation had stretched on for hours as Karen shared many private details about herself and her sexual experiences with her husband. Despite her so-called normal romantic life with him, I still found it difficult to believe that women enjoyed sex with men. After a while, the details of her sexual interludes not only disgusted me, but exhausted me. So I closed my eyes, hoping to take a short nap.

Moments later, I felt something touching my lips. Frightened, I opened my eyes. Karen's lips were pressed lightly against mine. I was startled, and yet surprised because she told me she believed that homosexuality was a sin.

I fearfully held my breath and wondered what I would say. But I remained silent as I had learned to do so many years ago. Not knowing what else to do, I slept with her.

Afterwards, I was stunned at how easily Karen had fallen into the freedom of making love with a woman, and that it didn't seem to tax her religious beliefs or personal view of herself one bit. Instead, I was the one who couldn't handle it. I was so confused. It was the first time I felt as if I had done something wrong after being sexually intimate with a woman. I wondered why I had never had those bad feelings after sleeping with Hillary. I tried to analyze what made this so different, but I didn't have any answers.

The next day at work I was so uncomfortable around Karen that I couldn't look at her. Guilt and remorse plagued my every thought. Why, I didn't know. I didn't know what to do.

Desperate for some type of resolution, I pulled Karen aside and tearfully told her, "I don't feel right about what we're doing. After all, you're still married, you're 15 years older than me and this goes against your religious beliefs."

I could sense that my words caught her off guard and made her nervous. But she looked deep into my eyes and said, "Being with you in a sexual way feels right to me, but it doesn't have to happen again if you don't want it to."

I knew I didn't want a sexual relationship with her, but I didn't know how to speak that truth. I was too afraid of hurting her feelings and was too desperate for someone to love me.

By the end of the day, Karen asked if she could come over so we could talk this through. I didn't see anything wrong with that so I agreed. Once at my place, the atmosphere grew thick with tension and I finally found the courage to say, "I can't sleep with you again because it's too difficult, and it brings up too many old memories for me."

Karen looked disappointed as she said, "OK then, I'll just be your friend." We talked a while longer and before we knew it, it was time for her to go home to her family. But when she stood up to leave she started crying and asked, "Can I move in with you? I'm miserable at home and I'm leaving my husband. I can't take living with him anymore."

Since she was now just my friend and I felt sorry for her, I allowed her to stay with me until she could find her own place. I knew it would be crowded in the room that was only large enough for a king-size bed and a dresser, but I couldn't let my friend end up homeless. Now that she had a new place to live, she seemed happy and asked to stay the night.

Lying in bed with Karen, I felt uncomfortable and nervous—almost like I did when I thought Gene might come into my room at night wanting sex. Moments later, she was kissing me. My breath grew shallow and my body tense. Afraid to say anything, we ended up having sex again.

The next morning, I felt just as guilty as I had before and it was eating at me. Karen, on the hand, kept saying, "I love you, and I was wrong about God, and about homosexuality being a sin."

Her words only confused and perplexed me further. How was I going to tell her how I felt without hurting her? And how could I throw away attention and love that someone was willing to give me, even if it didn't look the way I imagined it would? The truth was that I couldn't. So I comprised myself, pushed aside the fear and doubt I had about Karen, and jumped into a relationship with her.

Karen moved in and assumed the role of taking care of me. She gave me the physical attention I craved and a reason not to self-destruct. We spent every spare minute of our day with each other, as if we had been friends all our lives. There was a connection between us and I soon found it wonderful that she always made me laugh, even when things were dark and gloomy.

Just weeks after I moved out of Hillary's home, I received a call at work. "Come over right away—there's something wrong with Chelsey," Hillary screamed into the phone.

I threw the phone down and sped over to her house, dreading what I might find. I was afraid that Chelsey was sick, had broken a bone that would require surgery or even worse. By the time I got there, I had concocted just about every imaginable scenario except the one I was faced with. Without allowing the car to come to a complete stop, I threw the door open and ran to the porch as fast as I could. My eyes fell upon Chelsey lying motionless on the floor. Tears welled up in my eyes and my heart felt as if it were breaking in two. My knees buckled as I reached over to touch my lifeless friend who was now cold and unable to open her beautiful brown eyes to look at me. It was at that moment that my biggest fear came true, I had lost my best friend and confidante. Filled with overwhelming pain, I threw myself over Chelsey's body and cried and prayed that God would forgive me for being bad and that He would give Chelsey back to me. Agony and despair enveloped me much like it did when I had lost my pink kitty.

As Hillary witnessed the depth of my pain, she mournfully confessed that she had taken Chelsey to her sister's house without my permission. It was there that Chelsey had escaped from the backyard, found her way into the busy streets of Wilmington Island and was hit by a speeding motorist. I was so crushed I didn't know what I was going to do. I couldn't believe my best friend was dead and that I was truly alone now. I wondered what I had done to deserve this. I was convinced that my world and my life had just come to an end. I had no idea how I was going to handle this situation.

I just sat there and held Chelsey as I whispered, "I love you and I'm sorry. You were the best thing that ever happened to me, and I wish I could have been a better mother to you. No matter how angry I got with you, I loved you and I'm glad you were my girl." Stroking her head one last time, my heart finished breaking.

I glanced up to see a look of sorrow on Hillary's face, and that kept me from expressing my anger to her for what she had done. Instead, I fell back into my old childhood behaviors where it wasn't all right or safe enough for me to get angry or mad with anyone. I was still the scared child who was always too afraid of hurting someone else's feelings and never stood up for myself. I just walked away.

A week after Chelsey's death, I got a call from Mom. She decided it was time to start talking to me again. I immediately thought, "Why now?" In any case, I remained cautious and tried not to reveal too much information, especially about my being gay. I told her about work, the divorce, and that I was looking for a house to buy.

"You need help buying a house, so you don't make a mistake," she said. One part of me was afraid to tell her "You're wrong", while the other part longed for her love and attention, for us to be mother and daughter. So I didn't resist her assumption.

As I should have predicted, we looked at several houses together, she decided which house she thought I should buy and eventually hounded me into buying it. I was disappointed because it wasn't my dream home and it was more than I could afford. I felt like a child again—afraid that if I didn't do what she wanted, I would end up making a mistake and she would leave me again. So I gave in to my mother one more time.

Because the house was more than I could afford, I didn't have enough money to make the down payment. So Mom offered to make it for me. I think it provided her with a means of appearing like the perfect mother who always rescued her floundering daughter, and provided her a way of burying all the times she had hurt me.

The house needed a lot of renovations, so I got caught up in doing the repairs, painting and construction projects. Without warning, I started having those old feelings I had as a teenager in Felicity when I worked on the old farmhouse, afraid I wouldn't be able to finish it without going crazy. It put a strain on my relationship with Karen because I was easily frustrated, placed myself under impossible deadlines, and felt as if nothing I did was good enough.

To complicate things even further, Mom insisted that she was going to help with the restorations. I believed it was only so everyone would think, "Look what Sandy's mom is doing for her...look how great and supportive her mother is." As if that would erase, in her mind, everything that had ever happened to me. I became uncomfortable and angry with her because it was yet another convenient way for her to erase my childhood and invalidate everything I knew to be true. I was grateful for the help, but I didn't trust it. I was afraid she would use it against me for the rest of my life.

I tried to put the past aside long enough to give Mom a fair chance at behaving differently. But, as usual, it was difficult working with her because she turned into the mother I remembered in Felicity who was argumentative, overbearing and always provoking fights. Again, I survived another renovation ordeal by telling myself, "Hang in there...you can do it this time."

It wasn't long before Mom started expecting me to take care of her again, and I fell into the role of needing to do it, hoping it would erase her pain and make her love me. She would tell me how bad her life was with Gene and, and like the well-trained child, I felt responsible. She came over to my house regularly, wandering through my life and my home whenever she wanted. I pampered her with warm baths, dinner invitations, and let her hang out with Karen and me for "girls nights." For the first time, I actually enjoyed spending time with my mother and felt a spark of a connection.

However, taking care of her became a chore again. She wanted more and more of my time, even if it wasn't convenient for me or Karen. I grew to hate her unbearable and overwhelming expectations. Eventually, I tried to stand up for myself by asking for some personal space. All I got was her standing in front of me, wallowing in self-pity. It was all I could do not to lash out at her. But like the good little girl, I tolerated everything until one evening when Mom, Karen and I were outside on the porch having dinner.

Somehow we began talking about the past and some of the things that had happened when I was growing up. Without warning, Mom became defensive, started crying and screamed, "I did the best I could, and what happened to you wasn't my fault. I don't want to talk about it anymore!" As I sat there listening to her portrayal of innocence, I felt like I was suffocating. I wondered if Mom would ever acknowledge that she had hurt me. Or if she was ever going to help make it better so we could be mother and daughter without the constant reminder of the past hovering over us. Suddenly, I had an idea.

"Mom would you go see Susan with me so we can try to resolve the past and be mother and daughter?" Annoyed, she just glared at me. I begged and pleaded with her to go, and after much discussion, she reluctantly agreed.

Susan graciously welcomed Mom to the session and explained, "The purpose of you being here is to help Sandy overcome some of things that still haunt her, and not to find fault with anyone."

Susan looked at me and silently encouraged me to speak the truth. My heart pounded and my voice trembled as I said, "There was the incident in Kentucky where you whipped my brothers with a belt when they were wet in the bathtub. Then you beat me after you forced me to take off my shirt in front of my brothers and hold—"

"You're a liar," Mom screeched, interrupting me. She looked at Susan and started talking to her as if I wasn't even there. "I didn't do anything to Sandy—I only remember the terrible things Gene did to her! He was the one who molested her; I never did anything. She was the one who caused me to worry about her by drinking and doing all those drugs. I was the one who was terrified she was going to kill herself." She acted like she had been the perfect mother and had been a victim in everything that happened when I was a child. I couldn't believe it.

Susan tried to bring up the rest of the physical abuse; how I felt that Mom had never loved me. Again, she looked at me hatefully and spat, "She's a liar—I never hit any of my kids, much less, beat them." Without another word, she stood up and stormed out of Susan's office.

My spirit was broken as I just sat there in silence, wondering why Mom always walked out on me. I also realized that the truth was still a secret and there was still wasn't anyone to validate what happened to me. Susan watched the tears flow freely down my cheeks, and eventually broke the silence with, "I now understand what you've been trying to tell me."

I quickly learned just how angry Mom was about the counseling session. Before I could get home, she had broken into my home and taken several things. Most were things she had given me, but still she didn't have a right to break into my personal space. I was hurt, not only because she tried to punish me in Susan's office by leaving before anything could get resolved, but because she was doing it again by taking away things she had given me. I didn't suspect I would ever see her again.

The loss of my mother, again, rekindled the devastation and despair I felt about Chelsey's death because I didn't have her to love and distract me now that I was hurting. My heart cried out for another companion, another buddy I could depend on, and who would love me.

Chelsey left me devoted to strays and dogs no one else loved, so I went to the Humane Society to find a new friend. It was a heart-wrenching experience seeing all the caged animals looking for a loving home—they reminded me of myself. I was fighting back the tears when a beautiful little Beagle puppy found me. He looked at me, with his big, sad, brown eyes as if he was trying to subliminally convince me to take him home. As he jumped on me, I suddenly realized he was a boy. I was devastated because I didn't want anything male in my life. But after much thought, I couldn't leave him there, so I took him home. He was a great hit with everyone, and my co-worker Deborah named him Bo.

Bo was the cutest thing I had ever seen in all my life and I loved him. But my love didn't keep me from losing my patience with him either when he didn't obey me. Like Chelsey, I sometimes hurt him, even though I didn't mean to…it just happened before I could stop myself. I hated the rage I had inside me. Despite my anger, Bo and I did everything together, and he became my best friend. He was one compromise that worked out for the good.

Chapter 23

Attempting to Rectify the Past

THE LATEST LOSS OF MY MOTHER made everything seem overwhelming. Therapy with Susan became more difficult because it was getting harder and harder to access my emotions. And Susan's techniques now seemed limited, given the severity of the abuse I had suffered. I was faced once again with my old friend, suicide. It scared me because it started looking like the best option. I knew I had to do something quickly; I had to try something new.

I remembered hearing about a new program called New Haven. It was supposed to help people recover from childhood traumas and abuse. I thought it wouldn't hurt to give it a try, so I picked up the phone and called them.

"You're a perfect candidate for the program," a woman said. "We can give you an immediate two-week placement and a scholarship to cover the cost." As I hung up the phone, I whispered to myself, "Thank you God for helping me. Now please take the horrible pain and memories of my childhood away from me as I work my way through this program." For the first time in a long time, I felt a glimmer of hope that maybe someone would know what the missing piece of the puzzle was so I could finally be free.

It was now just three weeks before my thirtieth birthday and I was walking back into yet another treatment facility. Even though I was disappointed in myself, I thought, "At least this time I'm clean and sober."

As I walked into the building, I couldn't believe how beautiful and modern everything appeared. The bright colors and geometric shapes lifted my spirits, as did the large courtyard with picnic tables, luscious green grass, and a concrete bird feeder nestled underneath a large oak tree. I had a really good feeling about this place.

New Haven's program was designed to help people who had

dysfunctional and traumatic childhoods re-experience what happened to them when they were growing up. The goal was for me to go back to the anger and rage I felt as a child so I could face the feelings that were hidden underneath. In order to accomplish this, I was given a red plastic baseball bat to thrash pillows and was instructed to pound on couch cushions with my fists while screaming and yelling. When I was first asked to beat my feelings out onto the mound of pillows that lay before me, my heart clinched with fear as I remembered that revealing any family secrets was treason and a punishable offense, usually resulting in emotional exile and unbearable physical pain. However, I forced myself to the front of the room and meekly took hold of the red plastic bat. I stood there facing the other patients and my counselor, embarrassed and self-conscious. I was afraid everyone would be able to see my emotional pain and vulnerability if I did what was asked. But, because I wanted to get well, I began hitting the pillows with all my might. I tried to focus on the pain I had lived with as a child and, still as an adult. Then something strange started happening to me. Suddenly, my insides burned with hot rage and I wanted to hurt myself. I tried to move past the anger to the emotions that lay underneath, but I couldn't do it. All I could focus on was the pain of Mom beating me into submission while I crouched down in the kitchen corner. All I could feel was rage and overwhelming devastation. I felt as if I was going to break in two. Afterwards, I felt like a failure and was devastated because the calm seas I was promised were no where to be found. Instead, I was left with rage that was automatically replenished after each bout of pounding the pillows.

The counselor's methods weren't working on me and they didn't understand why. Instead, I was out of control again, much like the days when I was living with Hillary. It was then that I heard someone say that taking anti-depressants kept people stuck and it was like using a crutch to hide from the past. I wondered if that was the reason why I wasn't responding well to treatment. So I decided to go off my anti-depressants. The staff, surprisingly enough agreed with my idea, but didn't suggest I taper off the medication. So I stopped it cold turkey and flipped out a couple of days later. My vulnerability, suicidal thoughts, hostility, depression, and need for someone to love me escalated out of control. I was terrified, but the staff just kept pushing me harder and harder.

Then one day the therapist verbally pushed me until my fists were clenched. I held my breath as I tried to push the flood of emotions back into the depths of my soul to keep them from overwhelming me and making me want to hurt myself. Moments later, I felt as if I were drowning.

"No one cares or believes me!" I screamed as I started to sob. "Please believe me—I was hurt as a child and always told the truth about it—no matter what Mom said!" The staff didn't respond; no one seemed to understand what was happening to me. So I stormed out of the meeting, ran to my room, and hid beside my bed, rocking back and forth, trying to feel safe again. I kept mumbling to myself, "It's okay, it's okay, it's okay..." But it didn't work this time. I caved in on myself!

I suddenly felt someone touching my arm. I thought, Oh no—they're all here watching me—they can see my hiding place and know that I rock myself! They think I'm crazy—this is so degrading. But I just kept rocking, and rocking. They tried to talk to me, but I couldn't hear them—they seemed far away.

My counselor and the whole group stayed there and talked to me until I felt safe enough to come out of the corner. When I was able to stand up, I could tell by the look on their faces that they finally understood the severity of the abuse I had endured all my life. I was also embarrassed and ashamed because they now knew about my secret means of escape. I wondered how many of them thought I was crazy.

My return to hiding in corners was followed by an evening filled with torturous nightmares of childhood beatings and sexual abuse; memories of being alone, abandoned, and my desperate need to have my mother rescue me from my pain and validate the unspoken family secrets. As the sun began to shine through the window, I found it almost impossible to separate reality from my dreams.

I couldn't leave the room, so I wrapped myself in a blanket and crawled back into my corner. I rocked back and forth trying to make the pain go away, while hoping that someone would help me. I called for my counselor, but she never came. I started crying and couldn't stop. I rocked and rocked, and then became angry. I wondered why my counselor had abandoned me. Why had she been so caring the day before, but not now?

Desperate for answers, I walked down the long hall toward the nurses station, only to see that the morning meeting had begun and my counselor was leading the group. I stood there hurt and wondering why no one came to get me for the meeting like they did every morning. Angry, I walked into the activity room and asked why no one came to get me. My counselor looked at me with disdain and arrogance in her eyes as she said, "You're responsible to get yourself to the meeting." Her cold words made my fists clench and my blood boil with rage. I wanted to make her pay for abandoning me and changing the rules. I glared at her with hatred in my eyes as I screamed, "Someone always rounds us up for group every morning." She smugly called me a liar and talked down to me just like my mother used to. I was instantly transformed back into that teen-aged girl who could never win, who felt helpless and was unable to strike back because everyone else was always stronger.

I ran back to my room, crying and pacing back and forth. The more I paced, the more desperate I became. Completely out of control and crying, I marched back to the nurses station and screamed, "I demand to be discharged immediately. I'm done with everything," implying that I was going to kill myself. I ran back to my room to start packing when something happened that I didn't anticipate.

Anger seethed out of every pore of my body, desperation out of my heart and tears welled up in my eyes. I realized I had nowhere to go, and no one I could tell about my suicidal feelings. I began to believe that there wasn't anyone who could ever help me; that I was permanently defective and beyond repair. So I threw my clothes into a gym bag with the intention of walking out of the hospital, and killing myself in the Northeast Georgia mountains. Suddenly I realized there was something different about this suicide pact. For the first time my soul understood that I would likely succeed this time. My heart wrenched with emotional pain; I was mourning my own death. What a strange and hopeless feeling that was as I stood there grieving the failure of my life. In many ways, it reminded me of the grief stricken eight-year-old child I once was as I grieved the loss of my pink kitty with no one to help repair or mend the heart of that child.

I didn't want to leave without saying good-bye to the patients I had grown to know. So I went to the courtyard, tried to act as if nothing was wrong, and explained I was leaving because of what happened at the morning meeting. As I turned around to leave, I heard a voice calling my name. It was my counselor. She stood before me, and everyone else, with genuine remorse in her eyes as she said, "I'm sorry for how I talked to you, and you were right, someone always gathers everyone up for the morning meeting. I'm also sorry for not coming to talk to you this morning in your room. Please don't leave, stay and finish the program so you can get your life together." I didn't know what to think or if I could trust her, but I agreed to stay. More importantly, I was relieved that I wasn't going to have to die and could stop mourning my own death.

My next hurdle was surviving New Haven's Family Weekend. It was the part of the program that was supposed to help each patient with the transition back home. Since Karen was considered my only family at that time, she came to my first weekend meeting. She was a great support, but I felt sad and empty when I saw the other patients hugging and joking around with their parents, siblings and spouses. It reminded me that Mom was still angry at me, and it rekindled my need for her to love me and for us to have a mother-daughter relationship.

After much soul searching, I went to my counselor and asked if there was any hope of my mother and me ever having a relationship, or should I just give up? I explained how Mom hadn't spoken to me in several years because of the counseling session with Susan; how she always resurfaced and acted as if nothing bad had ever happened between us; and how she would get angry with me again and would stop talking to me for several years. She momentarily looked confused but said, "This might be the perfect time to see if your Mom would like to come to Family Weekend. I would encourage you to call her and then make it clear that the focus of the weekend would be on you, and not her."

A week later I found the courage to call and invite Mom to Family Weekend. "I'm in treatment again, trying to deal with what happened to me growing up. I'm trying to work on me, not point any fingers at anyone," I blurted out, trying to ignore her gruff voice and the painful memories that came flooding back.

"So it's about Gene?" she asked defensively.

"Yes, but there's more I'm trying to deal with as well."

"Look, you've hurt me. You're a terrible alcohol and drug-addicted daughter. I've spent too much time worrying about whether you're going to end up dead, and you never come home anymore."

I didn't dare correct her for fear that she would get angry and hang up.

Instead, I said, "Mom, I'm really trying to change my life and I need your help."

Silence filled the air, so I quickly reassured her, "The family weekend is about working on me, not attacking you." Still there was no response. "Please, Mom—"

"I can't come because I'm sick."

"No one will be pointing the finger at you. Please, I need you to be my mom."

"Well, I'll just have to think about it. If I come, I'll just show up; if not, then I won't," she said, sounding frustrated.

Family Weekend arrived and I felt like a child waiting to see if Santa Claus was coming to visit. The hours passed and it was time for the group session to begin. Mom still hadn't arrived. I gave up, and started walking down the hall with Karen toward the group room. When I heard the door behind me open, I turned around to see that it was Mom. I was so excited, but by the look on her face, I knew she wasn't happy about being there.

The group session began with everyone sitting around in a circle in the activity room listening to educational classes on birth order, and how diseases and behaviors were passed down from one generation to the next. I was in complete awe because it made such sense and explained so many things. It made me want to understand my own family in that context, so, during the break, I asked Mom if we could do our family tree in the next session. She just looked at me disdainfully and said nothing.

The session began with the counselor asking, "Would anyone like to do their family tree?"

I looked at Mom again. This time she leaped out of her chair, stood over me and looked at me as if she hated me, and screamed, "I'm not going to do anything!"

Immediately I became the frightened child again, cowered and waited for the first blow across my face.

Knowing she couldn't hit me with everyone watching, she stormed out of the room and abandoned me again. I tried to run after her, wailing, "Mom, please don't leave me—please forgive me."

Half way down the hall, a counselor grabbed Mom and tried to calm her down. I stood there trembling…waiting.

"I'm done with her, and I won't be back," she grunted, as she pulled away from the counselor and ran out the door.

Panicking, I yelled, "Please don't leave me, Mom…I'm sorry." She didn't look back.

The slamming of the door shattered my heart and left me feeling empty.

A counselor pulled me aside and asked what happened. I had no answer for her or myself. She asked, "Who do you think your mother is?"

I couldn't answer that question either—I didn't know who she was anymore.

The counselor went on to explain that, "She's a 'martyr'. She maintains the role of being a victim so she can get sympathy from other people, and so they will take care of her because she can't take care of herself. Martyrs survive by doing things like your mother did today—it's her identity."

I instinctively knew she was right and, for the first time in my life, *I saw my mother for who she was, instead of who I needed her to be.* It was as if someone had turned the lights on in a dark room to reveal the true color of the walls, instead of the imagined color that lingered in the protection of the darkness.

I could see that my mother claimed to be agoraphobic for sympathy purposes; that she had always played the victim when she was fighting with Gene; and, most of all, it was the reason why she had walked out on me.

I understood that she was afraid the counselor would have seen through her façade, and that would have forced her to take responsibility for the things she had personally done to me, as well as things she had let happen to me.

My expected two-week stay at New Haven turned into three long, eventful weeks. I was finally discharged on October 23, 1993, just one day before my thirtieth birthday. This was, supposedly, as good as I was ever going to get and although I didn't feel like I was ready to be discharged, I left.

After leaving New Haven, I realized there was something very different about me, but I didn't understand what it was. Instead of being occupied with a resounding sense of anger, or uplifted with a sense of freedom as promised, I was depressed, and apathetic. I had no hope for my life being any different, especially now that Mom was gone again. *I was left trying to live a life weighed down by painful memories, torturous feelings, a job I hated, and a mother who had abandoned me. I didn't care what happened to me. I wasn't suicidal, I just didn't care if I lived or died. I didn't care about anything.*

I woke up the next morning, at home with Karen, not caring that it was my birthday. I knew something had to change that day or I was going to quit. Out of nowhere, the thought came to me: Perhaps I could go to church—maybe that could help me. So Karen and I went to the Mountain Walk Tabernacle.

I walked into the sanctuary where I saw carpeted floors, a stage with all kinds of musical instruments, a balcony, recording studio, and about six hundred people. There was something special in the air, a presence. It was refreshing and full of life. I knew I was in the right place because of the contemporary Christian music that was playing and the enthusiasm the people displayed as they stood up and clapped their hands. I thought this was great.

The pastor preached a sermon like I had never heard before. She preached in a way that applied to people's lives, showed that she was a person just like everyone else, and taught us how to live. Since I had never really gone to church as a kid, I fell in love with this place. It felt good, made me feel at home and made me want to come back every Sunday, if not more often.

After the service, I spoke with the pastor and explained my situation. She said, "Your statements reflect authentic insight that can only be provided by God." She touched my hands and told me, "God loves you and He will help you if you ask."

I started going to church regularly, and began seeing Susan more frequently. I started studying the Bible: soaking up every bit of information and finding that it deeply touched me in a way I didn't expect. Slowly but surely, things began to change for the better. With my life revolving around the church and my dedicated search for God's mercy and truths, I looked at the world through different eyes.

The only problem I had with the church was with the belief that homosexuality was a sin. So Karen and I hid the true nature of our relationship. I'm sure that the pastor and everyone knew, but they were so loving and kind, they never judged us or confronted us about it. Instead, I was invited to study at their seminary, and graciously accepted their invitation.

The seminary program was extremely difficult and time consuming, but my soul thrived with the knowledge I ingested on a daily basis. My outlook on life continued to improve and became more positive. After receiving my black belt, I even quit Tae Kwon Do to study on a full-time basis.

My sessions with Susan changed as well, as we focused less on my past and more on the spiritual concepts of change. The marvelous thing about our time together was that she really seemed interested in what I was learning and it appeared to help her as much as it helped me. I was now giving back to someone who had given to me.

Chapter 24

First Taste of Death

It was the spring of 1995, and Mom was back in my life in a split second via a telephone call because she needed my help. "Gene's cancer is back—can you get him set up with disability benefits?" she asked, pretending nothing bad had ever happened between us. Hoping she would love me, I made the necessary arrangements for Medicare and Medicaid.

It didn't take long before she started complaining about her awful life and how she despised Gene and his doctors appointments. She went so far as to admit that she was making him drive himself to his radiation and chemotherapy treatments. Despite the things Gene had done to me, I felt sorry for him and called to see if he needed any help. I didn't want anyone to feel the loneliness and abandonment I had felt all my life, especially when it came to Mom.

In the meantime, Mom and I started developing what I thought was a relationship. She bought a business that she wanted to turn into a florist and restaurant and asked me to help her with the improvements and landscaping. Desperate to win her approval, I agreed and enlisted Karen's help. We spent many long hours, and every weekend, in the blistering summer heat and humidity working without pay. As usual though, when we were finished, Mom didn't even say thank you, and showed no signs of appreciation.

She also started coming back to my house for visits. Each time she came over she wanted me to give her something that I valued, like my antique ironing board, bricks, pond plants and decorative rocks. I worked hard and gave her whatever she asked of me. My childish ideas of being able to earn her love carried me for months.

Eventually, I became physically and emotionally exhausted. Too tired to crawl out of bed one Saturday morning, I called to tell her, "I can't help you today, I'm physically worn out and need a day to rest."

Her voice took on a hard and defiant tone. My whole body began to shake with fear, and even though I was talking to her on the phone, I physically backed into a corner like I used to when I was a child. She became so angry that she started yelling and screaming, "You're a horrible person for not helping me when I need it."

When I tried to explain how I felt, she began cursing at me and then hung up, like she had done so many times before. I couldn't believe it was happening again.

Knowing it would be several years before Mom would speak to me again, Karen and I drove to her place of business and picked up the personal things I had left behind. As we drove away, I realized we were close to the old trailer in Clyo, and decided to go visit Gene. I hadn't heard from him in a while and was concerned about how he was doing with the chemotherapy and radiation treatments.

As we drove up to the old, isolated home place, I tried to ignore the images that flashed through my mind; the memories of how Gene had molested me; my seventeenth birthday when Mom threw me out; and all the abuse I had endured. I nervously walked in the front door, trying to hold back tears. I was shocked to see Gene lying in a hospital bed in the living room, looking as pale as a ghost. He was emaciated, frail, and dirty. Old Jell-O pudding cups, dried out and crusty, lay next to his bed. It looked like no one had been there to help him for some time. It hurt to see that Mom had left him out there to die alone.

Gene looked up and seemed glad just to see another human being. My heart ached for him. I looked at Karen and saw sympathy on her face, so I knew she would understand when I said, "Hold on Gene, we're taking you to my house."

It was June of 1995 when I bought Gene a hospital bed and converted my study into a bedroom. I put in baby monitors in case he needed something during the night, and generally tried to make him feel at home. Karen cooked the meals, while I provide the direct care. Surprisingly, my compassion was stronger than my anger, although I didn't understand why.

Surprisingly, Mom had no problem with Gene staying with me. She agreed to help out with his care, but she never followed through.

Eventually, caring for Gene became more than I had bargained for. I had to take him to the clinic at least once a week for check-ups and radiation/chemotherapy treatments, and to the emergency room several times a week for acute problems. He was getting sicker by the day and I feared he would die soon. Through it all, the only thing he wanted was for Mom to visit him. But she only came to see him a couple of times. When she did, she brought another man and sat in my kitchen drinking and having a good time.

After the visits with Mom, Gene accepted that Karen and I were his only family and that we would be taking care of him until the end. He understood that Mom has given up on him and had abandoned him.

His only prized possession in the world was his little teacup Chihuahua named PB, which was a nickname for Precious Baby. I made Mom bring PB to my house to live with us, and she helped keep Gene's spirits high.

Gene grew progressively weaker by the day until he could barely get out of bed to use the bathroom or bathe, and was constantly in the emergency room. We were finally forced to admit him to hospice, so qualified medical staff could take care of him, and provide him with the pain medication he needed.

The hospice house was close to work so I visited Gene every morning before work, at lunch, and every night until I had to go to school. During the weekends, I spent all my time with him. I hoped my presence would ease his pain, but it was hard on me because I never had any time to myself. I was rarely at home with Karen, but she understood and helped out a great deal by visiting Gene, too.

The weeks passed slowly and everything started taking a toll on me physically. I got sick from exhaustion, was struggling at work, and was barely able to concentrate at school. Gene's mother and sister finally drove in from Mississippi to visit him and help with his care. Even though they were rude to me and didn't help much, at least their presence meant that I could modify my visitation schedule on the weekends and get some time for myself.

Gene started slipping closer and closer to death and I still had a dilemma that required Susan's help to resolve. Gene had never admitted out loud that he had sexually abused me. For both our sakes, I didn't want him to die before we had a chance to discuss and resolve that issue. I was afraid to bring the issue up again, and didn't feel I had a right to seek resolution from a dying man. So I spoke at great length with Susan about how to handle my fear and broach the subject.

She reminded me that I was the victim, that I had a right to have my questions answered and to seek closure about the horrible things he had done to me. After hours of discussion, we drew up a plan with goals. We outlined how I was going to start the conversation, listed the things I wanted to say, and how I was going to end the discussion. The goal was for me to understand that what happened wasn't my fault, for Gene to understand what the sexual abuse had done to me, and for him to know that I forgave him. It was also important that he validate the abuse so I could be free from the lingering guilt and shame.

I thought about it for days, and was terrified and unsure if I would be able to do it. I finally chose the day to speak with Gene about the molestation and incest. I rehearsed in my mind what I wanted and needed to say. I also prayed that God would allow Gene the strength and courage to admit what he had done so that I could be set free from my prison of unrelenting pain.

As I pulled into the parking lot, I again questioned my fortitude in being able to follow through with my mission. My heart pounded and my stomach was tied in such large knots I could barely stand upright when I reached his room. My lips were trembling as I sat down next to his bed and said, "I need to talk with you about something important."

The look of apprehension on his face told me he knew why I was there, and that it terrified him. For a few moments, we spoke about things that had happened in the family and how screwed up everything had been, but only in a general way. We were avoiding the real issue at hand because I still wasn't sure if I could handle it. I became overwhelmed with fear and the pain that came from my past; tears flowed down my face.

I took a deep breath, looked at Gene and blurted out, "I need to talk to you about what you did to me, so we can resolve it."

"I'm sorry for what you kids went through and what I did," he mumbled. "I was messed up back then and I regret a lot of things."

No matter what I said, he wouldn't admit what he did to me.

Disappointed, I did what I had done all my life, I pushed my feelings aside long enough to take care of the needs of someone else and said, "I'm not angry with you. I forgive you and I don't want you to pass from this life thinking that I harbor any bad feelings toward you."

The expression on his face changed from one of agony to relief. He looked at me and said, "I want you to patch things up with your mom and try to ignore her when she gets crazy."

I nodded my head, hugged him and walked out hiding my tears. I was disappointed that he didn't validate the sexual abuse and that I would have to live with what happened to me for the rest of my life. But I was relieved that he could die in peace.

The cancer continued to pop up all over Gene's body. Lumps were literally rising up under his skin. The cancer metastasized to his bones and brain and it wasn't going to be long before he died.

It was December 10, 1995, when the phone rang.

"You need to come and see Gene because he's not doing well," the nurse said. I drove straight to the hospice house dreading what I would have to face. I stood at the hospice door, and waited for someone to buzz me in.

The nurse opened the door, and said, "I'm sorry Gene died about thirty minutes ago."

I didn't know what to say. My breath grew shallow and I felt as if someone had just punched me in the stomach. My legs almost gave way beneath me, but I managed to hold back the tears until the nurse left me alone to deal with my first taste of a family member's death.

I didn't know what to do with what I was feeling. I felt lost and sad. It was confusing mourning the death of a man who caused me, and my family, so much pain. But then my compassionate side reminded me that Gene and I were alike in one way: we both wanted, more than anything else in the world, to feel the unconditional love of my mother.

I slowly made it to his room to say good bye. I walked in and saw him, completely void of color, with his mouth hanging open. I almost fell apart. My heart broke for him. I started crying and whispered, "I'm sorry. I love you and hate that you had such a sad and unhappy life."

I left his room and sat in the lobby for hours waiting for Mom to show up. She finally arrived, and as usual, immediately went into hysterics, acting like she was devastated by Gene's death. Everyone there, including the hospice staff, knew better than to fall for her theatrics. They just looked at her in disbelief. Not only did she play the hysterical wife, but she also went against Gene's burial wishes. Instead of laying him to rest in Mississippi next to his family, she decided to cremate him so she could put him in a vase and keep him on her mantle. That just about killed his family because they didn't believe in cremation. It just created more bad feelings in an already difficult situation. No one knew what to do with Mom and her lack of respect for anyone's wishes except her own.

Members of my church had been very supportive during Gene's illness and they helped him get right with God. They allowed me to have his memorial service at the church even though he wasn't a member. Their kindness and understanding helped provide a means to obtain closure, and I was grateful for their godly presence in my life.

After Gene's death, things in my life started moving quickly—almost too quickly. Susan and I continued with our spiritual sessions while my childhood remained a silent topic, even though I knew it was brewing just beneath the surface. We were now confiding in each other about everything. Our therapy had reached a new dimension I had never experienced with another person: one of pure spirituality. Even though we weren't actively engaged in counseling, or working on the issues that got me in trouble, I enjoyed my time with her and looked forward to each session.

Now that Karen was an integral part of my life, Lydia and I resumed our friendship and I introduced her to Karen. I was happy to see that they liked each other and that Lydia accepted Karen as a part of the family. They had a lot in common since they both liked to do the home maker stuff and go shopping. That was great for me and Dr. Russ because it gave us time to hang out and do our household repair projects. He always thought it was great when we could fix something or complete a project together, like cutting firewood.

Dr. Russ finally retired, and he and Lydia moved to a place called the Sautee-Nacoochee Valley. They bought a home on five acres of land, renovated it and built a second home, called "the little house," for friends and guests who visited.

It was now the spring of 1996, and I wanted to start looking at property in the Sautee-Nacoochee Valley so I could be close to Lydia and Dr. Russ. I also loved the mountains and could no longer deny how much I wanted to be closer to nature. So Karen and I started looking at property.

We fell in love with a piece of property about two miles from Lydia and Dr. Russ on 7.76 acres of land. The Cherokee Indians once lived there and it was breathtakingly beautiful. Hemlocks, dogwoods, and mountain laurel covered the land. There was also Monkey Pine, the last of a luscious ground cover that only grew in very fertile soils and denoted prosperity to the Native American Indians. I had a strong feeling that this was the property I was supposed to buy, so I made an offer on it.

Karen and I were thrilled when the seller accepted the offer. Now all we needed were jobs, a temporary place to live until we built a house, and money to do it all with.

While I was trying to finance the new property, I finished seminary school with honors, Magna Cum Laude. I was proud that I had made it. I also looked forward to being among the first to graduate from the Mountain Walk Bible Institute. The graduation was a huge event and I was honored for having the highest grade point average in the class. Susan added to my joy by coming to celebrate my academic and spiritual accomplishments.

After graduation, Karen and I started looking for jobs in the Northeast Georgia area. Somewhere inside, I knew I had fulfilled my destiny in Savannah, and it was time to move on. I had overcome my addictions and my eating disorder, earned my black belt in Tae Kwon Do, graduated from undergraduate and graduate school, graduated from seminary, and survived Gene's cancer and death.

I was confident that I could handle anything as a result of my counseling and spiritual training. The biggest step of all came when I took the bag of pills I had stashed to kill myself with and flushed them down the toilet. It was time for a fresh start at living.

Chapter 25

Endings and Beginnings

FINDING A JOB was a difficult, but after several months of searching, I learned about an opening at one of the large rehabilitation facilities. I immediately faxed my resume to them. About ten minutes later my phone rang with Vivian, the director, saying, "We have a vacancy and I want you to come up for an interview." My heart pounded with excitement, but I tried to act calm and professional as I politely accepted her offer. My dream of living in the mountains was about to come true.

The interview was extremely important because I was the one responsible for paying for the move and the house. A lot was resting on it.

At the same time, I was afraid I was making a mistake by leaving my life in Savannah, which had finally gotten on the right track. Second guessing myself required too much energy, so I told myself that everyone felt like that when they were making huge changes in their life.

I was under a lot of pressure as the primary provider and the one making all the moving arrangements. My mind whirled with constant questions: Where were we going to live while we built the house? How could I afford to pay for a place to live while building a new house? How was I going to have enough energy to devote to a new job, moving, and building a house all at the same time? There were more questions than answers.

Karen and I drove to Sautee for the weekend so I could interview for the job. When I walked into the huge rehab facility, I was terrified. I had never done anything this big before and I wasn't sure how I would fit in with such a professional group of people. I went through a series of grueling interviews over several days, and drove back to Savannah to await the outcome.

I was amazed and relieved when the Human Resources Department called from the rehab facility and offered me the job. My heart jumped for joy at my first hint of good luck in forever. Needless to say, I accepted the job. After I hung up the phone, I sat stunned that they had hired me, of all people. For the first time, I felt my life was about to change for the better and I was finally free from my past.

In a matter of a couple weeks, I had to put the house on the market, pack everything up, find a place to live, and say good-bye to Susan. I also had to move up to Sautee by myself because Karen hadn't found a job yet. Instead, she would stay on in Savannah to sell the house while trying to find employment in North Georgia. Fortunately, Lydia and Dr. Russ took some of the pressure off by letting me stay in their guesthouse. I was very grateful because their hospitality saved me a lot of money and allowed me to be close to them.

My last session with Susan was difficult, yet exciting, as we defined what our relationship would be from that day forward. We decided that we would write to each other, pursue a friendship, and dissolve the counseling relationship. Somehow we had moved past the patient-therapist alliance a long time ago. I was glad because I didn't want to play that role with her anymore. I was delighted and relieved she was in agreement and gave me her address and phone number. For me, that made our parting much easier.

On August 14, 1996, at the age of thirty-two, I packed my car, said good-bye to Karen and drove to the Northeast Georgia mountains to begin the first stage of my new life.

When I arrived in Sautee, I went directly to the guesthouse. I really liked it because it was a great little hideaway. The inside looked like a cabin with natural hardwood floors, a wooden staircase, and fireplace. It also had a loft, which I thought was fabulous because it reminded me of my little closet in Santa Monica. There was a front porch with a table and chairs and a gas grill. The extra bonus with staying at the little house was that I got to see Lydia and Dr. Russ almost every day.

On that first evening, when I finally got everything unpacked, I realized how nervous I was about starting my new job the next morning. I could hardly sleep. I wanted to be the best employee this place had ever had, and to prove to everyone that they didn't make a mistake by hiring me. I wanted to be good and do well so Vivian would be proud of me. Most of all, I wanted to fit in for a change, and I was sure the rehab facility was going to be a place where I could.

Chapter 26

Stumbling Blocks

MY FIRST DAY AT WORK felt like my first day at school. Rita, the supervisor of the department, greeted me without a smile, and then took me to meet, Sydnie, another manager who was to supervise my work. I'd never worked in a medical environment, so at first it was a bit overwhelming. But the first week went well and I really enjoyed it.

Sydnie seemed to be happy that I was there. She provided so much enthusiasm and encouragement that I felt special and wanted. I thought she walked on water and could do no wrong. She was the neatest person I had ever met in the professional world. I wanted to be just like her one day and wanted to make her proud of me. She also seemed to be a person I could talk to; someone I could be myself around her. Oddly enough, she seemed just as relaxed around me. There were many days that she called me into her office, and disclosed personal things about herself. She told me of her trials and tribulations, much as my mother had done with me when I was a child.

The more she told me about herself, the more I began to feel responsible for her, as if it were my job to make sure that nothing bothered her or hurt her. In return, she wanted me to open up and be just as honest with her about who I was as a person and about my past. I was so desperate that, without thought or caution, I told her how I longed to be loved, how much I needed a friend, and the things that were bothering me about work.

When our sessions of self-disclosure were over, Sydnie always hugged me before sending me on my way. As a matter of fact, she was always hugging everyone. All the staff lived for the day that she compensated their efforts with that show of affection. Unfortunately though, it re-awakened the part of me that desperately needed to feel loved, so I started clinging to Sydnie to meet my needs.

For some reason though, Sydnie's mood began to change. She began yelling at me in front of other people for things I hadn't done. When she was finished screaming at me, she would take me to her office, sit me down like I was her best friend again, and tell me negative things about my supervisors, Rita and Vivian, hoping to re-win my allegiance. She began making unrealistic demands of me, saying that I had to be perfect. I was confused because I couldn't figure out what she wanted from me.

Things were further complicated by her irrational decisions. She placed many impossible and unrealistic expectations on everyone and there was no consistency from one day to the next. She also played people against each other much like a chess game; it was office politics at its worst. It drove everyone crazy, and left all of us confused about what was expected.

My new job reeked of my childhood all over again because Sydnie was nothing but a reincarnation of my mother, and this was the last thing I wanted to deal with. Thus, any hope I had left of my life being better was now snuffed out. Depressed and feeling hopeless again, I didn't know what to do, who to tell, or who would believe me if I did tell.

As time went on, I realized that I couldn't take working with Sydnie, or her erratic and punitive behavior, anymore. I'd had enough and was either going to hurt myself or quit. Crying, I ran down to Rita and Vivian's office and disclosed what had been going on with Sydnie. They weren't surprised. They said this had been going on for six years and with every person they had put under Sydnie's supervision. They offered suggestions, but they only exacerbated the situation and caused Sydnie to act even more like my mother every day.

I went to see Rita and Vivian several more times, crying because Sydnie maintained her unprofessional behavior and made work unbearable. But still they did nothing about her. I was barely surviving. At the end of each day, I would go home and sit in the corner, crying and rocking back and forth trying to soothe myself from the nightmare I had unknowingly entered into. I was sad and disheartened because the old feelings I thought I was rid of were resurfacing and I didn't know what to do with them, especially without Susan to talk to.

I was convinced that I couldn't go on, that I couldn't keep living in dysfunctional situations that reminded me of my mother and my torturous childhood. At my breaking point, I went to Vivian's office and tried to tell her, "I'm hanging on by a thread."

She didn't understand what I was trying to tell her, so she only suggested that I talk with someone in the Employee Assistance Program (EAP). Maybe they could help me deal with my feelings about Sydnie so they wouldn't be so confusing. Since I didn't trust anyone at that point,

I didn't take her advice.

The day finally came when I had complained and cried so much to Rita and Vivian that they suggested I tell the vice-presidents what was happening. Despite an overwhelming fear of the repercussions, I met with them and told them about the problems everyone in the program was having with Sydnie.

"We're appalled that she has been allowed to get away with her unprofessional behavior for six years. A full investigation will be completed and action will be taken," they said confidently.

I felt like a traitor, and yet was afraid because I knew that if Sydnie learned of my betrayal she would find some way to turn everything back on me, to make me look like the bad guy. From that day forward, she treated me like I was nothing more than dirt that had been swept under an old rug. She talked badly about me to my peers and anyone who would lend an ear to her blithering and unfounded accusations about who I was as a professional, and as a person.

Each time I saw her cornering someone and talking about me, I felt as if I wanted to die. I wanted to scream, "Why are you doing this to me after I loved you and trusted you?" But I remained silent, like a well-trained child, while Sydnie made my life a living hell.

There were many more days when I found myself sitting in Rita and Vivian's office with tears rolling down my face, telling them, "I'm barely hanging on. I'm not sure I can see this thing through to the end with Sydnie. I can't handle being in a situation with someone who acts like my mother, doesn't listen to me, mistreats me, makes me responsible to save her and her program, and who tries to make me out to be the bad guy. It is more than I can stand!" But nothing changed.

To complicate things further I didn't have a support system outside of work to help me with my feelings about Sydnie, much less the move, the new job, and building the house. I didn't have Karen, Susan, my church, or my dogs. And I was so new to the area that I hadn't had enough time to establish a new support system, or know of anyone I could trust to be my counselor if I needed another one. I felt lost.

I tried to talk to Lydia about work. All I wanted was for her to listen and understand what I was saying, to give me a sign that she comprehended my dilemma and to throw a little attention my way. I wanted her to hug me and tell me, "Everything is going to be all right." Instead, she looked at me apathetically and suggested that I go to an AA meeting. I'd been clean and sober for years now, and wondered what made her think that AA was going to do me any good, especially for a problem that wasn't alcohol related. Her suggestion made me feel that she hadn't heard a word

I'd said. I bowed my head feeling disappointed and hopeless, and left believing there was no one who could help me.

My life was further complicated by my builder who was several months behind on the house and was going through my money faster than I could keep up with. The constant and ongoing battle with him began wearing me out, emotionally and financially.

I was becoming more and more depressed by the day. I was seriously contemplating suicide again, and resorted back to my old behaviors. Night after night, I locked myself up in the dark, sat in the corner rocking back and forth, and listened to sad music while I tried to figure out what had gone wrong with my new start on life.

Four months later, Karen finally sold the house in Savannah and found a job. That meant she was ready to join me. Now I had even more stress—I had to find us another place to live, because Lydia and Dr. Russ wouldn't allow my dogs in the guesthouse.

With the building costs draining me dry, the only thing I could find in my price range was a dirty, moldy trailer about five minutes down the road where several flying squirrels had taken up residence.

As soon as Karen moved up to Sautee, I realized something was different between us. I was barely hanging on from the move, the pressure at work, trying to build us a house, and financially keeping us afloat while Karen was trying to cope with the separation from her family.

We both silently realized that something had changed, but neither of us knew what it was. The only thing I knew was that I wanted her to leave me alone and give me some space so I could deal with everything that had been happening since I had left Savannah, and with the fact that my dream of a new life was turning into a nightmare.

My saving grace was my dog, Bo, and it was good to have him back in my life. He was still my best friend and the only one who loved me unconditionally. I found it comforting and therapeutic that I could take him for walks out in the woods and watch him run and play freely without a care in the world. I often wished that I knew what being carefree and happy was like. He seemed to like the mountains as much as I did, and having all that room to roam around in appeared to be quite liberating for him.

Bo was a typical Beagle though. He liked to sniff things out and once he got on the trail of something there was no stopping him. He had a one-track mind. It didn't matter how much I called him, he wasn't going to stop until he followed and then found whatever scent he was on. I began worrying about his wandering off because the trailer wasn't too far from the road and it scared me that something bad might happen to him.

I knew I couldn't handle that, so Karen and I agreed that one of us would go outside with him from then on. That was one burden off my shoulders.

The next morning, Karen and I were lying in bed a little longer than usual, basking in the knowledge that it was the weekend. For the first time in a long while, I was able to relax, let my worries briefly slip away and drift back off to that dreamy, ethereal place between consciousness and sleep while Karen volunteered to let Bo outside.

My peaceful sleep was interrupted when I heard water running in the bathtub. I was momentarily confused because I thought Karen was outside with Bo. I quickly jumped out of bed to make sure he was all right. I stood at the door calling him, but he didn't come. Terrified, I stood outside in the cold calling, "Bo !...Bo! ...Bo...!" He still didn't come.

I immediately knew something was wrong. Karen finally came outside to join me in my frenzied and emotional search. The look on her face told me she knew she had messed up by not following our plan. I walked around the large wooded area for several more minutes afraid and with tears rolling down my face.

"Sandy!" Karen screamed. I ran up a huge hill toward her and froze—Karen was holding Bo in her arms. His head was slumped down, and blood was dripping off his head and out of his mouth.

"I found him lying on the side of the road," she shrieked. "They hit him and didn't even stop to make sure he was all right!"

For a split second, I stood there unable to believe what I saw. My heart sank with unbearable, gut-wrenching pain. I thought I was going to pass out. The sight of my friend lying lifeless in my partner's arms left me fearing that he was dead. I didn't know what to do.

Without thinking, I ran into the trailer, called Lydia and a vet who lived down the road, and begged them to please help me. I slammed the phone down, ran outside, and grabbed Bo from Karen's trembling arms.

As soon as I took him from her, I could feel that he was cold. I laid him gently on the porch and cried hysterically. In my mind I understood that he was dead, but I covered him up anyway with some blankets to keep him warm. I held onto the hope that he would wake up from his deep sleep. Tears ran down my face as I whispered in his ear, "Hold on just a little while longer." With each word I uttered, my heart broke a little more. I felt as if my whole world were ending at that very moment.

Each time I thought about Bo dying, I cried and screamed, "Someone, please help me!" I rocked back and forth trying to convince myself that he wasn't dead and he wouldn't leave me.

Finally, Lydia and the vet arrived. The vet just looked at me with tears in her eyes, and said, "There's nothing I can do."

Her words splintered my already breaking heart and I wondered how much more I could take. How much longer God was going to punish me? Why had He taken Bo from me, now of all times? I really didn't think I was going to be able to take the hurt, sorrow and pain that went so deep it penetrated the very core of my being, much like the loss of my pink kitty. But I gathered the courage to take Bo over to the new house and buried him. Afterwards, I just sat there, grieving and praying that I could survive the loss of my best friend.

I was really angry with Karen because we had just agreed the night before that Bo couldn't go outside alone. But, as usual, I couldn't express my anger to her, just like I couldn't with Hillary when she let Chelsey get run over. I was still too afraid. I didn't want to hurt Karen's feelings, just like I didn't want to hurt Hillary's. I asked myself over and over why I couldn't get mad at the people who hurt me and killed my best friends.

Several months later, Karen and I moved into the new house. That in itself was a major feat since the builder went over the estimated cost by about $20,000. It took all my savings, all the profits from the sale of the house in Savannah, and left me having to borrow more money than planned from the bank.

Karen and I were now at each other's throats almost every day. I was slipping deeper into anger and depression. I contemplated killing myself almost every day and stopped taking my anti-depressant because it wasn't helping.

At work, things progressively worsened with Sydnie, leaving me more desperate than ever. I didn't know what to do or who to turn to except for Rita and Vivian, even though they weren't any help.

Then one day at work, I heard that the vice presidents had given Sydnie two options— she could resign or be fired. Of course, she chose to resign, but not before figuring out that it was me who had betrayed her. Her mission for the last six weeks of her employment was to seek revenge. Every day I was left sitting in my office crying and wanting to hurt myself. It got so bad I knew I was either going to find someone to help me or I was going to end my life.

I had no choice but to follow Vivian's advice, so I went to the EAP office.

Chapter 27

The Final Fall

"**I**'M DESPERATE. I have no support system. My best friend has been killed. My builder took all my money. I'm being treated horribly at work. I stopped taking my medication. Everything is bringing up unwanted emotions from my childhood. I'm trying to fight off the need to end my life and need someone to talk to so I won't have to hurt myself," I confessed to the EAP counselor.

But I must have been too honest for her because she became exceedingly concerned and started acting as if it were her professional duty to protect me.

"All I want is for you to understand what I'm thinking and feeling so it will relieve some of the pressure that is building inside me," I tried to explain.

However, instead of listening she continued to panic. Frustrated, I repeated, "I just need someone to talk to—not to protect me."

When I realized she didn't understand what I needed, I got up to leave. She shot up out of her chair and said in a strained and forthright tone of voice, "You can't leave my office unless you promise not to kill yourself and give me time to find you a counselor."

Annoyed, I said as I left, "I'll see you tomorrow for a follow-up visit and the name of my new counselor."

Barely hanging on, and as promised, I went back to see Lindsey the next morning. She looked aggravated and admitted that she was having difficulty finding me a counselor. I told her I was fine, even though I felt helpless and wanted to quit. She made me promise that I'd call 911 if I became suicidal over the weekend. I really didn't know who I thought I was kidding, but the promise sounded good and I was relieved that I had escaped the narrow confines of the psychiatric hospital one more time.

On my way out of the building I heard someone calling my name, and turned around to see that it was Denise, another EAP counselor. She asked me to come into her office so we could talk for a few minutes. She had heard about my problems and suicidal feelings and demanded I stay until she called Karen.

As Denise dialed the phone, I silently prayed that God would keep Karen from getting angry with me and thinking I was truly crazy. In the end, Karen was rather nonchalant about the whole thing and told Denise, "So what? Sandy's always suicidal." Now convinced that my significant other was aware of my suicidal thoughts, she allowed me to leave her office.

It was the weekend so I had to figure out how I was going to survive it and manage to be in my own skin without going crazy. I couldn't stand being with myself, much less anyone else. It was as if my body needed to explode from the excess energy running around inside. I was so angry that I walked around clenching my fists, wanting to hit something. I paced back and forth like a caged animal, ranting and raving about things that were bothering me.

I tried to control myself, but no matter what I did, I didn't know how to make the agitation and pain stop. I needed to erupt, but I didn't know how to do it without going off on Karen and hurting her or killing myself. It was energy I didn't know how to access for constructive purposes; only destructive baggage left over from my insidious childhood.

Karen and I tried to do some household projects together like a normal couple would do on a weekend, but there wasn't anything remotely normal about our life. In a fit of fury over something stupid and insignificant, I got angry with her. I grabbed two bottles of pills I'd stashed, jumped into my car and sped off down the road. My hands gripped the steering wheel with frustration and hopelessness. Tears began streaming down my face. I had absolutely no idea where I was going, but I knew it had to be somewhere where I could end my pain once and for all.

I went to my office, locked myself inside, turned the lights off and closed the blinds on the door. I sat on the floor contemplating how I was going to take the pills without anyone finding me, and without vomiting so I didn't inadvertently increase my chances of survival. My heart was heavy with the understanding that I was about to die and there still wasn't anyone to love or help me. Even though I was afraid I might succeed this time, I was even more terrified of someone rescuing me and forcing me to live in a world that didn't like me; a world where I felt completely alienated from everyone.

The minutes turned into hours as I sat on the floor trying to gather the courage to follow through with my plan. Each time I tried to put the pills in my mouth, I gasped with horrible bouts of grief. Overcome with mourning my own death once again, I forced myself off the floor and into my chair where I paged the EAP counselor, Denise, over and over again so I could tell her what I was about to do.

However, she never responded to any of my calls. Panicked that I couldn't get her to call me back, I had the facility operator page her, but to no avail. When I realized there wasn't a soul who could help me, I crumbled. I had no choice but to complete my mission.

I turned to my computer with shaking hands and wrote a letter to Karen. I told her how much I loved her and how sorry I was for what I was about to do. I also taped her a short message because I couldn't quite get on paper what I wanted and needed to say. I put them in an envelope and placed them on my desk for someone to find.

I sat back down on the floor again and tried to swallow the pills, but for some reason I kept breaking down and crying. I just couldn't do it. I only found myself caught up in the same vicious cycle over and over again of trying to swallow the pills, getting scared, becoming sad, reaching out for help without any response, and then trying to take the pills again.

Five hours later I became so emotionally and physical exhausted that I made myself get up and drive back home.

The next day was June 16, 1997. I woke up emotionally depressed and exhausted from the day before. Because I was a faithful employee, I forced myself to go to work even though I was still decidedly despondent and suicidal. I was in my office trying to figure out how I was going to endure another day of Sydnie's caustic attacks, when Rita came in to discuss some work things. Unintentionally, I emotionally collapsed in front of her.

"I can't take what Sydnie is doing anymore. I just want to die."

Her face changed from her usual rigid and stone-like appearance to one of concern. "Do you have a plan for how you want to end your life?" she asked.

Embarrassed and desperate for help, I admitted that I had 180 pills on standby. She was obviously dumbfounded at my honesty, but she managed to keep it together long enough to be supportive without panicking. I was surprised that she even cared enough to ask since she had always been distant with me and never acted as if she liked me.

I headed back to the EAP office again, but this time with Rita following close behind. I sat there desperately trying not to hurt myself while Lindsay kept saying, "I can't get anyone to call me back about being your counselor." After a great deal of discussion, neither of them seemed to understand the huge stumbling blocks in life, or how this job had created most of them, so I gave up.

Without any tolerable options left, I excused myself to the bathroom with the intent of swallowing every pill I had in my possession. I stood there for a moment with the pills clutched tightly in my hands wondering how I had gotten myself into this mess again. I glanced up and saw my tear-stained face in the mirror and then watched as I swallowed every one of the pills.

I walked out of the bathroom and tried to act as if nothing had happened. But fear gripped me. I told Rita, "I have to get out of here because I can't stand the tension in here anymore."

"You're not leaving unless you give up the pills," she said.

I slammed open the bathroom door, showed them the empty bag and said, "I flushed them down the toilet."

Rita looked relieved, "You can leave the office, but you'll have to stay with me until you get an appointment with a counselor or psychiatrist."

Rita and I walked out into the fresh air. My hands started trembling, my body was shaking and my breath grew shallow.

"Let's walk around to relieve your anxiety," Rita said.

As we walked, she reached up and put her arm around my shoulder and said, "Everything is going to be all right."

My heart melted and I cried. I wanted to tell her so badly what I had done, but I couldn't. I was afraid she would be mad at me and would hate me again.

Not feeling too well, I told Rita I needed to sit down. We walked back to her office where I was instructed to sit and wait. Moments later, the pills started taking over: my heart started racing; my body violently shook; and I couldn't breath.

"Rita, if anything should happen to me, call Karen at _____." I tried to give her the phone number, but I couldn't say the right numbers.

"Are you all right?" Rita asked.

I couldn't respond to her. Panicked and frightened, I knew I had to get out of there but my legs wouldn't move. I fell to the floor, passed out.

In the emergency room, no one knew what I had taken, so the doctor tried to pump my stomach full of charcoal. But it didn't absorb the pills fast enough. Every organ in my thin body began shutting down. I was having one uncontrollable seizure after another. My heart rate was virtually non-existent, and my face was a ghostly, corpse-like shade of white. My skin was cold and clammy as my body temperature dropped too low to sustain life. No longer able to support my own breath, the doctors forced a long tube down my throat so a machine could breathe for me. Moments later, I lay in a lifeless, fetal position in a coma.

There was nothing left for the doctors to do but wait, so I was transferred to the intensive care unit to see if I would ever regain consciousness. The hours slipped by and then I took a potentially irreversible turn for the worse: while experiencing hallucinations in an extremely combative unconscious state, I tried to pull out the IVs, and the tube in my throat that allowed me to breathe. Although the medical staff prevented me from ripping out the tubes, there was now deep concern—my actions and unresponsiveness to pain were clinical signs of brain damage. To make matters worse, aspiration pneumonia had developed from the charcoal used to pump out my stomach.

On the fifth day, I finally awoke from my coma, reasonably intact. For a few moments, I wasn't sure what had happened, and why I was lying in the hospital hooked up to machines in an intensive care unit. Suddenly, I remembered the overwhelming need to kill myself, and the overdose in the bathroom at work with my supervisor and employee assistance counselor sitting in the next room. I was instantly horrified and disappointed that I hadn't died.

Lying in the hospital bed, I was immersed in a resurgence of memories about why I tried to take my own life at a mere thirty-three years of age: the intense feelings of worthlessness; fear that things in my life would never be any different; and exhaustion from the constant strain of trying to survive emotionally from one day to the next.

Those memories kept rolling over me, as did all my fears. The fear that I might do or say something wrong; that I would never fit in anywhere and would always drown in loneliness because I didn't know how to have a "normal" relationship with anyone.

Finally, the most painful memories resurfaced: believing that I would never know how it felt to be loved in a good way, and that I would never be able to forget the terrible pain of the child who resided inside me. It was her pain and memories of unspoken secrets and forbidden memories that I couldn't bear for even one more day.

After remembering why I chose death over life, a small voice within me spoke: This isn't supposed to be happening again...I'm supposed to be dead this time. I don't want my life back, to continue living with my past hurts, or to be alone anymore. I don't want to be alive!

I was afraid of being in trouble now that I had survived my worst suicide attempt. Would I lose my job? Who was mad at me? How would I explain what happened? Would I be locked up again? I felt alone, with the sinking feeling in the pit of my stomach that I would have been better off if I had died.

My body felt as if it had been beaten and left for dead on the side of the road. There were bruises all over my arms from the IVs, and every muscle in my body ached from the convulsions and vomiting. My throat was swollen and raw from the breathing tube, and my lungs were tight and full of mucus from the pneumonia. I wasn't able to talk because of the rigid tube that had been down my throat for almost a week. I was so weak and physically ill I could barely get out of bed.

Almost immediately, I was placed in a police car and taken across the street to the psychiatric unit where I was placed on a 24-hour suicide watch. I thought to myself, "Not again! I wish my life was over."

My room only had a bed and dresser in it, and the bathroom was kept locked. The terrible memories of the many nights I had spent in the Maximum Care Unit at Turning Point flooded back. The only difference was that this place had cameras securely affixed to the walls so I could be monitored at all times.

I sat on the edge of my bed and cried, "God, please help me understand why You didn't let me die, and when You'll stop punishing me."

At that moment, I didn't care if I rotted away in that room. I didn't want to eat, talk, or do anything. My body felt so heavy I could barely breathe. I just curled up on my bed in a fetal position and prayed that death would finally come to me.

Realizing someone had entered my room, I looked up to see that it was Karen and Lydia. I could tell they were angry, so I sat up and just stared at the floor. I wanted to scream that I was sorry and to beg them to forgive me, but I was too afraid. I just sat there and cried.

Eventually I heard myself whisper, "I'm so sorry—please forgive me— please don't be angry with me."

Karen held me and said, "Everything is going to be all right."

But Lydia couldn't let go of her anger, and said, "You need to do what the doctors tell you and not manipulate them into letting you go home too soon. And you won't be allowed back into mine or Dr. Russ' lives unless you go back to AA meetings."

I was shocked that AA was still her answer to everything—including suicide. My spirit plummeted now that Lydia had abandoned me and withdrew her love in my darkest hour. All I wanted and needed was for her to support and understand what was happening to me—not to chastise me like a bad child, like my mother would have done if she had been there.

I never fathomed for one moment that anyone would be mad at me for trying to kill myself. It surprised me more than surviving the suicide attempt.

Sitting in the psychiatric facility feeling alone and misunderstood, I continued to battle the physical ramifications of my suicide attempt—aspiration pneumonia and a limited ability to talk.

I also hit a new emotional low. I became quiet and withdrew deep into myself. I didn't want to interact with anyone or participate in life at all. I felt so alone that I didn't know what to do with myself. I only knew that if I'd had a way to kill myself at that moment, and could have gotten away with it, I would have done it. I had nothing left to live for.

On Monday morning I got to see my psychiatrist, Dr. Jones. I did my usual thing, putting on my professional face so I could convince him that I wouldn't try to kill myself again. I used the excuse that I had stopped taking my medication as the reason why I had tried to end my life, even though I knew that wasn't entirely true.

My professional performance was more effective than usual and Dr. Jones appeared to believe me. He put me back on the anti-depressant, and called Karen to come in for a meeting with us the next morning. He wanted to make sure I had a safe discharge plan and to ensure that she knew what he expected from me.

I was ecstatic about being able to go home the next morning, even though somewhere in the back of my mind I was afraid I would try to kill myself again when no one was looking.

The meeting took place the next morning and Dr. Jones decided that it was safe to discharge me, even though he understood that I was still very emotionally fragile. Trying to hold back the tears, I asked, "Can I go back to work?"

"I don't see any reason why not, if you still have a job to go back to."

The reality of his words hit hard because I knew he was right, I might not have a job left. In front of Dr. Jones, I called Vivian to relieve my own uncertainty about work. I couldn't help it. I started crying and begging her forgiveness. I then asked, "Do I still have a job?"

"I'm amazed Dr. Jones is discharging you so soon," Vivian replied. No matter how many times I asked, she wouldn't answer any of my questions about work. She only said, "We'll talk about it later."

Terrified and crying that I had lost my job, I hung up the phone. Dr. Jones just sat there, ignored my emotional state, and carefully outlined his expectations which included meeting with him two times a week and taking my medication as prescribed. At that point, I didn't care what I had to do as long as I could get out of there.

I was finally discharged into Karen's custody just five days after my admission. As I walked out the front door, I felt nauseous at the idea and sight of the real world again. What was I going to do with my freedom?

Was I going to live or finish what I had started?

It felt strange not to be at work on a weekday and it left me feeling awkward and out of sync with normalcy. All the way home I just sat on my side of the car and stared silently out the window thinking about everything that had happened in the last week. I felt like such a failure. By the time we got home, I was exhausted and afraid about what was going to happen to me.

After my unexpected discharge from the hospital, my relationship with Lydia wasn't the same. She remained furious with me and basically didn't want to have anything to do with me. I tried on several occasions to talk with her, begged her to please love and forgive me, but she remained angry. Each conversation resulted in me crying, feeling abandoned and unloved all over again. There was no way to right my wrong in her eyes.

The task of trying to return to work was long and fraught with bureaucratic red tape. No one at the rehab facility cared about what was best for me, only with how they looked. My suicide attempt made the EAP department appear incompetent, and upper management look bad for not correcting the supervisory problems sooner than they did.

After a month of telephone conversations and one formal meeting at Dr. Jones' office, a meeting was arranged with me, Vivian, and the Human Resources Director, to talk about my possible return to work. I was afraid I might start feeling vulnerable and cry at the meeting, so all the way to the meeting I tried to convince myself that I was all right. I also rehearsed the idea that the suicide attempt was a thing of the past, and I am now emotionally stable and ready for work. I really thought that if I could trick myself into believing those things, I would appear confident, stable and ready for work.

I walked into the meeting room where Vivian and the director of human resources greeted me. They both appeared distant and cold, like they were meeting me for the first time. I was so scared I thought I was absolutely going to stop breathing. I felt like everyone could see how nervous I was, so I just kept telling myself I am going to act professionally, like everything that has happened is history and nothing more.

"I'm doing really well and want to return to work," I said positively.

"The rehab administration wants you to resign with three months severance pay," the director coldly spat.

I gasped, and did exactly what I didn't want to do—I allowed his words to reach my heart. I tried to hide how I felt, but tears welled up in my eyes and my voice trembled as I said, "I can't believe you want me to resign, especially after everything you put me through with Sydnie. I've stuck with you for the past ten months and did everything you've asked of me. But now that I'm having a problem and need your help, you're not willing to stand by me? Why doesn't the organization stick by its employees?" I paused for their response, but they just stared at me. So I continued, "I won't resign because I won't let everyone think I'm emotionally unstable or crazy. I'm determined to prove that I can do my job and change everyone's perception of me, no matter what it takes."

Only silence filled the air. Nothing was said in return to either support or help me. Instead, the director of human resources abruptly ended the meeting and said that he would call me with the next step since I wasn't willing to resign.

I left the meeting feeling shattered and overwhelmed. By the time I reached my car, I broke down crying and wishing once again that I had succeeded in killing myself. I really didn't think I had the energy to fight the facility and I questioned how much more I was going to be able to take before I cracked.

Several days later, someone from work called to explain that I wouldn't be allowed to return until I had successfully completed a neuropsychological evaluation. They used the excuse that they were concerned that the overdose and coma could have left me with brain damage and were skeptical as to whether I could emotionally handle my work duties.

I was beginning to think they were trying to put me through as many hoops as they could so I would just give up and quit, but I wasn't about to let them win. I reluctantly agreed to the neuropsychological evaluation, and to let them choose the psychologist to do the testing.

While I waited to be evaluated, I made it a daily practice to wear myself out at home so I didn't have enough time to think about killing myself before I could get my job back.

My appointment for the neuropsychological evaluation was scheduled for July 25, 1997 with a psychologist named Dr. David Bailey. Terrified that I wouldn't to be able to hold it together for an entire evaluation with someone I didn't know or trust, I made an appointment with my psychiatrist so he could help me figure out how to accomplish this. In his usual nonchalant and arrogant manner, Dr. Jones gave me quite a few pointers.

He advised, "The best thing you can do is to answer the questions that you're asked with as little information as possible. Just answer the questions and don't add anything extra. Be professional and maintain a safe distance from the psychologist so that your emotional undertow won't be detected."

It seemed like an insurmountable task, especially for someone like me whose emotions always sat just beneath the surface. I wasn't sure if I could do what he was suggesting, but I knew I had no choice if I wanted my job back.

As I drove to the evaluation I rehearsed in my mind over and over again, It's not acceptable to let David into my private thoughts, or to show my emotions to anyone. I had to maintain a professional demeanor and paste on my "I'm okay" face. I practiced providing only enough information to squeak by any questions that were asked of me.

I made my way into David's office and knocked on the sliding glass door. A secretary handed me a clipboard full of paperwork to complete and told me to have a seat. I was shocked to see that they wanted to know everything, not just about my insurance, but my most private feelings and what brought me into their office.

When I finished the forms with only the information I was willing to disclose, David came to the door of the waiting room. He didn't look anything like I had pictured. He was a thin man in his mid to late fifties with white hair, combed straight back. He looked like a charismatic preacher, and was dressed very professionally with a starched white shirt, colorful tie, and neatly pressed pants.

My first thought about this guy was that he was arrogant and staunch. That he thought of himself as the all knowing psychologist who was having to deal with a lowly employee who tried to kill herself and was less than worthy of his attention and consideration.

My impression didn't seem too far off since David didn't spend much time with me that first day. He merely asked me several questions and then put me in a really small room with a desk to complete several personality tests. Thankfully, I had the advantage because of my undergraduate degree in psychology and a master's degree in counseling. I knew how to answer the questions in a way that wouldn't disclose my true feelings. So I minimized anything that dealt with depression, anger, and wanting to hurt myself.

After more tests and a session with David, I grew comfortable with him and started to like him. I was still wary of the power he had over my future and made sure I tried to say all the things he would want to hear. I didn't volunteer any additional details about myself or show any emotions whatsoever. But I felt guilty about not being truthful with him. I wasn't trying to lie, but I knew that if I told him the truth he would think there really was something wrong with me. I couldn't take the chance of allowing him to figure out who I really was.

When it was time for me to learn about his recommendations, he handed me a copy of his report and suggested I read it. I held my breath as I carefully read through it. His interpretation of my personality and how my childhood affected me were so accurate I wanted to cry. I was completely in awe that someone had finally seen me, even if it was just on paper.

He looked at me sympathetically as he stated, "I am recommending that you be allowed to return to work, but only if you agree to go to therapy on a regular basis to deal with the childhood issues that have left you with an overwhelming sense of desperation and need to hurt yourself." My soul leapt with joy and relief that someone was finally on my side.

One thing concerned me though—I was able to fool him into believing that I was experiencing a "flight into health," which meant I was on an emotional high and was rebounding from the traumatic events I had just survived. I didn't want him to believe this because I really wanted him to see and understand me so I wouldn't try to kill myself again. But I kept quiet so I could go back to work.

Before leaving David's office that day, he stared at me and said, "I'm willing to see you for therapy."

I was momentarily speechless and then admitted in a trembling voice, "I'm not sure I can see a male therapist, especially after what happened to me growing up."

"A change might be good—maybe it's time you talked with a man in light of your past sexual abuse."

Looking directly into David's eyes, I challenged him, "Can you help me overcome my problems so I won't ever have to be in therapy again?"

With great confidence, he said, "I can help you overcome your problems with about a year of therapy, I have a unique approach."

Impressed with his confidence and belief that he could help me, I said, "I'll see you next week."

PART III

THE JOURNEY OF HEALING

Chapter 28

The Difficult Path to Understanding

AUGUST 14, 1997, finally arrived, and I was terrified about going back to work. I wondered where I would be working, who I would be working with, and what I would be doing. No one explained anything to me, only that I was to show up.

"We're not putting you back in your old position—you will now do the nursing home admissions for the long-term-care patients," Rita announced. "We want you to start off in a no-stress situation to see how you handle it emotionally."

Her words were like a slap in my face because the job was well below my level of education and experience.

Trying to hide my disappointment, I said, "Thanks for giving me the chance to prove myself—I promise I won't fail you."

Rita then escorted me to my new office. It was a very small cubbyhole, far away from my co-workers, in the basement of the building where old rehab records were stored in large brown boxes. There were no windows or people—just huge brown containers of old charts lining the walls.

I knew my new position was going to be extremely boring and redundant since the bulk of my job duties entailed filling out forms. After quickly becoming irritated with the repetition of my "no-stress" assignment, I came up with numerous ideas on how to improve the nursing home intake process. Surprisingly, I was given permission to make the necessary changes. Everyone was delighted with the time it saved, and dazzled with how professional the forms looked compared to the old hand-written originals. Rita was so pleased with the new process that she gave me the task of orienting and training the entire department on the new system. Quite an accomplishment for the undesirable who had only been back to work less than a month.

Although the people at work were nice to my face, I could sense that my suicide attempt was in the forefront of everyone's mind. It was obvious that I didn't fit in anywhere and I was seen as a charity case with this new job assignment. It was also apparent that everyone thought I was crazy and should have been fired rather than being given the chance to prove that I wasn't who they thought I was. That didn't help how I felt on the inside; it really bothered me. There were many days I just wanted to quit. But I knew I had a mission to complete so I had to persevere as long as I could.

About a week after I returned to work, Rita informed me in a stern voice, "It's time for your annual success review." It was obvious by the tone of her voice and the rigid look on her face that she didn't like that I had returned to work. It was also apparent that the timing of the performance review was a political one and something that would hopefully make me resign. Realizing all of these things, I felt as if someone had punched me in the stomach.

As anticipated, the review didn't go well. Rita just sat there and said over and over again that I had really "hurt the department." Each time she said that, I became more and more upset until it was apparent to both of us that I was still very fragile. I couldn't hold back the tears that freely streamed down my face.

I confessed, with a trembling voice, "I don't have anyone I can talk to about my return to work and how I feel about it—I need someone to talk to."

Rita looked directly at me as she picked up the phone and arranged for David to see me for an emergency appointment.

As I walked over to David's office, I was deathly afraid of seeing him even though he was the one I had survived the neuropsychological evaluation with and grew to like. I was afraid he wasn't going to believe anything I said, just like everyone else when I was growing up. At the same time, I was so desperate for his help and understanding that I went to see him anyway, praying that he could make all of the bad feelings and the need to hurt myself go away.

David immediately won my respect when he squeezed me into his busy schedule. It told me that he understood I was desperate; that he wanted to help me; that he understood the emergent nature of my feelings; and how easily they overwhelmed me. It was refreshing that someone understood I was about to fall apart. I'm sure my suicide attempt, just three months earlier, was also fresh in his mind. Thus, he understood I wasn't far from stepping back into the realm of self-destruction.

As soon as I sat down on the striped couch across from the fireplace in David's office, I found it difficult to remain still. My hands were electrified with nervous energy. Everything about me raced with fear that I would fall apart emotionally from the forbidden family secrets that needed permission to come out and be heard. I flashed back to when I used to hide; when I rocked back and forth in the corner to keep myself from skipping off into the dark, ethereal world of insanity. I silently sat there doing the same thing in the dark recesses of my mind, trying to feel safe. I wondered how I could have wanted this person to help me, but I was already too afraid to open up to him. It then occurred to me that I was afraid that David was going to see inside my heart, and he would think badly of me when he saw how messed up I was. Tears began to fall from my eyes as I realized that I desperately wanted him to help me, and that I had to trust and confide in him or I would die.

This stark realization left me trembling and mumbling, "I feel so bad, so alone. I'm not coping with my having to work in a place where everyone knows about my suicide attempt. They're watching me all the time—looking to see if I'm really crazy. I feel so self-conscious, so out of place—like I should give up on work and life. Every day I have to try really hard not to kill myself."

David listened to my vague ramblings, and immediately explained what he thought I should do to fix what was happening. He jumped right into problem-solving mode because he was a cognitive-behavioral therapist: that meant that he was someone who primarily focused on the mind and its thoughts to heal the psyche. It meant that we didn't really discuss what was going on with my feelings, but worked on solving my problems intellectually. After all, I had to be able to function at work or I was going to lose my job.

The first task with therapy was instilling in me that *thinking leads to feelings and feelings lead to behaviors*. This was how I was going to be able to change who I was. This was the core philosophy of David's therapeutic beliefs. With this, he began educating me so we would be operating from the same knowledge base.

The first lesson came with David informing me, "You're operating out of a child and critical parent ego state, rather than an adult ego state." He went on to explain that each of us has three distinct ego states from which we operate: *parent, adult, and child.* The parent represented my thoughts and the messages I gave myself, especially the critical ones my mother ingrained in me when I was a child—the ones I continued to carry as an adult. The child represented the unbearable and overwhelming feelings I felt as a child growing up. The ones that were filled with hurt, torture, unworthiness, and self-hatred. In essence, I was letting my parent (my mind and thoughts) bombard my adult self with thoughts of what a bad person I was, while my child (my emotions) was barraging my adult self with the horrible and torturous feelings from my past. This wasn't healthy because my adult self wasn't strong enough and didn't have firm enough barriers to keep the parent and child parts of me from spilling over and reeking havoc in my adult life. Thus, the goal was to make my adult-self healthier and stronger so I could operate solely from this adult ego state, while keeping the other two ego states in their proper places.

Even though I knew this made perfect sense, I had no idea how I was going to do it and how I was going to survive until I could make this technique part of me and my life.

I also learned that only about ten percent of a person's mind consciously operates out of the present and thinks in linear and ordered terms. The other ninety percent is the unconscious mind that operates out of the past and thinks in non-linear and unordered terms. In other words, there wasn't much order in my unconscious mind—just a lot of scattered, hurtful feelings and bad memories that I didn't know how to access and that weren't accessible for understanding and healing.

The primary problem was that I didn't have any way of knowing how anything in my unconscious mind was ordered, so I didn't know how to access it. It was like having a file cabinet with papers randomly dumped into it and trying to find one specific piece of paper that dealt with one specific period of time or one specific incident that happened over twenty years ago. It was almost impossible to find that one piece of paper without having to go through the entire filing cabinet—that is why the unconscious mind is considered to be non-linear and without order.

After I was educated on these things, David said that I had to learn the basics because I didn't get them growing up. Apparently, most people learn *three basic concepts* as children and these concepts shape their whole lives. These concepts escaped me because of the way I was raised, and because of the abuse and dysfunction I was involved in at such a young, vulnerable age. The three basic concepts were:

1.   I am a good person;
2.   There is order in the universe;
3.   I have a certain amount of invulnerability
     (Things happen to other people, not to me).

I lacked all three of these fundamental concepts, so I began the journey of trying to ingrain these concepts into myself. The only way I would be able to learn these fundamental beliefs and be able to incorporate them into my life was through conscious repetitious input. I had to change the way I thought, in order to change the way I felt, in order to change the way I behaved. So phrases were written down on cards for me to say to myself over and over again during the times I wasn't in therapy. I started off with three basic phrases:

> *People don't do things against me, they do things to meet their own needs.*

> *How I behave is about me, how other people behave is about them.*

> *I am not disturbed by things, but by the view I take of those things.*

> *How others treat me tells me more about them than it does me.*

"These phrases are called *cognitive hooks*," David explained. "When things start getting out of control or when you begin feeling emotionally overwhelmed, these phrases will help reel in your thinking so you can change the way you feel."

I eventually called the cognitive hooks my guardrails because I saw my life as a highway needing guardrails on both sides of it to keep me, and my life, on the road—free from crashing off the highway of life and ending up dead.

The cognitive hooks were important because the way I saw and perceived the world was skewed and extremely distorted. I thought the way everyone acted was directly related to me, and was about me: if someone were in a bad mood—I must have done something to put them in that bad mood; if someone were angry—I must have done something to have angered them; if someone yelled at me—I must have done something to deserve being yelled at. No matter what it was, I felt responsible for it. *These phrases were supposed to teach me that I was responsible for myself and no one else, and in turn, that meant that everyone else was responsible for their own behavior.*

Not only did I feel responsible for everyone and everything around me, but I believed that people instinctively didn't like me and treated me badly because I was unlovable. I was convinced that people were doing bad things to me because I was a bad person. I thought I deserved the treatment I was getting, and I believed that everything bad that happened to me or in the world was my fault. I basically let people treat me however they wanted to and I took it, without question or defense. I didn't realize that people acted like they did, not to hurt me, but to meet their own needs.

Before I left my first session with David I asked, "Am I ever going to be different? Will I ever be all right? Will the day ever come when I can forget what happened to me? Will I ever like me and not want to hurt myself?" He answered my question by writing down this cognitive hook:

> *I learned to be this way, so I can learn to be different.*

As I walked down the hall back to my cubbyhole in the basement, I didn't understand how repeating those phrases to myself was going to help. But, I was told to do it and I did it because I wanted, more than anything else in life, to be happy and to be all right.

Every day that I wasn't in therapy I carried my cards around with me and said them to myself over and over again until I had memorized them. After I memorized them, I just kept repeating them to myself, hoping I would see some change in how I felt. It was very frustrating saying those words to myself because I didn't believe, on a feeling level, what I was saying. I was tired of trying to fake it until I can make it, but I believed I had to do it in order to survive.

All during my therapy, I collected different phrases to help me change my thinking and to get through each situation that troubled me. I came to love my cards and began relying on them almost like a security blanket. If I didn't have anything else in my life to hold onto, I had my cards.

On the home front, Karen and I were still living together, even though everything was falling apart. The primary problem was that I was working extremely hard with David, while trying my best to work in a place where I still felt like I didn't fit in and no one liked me. I still felt like the black sheep of the facility, and it reminded me of the days at home when I felt alone and unworthy. I was also at a point in my life where I realized that I didn't know who I was, and that maybe I had never known.

I had spent my entire life trying to take care of everyone around me and then, as an adult, trying to hurt myself—for what—I wasn't sure. I never had the opportunity to figure out who I was and what I wanted out of life. But I now knew that I had to figure out how to get over my past, so I could answer my questions and learn how to be happy. This meant that I had to eat, drink, and sleep therapy and what I was learning, so that maybe it would take charge of my life and become second nature to me. In essence, it was a full time job, leaving little time for anything outside of work and therapy, and consequently taking a lot of time away from Karen.

My need for real help, just to stay alive, meant that David worked with me in two-hour twice-weekly sessions. Most of his patients could get finished with a session in an hour, but I couldn't. It took him that long just to break through my defenses so I could talk to him and so we could get some work done. I didn't do it on purpose: I was just afraid of being abandoned again—afraid he would hurt me like my mother and all the other adults in my life had done.

My mistrust was confusing because I really liked David and was glad that he was my therapist. He was the only person I had ever met who wasn't afraid to really talk to me and share things about himself, especially about his own physically abusive childhood. It was good to know that there was someone else in the world like me. For so many years I had thought I was the only one who was messed up, and that fallacy had separated me from everyone around me. It was really good for me to hear about the things that happened to him because it allowed me the opportunity to understand that despite the bad things that happened to him, he turned out to be all right and so could I. He was my hope, and I loved listening to his stories.

I began feeling the need to separate myself from my Karen; to isolate myself from everyone around me so I could focus only on myself. I then became confused about whether or not I was gay. And if I were gay, then I wanted to know how I ended up that way.

I wondered if I was born straight and turned gay because of the sexual abuse or if I was born gay. For some reason, I wasn't sure anymore and it left me confused, frustrated and feeling as if I was drifting farther away from the truth of who I was as an individual. It seemed like I pondered this question for a long time before gathering the courage to ask David his opinion. I stared at the floor, embarrassed and with my hands clenched tightly together, as I asked his opinion.

Without a moments hesitation, David confidently looked at me, and professed, "I think you were born heterosexual, but you became emotionally gay because of the abuse you sustained growing up—especially the sexual abuse. You've remained gay because women are more nurturing than men; women feel safer to you; and their anatomy is easier for you to deal with."

Somewhere in my heart I knew there was truth in his words. I didn't like men: I hated having sex with them because I always ended up feeling dirty, ashamed, and used. However, I was now more confused than ever because I thought I had been comfortable with my sexual orientation for the last seven years.

David wanted to further understand what prompted my change of sexuality, so he probed deeper into my psyche. "Sandy, tell me more about the sexual abuse. What exactly did Gene do to you? How often did he do it? Did you have to do things to him? Did anyone else abuse you? Can you give me more details?"

I had no idea that my asking a single question about the cause and nature of my sexual orientation would have led to this. But, as soon as I realized where David was going with his questions, I froze in fear at the thought of revealing the disgusting and horrible secrets that made me feel dirty and ashamed. As I sat in his office trying to hide my immense fear and apprehension, I meekly recounted what had happened with Gene. But when it came time for me to tell the truth about Miguel, something happened that I wasn't prepared for. My mind raced and I found myself saying, I feel so cold. I've got to get closer to the fire. David is waiting for more details but I've got to get warm. I really like sitting in front of his fireplace, I seem most at ease in front of the warm hearth. And I don't have to look directly at him. I still can't look at him and reveal my secrets, my feelings. I'm still afraid that he might hurt or abandon me.

I've never told anyone what Miguel did to me. It's so disgusting. How am I going to tell David now? How? What will he think of me and about why I couldn't make Miguel stop? I can't get any words to come out of my mouth? The memories burn inside me like a fire. They've made it impossible to trust anyone, especially men.

I hate myself because of the things I've let happen. I hate feeling like a victim who will always be burdened with overwhelming feelings of guilt and shame; a victim who can't escape the feelings. I'm tired of reliving the abuse over and over again in my heart and in my mind, and acting it out with the people in my life who I want to have a relationship with.

How am I going to explain all this to David? Make him believe me? Face him and say the things I need to say? Will he think I deserved what I got? That I'm a bad person? I'm a prisoner in my own mind.

I sat on the pillow in front of the fireplace, trying my best to find the words to explain the unconscionable events I had to endure. I was so terribly frightened. I felt like such a small child on the inside—like I was going to fade away. David kept prodding me to answer his questions. All I could do was mouth the words, "Miguel sexually abused me."

When it came time to tell David that Miguel had held my head and stuck his penis so far back in my throat that I thought I was going to die, I couldn't say anything.

David sat firmly in his chair quietly encouraging me, "Just relax, Sandy, and say whatever you need to say—you won't shock me. Really, it's OK—it isn't a big deal."

I didn't understand why he was saying that. It was a big deal—it had ruined my life for over twenty years!

After a great deal of prodding, and still sitting in front of the fireplace rocking back and forth, my trembling lips eked out, in a barely audible voice, what Miguel had done to me. With the words out in the open, I felt overwhelmingly vulnerable and ashamed. As I sat and listened to David's response to my confession, my eyes locked onto the flames in the fireplace. Suddenly, I felt like the worst person in the world. I was consumed with the need to hurt and punish myself for what Miguel had done to me. As the feelings began to overtake me, I went away somewhere in my mind.

My mind momentarily went blank and then I saw myself, not being sexually abused, but back in Lexington hiding in a corner with my mother beating me. I heard the children's song "Hush little baby don't you cry" playing over and over again in my heart. I felt my throat starting to close up, and I couldn't breathe or swallow. My ears could hear David talking to me, but it was like I was too far inside of myself to respond to him. No sooner than he would stop talking to me, I would feel myself drifting further and further into my mind, huddled in a corner somewhere begging, "Mom, please stop hitting me."

The next thing I knew there was another therapist sitting in the room with us. Her sweet, gentle voice began talking to me, trying to bring me back to the present using guided imagery. It seemed to help center me back into reality, to detach from what I was seeing in my mind's eye.

I managed to get back to the reality that I was sitting in front of the fireplace in David's office. I was in a terrible emotional state, unable to function or drive. David explained that what happened to me that night was called *dissociating*. It was a defense mechanism I had adopted to separate myself from the pain I was experiencing. I learned to do it as a child so I could deal with the abuse without going insane.

The whole sexual abuse issue was hard for me because I felt as if I had caused all of it to happen, and that I was a bad little girl because I didn't make it stop. I felt dirty and ashamed of myself, like a vile and wicked person who deserved only pain and anguish for letting it happen. But I now saw that all of this greatly interfered with my relationships with men and people in general. I didn't trust anyone because I was afraid that they would hurt me and make me do things I didn't want to do. At the same time, I was afraid I would do things I didn't want to do because of my desperate need for someone to love and hold me. I was terrified of getting close to anyone for fear of being smothered and trapped.

David and I continued to talk occasionally about the sexual abuse, but I couldn't heal from it because I still couldn't talk about it or feel it without dissociating. So, I remained a prisoner to my worst memories and fears.

Not too far into my therapy I started getting ferocious migraine headaches. It was suggested that the headaches were caused by my unconscious mind not wanting to deal with the things I was trying to force myself to talk about. The nightmares also continued, leaving me extremely tired from the lack of sleep.

Because I wasn't obtaining much resolve in therapy, I was becoming more depressed and angry by the day. I maintained my relationship with Karen, even though it was difficult. I was still the outcast at work. I wasn't happy anywhere and I surely wasn't happy with myself. I really wished I had died on June 16.

I was especially angry with Karen because she had been my power of attorney during my last suicide attempt, and it was her job to take me off life support so I could fulfill my wish to die. I believed it was Karen's fault that I was still alive. It was her fault I was having to deal with the horrendous and insurmountable pain and hurtful memories of my past. I didn't want to be going through that anymore. I was angry. I was tired.

Because I was continuing to stay depressed and suicidal, David and I started spending a great deal of time trying to figure out what the self-destructive feelings were that kept running around inside me. Every time we investigated it, the same issues surfaced: my mother and the feelings I had about her. This caused us to explore my relationship with her, what it was about her that made me want to hurt myself and why my heart hurt so badly.

The first thing that always came to my mind was that I never felt that she loved me. Somewhere in my mind I knew that she had to have loved me because she was a mother, but my heart and the core of my being never felt as if she did, especially after my eye accident. I couldn't figure out what I had done that was so wrong that my own mother couldn't love me and couldn't instill her love inside me as a child. I wanted her to hold me and tell me how special I was. I wanted to feel in my heart that she loved me. Without this I felt as if I had missed out on something important—something that would have made me feel like a whole person. I was left without the love that only a mother could give a child.

When I thought about growing up without any affection or warmth, it always reminded me of the psychological studies by Harlow and his monkeys. The well-adjusted monkeys grew up on surrogate mothers made from a soft terry cloth that felt warm and comforting. The other monkeys that weren't emotionally or psychologically stable, and who had difficulties with self-esteem and interacting with others, grew up on surrogate mothers made from a cold wire mesh. As I remembered this important psychological study, my soul sank with the understanding that I was definitely the monkey who had nothing but wire mesh for a mother.

Secondly, I remembered how much my mother and I were unhealthily intertwined because of the horrible stories she flooded me with about her childhood. I had no choice but to embrace her and her stories because they made me feel sorry for her. In turn, I felt responsible for her, and became my mother's mother. The frustrating thing about this was that I was given the *responsibility* to take care of her but without the *authority* that normally went along with it. It resulted in me feeling confused and powerless; weak and unworthy; lost and not knowing who I was. Then I remembered the question I had been asking myself, "Who was there to take care of me, to make sure I felt loved, and to teach me what I needed to learn as a child?" The answer echoed through the years: "No one!"

Thirdly, I remembered that I was my mother's protector, making sure on a daily basis, year after year, that no one would hurt her. This made it impossible for me to tell her when someone was hurting me, how the dysfunction and abuse made me feel, and how I needed her to love me. It left no one to understand my needs or to meet them. Instead, I was placed in the role of feeling sorry for Mom, so much so that my heart literally ached for her. So as the good little girl who was the protector of my mother and the family, I was given the insurmountable job of making sure that she felt loved since no one in her life ever had.

Unfortunately, this left me afraid of getting angry with my mother for the way she treated me growing up. I was afraid that if I stood up for myself, I would make her feel unloved and abandoned, like I had felt all my life. I couldn't bear the thought of making anyone feel like I already felt. I couldn't endure the thought of hurting my mother in any way—even though she had hurt me immensely and continued to do so.

I cried to David, trying to explain my feelings, "Mom emotionally abandoned me when I was a small child. She didn't spend any quality time with me, didn't hold me, and didn't tell me that she loved me. Instead, she saw me as a blemished child who was no longer perfect because of an accident that left me with an ugly eye. I was so hurt and confused about why Mom didn't stop all of the bad things that were happening to me. Why couldn't she just get out of the relationships with all of the abusive men, so my brothers and I could be all right?"

David, being the intellectually-oriented therapist he was said, "Let's talk about what the *thoughts* were that led to your feelings, how you have given your mother so much power over your life, and how you continue to do so." We went on to explore the cognitive avenues that would keep me from giving my mother control over me, and would help me think about her differently.

"Your mother loved you, but not in the way that you needed her to. You have to learn how to *separate, individuate, and reintegrate* with your mother before you will ever be okay with her and what happened to you," David said.

My mind knew that he was right, but my heart and soul were afraid that if I separated myself from her that she would abandon me, especially if she figured out what I was doing. I was terrified that if I acted like an adult and like I didn't need anything from her, she would think I was mad at her for the way I grew up and thus reject me. I was continually afraid of losing my mother's love and being abandoned again. This was ludicrous since I had never been granted the privilege of her love and had always been abandoned in the first place.

David also pointed out, "You're still living the role of the tortured child and this perception will never go away until you change the way you view your situation and your mother."

With this new understanding, I got more cards to remind me that I wasn't the tortured child anymore and that I needed to start changing my perspective about my mother and how I thought about her. *I needed to substitute the child's perception with the insight of an adult.* I still wasn't sure how I was actually going to be able to accomplish the separation, individuation, and reintegration thing, but I practiced the new cards anyway.

I torture myself as my mother tortured me because I have taken the mother role assigned. Soon the time will come for me to say "No" and become who I am.

Separate the distortions of a child's perspective and substitute the insight and understanding of an adult.

Remember the vampire in the turnip patch. You can't get blood out of a turnip, and you can't get love out of an emotionally bankrupt Mom.

It's not true that I was unlovable and unacceptable— only that I was a vampire in a turnip patch.

I am accepting the fact that my mother loved me the best she could given her own pathology, but she did love me.

I had a right to be angry about the lack of attention and the abuse I got from my mother. I am carrying around the role my mother assigned to me, but it was never a role that I was supposed to fill—so anytime I am ready I can lay it down and walk away. Then I become who I am, instead of filling a false role forced upon a child.

Hearing all of these things really made sense to my intellectual adult self, and I knew there was power in these thoughts. But my heart, and my child self that was filled with destructive feelings, didn't know how I was going to accomplish the goal of separating myself from my mother. I was afraid that if I did, I would risk messing up the possibility of ever having her love me one day. It made me wonder when I would be adult enough to stand up for myself and say, "Enough is enough!" and be able to do what I needed to do to be free of my mother's hold on me, once and for all.

The more I worked on the issues about my mother and my past, the harder it became for me to be involved with, and dedicated to, my relationship with Karen. Everything seemed so crazy. The lessons David was teaching me were whirling around inside of me so fast I almost couldn't keep up with them. Somewhere inside I understood that I couldn't be in a relationship with Karen right now because she was more like a mother to me than my partner. When I realized this haunting fact, I was truly stunned and afraid. I had no idea what I was going to do, and how I could remain in this relationship with her while I worked on myself.

One night after seeing David, I reached my breaking point. I sat Karen down and nervously confessed, "I'm struggling terribly. I'm trying my hardest to hold on to my life and deal with the issues of my past all at the same time. I need you to give me a little bit of space to figure things out, especially with the question of who I am and what I want out of life."

Karen broke down crying as we talked about my proposal but finally agreed to give me the space I had asked for. I was immensely relieved that she seemed to understand what I was saying, and I held onto the hope that maybe our relationship could be salvaged once I worked though my issues and knew who I was.

But the next couple of weeks proved that Karen didn't have a clue as to what I was asking for. Instead of giving me space, she became more clingy, to the point of smothering me. I was becoming angrier and angrier and felt as if I wanted to explode. I didn't know what to do. I knew there had to be room made in my life to work out my childhood because I couldn't stand how desperate I felt.

My first thought was to kill myself and get it over with, but as soon as I remembered how much trouble I had gotten into the last time, I quickly dismissed that unforgivable thought. I then fantasized about drinking and drugging, until I realized that this option was also fraught with enormous consequences that would lead me further into the pit of self-destruction. I began dreaming about packing my bags and moving to Arizona without telling anyone, hoping I could leave my old ways and my past behind so I could start my life over. I thought about moving to the mountains of Montana where I could live off the land. Then I realized that I would be taking me, and my feelings, wherever I went. I would ultimately be faced with the same problems and dealing with myself.

I managed to hang on until Christmas before I got depressed and my spirit began growing weary. I discovered that I wasn't only mired down in the difficulties of work and my suffocating relationship with Karen, but I was also becoming frustrated with David because he only appeared interested in my thoughts and not with exploring my feelings. It made me feel like he wasn't interested in understanding my emotional pain. It seemed he was only interested in finding and announcing the solutions to my thought processes rather than helping me work through and understand my emotional pain and how I became who I was.

I really didn't want to celebrate Christmas at all that year (1997), and I truly didn't care about getting a tree or decorating it, getting or giving presents, or anything. I only wanted to be left alone to sort out what was happening inside me. I didn't have enough energy to devote to therapy, working, being in a relationship that I wasn't sure I wanted to be in, and still have enough energy left over for Christmas and everything that went with it.

In quiet desperation, I beseeched, "Karen, please give me the space I asked for. I'm not handling the feelings and memories that are surfacing in the therapy very well, and I'm having problems figuring things out."

A look of surprise came over her face, as she declared in a firm and defensive tone of voice, "I am giving you space."

My heart was now beating fast. I was afraid of making her angry with me and not loving me anymore if I continued to speak my truth. But, I forced my quivering lips and tear-filled eyes to communicate, "You have become more and more clingy, almost to the point of smothering me. I can't get better if you don't leave room for me to change. Please give me the space I need before I absolutely lose or hurt myself again—it's imperative that I have the time to devote to understanding the journey I'm now on and what is causing my pain."

Karen always cried whenever we talked about anything and this proved to be no exception. She cried hysterically about my request and turned the conversation around to make it look as if I was *doing something to her* rather than *asking for something for myself*. She became defensive and screamed, "You just want to end the relationship!"

This wasn't what I was saying and her lack of understanding only frustrated me more. "Look, I just need us to take a few steps back from our relationship, to become friends again and rebuild our relationship on something more lasting and more solid," I said. This was true more than ever because I felt that our relationship had been built on what I needed from her emotionally and what she needed from me that her husband used to provide her—not on unconditional love for one another.

I could hear the frustration and separation in Karen's voice as she finally agreed one more time to give me a wide berth for healing.

Basking in a little bit of relief, even though I knew the timing wasn't great, I went ahead and asked for the other thing I needed. I stared at the floor as I meekly said, "I can't do Christmas this year. Would it be all right for us to skip it this one time?"

This was the straw that broke the camel's back for Karen, and it was now obvious that her feelings were hurt. "This is just an excuse—it's about me isn't it?"

"No Karen! It's about me—not you!"

"I don't believe you!" she cried.

"Really, it's about my issues." She still wasn't listening.

Despite the fact that I had asked for what I needed for the first time in my life, and was able to skip Christmas, I felt like such a bad person for causing Karen pain. But, I knew that I had to do this or I was destined to repeat June 16 again—maybe successfully the next time.

Karen and I continued living together for several months as friends, but the more we tried to pretend that we were friends instead of partners, the worse things got between us.

By spring, Karen declared, "I can't be in a relationship with you anymore—I'm ending it. I can't tolerate the space you've asked for—it's just another way of you saying that you want out of our relationship."

I felt defeated as I realized I was left alone again because someone wasn't willing to give me the space I needed for the healing process. In many ways, it reminded me of Randy's inability to allow me the same opportunity for change.

Chapter 29

Road Blocks

AFTER KAREN and I split up, things at work started changing rapidly. Rita reinstated me to my original position but moved me to a different floor of the facility to work. I was concerned about my transfer to this floor because it required a nursing degree to be able to understand the medical jargon and to do the job. But, Rita said this floor was the best place for me to start even though it was the hardest section of the facility to learn and understand. I was definitely torn about my promotion. One part of me was happy that I was maintaining enough emotionally stability to be promoted while the other part was afraid I would buckle under the pressure of having to prove myself again, especially in an area that required a level of expertise I didn't possess. The more I thought about my new job assignment, the more afraid I became. I realized I still didn't have any self-confidence.

The first couple of weeks of my new assignment proved to be more overwhelming than I had anticipated. I struggled with the fear that my imperfections would eventually lead to punishment and I would be viewed as less than worthy. I was also faced with the terrible revelation that I had to learn how to interact with the staff and the patients in a way that was professional and that left my emotions outside of work. I was frustrated because it felt like I had to learn each person's personality so I could do what they wanted and so they would like me. I lived in fear every day that I was going to do something to make someone mad at me and I would get in trouble for just being myself. It reminded me of my life at home with Mom

Everything became overwhelming. Day after day, I went to work depressed, angry, suicidal, and feeling as if everything were caving in on me. I believed that everyone around me always felt competent, did everything perfectly, and felt self-assured. While I, on the other hand, felt ill-prepared and unable to handle anything. I was constantly nervous, afraid, and felt as if I were suffocating with the belief that I couldn't be myself at work or anywhere else. I was stricken with a sense of extreme incompetence.

Then one of my co-workers, Joyce, seemed to sense my vulnerability. She made it her mission in life to be hostile to me and to verbalize hateful, hurtful comments to damage my already fragile self-esteem. It was like she could see my weaknesses and couldn't resist taking advantage of my deteriorating condition. Each time she said those terrible things to me, my spirit broke with misgivings of unworthiness. And inevitably, she always won because I would become so distraught that I would run out of the office crying and harboring the feelings that I still didn't fit in anywhere. I eventually learned that I had to separate myself from her in order to protect myself, just like I did at home when I was growing up, so I retreated deep into my shell.

It eventually got to the point where I was very defensive around Joyce because I never knew when she was going to strike. So I resorted to pasting on my "I'm okay" face and became nothing more than a chameleon who changed behaviors and personalities to match whatever situation or person I was dealing with at any given time. This was safer than letting anyone know how vulnerable and afraid I was. It was also safer than running the risk of getting hurt again. However, not being able to be myself further complicated my confusion about who I was and where I was going.

I found it extremely difficult dealing with all of the changes at work in conjunction with everything I was working on in therapy, and with losing Karen. I felt like I was drowning, like I needed to hurt myself more than ever. The stress and inherent risk of failure made me feel worse about myself as a person. In many ways I returned to the all-too-familiar need to explode or to jump out of my skin because no one understood the incredible strain this new position was placing on me. And, how it brought back the feared consequences of being punished if I wasn't perfect. It got so bad that I called in sick several days and admitted that I couldn't emotionally handle therapy and work at the same time.

On the days I called in sick to work, I went to see David and tried my best to explain what I was feeling. "I'm an emotional basket-case! How do I handle my extreme fright and nervousness? The fear that people aren't going to like me? The daily apprehension of getting in trouble if I'm not perfect and don't people-please?"

David looked bewildered and said, "I don't understand why you're plagued with those feelings because I don't see you that way. The way you see yourself is distorted. No one around you can see the nervousness and fear that you're convinced is 'oozing from every pore of your being'." Smiling, he continued, "From the outside looking in you come across as confident, intelligent, and quite capable of doing anything you set your mind to. Only you can feel what's happening inside—no one can see it from the outside."

David tried to get me to see that I was a good, likable person, and that my problem was that I had spent so much time shooting down any compliments anyone ever gave me that I maintained the poor self-image I developed growing up. His metaphor for my condition was, "You have bad dark soldiers guarding the gates of your mind. Their job is to shoot down any good, light-filled soldiers that have anything to do with any good thoughts or good comments about yourself." He then gave me another card that read:

> *You are wonderful, attractive, charismatic, likable, lovable, cute, intelligent, and entirely acceptable and competent.*

I definitely had a hard time with this because in my mind, and in my heart, I didn't understand how he, or anyone else, could think those nice things about me. After all, I believed that if he knew who I truly was and understood how I really felt, he would know that those things weren't true.

David tried to convince me of my worth by providing me with some suggestions on how to deal with Joyce and my fear at work. He insisted:

> *My attitudes, feelings, values, beliefs, and opinions are just as good as anyone else's.*

> *I don't have to be different than I am in order to be competent.*

> *Everybody else out there is making it up as they go along or they're following somebody else.*

Everybody (almost) is afraid to acknowledge the fact that nobody knows what they are doing.

Nobody knows what they are doing, but that's OK— it means that I don't have to know what I 'm doing to be OK.

And "Your attitudes, values, beliefs, and opinions don't have to match other people's to be valid," he said.

Despite my new cards, my self-destructive needs were resurfacing. So I spent more and more time with David in emergency sessions. One day he looked at me seriously and said, "I'm still amazed at your continued need to hurt and kill yourself, despite the cognitive retraining I've been doing with you. I can't understand why the cognitive phrases aren't taking hold of your mind so that your feelings can be more positive and self-affirming."

I didn't understand either. I didn't know why I instinctively became frustrated, desperate, and suicidal every time something overwhelmed me and every time we had a rough session.

It was during this time that I made both of us nervous because I had thrown together a stash of about 300 pills and bought a gun in case I needed a quick way out. David was concerned because of the lethality of my previous suicide attempts, and it left him all too aware that I might very well succeed at killing myself the next time. We both were afraid that I was going to get overwhelmed and kill myself out of desperation, especially since I wasn't able to envision how my life could be once I was free from the clutches of my mother, the abuse, and the dysfunction of my childhood.

I must give David credit though—to help me trust him and feel comfortable enough to discuss things—he promised he wouldn't have me committed to the hospital as long as I promised to call him before I did anything stupid. I know there were many days and many nights when he wasn't sure if I was going to survive, but he always kept his word and I really appreciated that I could trust him. He knew, as well as I did, that any other therapist would have hospitalized me. And, if something had ever happened to me, he would have been held responsible. But, David always kept his word and I always called him first.

To further complicate my life, when I was getting ready for work on

June 30, 1998 my phone rang. I instinctively knew something had to be terribly wrong for the phone to be ringing that early in the morning, but I just couldn't imagine what it could be.

When I picked up the receiver, there was a familiar voice on the other end telling me that Dr. Russ had died last night and that Lydia was on her way back from out of town. For a brief moment nothing seemed real. I couldn't believe the words that were piercing my ears, causing shock and my knees to buckle. I fell to the floor with grief, not knowing what to think or feel, and rocking back and forth telling myself, "This can't be true!"

Dr. Russ' death hit me hard because I loved him with all my being. No matter how badly Lydia treated me after my suicide attempt, Dr. Russ was always objective and unconditional with me. We used to do little projects that he couldn't do by himself. We cut down trees, sawed firewood, fixed the toilets, repaired the dog doors, mended the porch, and anything else we could get into. We were buddies and we both loved the same things. It was great hanging out with him. He always appreciated that I could fix anything and he seemed to thrive on my expertise, which in turn made me feel good about myself.

The most important thing though was that I learned a great deal from Dr. Russ and I admired him. I wished that I had his inner peace and sage-like wisdom so my soul would become quiet, and my heart would become filled with something other than pain. I wanted to like and enjoy life like he did. I loved him the most because no matter what happened in his life, he was always calm. No matter what I did, he always accepted me just the way I was. This was true from the time he was my doctor at Castwick Recovery Center, until the day he died.

When Dr. Russ passed away, I felt as if I had lost a part of me. However, I didn't believe that I had a right to grieve his death because Lydia still considered me to be an outcast and made it very clear that I was no longer a part of their family. I wasn't even allowed to sit with the family at the funeral, and was treated as if I had no right to mourn my loss. Lydia still hung onto the memory that I tried to kill myself and it was her anger that wouldn't allow her to get close to me again. She had never forgiven me, and I was going to have to live with that for the rest of my life. No matter what I did or what I said, I was never going to be able to redeem myself in her eyes.

Drowning in a sea of grief, I called David. He was the only person I could talk to about Dr. Russ' death, and the only one who wouldn't hold my suicide attempt against me. As always, David fit me into his busy schedule. I sat in my designated place on the striped couch, feeling abandoned and alone. Tears ran down my face, as I stared at the floor, thinking about how badly Lydia was treating me and how my soul ached at the loss of my friend.

By the time I had managed to reveal the pain I felt about Lydia's betrayal and unrelenting anger, and Dr. Russ' death, all of the painful feelings of my past resurfaced like an unwanted tidal wave. In a matter of seconds, I was in contact with feelings of being unwanted, unloved, unworthy, not good enough, not fitting in, and not being a good person. I was struggling with the horrendous emotions running around inside me. I knew in my mind that what was happening was about Lydia and not about me, but I just couldn't figure out what to do with the feelings all of this was tapping into.

David relied on his cognitive approaches to help me figure out what I must have been thinking. After all, we knew that *thinking leads to feelings, and feelings lead to behaviors*. No matter how hard I tried, I couldn't let my defenses down long enough to figure out what I was thinking, and what would cause such feelings to surface now. It was like the thoughts were coming from somewhere other than my conscious mind. The only thing I knew to be true was the way Lydia was treating me reminded me of my mother, but I tried my best to follow David's advice and say, "this is about her, not about me."

The one thing I really learned and took with me from that experience was something David wrote down on one of my cards. He called it "Pop's Legacy:"

> *It is good to allow others to pursue their own path— and in allowing them to do so, I can accept them even though I do not wish to follow their path.*

I was granted three bereavement days by Rita to mourn my loss. At the end of my designated time of sorrow, I made my way back to work. I knew I should have taken a couple of extra days off to attend to my wounds, but instead, I forced my way back into the office with a pasted professional face, trying to convince everyone I was all right. By the end of the morning, I was consumed with such sadness and depression I could hardly breathe. I didn't want to be at work—everything I did felt wrong. Everyone seemed to be keeping a close eye on me, wondering if my loss would be the straw that would cause me to make another attempt on my life.

I tried my best to ignore the barrage of painful feelings, but no matter how hard I tried, I just couldn't. I was so worried that everyone could see right through me that I finally gave in to my paranoia. I went to talk with Rita to see if I could get what I called a reality check so my soul could be at rest once again.

I sat in her office with my body shaking and my voice trembling as I asked, "Do you think I'm doing all right at work? Are you happy with my job performance?"

"Everything is fine," Rita replied in her usual stone-like demeanor and vacant tone of voice,

"I asked about my job performance because everything in my life feels like it's falling apart," I meekly declared.

Rita looked at me with concern in her eyes and asked, "How are you handling Dr. Russ' death?"

My heart exploded with a surge of uncontrollable grief and with needing someone to understand how badly I was hurting inside. Not only because of Dr. Russ' passing away, but also because Lydia still hated me. I began crying. I wanted to tell her everything, but I couldn't. I was too embarrassed about being an outcast.

The more I talked and tried to get Rita to help me feel better about myself, the more I found that I couldn't control my emotions. All the old feelings I always carried around with me started oozing to the surface so fast that I almost couldn't keep up with them. I felt weary and wanted to give up again. When I realized that I was becoming the scared child again, I didn't dare admit it to Rita since she was the one who was involved with my last suicide attempt. I was now barely hanging on. The pain was getting too great to bear. I could feel in my body that I was about to go into one of my dissociative states. That was my clue that I had to get out of her office before I disappeared into my mind and ended up in trouble again.

In a matter of seconds, I made a swift exit, found myself sitting in my car crying and wondering if I was going to be able to drive home without killing myself. I truly wanted to die and get it over with so there would no longer be any pain or a need for anyone to love and hold me.

To my surprise, I made it through the weekend using my cards and hanging on by my fingernails. I went to work Monday morning as usual, but I could sense there was something different about me. I recognized, for the first time in my life, that I had crossed some magical boundary with another person, and that person was Rita. I understood that I had let my emotions get too far out of control in front of her, and it would get me in trouble because it was inappropriate for a work relationship. I didn't want to be a person who crossed boundaries and who was vulnerable at work or with anyone. I wanted to be the way I perceived everyone else: as self-assured adults who could do anything without a care in the world. I wanted internal stability.

I then remembered how David told me that change comes from the conscious repetitious input of my cognitive phrases. So I made a promise to myself that I would paste on my professional face every day, and I would repeat my cards over and over again so I could push my feelings aside and act as if nothing bad had ever happened to me. As I practiced my new role, I could see Rita was surprised at how together I acted that Monday morning and that helped me to avoid any consequences she might have been planning.

With the improvement in my work performance and demeanor, I was asked to do the long-term care admissions again in addition to all of my regular work duties because the admissions person had quit. Thus, I was now doing two jobs, trying to maintain my professional demeanor, and trying to keep my feelings under control. Initially, having to do the long term care admissions again was a breath of fresh air compared to what I was doing on a daily basis, but it was hard keeping up with my regular job duties at the same time. I was surprised though at how well I was able to handle being pulled in several different directions, and how I felt more in control at work. Finally, the things I was learning in therapy and practicing my cards were paying off. I was amazed that I was able to feel good about myself just because I was able to cope with something as mundane as work.

This extra assignment was only supposed to have been a temporary one, but it turned into a two-month ordeal. Before it was over, I was asked to train the new admissions person on her duties on top of everything else. I was able to keep my emotions under control by stuffing my feelings and using the cognitive phrases that stayed with me everywhere I went. I didn't know why the change occurred at that particular point in my life, but from there on I was basically able to keep my feelings under control at work and maintain a professional disposition.

A year had now passed since my return to work and it was time for my success review. On one hand, I was convinced I would do well because of my new ability to maintain professional poise and successfully hide my emotions. But, I was also nervous because my past had taught me that it was never safe to let down my guard. Whenever I felt safe or confident, I would get in trouble for something I didn't expect or someone would hurt me. However, I just tried to focus on the fact that I had made so many positive changes in the last several months, and surely my review would reflect it.

I went into the small sterile conference room where I first met Rita during my job interviews and my last success review. I never liked that room because it was usually used for official business and rarely for things that weren't stressful. Despite the nervous anticipation that ran freely through my body, I tried to act confident while repeating in my mind, "Everything is going to be all right and no one can hurt me unless I allow them to. I have made a lot of good changes, and I deserve a good appraisal."

I practiced these sayings over and over in my mind until Rita walked in and announced, "Vivian is going to sit in on your review with us." My heart started beating fast and my breath grew shallow. I instinctively anticipated that Vivian's presence meant that the review wasn't going to be a good one.

Fear and apprehension ran through me as Rita and Vivian explained, "A success review takes into account everything that happens over the whole year, not just a part of it." They went on to mention all the problems they had seen over the past twelve months, which included my depression, letting my personal problems affect my work and co-workers, meeting with Rita for "reality checks," and missing work because I was having problems dealing with things. "In particular, the last 'reality check' you had with me, right after Dr. Russ' death, upset me because it reminded me of the day you tried to kill yourself," Rita said.

Their reminders of everything I had done wrong caused tears to well up in my eyes. I tried to choke back the tremendous hurt and pain that came from the belief that no one understood how hard I had been trying and that nothing good could come from this review.

"Sandy, we have seen a huge change in you since your last 'reality check' and we are happy with how you have been acting at work. We have no complaints with your new approach to work, but because these changes are only a few months old, we're placing you on probation for six months."

I sat in front of Rita and Vivian enduring the devastating blow of being placed on probation. I was crushed and didn't know what to think or how to feel about it. In my heart, I knew this success review wasn't an accurate representation of the new me because so much of the emphasis was placed on how I had behaved months ago. It didn't give the new work me enough credit, and left me believing that nothing I ever did was good enough for anyone.

Despite the fact that I was falling apart on the inside and feeling as if everything I had done was in vain, I managed to make it through the meeting without getting upset or crying in front of anyone. Instead, I sat in front of them with my hands clinched tightly together, listened intently to their words and maintained my professional demeanor. I dared not open my mouth for fear that I wouldn't be able to control the words and emotions that would follow. At the end of the meeting, I politely walked out the room. I counted the seconds until I could make it to my car so I could let out the emotions that had been building.

As I sat alone in my car waiting on my appointment with David, I was inundated with the same old feelings of not being heard or understood. I was reminded of the terrible fact that no matter what I did, nothing was ever good enough: not for my mother, not for Rita, and not for Vivian. I was drowning in my own miserable and painful existence of unworthiness and ineptness. Suicidal thoughts raced through my mind, reminding me that relief could be at hand. I was torn between needing to hold on to David so he could help make me well, and the need for immediate relief as I was once again the helpless child who didn't understand how to make the horrible feelings go away. Despite the fact that I tried to hold on to David's words of wisdom from past sessions, I felt as if the bottom was falling out from under me. That no matter how hard I tried, I wasn't ever going to be good enough for anyone, including myself.

Since my appointment with David wasn't for another hour and a half, I had to figure out what I was going to do, so I wouldn't end up hurting myself. I paced back and forth in the parking deck, crying. My hands were balled up into fists; I needed to strike out at something. Desperate, I finally called David's secretary, "Bobbie, I need to come up to the office early before I do something stupid."

By the time I made my way upstairs to David's office, tears were streaming down my face, and I wanted to hurt myself in the worst way. Bobbie took one look at me and knew that I needed somewhere besides the waiting room to sit. With her look of compassion and soft tone of voice, she guided me safely to the biofeedback room where I could sit in silence and safety. I was so messed up and so emotionally wrought with sadness and self-loathing that I kept the lights off and sat on the floor in the corner of the room rocking back and forth, crying uncontrollably. Time passed slowly as I drifted, without awareness, into one of my dissociative states, oblivious to my surroundings.

David walked in and found me in the corner, lost to myself and the world around me. My heart was consumed with hopelessness and no desire to go on anymore. The despair that surrounded me left me unable to get out of the corner, or respond to his request. I only wanted to lie down and die. When he realized the seriousness of my state, he came over and started talking to me, trying to help me get connected with reality enough to get out of the corner so he could help me resolve whatever was wrong. For some reason, none of his words helped, but as soon as he reached out his hand, I instinctively grabbed hold of it for dear life, allowing him to help me out of the corner and down the long corridor to his office.

After helping me to the couch, David looked at me with bewilderment in his eyes and asked, "What happened to put you in such a state?"

His question embarrassed me. I didn't want to tell him about my review. I was convinced that because Vivian and Rita wrote those things down on paper and they believed what they said about me, that those things made me a bad person. I was afraid that if he knew what they said, or saw the review that he would think I was a bad person, too. I just couldn't take that. I already felt bad enough about myself without losing the only person I was holding to.

After a great deal of prodding, I bowed my head in submission and clinched my hands tightly together as I told David what happened and showed him the review. After reading the unbearable words of my so-called performance, he acted as if the whole thing was no big deal.

I was confused, but I listened intently as he explained, "A review is designed to give you a picture of how you did the whole year, and most of the problems that are on the review are no longer an issue for you. You have already resolved most of these problems, and you should focus only on the parts that show how you have changed for the better." He continued, "This doesn't mean you are a bad person and that you aren't as good as anyone else. We just need to make sure that for the next six months you keep your personal problems away from work, you don't miss any work days due to emotional crisis, and you maintain your professional demeanor." In other words, just keep up the new "work me."

From that day forward I went to work and did my best to keep my feelings safely tucked away out of everyone's sight, even though I still felt like I didn't fit in. Hiding my true feelings from the world was labor intensive, and went against everything I thought I needed to do because I still possessed the incredible need for someone to understand and love me. I needed to show and own my feelings, since that was never allowed at home when I was a child. I wanted my thoughts and feelings to be appropriate and to be accepted like everyone else's. However, mine still weren't.

Even though I was now able to function better at work, I was still an emotional wreck on the inside, despite the fact that no one at work could tell anymore. No matter what I did with all the cards David gave me, and with all of the time we were spending together in therapy each week, I continued to have problems with depression and wanting to kill myself. It was all I could do to make it from one day to the next.

I was only hanging on at this point because David said that if I ever tried to kill myself again and I survived it, he couldn't continue seeing me. I couldn't take a chance of losing him; I needed him to help me get better. I needed him to hear and understand what I was saying. I needed his validation.

My life became nothing more than working all day, seeing David several times a week for several hours at a time, and trying to stay alive in between my appointments and until my next Success Review. I did nothing but eat, sleep, and breathe therapy while trying to figure out what was bothering me so badly that I couldn't get off the spiraling staircase of self-hatred and self-destruction to become happy and content with myself and life.

The next six months were very difficult for both David and me. We hit some type of therapeutic impasse. I was becoming extremely frustrated with him because I felt that he was ignoring a very vital part of me. He continued to only focus on the thinking part of my problems, rather than dealing with the emotional side of the abuse and my feelings. We argued about that until he finally stated, "I don't believe you need to address your emotions or relive the abuse in order to get well. You've done enough of that."

I kept trying to explain, "I feel as if there are two people that make up Sandy: the adult who is thirty something years old, and the child who is emotionally stuck at about two years old. I believe the adult part of me is emotionally healthy; can handle things in the real world because of the cognitive techniques you've taught me; and is the thriving part of me who wants to be positive and self-sufficient. But, I also have a child part who always gets me in trouble. She needs to be heard and desperately needs to have a voice about everything that happened to her. She feels trapped because no one has ever shown her any understanding and has never validated anything that happened to her. She needs to come out and be heard! She needs to let go of and share the forbidden family secrets!"

To my utter dismay and frustration, David didn't see the validity in those words. Instead, he insisted, "I don't understand how exploring the abuse and your feelings about it are going to change anything, especially since you usually go into a dissociative state when we talk about them."

"Then I need you to talk me through the dissociative state because that is where my scared child lives! I need you to help me get her safely to the other side of her pain so I can learn what she is afraid of. Surely, once the unspeakable fears and memories are out in the open, I can apply the cognitive techniques and respond differently to my feelings and past hurts" I said.

David just shook his head and said, "I'm sorry Sandy, I don't agree. The only way to change the little girl who resides deep inside your heart is by changing the way she responds to things that happened to her, and this can only be accomplished by changing the way she thinks about those things."

The continued dismissal of my emotional needs, and sole concentration on the cognitive therapeutic style, absolutely frustrated me to no end. In many ways, I felt David wasn't hearing a word I was saying and there was no way to get what I needed so I could heal and help my child self to grow up.

Even though I didn't have multiple personalities, when I thought about what help I needed from David, it always reminded me of what happened with the woman in the movie Sybil. Due to her traumatic childhood, Sybil was fragmented into many different parts. This left her with numerous personalities who came out at very inopportune times, wreaking havoc on her life until she couldn't control what was happening to her. In order for her to get well, she went back into her childhood, to the times that were filled with enormous pain and abuse. The emotional events in turn revealed to her therapist her hidden identities and the true cause of her emotional malady. Sybil was then assisted with meeting each part of herself and then integrating them until she became one whole person: an adult who could deal with life on its own terms.

This was what I thought I needed to do. I needed David to see my little girl who was hiding in the corner and being beaten, being sexually abused, and witnessing the domestic violence. The little girl who lost her pink kitty, who hid in the closet and trash-bins for safety, who protected her mother when there was no one left to protect her, who learned to self-destruct, and who didn't feel loved. I needed him to help my child self to walk through the terrible memories and feelings of my past so I could integrate them into a healthy adult with the use of the cognitive techniques. I firmly believed that if someone could see and experience the pain of my inner child and help her to feel validated, then her pain would become bearable and she wouldn't have to act out any more or hurt herself.

I was also frustrated because I couldn't find a way to feel what I was saying when I was in session with David. When I was trying to tell him what happened to me, I couldn't get my feelings to come out at the same time as my words. If I was trying to relay how it felt when my mother beat me, or when Gene to sexually abused me, my feelings would mysteriously disappear—I felt like I was telling a story about someone else. It made me feel like I wasn't real, and that what happened to me wasn't real either. It led me to perpetuate, in my own mind, what my mother had always done when she told people (from whom I was trying to get help) that I was lying about everything. David finally convinced me that when I was doing this it was just another form of dissociating. It was a defense mechanism I learned as a child to protect myself when I was feeling vulnerable. But the problem now was that I had perfected this defense mechanism so well that I couldn't even let anyone, including David, in to help, even though I was now an adult.

Instead, I was left talking about things in his office, and then emotionally falling apart and becoming suicidal after I went home from the barrage of overwhelming feelings that I couldn't feel around him. This also kept David ignorant of my real feelings because he had no way of really knowing or understanding what was happening inside me, and this was a vicious cycle that kept me trapped and self-destructive.

I knew I had to find a way to let David in or I was going to die. I had to find a way to let him know what happened to me even though I couldn't verbalize the horrible and debilitating memories. I began writing down some of the things I needed to tell him. I thought that, just maybe, if I could put my feelings down on paper, then we could talk about what I wrote, and it would force me to feel what happened to me and keep me from being suicidal. This book evolved from those writings.

Writing about the sexual abuse led to more exploration in our therapy sessions about whether I was straight or gay. I was truly confused about it, and needed resolution to this poignant and moral mystery.

David explained, "You need to take it one step at a time and to accept the fact that you just don't know what your sexual orientation is right now. You are to be the good observer and say, 'So this is how it is,' and accept where you are at this point in your life and in your recovery."

In many ways, I felt as if this was an insurmountable task. I needed to know who I was and where I was going. I needed to know if my soul mate was going to be a man or a woman, or if I was destined to be alone the rest of my life because of my inability to be intimate.

For the next several months, David and I argued about therapeutic technique. I was now convinced beyond a shadow of a doubt that I didn't need to ignore my feelings, but rather, I needed to allow them to be heard and explored. The more we talked about it and the more we didn't work on what I thought needed to be worked on, the more frustrated, depressed and suicidal I became. There were many days when I became so furious with David, because I didn't feel he was hearing me, that I stormed out of his office determined that I was going to end my life. Sometimes I would make it as far as his door and then stop cold in my tracks because I really didn't want to have to resort to killing myself.

I would stand there angry, crying and pleading, "I'm serious about needing you to hear me and to understand my feelings. If you can't do that, then I'm left with no choice but to kill myself. I really want you to help me not to get this way anymore."

But it was like he didn't understand what I was saying. My mind wanted to fight for my life, and stay with him so he could help me figure out what was wrong with me, but my desperate inner child didn't have the coping skills to handle the life-threatening feelings that were engulfing me. Even more disappointing was the fact that I obviously lacked the skills necessary to help David understand this plight that was causing me such pain, and him such frustration.

As I continued to spiral down the tunnel of emotional misunderstanding, I started clinging to David for dear life. I was constantly calling him for emergency appointments so he could help me contain my overwhelming feelings. I frequently paged him over the weekends because I was so depressed and suicidal that I needed his voice to provide me with a sense of safety. Somewhere inside I knew he had to have been getting tired of me, but I didn't know what else to do or who else to turn to. I was doing the best I could.

The weekend cycle began with me getting depressed, until I was left with an overwhelming need to talk with someone. Of course, I didn't have anyone in my personal life to do that with. When I couldn't take it anymore, and when I understood that I was about to kill myself so the pain would go away, I would call David and cry, "Please, I'm begging you, please help me!"

At that moment I wanted David to help me figure out what was going on inside me; to feel that he cared about what was happening to me; and for him to hold me and make me feel that everything was going to be okay. I wanted him to love me like a parent would love a child. I wanted him to understand what I was saying but I could never come out and tell him those things, and he never did.

Instead, David would reply, "Sandy, just find something to do and stay busy."

Instead of feeling helped, I felt frustrated and more desperate than ever. Because I couldn't get David to understand my hidden messages and what I wanted from him, I became more enraged and more convinced that I needed to kill myself. That, in turn, threw me back to the beginning of the vicious cycle that began with overwhelming depression and thoughts of suicide that neither I nor David knew how to me get out of.

David finally said, "Until you let go of your desire and need to kill yourself, you are never going to get well. You are keeping suicide as a way out, as an escape, and it is that means of escape that keeps you a prisoner to your innermost demons. You won't ever be able to resolve what you need to because you always have a way out when things get too tough."

I heard his words, but I didn't know how to do what he was telling me. After all these years I didn't know how not to want to kill myself.

I thought a lot about what David said and was afraid he was right. I broke down and asked him, "What am I supposed to put in place of the suicide when I'm in a difficult situation and really want to hurt myself?"

He hesitated before answering, "Just stay busy and use the cognitive phrases I have given you."

I wondered how that was going to change anything since I had been trying to stay busy and had been using my cards for a while now. "That's not good enough David—I need a solid plan that doesn't just include occupying my mind. I need a detailed way of doing things differently when I get into trouble."

David maintained, "You only need to think your way out of any difficult situation by using your cognitive phrases!"

I grew angry as I now believed that I wouldn't ever be able to give up the need to hurt myself, especially since David couldn't understand or give me an alternate plan for when things seemed out of control. I desperately needed to know if I was supposed to call someone, or if I was supposed to do something special, what I was supposed to say to myself, and how I was to control my feelings and emotions. What was I supposed to do differently? I didn't understand!

David was frustrated because the cognitive model wasn't working as effectively as he would have liked and he didn't know how to get me to give up the suicidal thoughts. I was also frustrated because he still wouldn't take me to the forbidden places of my childhood so I could face my demons and deal with the insurmountable rage, anger, and hurt that my child harbored deep inside of me. So we muddled around for a while longer trying to figure out what to do next. At the same time, I was proud of myself because I didn't let my therapy or anything else personal spill over into my work. I went to my job every day and pasted on a professional face while repeating my cognitive phrases over and over to myself. I couldn't believe it, but those cards and phrases were really paying off in my professional life. I could now see how things at work weren't about me and how people were doing things to meet their own needs and not to hurt me. I was a grown up at work. It felt good to be a professional and to be able to do my job.

Six months had passed by rather quickly and it was time for my probationary review. I passed it with flying colors. The only area that Rita and Vivian thought I needed improvement in was getting my emotions to match whatever work situation I was in. I knew exactly what they were talking about. Whenever I was interacting with people, I became nervous and it came out as hyperactivity and an abundance of raw energy. I believed it was only permissible for me to show superficial emotions and act as if nothing bothered me. Even if I were in a situation that was sad, my response would be one that echoed no emotions whatsoever, only professional jargon. It was merely a way of protecting myself because I was afraid to let anyone see me for who I really was. I accepted their suggestion, even though I already knew it was a problem. The important thing was that I was off probation.

David and I continued muddling our way through each therapy session, while I continued becoming more frustrated at my limited and sporadic progress. I was still seeing him twice a week for two hours a session and was feeling pretty burned out. My sleeping continued to be interrupted with terrible nightmares and early morning awakenings, and I continued to have headaches that left me incapacitated. I began wondering how much longer I could keep up this pace. I also found myself questioning if David and I were ever going to figure out what I needed. Was I ever going to be well, or was I just kidding myself?

David and I persisted in our debate about dealing with my inner child and the emotional parts of my self, while he remained confused as to why the cognitive techniques weren't working for my inner child. So I made one last attempt at explaining how I saw therapy as a linear process and how I needed it to move from:

Point A (where I was now) to
Point B (exploring my emotions) to
Point C (incorporating the cognitive techniques) to
Point D (recovery).

Throughout my therapy with David, I felt as if he wanted me to skip Point B (dealing with my emotions) and to go directly to Point C (using the cognitive techniques). But my heart and soul screamed out that if I didn't deal with my emotions first, then I wouldn't ever be able to make the cognitive techniques work for me. Once again, David disagreed, "Therapy isn't a linear process—you can deal with your emotions through a cognitive means, without having to get knee-deep in your feelings. And I'm not the kind of therapist who is trained in how to do the kind of emotional work you want and need."

I didn't believe him, so I begged, "I'm sure that if you will just push me hard enough then the emotional toxic waste of my past will come to the surface so we can deal with it and you can teach me a new way of responding to it."

"Look Sandy, I could push you, but I don't feel safe enough doing it. I'm afraid you will kill yourself after you leave my office—especially since I'm your only support system."

I tried to disagree, but he continued, "Also, it would take two people to do it because I couldn't be the one pushing you and the one helping you work through your issues at the same time. I can't be the bad guy and the good guy simultaneously." He continued, "Sandy, the bottom line is that I won't and can't push you until you meet three criteria: you have to give me your stash of pills, your gun, and give up suicide as an option. Can you do that?"

"I'm begging you, please don't make me give up my only way out! Help me walk through this process so I will give these things up because I want to, not because I have to."

But no matter how much I begged and pleaded, David stood firm with his demands and wouldn't budge. Frustrated, confused, and desperate, I asked him over and over again, "How am I supposed to give up suicide? And if I do, what am I supposed to put in its place?"

It was obvious that he didn't understand what I was asking, and that he didn't know how much I really wanted to give him everything he had asked for. I wanted to tell him that I wouldn't hurt myself anymore, but I truly didn't know how to do it. I didn't understand how I was supposed to instantly quit feeling the way I had felt for so many years. I didn't understand what I was supposed to put in its place.

The more helpless everything looked, the more I wanted to kill myself. So I said, "We just need to be realistic about this whole thing. We need to accept the fact that I'm never going to be any different on the inside, and it's inevitable that I'm going to end up taking my own life one day. Why should we put ourselves through all of these changes when I am hopeless?"

I didn't expect it, but my reasoning only infuriated David. He said, "That's ridiculous—there is a solution to every problem—we just need to keep working until we find it! I don't understand why you can't think this way and what makes you want to give up so easily."

I couldn't answer him.

I was now a pressure cooker. All I was doing was getting depressed, getting suicidal, calling David, getting angry and letting off a little steam. The release of the metaphorical steam made me feel better for a day or so until the pressure cooker was full again.

As David watched the pressure cooker syndrome cycle round and round, he finally came to the conclusion that I was full of something called *retroflexed rage* and this was what was perpetuating the suicidal thoughts. Retroflexed rage was the anger I turned back on myself rather than expending on someone or something else. Since I couldn't get angry with my mother, I took it out on myself. Since I couldn't take out what I was feeling about the sexual abuse on Gene or Miguel or anyone else, I turned it back on myself. This retroflexed rage was also what was fueling the depression and the bad thoughts I had about myself. It was the keeper of my depression and suicidal desires. The question now was, how was I going to get rid of the retroflexed rage and how could I learn to deal with it on my own?

It was now June 14, 1999 and I was 35 years old. I had been in therapy with David one year and ten months, and it was almost two years to the day when I last tried to kill myself with the lethal overdose of pills. It was also the day that I learned David was planning on retiring. I was completely terrified at the potential loss of the only thing I was holding on to in life. It was also the day I hit my emotional therapeutic bottom and came to terms with the suicidal side of me for the first time in my life.

David and I were arguing again about his therapeutic style, what I felt I needed, and why he wouldn't do what I wanted and needed him to do. With David not buying into my avoidance of his earlier criteria, he reiterated in a stern voice, "I'm not going to honor your request because you still haven't followed through with my three requirements: give up your gun, your pills, and suicide as an option."

With my fists clinched in anger, tears streaming down my face, and my spirit drowning with hopelessness, I continued pleading, "David, I don't want suicide to be an option. But if you won't push me so I can resolve my past, then what is my option? I might as well kill myself and get it over with because I'm sure as hell not going to live the rest of my life the way I am and with who I am!"

My statement only left David angry and declaring again, "As long as you see killing yourself as an option, you won't ever accomplish what you need to with me."

I truly didn't understand and I tried to explain, "I really don't want to have to kill myself. I want to do what you're asking of me, but I also want you to do what I'm asking."

I didn't feel like David was hearing a word I was saying and he didn't think I was hearing him. The more we fought, the more I wanted to go down to my car, get my gun, pull the trigger and viola—no more pain and no more begging for help. No more wanting him or anyone else to love and hold me until I could do those things for my self.

David just kept looking at me with frustration in his eyes, and reiterating in a stern and non-compromising voice that I hadn't met his requirements in order for him to push me. I felt as if I were a mink caught in a steel trap and would rather chew my leg off than risk the amount of vulnerability that would come from handing over my gun, pills, and suicide.

I became so angry with him and his refusal to compromise that I stormed out of his office and ran down to my car to blow my brains out. While standing at my car with the barrel of the gun to my head, I began developing a sense of clarity somewhere deep inside that said that I was at a fork in the road. I had a serious decision to make. Afraid, I slowly lowered the gun away from my head. I quickly and safely tucked the gun and my pills inside my clothes and ran back upstairs to David's office.

I threw open the door and slammed my gun down on his desk and demanded to know, "Is this what you want? Are you going to help me now?"

His hand quickly reached across the desk, grabbed the gun and put it in his drawer. Then he said, "Sandy, sit down." I was far too angry and shaky to sit on the couch. So I remained standing and begged David to please just help me because I didn't know how to make all of this stop.

After a great deal of discussion about the whole suicide thing versus him pushing me, David finally said, "You don't know what you are asking me to do—it is definitely contraindicated by everyone I have discussed it with. I would no longer just be out on a limb with you, I would be standing in mid-air from a therapeutic and ethical standpoint! I don't even know if I could do what you're asking because I can't be sure that you wouldn't kill yourself." He paused for a moment and then continued, "Sandy, you know that as a therapist it is my responsibility to make sure you are safe— I can't do anything to hurt you or make you want to hurt yourself."

About two-and-a-half-hours later, we were both exhausted, frustrated, and angry. I was feeling extremely suicidal because I knew that I wasn't going to be able to get what I needed from David before he retired, and I didn't know how to do what he was asking me to do with removing suicide as an option. The more I thought about this, the more my wounded child started easing her way out of her hidden abyss of pain. In a matter of minutes, tears started pouring down my face. My body was curled up in a fetal position on the couch. I rocked back and forth with my trembling lips mumbling the same thing over and over again, "It's okay, it's okay, it's okay…" Then my inner child who held the pain and hurt associated with my mother began barreling its way to the surface. I cried uncontrollably and wondered if I was about to skip off into the unforeseen world of insanity. This was my core and the suicidal part of me that had never come out in front of David.

As soon as David saw her, it was as if a light bulb went off in his head.

"Is what's happening to you right now what you have been trying to get me to understand?"

Relieved that he was finally getting a glimpse of what I was saying, I nodded my head in affirmation while explaining, "This is the center of my pain."

With the look of insight on David's face, I instinctively knew he was starting to understand.

Desperate, I begged, "Please help my child self to be all right and help her work through her problems."

David continued to insist, "The way you will get over this is by changing the way in which you think and respond to your pain, to you mother, and to your childhood. If you will consciously give yourself different messages, then after a while your perspective will change and the feelings will no longer have power over you."

My mind and feelings were telling me that this was a huge task. It led me to delving further into my pain until I was almost a child again, alone in my suffering. David then repeated himself, but for some reason I heard his words with a new meaning. "No one can do this for you. No one can make you whole. No one can fill up the hole inside of you—You have to help yourself."

I finally understood that I had to change the way I responded to what happened to me growing up through conscious repetitious input. When I started feeling those overwhelming feelings, I was going to have to talk myself through them. When I wanted to hurt myself, I had to tell myself over and over again, "I'm all right, I can get through this . I learned to be this way, so I can learn to be different." I had to stand up and look my fears in the face. I had to let go of the emotional baggage and replace it with a cognitive perspective that made sense until I could find someone special with whom I could have a good, healthy relationship. Then hopefully, what I would get out of the relationship would, in a healthy way, satisfy what I had been yearning for all of my life.

Even though David seemed to now understand what I was saying and I understood what he was saying, it was time for both of us to go home. However, I felt like hell because I still hadn't given him my pills. I was still too afraid to let go of my only way out.

Utterly exhausted, I walked out of David's office and down the long, dark hallway towards the back door. All I could do was cry because I was leaving without giving up suicide as an option, and without giving up my stash of pills. I was an emotional wreck and had no idea how I was going to get through the rest of the night. As I stood alone in the dark hallway, I knew that if I didn't go back and give him the pills, I was never going to be well and I was never going to change. So I took the pills out of my pocket and held on to them for dear life, contemplating what I should do. Afraid, I turned around and slowly walked back down the hall to David's office.

As soon as I turned the corner, I saw that he was already standing outside his office, locking his door to go home. With my heart beating fast, sweat pouring off my brow, and my knees quivering with fear, I walked up to him and held out my trembling hand, placing the bag of pills in his hand. I held onto his hand tightly for a brief moment while bowing my head in submission and meekly exclaiming, "I need you to help me. Will you please help me?" I then reached out and held David's other hand and said, "Please don't give up on me. Please continue trying to help me." For a brief moment I could sense that he was frustrated with me, so I squeezed his hand and repeated in a trembling voice, "I need your help and I need you to understand that I am serious."

I waited for a moment, hoping that David would give me some kind of a sign that we were okay and that he wasn't going to give up on me. Finally, he looked at me with compassion in his eyes and squeezed my hand back, showing me that he understood how big a step this was for me and that he wasn't going to give up. I was instantly relieved and thankful. I then took another chance with David and asked, "Could I have a hug because I desperately need one?"

He was always such a kind and gentle person, so he hugged me until I could sense that he was going to continue trying to help me the best he could. I can't begin to explain how much I needed David to understand what I had just done; for the first time in my life I trusted someone.

I turned around and walked back down the hall, a different person somehow. I talked to myself the rest of the evening and told myself the things David wanted me to say. I tried to convince myself that I was all right; that things were going to get better; that I learned to be this way so I could learn to be different; that I had to face my fears; that someday I was going to find someone special who would love me; that suicide wasn't an option; and that I CAN DO THIS. I repeated those things over and over to myself.

I also figured out where I had gone wrong with my views about suicide. I thought David wanted me to change the way I *felt* about wanting to kill myself, when in fact all he wanted was for me to make a *conscious decision* that suicide wasn't an option any longer. I now understood that it would be my telling myself over and over again that, "Suicide is no longer an option" that would change the feelings about my wanting and needing to kill myself. I just had to figure out how to make it work for me, and how to quiet my inner child once and for all.

Chapter 30

The Beginning of the End

THE NEXT MORNING, I knew I was different somehow. There was something about giving up my permanent means of escape that brought all of my vulnerabilities and feelings about my past to the surface. I was absolutely exhausted and felt as if I had committed suicide emotionally, rather than physically. It confused me because I felt the same way I did on June 16 when I had overdosed, but without the fallout of comas, intensive care units, and psychiatric hospitals. I also had the guilt that went along with it; like I was in trouble. Yet I realized this being different was somehow for the better, even though it scared me so much that I started feeling as if this journey to healing was too big for me to handle, now that I was embarking on unfamiliar territory.

I felt so vulnerable that I didn't know how to act, how to feel, or what to think. Something inside had changed and I didn't know what to do with it, or how to cope with it. I felt exposed, like all my defenses had been penetrated and laid open. I couldn't even decide if I should go to work that morning, afraid that everyone would be able see my vulnerability. I had never been at this juncture in my recovery process, and I didn't know what to do.

Out of a pure, innocent need to understand what I should do and to get the help I needed with these new experiences, I called David. Phoning him was very different this time though. I didn't reach out to him in my usual I want to kill myself mode, but in a problem-solving manner, willing to do whatever he advised. My trembling voice confessed, "Something strange has happened to me. I'm different somehow. My defenses are filleted open, and I don't know what to think about how I feel. I need to know what I'm supposed to be telling myself so I can help myself. Should I go to work and run the risk of not being able to function? Should I skip work to see you so we can explore this uncharted territory together?"

David's voice reverberated with a sense of relief at my unpredicted progress, and suggested that I call in sick.

Once again, David squeezed me into his busy schedule and I confessed everything I was feeling. He reassured me that I wasn't crazy, wasn't mentally ill, wasn't in trouble, had a job I was doing well at, and I was okay. He went on to explain, "The feelings you are having are distorted. They are fueled by your child's fears, and it is your focusing on those fears that is making you feel this way."

In essence, he was once again telling me that I needed to change the way I was thinking so I could change the way I was feeling. The more we talked, the more my terrified inner child began coming out. In a matter of moments, I was curled up in a ball, rocking back and forth, crying uncontrollably and begging, "David, please help me! Please make my mother stop hurting me inside!"

This was the same wounded part of my core-self that came out last night and prompted David to ask more questions about her. This was the part of me that harbored the abandonment from everyone in my child's life, where all of my hurt was rolled up into one, and where the child who was beaten and emotionally wounded lived. This was the part of me that wanted to hurt myself.

Desperate, I looked up at David and said, "If I can work through this part of me and deal with it, then I know I will be all right. But I can't do it without your help."

With a confused look on his face, he asked, "What is keeping you from just sitting there and allowing yourself to experience what you are feeling without dissociating?"

In a child-like manner, I dared not look at him while I said, "This part of me scares me. I'm afraid these terrible feelings will consume me, or break me beyond repair. And, if I break, there won't be anyone to help put me back together again. No one, including you, knows how to deal with this part of me and I have enough common sense to know that it is too big for me to deal with by myself."

Insight lit up David's face as he declared, "The reason you can't share or resolve this part of yourself is because there are only small parts of it available to your conscious mind for you to work on. The rest of it is locked away in your unconscious mind. A little bit of it got locked away each time you tried to protect yourself as a child by going into a dissociative state."

As soon as he said that, my heart and mind instinctively knew that he was right. Maybe this was the reason why every time I felt my inner child resurface, I remembered Mom beating me until I was hiding in the corner. There was something about her doing that that really messed me up, kept me separating and dissociating, but I didn't know what is was because it was locked away in my unconscious mind.

He continued, "This is also the reason why you continue to see suicide as an option when it is really a conscious decision, and nothing more." I didn't know why, but that statement caused me to realize that starting at the age of thirteen, I had been anesthetizing and drowning my feelings in a number of different ways. I had done drugs, drank alcohol, exercised excessively, starved, binged and purged. Each of these things helped me push the abuse further into my unconscious mind. And each time I gave up one of these means of escape, the feelings I had been running from began mysteriously re-emerging. Now that I was trying to give up suicide as an option, I was aware of those same feelings resurfacing all over again and that was what I had been experiencing all that morning. In essence, when I felt vulnerable, I used self-destruction and suicide as a means of hiding from my feelings. I had been using suicide as a means of coping because killing myself was easier than having to face my past, my feelings and my wounded child. It was also easier than getting well because *I equated recovery with abandonment.* If I were healthy and appeared self-sufficient, I believed there wouldn't be anyone to love and take care of me, to make sure I was all right and I would be forced back into the role of taking care of everyone around me. I believed there wouldn't be anyone left to help me when I was struggling or when the bad feelings crept back in! I would be like an old glass jar that had been slightly polished and put back on the shelf to look pretty and gather dust, even though I was still breakable.

This insight was paradoxical because I was the one who was pushing people away and causing myself to feel abandoned because I didn't like who I was. I was needy, emotionally desperate, and had given everyone around me the responsibility of making me okay. As an adult, I still gave everyone unlimited power and authority over me. I gave away my power by wanting people to tell me what to do, how to get well, to make me feel loved, and by not thinking for myself or taking care of myself. I was sabotaging my own friendships and relationships. I needed to start taking responsibility for my own recovery, even though I still didn't understand how I could do this if the emotional part of my past still hadn't been dealt with.

I was also afraid that if I got well, then people would start expecting things out of me and I would crack under this kind of pressure. I was already so burnt out from my mother and my family needing me to take care of them, that I couldn't fathom giving anyone else anything, including myself.

From that infamous day on June 14, 1999 forward, therapy was very different. It was filled with numerous insights about myself and what I needed to do, even though I didn't realize the battle was just beginning. Thus, I grew more in the next six months of therapy than I had in the previous two years.

In the war I was waging on my past, I understood that I couldn't just live with the knowledge of what was wrong with me—I had to actually *change* my thinking and perspective about the things that were wrong. The more I began to understand that simple yet complicated truth, the more I started feeling physically unwell without understanding why. I was exhausted and unsettled from my usual problems with not sleeping. And with each day that passed, it was increasingly more difficult for me to put any food in my mouth and get it down my throat without almost vomiting. Once again, I wasn't hungry and food was repulsive. To make sure there wasn't anything wrong with me physically, I went to see a doctor where I learned that I had lost seven pounds in about a week's time. There was nothing wrong with me from a medical standpoint. I then figured out what was happening. Because I was trying to give up my last means of escape (suicide), my eating disorder was trying to resurface as an alternate coping mechanism so I wouldn't have to deal with my feelings and hidden issues.

This was the first time in my life that I saw the pattern and realized what was happening. So I sat myself down and told my child self, "I am not doing this again. I am not going to starve myself again so you can continue hiding from the truth. I *will* eat and I *will* deal with the issues I need to face."

David was proud of my progress and I got another treasured card with a quote from Eleanor Roosevelt, which read:

> "Believe in yourself…You gain strength, courage, and confidence by every experience in which you stop and look fear in the face. You must do that which you think you cannot do."

He also gave me another quote by an unknown person:

> *"Watch your thoughts, for they become your words.*
> *Choose your words, for they become your actions.*
> *Understand your actions, for they become your habits.*
> *Study your habits, for they will become your character.*
> *Develop your character, for it becomes your destiny."*

His timing was perfect. I needed to hear those words of truth because they made so much sense to me. I intuitively understood what he was saying, and somehow this gave me the added boost to face the fears that enslaved me.

As the weeks passed, some of the things David had been saying all along started making sense. The phrases I had been saying became clearer and clearer until I could see how they worked and how they could elicit change. I instinctively recognized that I was on a new path. A path of understanding that I desperately wanted to get right. I was now seeing that there was validity in David's methods, even though I was still convinced it was only one part of the puzzle.

I remained frustrated with David because he continued to ignore my feelings and maintained that I only needed to operate out of my mind and control my thoughts. His style of therapy left me with the assumption that he wanted me to fake it until I could make it. Then one day, David stopped our session and proclaimed, "Ignoring your feelings and emotions isn't my message. It is permissible to *acknowledge* your feelings, but you have to change how you respond to them by changing the things you say to yourself about them."

In other words, I had to use my cards to think myself into being different. Not to ignore what I felt, but rather *choose* how I was going to deal with my feelings, my past and how I was going to respond to them. *I had to stop being the victim and become the observer.* I had to learn how to say, "So this is how it is," identify my feelings, choose how to think and then what to feel. I had to understand that at the core of my being I wasn't the wounded child, but an observer, a witness who could choose what I wanted to think and feel, and how I wanted to act.

The desire to take hold of my thoughts and become the observer made me want to conquer my inner conflicts about my mother; to figure out what bothered me so much about her abandoning me. David kept trying to get me to see that *I wasn't abandoned by her because she had never been there to begin with.* Somehow this didn't fix the gaping hole in my heart that still wanted, and needed, my mother's love and understanding; for her to sit down and hold me and to tell me, "Everything is going to be all right." I couldn't figure out what to put in the hole in my heart, or how to fill it up so it wouldn't hurt anymore.

It then occurred to me that *if I learned how to take care of and love myself, then I couldn't ever be abandoned again because I would always have myself.* And, the only way I could ever be abandoned again was if I abandoned myself. I realized I had to take responsibility for myself and to stop being the victim. I had to get to the place where I could take care of myself and take full responsibility for my thoughts, feelings, and actions. Whatever happened in my life from here on out, I would choose. Taking responsibility for myself also meant that *I could take care of myself,* solve my own problems, learn to love myself, and accept myself for who I was and where I was at any given moment. To be the good observer who says "So this is how it is."

I had to understand that I couldn't change my past—I could only change how I responded to it, how I saw it, and learn from it. I had learned to be the quintessential victim because of the way everyone exploited me growing up, and because of the horrible things that happened to me. *But, it was me who continued to play the role of the victim as an adult.* Being the victim assured me, in my mind, that I wouldn't be abandoned again. But, in reality, it caused everyone to leave me because they couldn't cope with my dysfunction and what I *needed* from them in order to survive.

I learned that no one could make this journey for me and no one could heal me...that I had to heal myself. That no one was coming to my rescue like I needed as a child, and that I had to learn how to do it for myself. I had to love and care for me and to make myself feel okay and acceptable. Most importantly, when I could do this, then other people would want to be around me because I would no longer be needy and overwhelm them. Instead, there would be an air about me that would say, "I'm okay and so are you."

The most important thing that I learned about my overwhelming need for others to love and take care of me was that *it wasn't my needs that were the problem, but it was my being "needy."* Everyone has the need to be loved and accepted, but my problem was that I allowed that need to take control of my life. I had transformed a basic human need into one of neediness. It was true that I needed my mother to love me as child, but the erroneous fact was I thought I needed her to do it now, when what I really needed was to find myself and to take responsibility for me. I needed to change my perspective, to relax and to let things happen the way God saw fit and to trust that things would work out for my own good.

I also learned that I had to take the anger and rage that lived deep inside me and redirect it so I was using it to make myself better, to respond to my emotions differently, and to do whatever it took to make myself well. I had to use this anger and rage to give me the energy to do what needed to be done so I could emotionally survive my past. *For so long, the feelings of anger and rage left me feeling exhausted, depressed, and suicidal. I now had to figure out how to convert this energy into something I could use to heal myself rather than tearing myself down.*

And, because the feelings associated with my mother's lack of love for me were overwhelming, even as an adult, I had to get to the place where I could accept this part of myself. I had to tell myself that, "I am not little and helpless—nothing can, or will, consume me without my permission." It was my ability to think and reason that would give me the competency to control my emotions. So when I started feeling that something was insurmountable, I had to tell myself, "Sandy, you are in control of what you think and feel. You are the observer and you decide how you will respond to things."

I also learned of another self-induced fallacy—I believed I needed to model myself after someone else, when what I really needed to do was to figure out who I was and accept myself. Then if there were parts of me that I didn't like, I could go about changing them in a constructive and self-affirming way, rather than in a self-destructive and self-condemning way.

Although these insights started manifesting themselves in my life, the emotional part of myself knew that all was not well and that I still had a hell of a long way to go before my emotions caught up with my mind and the unbelievably accurate insights. I was definitely healthier in my mind than I was in my heart.

With David's keen sense of therapeutic poise, he took this insight-filled opportunity to begin trying to push me to make me angry. The purpose of this was to force out into the open the anger and rage I silently held onto. However, my unconscious mind blocked him each step of the way and left me a perpetual slave to its moods and poisonous aftermath.

With all of my great intellectual progress, I didn't understand why this was happening and why I still couldn't access my anger and rage. I understood, as well as David did, that I had mounds and mounds of rage running around inside of me, but when he started pushing me, it wouldn't budge. I realized that I was back to the same problem of not being able to feel my emotions around him, or anyone else for that matter.

I was tired and exhausted, especially with the realization that I still couldn't feel around David. I had so much work that needed to be done before he retired that I kept pushing myself. I just didn't know how I was going to muster up the energy to do it, especially since I still wasn't sleeping, I was emotionally exhausted from the countless hours of therapy, and I was still expending energy at work pasting on a face. It was obvious to David that I was growing weary. So he tried to encourage me with the explanation, "You have one last huge tree lying in the road, and you have to figure out what needs to be done in order to move the tree so you can be free."

I pondered his statement over and over in my mind, and in my heart I knew he was right, but I just didn't know how to move the stupid tree. Each day that passed with the metaphorical hardwood lying in the road of recovery, I began growing more frustrated until I drifted back into one of my old patterns of trying to take over the therapeutic process. I jumped back into the driver's seat—back to my beliefs about what I needed David to do—instead of trusting his objective therapeutic understanding of what needed to be done.

My mind understood that I needed to stop pushing and to let therapy unfold, as it should, because this was a therapeutic process, not one giant cathartic experience like I wanted it to be. I wanted a rush of emotions to cascade over me like a waterfall so I could address everything that happened to me growing up at one time, instead of conquering one emotional battle at a time. After two years, I realized the cathartic experience wasn't ever going to happen. I had to trust that I would recover when the time was right.

As I fell back into my original belief that David needed to help my inner child face her feelings and the incidences that happened to her, he also retreated into his original thoughts. He went on to declare, "I don't think the key to unlocking your anger and rage is my pushing you until you explode. You have been blowing off anger and steam your whole life through alcohol, drugs, anorexia, bulimia, compulsive exercising, and suicide, and none of that helped. There has to be something causing your anger and rage to regenerate."

In my efforts to understand what was fueling my anger and rage, I continued writing down my thoughts and memories for David's review, especially since I still couldn't talk openly or with feeling. Through this process it became clear to me that the core issues surrounding my mother was the tree that was lying in the road and was regenerating my anger and rage.

Somehow along the path from childhood to adulthood, the issues surrounding my mother took control of my heart and became my core self…my identity. It was the part of me who wanted her to love and take care of me, but then felt abandoned with no self-esteem. It was the part of me that always came out when I got depressed, when I became suicidal, and when I called David at home on the verge of killing myself. When I wanted to do drugs or drink myself into oblivion. When I felt the need to punish or hurt myself. It was my child who was desperately crying out for my mother to love me, and if not her, then anyone until I could learn how to do it for myself.

The desperate and needy part of me got locked away in my unconscious mind when I was being beaten by my mother, and when I was hiding in the corner trying to protect myself and dissociating. This was what changed my core self from a sweet and innocent child to one who was afraid all of the time and desperately seeking and needing other people to care for her. This kept me stuck in a perpetual cycle of neediness and dependency. My adult self had never faced the overwhelmingly desperate and vulnerable child who lived inside; the child who needed someone to love her, in particular, her mother. I had never let her come out and be seen because I was too afraid of losing control; too terrified of going crazy from the overwhelming emotions; and too ashamed and embarrassed about how I felt.

For many sessions, David and I discussed this at great length until we both had a firm grasp on what was happening to me, and until I learned that I had yet another vicious cycle that needed to either be destroyed or re-routed. We called it the *"Self-Perpetuating Rage Regenerator"* because I was regenerating and perpetuating my own anger, rage, and self-destructive behaviors, despite the fact that I hadn't lived at home or been a child in years. I was taking my core problem with my mother, and the old traumas associated with her, and regenerating my feelings about them over and over again. Despite the fact that I no longer lived in an abusive situation I continued regenerating how I felt about it every day of my life. The Self-Perpetuating Rage Regenerator worked like this:

- I had the core emotional problem of not feeling loved by my mother hiding in my heart. It left me feeling insecure, lonely, depressed, abandoned, unlovable, unlikable, and made me dependent on others to meet my needs.
- Because I didn't like the residual feelings I had inside me, I didn't like who I was as a person. So I eventually began equating who

I was with how I felt. If I felt unloved by my mother, or anyone else, then I instinctively believed, "I am a bad person, unworthy of anyone's love."

- I then took these overbearing and caustic feelings, coupled with how I felt about myself, and projected them onto other people.
- When I perceived that people didn't like me, it reinforced how I already felt about myself: thus strengthening the feelings my mother left me with and making this a self-fulfilling prophecy.
- I would then get mad at how other people were treating me, and how I didn't feel as if I was a good person or worthy of being loved. This, in turn, sent me spiraling into a hole of depression.
- After I got depressed, I had no one to talk to (because I had isolated myself by pushing everyone away in this vicious cycle) which resulted in suicidal feeling because I was alone and felt unlovable.
- I then got stuck in a double bind, being angry at people for how I *perceived* they were treating me, and my neediness for them to love me and make me feel okay. Thus, I was constantly stuck in *mutually hostile* and *mutually dependent relationships* with everyone around me.
- The mutually hostile and dependent relationships left me feeling confused, unloved, and desperate which led me back to the way my mother made me feel, thus causing the cycle to start all over again.

Summarized: Core problems →Internal feelings about self →Projected feelings onto others →Perceived Rejection (Self Fulfilling Prophecy) →Bad feelings about self →Isolation and depression →Mutually hostile and dependent relationships →Back to core problem.

In essence, I was seeing everyone around me as I saw myself.

The question now was how was I going to stop retroflexing my rage? The only obvious answer was that I needed to come to terms with what was causing me to stay in this vicious, perpetual cycle. I needed to deal with the core issues of my pain—the grief I felt about my mother. This, in turn, meant that *if I could change how I saw my mother and what she did to me, then I could change how I saw myself, and then, by default, I would be changing how I saw everyone around me.* If I liked myself, was confident, secure, independent, and had good self-esteem, then I would project this onto other people, and in turn I would see myself the same way. This was the goal and key to me being happy and free.

The flip side of this insightful understanding was that it also presented another problem. I didn't know how I was going to deal with the core issues surrounding my mother if I had never been able to feel the things that happened to me, especially in front of anyone else. I became terribly frustrated when I tried to talk about these things, especially with David, and I couldn't feel what I was saying. I felt like I was a liar, and as if no one was ever going to believe me. It reminded me how I felt growing up when Mom constantly told everyone that I fabricated what was happening in our home—even though I was the only one telling the truth. I wondered how I was going to fully recover if I couldn't allow anyone else to see my feelings that were buried deep inside my heart.

The new question became why couldn't I feel the pain of my past memories in front of people like David who needed to see them? One problem was that my heart understood that David didn't believe in the emotional side of me or of its importance in my healing process. But, I equally understood that I was mortified at the bad things other people had done to me and was ashamed of what I had done. Thus, I was terribly self-conscious when I tried to talk about them. I felt like *I was what happened to me; I equated my self-esteem with what other people had done to me; and was afraid David would do the same.*

My fear of being seen as a liar, and no one believing me, kept me separated from my true feelings and in constant fear of sharing things.

Simultaneously, I was captured in a relentless need for someone to validate what happened to me —to hear and believe me. David explained, "Because you have feelings and memories about what happened to you, your feelings about them are real—no matter what anyone says— because they are your feelings. *Feelings only exist because an event has occurred to produce them.*" In other words, I couldn't make up what I was feeling and this meant that my feelings were real. My feelings weren't a lie, because people can't make up or produce feelings to suit their own needs. So, *my feelings had always been inherently valid and therefore, I could rely on myself to validate my own feelings and experiences.*

Because therapy felt like it was taking forever, I started exploring what else I could do to speed up the process. I felt compelled to research and discover how I could reach my destination of recovery and happiness more quickly. I submerged myself in biofeedback and EEG training tapes to help loosen up the things that were continuing to hide in my unconscious mind, so David and I could work on them in our therapy sessions. Every night before I went to bed, I listened to tapes that either dealt with my unconscious mind, or helped me to sleep. I also started reading a lot of books and researching articles to better understand the plight surrounding my unresolved emotions.

In my everyday life I continued doing all of the cognitive things that I was supposed to be doing, such as talking to myself, saying my cards, and thinking through situations. However, I still found that I couldn't get a handle on my feelings, much less control them. I found this particularly frustrating in my professional life because I felt like two different people trying to survive in one body. This dichotomy became all too apparent when someone would hurt my feelings or got angry with me. I would try to act professional, like a secure and confident adult, but inside, I instinctively resorted back to the terribly hurt and wounded child. I was an adult who was able to use cognitive phrases and maintain a professional poise to the outside world, but I was still a frightened, traumatized and lonely child in my inside world who couldn't make the magical phrases work for her. It was very difficult not letting those two worlds collide on a daily basis. I didn't understand how I could be doing all of the right things in my mind, but I still wasn't able to control my emotions.

The difficulty with harboring two people inside of me taught me that I was splitting my life into parts. I was seeing my mind with the new cognitive phrases and new thought patterns as one part of me (the adult), and my unconscious mind with the wounded child and horrible feelings as a completely separate part (child part). Much like opposite ends of a spectrum, a dichotomy. I was also separating my past from my present situations, acting like neither one had any influence on the other. I was two different people living in the same body, if you will. I was an adult and a wounded child. This perspective looked much like this:

Present Situations/Conscious Mind/Adult Self vs.

Past Situations/Unconscious Mind/Wounded Child/Emotions

This perspective wasn't working because it meant I was trying to ignore the old parts of myself and thinking that if I could ignore them long enough then they would eventually go away. However, the more I tried to ignore my child self and her feelings, as instructed by David, the more my past and wounded child manifested herself at inopportune times.

The continued difficulty with my emotions reinforced in my soul that I would never be able to handle life and be okay unless I addressed and resolved the emotional component of my past.

Continuing to abandon the emotional work, David taught me that I was reacting to the world from an *external locus of control*, rather than an *internal locus of control*. I had an external locus of control because I didn't feel as if I had any control over my life or what happened to me, that if anything good or bad happened, it was by sheer luck. I felt as if I was stuck with no choices, that I was a mere victim of people and circumstances. No matter what I did, it wasn't ever enough. If I had a problem, I couldn't fix it by myself. If I needed something, then I had to get it from someone else. If someone did something to me, then I couldn't defend or take care myself. This by definition was an external locus of control because I believed and felt like I had no control over my life and everything that happened to me was controlled by external forces.

In contrast, people with an internal locus of control believe and feel that they have control over theirs lives. If they don't like something in their life or themselves, they believe they can change it. They also understand that the way in which they control their lives is by the choices they make. If they don't like something, they understand that they possess the power within themselves to change it, and believe there is always a way out that will ultimately be in their best interest.

I was giving everyone and everything around me *power* over me, my life, my happiness and lack of happiness. I was giving everyone else *responsibility* for my life and I was remaining the victim. So now I had to figure out how to shift my focus from an external to an internal locus of control so I could take charge and feel empowered with what I wanted out of life and how I wanted to be treated. The answer to yet another dilemma, was changing my perspective through conscious repetitious input. I had to start telling myself everyday "I am responsible for my thoughts, feelings, choices, and actions. I am responsible for me and how I respond to everything that happens to me. I am responsible for my life." I also had to start telling myself that "I am in control of my life and I can change whatever I don't like about it."

David reinforced, "You are also like you are, and where you are, because of the choices you made." When I initially heard his words I was angry and confused. My child self thought he was saying that I was who I was as a person because I wanted and chose to be that way, and I was emotionally impaired because I wanted to be. I believed in my heart that this was the furthest thing from the truth. I knew that I hadn't spent all of this time in therapy because I chose to be unhappy and miserable. After much discussion, I came to understand what he was really saying.

David was merely pointing out that, in my early adult life, I had several different paths I could have chosen, but I elected the course that led me to where I was at that very moment in my life. I chose this path out of ignorance, not out of a desire to be miserable or self-destructive. Despite my new awareness, I also had to understand that I couldn't sit around and beat myself up over the choices I had made, because I did the best I could with what I had to work with. Once I realized that, I began to see how this was also true for other people, even my mother. Maybe she did the best she could. The understanding presented me with new choices. I could continue to be angry with her and continue hurting myself, or I could say, "So that's how it was" and get on with my life. *I understood that this by no means excused what she did to me and how she made me feel growing up—it just allowed acceptance, and for me to release myself from my bondage to her and my horrific childhood.* It released me from feeling the need to punish her and everyone else for all of the bad and unconscionable things they did to me.

Once I understood that my life was like it was because of the choices I made as an adult, and that I could change my life from that day forward, it was a true taste of insight and freedom.

After much thought and therapy, I learned that I needed to develop a different perspective about how I saw my whole situation. I needed to understand that my childhood and all of the terrible things that happened to me were indeed a part of me and always would be. However, *it was up to me to change the extent to which these old things affected me.* But how was I going to change how much these old thoughts and feelings had affected me? How was I going to be able to respond differently to my present day situations that triggered thoughts and feelings about past experiences? How could I incorporate what I had already learned in therapy to diffuse the terribly overwhelming feelings that always resulted in me feeling like I needed to give up and/or kill myself?

One of the things I needed to do was to *learn how to make the things in my unconscious mind accessible to my conscious mind so I could identify them and learn different ways to deal with them.* I remembered earlier lessons from David that taught me that things in my unconscious mind weren't linear in time. So whatever happened to me a long time ago continued to feel as if it were happening to me right now. For example, my mother may have beaten me twenty years ago, and it caused me to feel small and helpless. But, now as an adult, when I became afraid, I automatically drifted back to feeling small and helpless again—just like I did when my mother was beating me in the corner.

The problem was that present day situations were triggering old feelings and keeping me stuck in the role of the victim. So I had to give the things in my non-linear unconscious mind linearity. I had to get the terrible things that happened to me out of my unconscious mind and bring them to my conscious mind so I could learn new ways of dealing with them. I also had to learn how to *connect* the things in my *present life* that were causing emotional turmoil, with the old *unconscious thoughts and feelings about my past*. I then had to choose how I was going to handle the old thoughts and feelings in a new way with my cognitive phrases. It looked like this:

Present Situation → Unconscious Mind/Wounded Child/Emotions

↑   ↓

New Response   ↓

↑   ↓

New Perspective   ↓

↑   ↓

Cognitive Shelters ← ← ← ← ← ← Cognitive Hooks/Phrases

For example, say I am in a stressful situation at work and I begin feeling emotionally overwhelmed, like I can't handle the situation (Present Situation). Feeling "emotionally overwhelmed and like I can't handle the situation" clues me into the fact that I need to see what this situation is triggering from my past. So I ask myself, "Sandy, what are you feeling and what do these feelings remind you of?" I then understand that I am feeling afraid of getting in trouble and that I'm going to get hurt somehow.

That in turn reminds me of how I felt when my mother beat me (Unconscious Mind/Wounded Child/Emotions). I then think about the cognitive phrases I learned in therapy and choose which ones best fit my situation. For this situation it would be:

> *That was then and this is now.*

> *I am no longer a wounded and helpless child.*

> *Nothing can happen to me unless I allow it to.*

I then take my cognitive phrases and think about them in a safe place in my mind (cognitive shelters). When I am ready, I then take my new thoughts and new perspective, created by my cognitive phrases, back to my current situation so I can respond to it differently and thus not end up in the Self-Perpetuating Rage Regenerator.

The purpose of this process was to put space between how long it took for my old feelings to get triggered and for me to act out (i.e. suicide attempts). To allow me time to enlist the help of the observer and to use my cognitive phrases so I could choose a new perspective about the situation and a healthier way to respond to it, rather than hurting myself. The hope was that my new responses would eventually become automatic with *practice*.

I called this way of obtaining a new perspective the *New Perspective Paradigm*. The following diagram denotes how situations can lead to the Self Perpetuating Rage Regenerator or the New Perspective Paradigm:

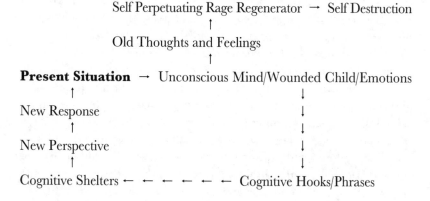

This understanding was incredibly beneficial in my everyday life, especially at work where I had to deal with difficult people in difficult situations. It also gave me the control and the power I needed to change things rather than remaining in the victim role. This was my internal locus of control.

Shortly after this tremendous discovery of truth, I actually started looking to my future to see what I wanted to do when my therapy with David was over. I went back to a previous goal: wanting to become a counseling psychologist to help children and adults who had grown up in abusive families like I did. I wanted to help them so they wouldn't suffer as long as I did and spend their entire lives listening to people tell them that they didn't know how to help them. I didn't want anyone else to pray for death because they couldn't stand the burdensome pain of carrying around a toxic, painful past. I didn't know how else I was going to be able to help others except by going back to school and writing this book.

On several occasions I had almost gone back to graduate school to become a psychologist, but I had never been at a point in my own recovery where I thought I was ready to impact someone else's life, especially since I hadn't resolved my own issues yet. But something was different now and I felt, for the first time in my life, that I was truly learning how to respond to my childhood differently and was choosing to be a different person, even if it was only from an intellectual standpoint. I was choosing to be the adult who could take care of herself rather than the wounded and tortured child. I knew this child would always be a part of me, but I would now have the choice as to how I responded to her.

David said that going back to school was a good idea, and went onto to explain why. He said, "I think you will make a great psychologist because you have already been through so many things and have tried just about every means possible to cope. But I also think school is a great idea because there are three things needed in order for change to occur: *the desire to change, the knowledge about how to change, and an environment where the change can take place.* I think school will provide you with an environment in which you can try out your new perspectives and obtain new healthy responses to your new behaviors." In other words, school was supposedly going to be the place where the changes in my thoughts, feelings, and behaviors, as a result of the cognitive techniques, could be explored and experienced. A place where I could be around other emotionally-stable individuals who could provide me with the responses that would reinforce and continue fostering growth in the new me.

Much to my surprise, I simultaneously passed the Licensed Professional Counselors exam and was offered a position in a graduate school program in Atlanta. But I decided to postpone school for nine months while I finished my therapy with David.

As I started working towards going back to school and getting prepared for David's retirement, I realized I needed his help with some other key issues. One of the biggest issues was how afraid and nervous I was whenever I was around people. How I couldn't relax and be myself around anyone, even if I had known that person for a long time. How I couldn't be myself around David, even though he knew just about everything about me. How I isolated myself and had difficulty meeting and feeling connected with anyone. I also wanted to overcome my fear of men.

David and I tried to explore why I was still afraid of both of these things. I confessed I was afraid of people because I was terrified that I would get hurt again or I would find myself in a situation where I couldn't stand up for myself. I worried I wouldn't be able to take care of myself if someone tried to hurt me, talked badly to me, or tried to force themselves on me in a sexual way. Instead of standing up and fighting, I would emotionally shrivel up, hide, and get hurt again. I was afraid that if I stood up for myself that I would make the other person angry, and they would abandon me.

I instinctively knew that there had to be a reason why I lost my ability to stand up for myself. Then one day while I was walking down the hall at work it hit me like a flash of light. I saw myself as a young girl in our house in Felicity, reliving the incident where I pointed a gun at Gene to try and make him stop hitting my mother. I could feel how terrified I was that he was going to hurt me. I saw Gene running towards me, grabbing the gun, and pointing it at me, threatening to kill me. While standing motionless in the hall, afraid and holding my breath, I realized this was why I couldn't stand up for myself. *As a child, whenever I had tried to protect myself, someone bigger and more powerful always overtook me, and scared me by literally trying to hurt me or threatening to kill me.*

I also realized that *I saw everyone as I saw my mother and I assigned them the role of being my parent.* I believed everyone was waiting to hurt me, waiting for me to make a mistake so I could be punished, and wanting me to meet all their needs and none of my own. I was afraid that sooner or later anyone I came in contact with would hurt me like my mother did. So in essence, I was giving away my power to the people in my life, like Rita and Joyce, and remaining the frightened child.

This finally explained why I was nervous around people, why I was afraid to be myself, and why I was afraid to stand up for myself with men.

Despite my strides of progress in controlling my thoughts, I continued to believe that if I didn't resolve what was happening to me emotionally, I would end up killing myself when David was no longer a part of my life. Thus, wanting to be a psychologist would be a moot point. I understood I was a very different person *intellectually* than when I began therapy with David. But, I also knew that my core issues remained at large, and I needed to work on them so I could be all right, once and for all. I knew that David was right about the cognitive techniques, but I also believed in my heart that if my child didn't find her voice and tell someone what was going on inside of her and figure out how to feel loved, then my life expectancy was very limited. My child self had to tell everything that she had been forbidden to speak about when she was a young girl, and still as an adult. I had to find a way that she could feel safe enough to come out and speak the unconscionable things that happened to her and be able to feel what she was saying at the same time. I had to find a way to help her claim and validate her past hurts and mend the broken shards of her spirit and core being. I had about nine months to get my act together so I could have a chance of surviving and before David retired.

Despite the fact that I understood the *Self-Perpetuating Rage Regenerator* and the *New Perspective Paradigm*, I still couldn't pacify or subdue the child who lived inside of me. She was screaming and begging to be heard, validated and loved. I had to work on the part of me that fell into a pit of dissociation whenever I encountered emotional pressure or found myself in a crisis situation. I had to find a way to help my inner child feel and understand what happened to her so my strong, intellectual, adult self could apply the cognitive techniques that would give her a different perspective. I saw the process working like this:

Current pressures or crisis →feel overwhelmed →dissociate →experience, understand, and talk about feelings about past →apply cognitive techniques →gain new perspective →change responses.

I needed to work on analyzing why I still wanted to hurt myself and the issues related to the sexual abuse. I wasn't only searching for happiness, but I wanted more than anything to have a chance of at least doing something normal in my life. I wanted to know what it felt like for a man to love me, and for it to feel safe. More importantly, there were still the emotional issues surrounding my mother. I needed to emotionally resolve these issues so I could like myself and be able to participate in a friendship that didn't illicit painful feelings and dysfunctional responses.

David and I came to the understanding that it was imperative to have a third party in our sessions to help me with the emotional component of the abuse. Someone to furnish my hidden child with the physical nurturing that David couldn't provide since he was a male therapist. David suggested that we enlist the assistance of one of his interns named, Tara Skakum. We initially only enlisted her help with EEG and biofeedback training hoping that these tools, designed to tap into the unconscious mind, would be the catalyst to bring my hidden child to the surface.

When I first met Tara, I was thrown into a dichotomous dilemma. One part of me was immediately afraid of her, and felt the need to keep my defenses up in order to protect myself from getting hurt again. The other part hoped that she would be the one person who wouldn't be afraid to provide me with the physical nurturing I needed and who could help me face my feelings when I became dissociative. I prayed she was the miracle I was looking for.

I met with Tara two to three days a week. I allowed her to hook me up to the machine that would hopefully help me sleep better and would crack open my unconscious mind that kept my forbidden memories a secret. While sitting in my chair in the tiny cubicle of an office, I was extremely frightened of the idea of letting someone other than David inside my heart.

After each session, I was surprised to find that I was beginning to trust her and wanting her to know who I was. At the same time I was still too afraid to let her see me or know what I was feeling. I wanted to let her into my world, but I just couldn't. Although I believed that Tara was a special person, I also remembered that she could very well turn out to be just like everyone else who had ever hurt me. Despite the fact that my intuition conveyed there was something unique about her, I kept a safe distance.

Week after week, Tara and I plugged away at the EEG and biofeedback training until my biggest fear came true. Without warning, the programs started bringing up feelings and visual images about the physical abuse and abandonment issues associated with my mother, and more so, the sexual abuse I sustained from Gene. Then it happened: I had one of my dissociative episodes right in front of her. As I sat in my chair curled up into a ball, rocking back and forth trying to protect myself, something happened that I didn't expect. She reached out and gently took hold of my hand. She began talking to me in a calm and compassionate voice. She asked questions so she could understand what was happening and where it was that I had escaped to in my mind.

Her kind and benevolent words grazed the surface of my soul and the touch of her hand penetrated the center of my desperate and frightened heart, causing tears to well up in my eyes. My parched spirit soaked up every second of this needed kindness and physical affection. I began crying uncontrollably. Her touch reminded me of what I had craved for some many years from my mother. This was what I had been looking for and what my child self had needed.

By the time I managed to find my way back to the present moment, I was embarrassed, staring at the floor, and profusely apologized for what had just happened. My plea was quickly pushed aside by more kind and compassionate words. I glanced up at Tara's face to discover that she wasn't looking at me like I was crazy either. I was so relieved that she seemed capable of handling this. To my dismay, though, the dissociating started occurring more and more frequently in front of her until it began happening almost every session.

My trust in Tara grew with each session that passed. Because of this, David suggested that she start participating in the therapy sessions with us.

While Tara, David and I were trying to chip away at my problems,

I embarked on a spree of intellectual and emotional understandings that caused many things to make sense to me. I came to understand that, as I had done with everyone else important in my life, I was expecting David and Tara to give me what my mother never gave me. I wanted David to be my dad, and Tara to care for like a mother and support me. I wanted them to sit and hold me, to spend time with me, and to just love me. I wanted someone to love me until I could learn how to love myself. It was now obvious to me that *I didn't know how to love or take care of myself since I never experienced it as a child.* I had been so busy taking care of everyone else around me that I never learned how to love or take care of myself. I was convinced that I needed David to be my parent just long enough so I could work out what was bothering me about my own parents.

Because David continued to only want to work on my issues from a cognitive standpoint, while Tara and I were in agreement about the emotional work that needed to be done before the cognitive lessons could be effective to the emotional part of my being, I made a decision. I needed to understand what was wrong with me, so I could better comprehend what it was that I needed to do in order to help fix me. My frustration caused me to embark on a different kind of a quest that eventually led to a great deal of understanding and insight.

My first course of action was reading as many books as I could about different psychological theories and treatments, especially those surrounding traumatic childhoods. One of the most profound things I discovered and studied was a branch of psychology called *Attachment Theory.* My heart leapt with joy that there was something out there in the real world to help me understand what happened with my mother, and why I found it almost impossible to break away from her. Not only did this theory explain a great deal about what was wrong with me, it also explained my desperate need for love and to connect with another human being.

Attachment Theory, according to John Bowlby and Mary Ainsworth's body of work (and in very basic terms), states that the way a person feels, handles interpersonal relationships, copes with life, connects with other people, and feels about themselves, is a direct result of the relationship they had with their primary caregiver as an infant. The type of relationship, as well as the quantity and quality of nurturing the infant received from its primary caregiver, determines how well the infant will function in adulthood in relation to interpersonal relationships and how much self-esteem they will possess. Each person can identify how much nurturing and closeness they had as a child, what kind of a parent they inherited, and the residuals they are left with by examining which of the four attachment styles they fall into.   They are secure, avoidant, ambivalent/resistant, and disorganized/disobedient.

I fell into the ambivalent/resistant attachment style. This basically meant that I had a strong need to be attached to my mother, but lacked the confidence in her availability to me because she didn't meet my needs *consistently*. Since my mother was inconsistent in her responses in caring for me, I couldn't count on being comforted by her, only with being frustrated. Even though I desperately wanted my mother to love, care, and comfort me, I couldn't get this from her on a consistent basis. *Thus, as an adult, I was still trying to attach myself to other people so I could get from them what I had missed from my mother, and hopefully in a consistent and reliable way.* I was doing this with David and with Tara. I was still trying to get them to love me like I needed my mother to love me, to fill the hole in my heart that I had tried to stuff with alcohol, drugs, anorexia, bulimia, excessive exercising, and suicide.

I also read books on self-esteem, Transactional Analysis, Reality Therapy, and the physiological effects of severe childhood trauma on the body and brain. They were very beneficial to my understanding of me and my ongoing dilemma.

By now, Tara and I had developed a rapport and I really liked her. We spent time together outside of therapy. It began with her coming to my house for visits. I was excited that someone like Tara would drive forty minutes to come and visit me, of all people.

During Tara's first visit to my house, we sat on my front porch and talked for hours. Her kindness reminded me of the love my inner child desperately searched for. I was overwhelmed with emotion at how she could inadvertently trigger my desperateness. Because she could trigger things that I couldn't feel in front of David, I became convinced that Tara could help me in a way that David couldn't. I then took the biggest step of my life—I asked her, "Would you be willing to work with me independently on the emotional and dissociative issues? As you know David has admitted that he really doesn't know how to do it."

Tara looked at me with assurance in her eyes and said, "I agree with your rationale and would be happy to help you."

Tara's weekly visits to my house allowed me the invaluable opportunity to experiment with my emotional theory and to determine if I was correct in my belief that I needed to address my child's memories and feelings in order to recover. To determine whether my inner child needed to come out and be seen. When it was official that she was going to help me, I noticed that I began having difficulty accessing my emotions in front of her just as I did with David. I was afraid of being hurt, afraid to let anyone see my vulnerability and desperation. However, because she was able to comfort and talk to me when I was in a dissociative state, my child self quickly figured out it was safe to show up in front of her.

Tara would try to help me figure out where the overwhelming hurt and horrific memories were coming from while sitting on the floor and holding me. It was my child coming out in front of her, in combination with her compassion, that made a great deal of difference in my recovery. I found that the more I experienced and talked about my pain, even in my dissociative states, the less afraid my inner child became with showing herself. She was learning that it was okay to claim who she was.

I now found myself needing Tori as much as I needed David.

We spent the next several weeks talking about the painful events of my past while Tara sat with me and gave my child self the things she so desperately needed. She talked to me, held my hand, and helped me feel safe. I was amazed that it was all right with her that I went away in my emotions in search of my pain. It was the relief I felt afterwards that allowed me to understand that I needed more of these experiences with her so I could be done with my past once and for all. However, just as I became assured of the correctness of my theory, and comfortable with this process, Tara had to stop coming to the house because her internship and school required a great deal of her time. To my dismay, this left us only working together in our formal twice-weekly sessions in David's office where she just sat quietly in her chair and said nothing. She just listened to me and David debate about what we each thought I needed to do and how I needed to do it.

The many months of therapeutic debate caused my suicidal undercurrents to flare up, but I tried not to dwell on them. I continued to feel alone and unable to fix the last ten percent of what was wrong with me. But, to my relief, I had one sure constant in my life: I could talk to Tara. Despite the fact that she didn't say much in our sessions, she and I talked quite a bit outside of them, and we got to know each other rather well. She helped me to see how things were for normal people in normal relationships, and she helped me to feel like someone cared about me. I felt as if she were my friend, and a person I could call on in time of great need. When I was overly-emotional, or about to hurt myself, I could pick up the phone and say to her, "I need your help." She would spend time talking with me, not just telling me that I needed to remain busy. There were no patient/therapist lines to be crossed and no threats of hospitalization. It was just one human being to another.

As my time with David was drawing to an end, I became quite desperate to be healed and fixed. I knew that if I didn't get my issues resolved that I would be dead shortly after therapy ceased, even though I continued to tell myself, "Suicide isn't an option." My mind understood this, but I still couldn't figure out what the key was to make the suicidal undertow in my heart disappear, especially in times of desperation.

Because of my almost impenetrable defense system, I continued having difficulty getting in contact with my emotions before the sessions were over. David suggested, "To give us more time, why don't you and Tara meet an hour before the formal session to see if you can get your emotions close to the surface before I come in." I thought this was a brilliant idea and it really seemed to help.

I now only had about four months left with David before he retired. This began to weigh heavily on me. I couldn't fathom how I was supposed to live without him in my life. He was the only person who had never given up on me, and who was willing to work with me until the end. I also found my soulful need for him to be my family, and my friend, greatly escalate, until my heart felt as if it were breaking each time I remembered his retirement. But, David being the good and ethical psychologist, made it clear that he could do neither. I wondered how I could have ended up with a mother and a therapist who couldn't love me. How was it that the only two people I ever wanted to love me couldn't reciprocate my affections and love me in return?

Chapter 31

New Steps

Terrified about David's retirement, I walked into his office and declared, "It's now time for us to work on my emotions; it's imperative for us to start doing things my way!" Trying to hide my nervousness, I continued, "I agree with your cognitive techniques, but there is no way I can incorporate them until I have dealt with my inner child's emotions that need to be verbalized and worked through to a point of understanding."

Surprisingly, David looked at me with a sense of surrender in his eyes as he admitted, "I concur with you. Research has documented that patients know what they need to do in order to heal themselves—I'm now with you on this. We'll start by using a mirror technique to help you get in touch with your inner child and then integrate her with your adult self." Thus, the next session would be my new beginning. The dawn of a new age in my recovery that would set me free—that would be filled with new techniques and insights.

The day finally arrived when I was to begin therapy the way I wanted and needed to do it, the way I believed that would set my soul and inner child free from the tormenting pain and memories. As usual, Tara and I met first in hopes of bringing my emotions close to the surface. At the designated time, we made our way to David's office where I sat on the magical striped couch anxiously awaiting the new mirror technique and my new steps on the road to recovery.

David had me sit down in front of the full-length mirror. I wanted to jump out of my skin because I couldn't stand to look at my own reflection. I hated the way I looked. Everything about me appeared distorted and ugly, especially my bad eye. Without warning, my throat became tight. My body grew tense until my hands began shaking. My legs swung back and forth in a nervous fashion. My level of self-consciousness and nervousness grew exponentially as I realized that David was sitting on one side while Tara sat on the other. I wasn't only nervous about who I was looking at in the mirror, but about the secrets that this person was supposed to reveal. I was drowning in a sea of self-imposed pressure—I had to do this perfectly, or I would end up feeling like a fool. This had to have been my most vulnerable moment yet with David.

The amount of emotional distress and tension I was experiencing was obvious. "I'm having difficulty breathing and my throat is so tight that it feels as if someone is strangling me, I can barely swallow," I confessed. To help calm me down, David spoke to me in a calm and soothing voice while instructing me to close my eyes as he walked me through some relaxation techniques. As I envisioned that I was surrounded by safety, my body became calmer and my breathing less restricted.

In my relaxed state, David instructed, "Open your eyes again and look at yourself in the mirror." I slowly opened my eyes and lifted them to the tall mirror. I quickly felt and saw my throat tightening up again. I instinctively took my right hand and placed it on my throat hoping that I would understand the source of the overwhelming discomfort. As soon as I did this, I could feel my child's pain emanating from the core of my being. I became so scared that I felt as if I needed to curl up and hide deep inside myself so no one would hurt me. Tara reached over and took hold of my hand to keep me from dissociating. I continued moving my fingers over different parts of my throat, and I found, beyond a means of comprehension, that when I did this it elicited different feelings from different places within me. I found my fingers pushing in on the top left hand side of my throat until it caused the emotions associated with my need to hurt myself quickly emerge. I then closed my eyes, and for the first time in my life, *I could feel in my body where the self-destructive part of me lived, and I could describe the visions associated with it.*

"I see a very long and extremely deep pit that leads to the core of my being. At the very bottom of the dark pit is a small yellow image of light. I'm looking at it very closely—it's my child self! I'm just sitting at the bottom of the pit with my legs pulled tightly to my chest. A sense of fear, loneliness, and helplessness emanate from my small being. I can't see any of her features, but I know it's me—it's surreal. My very small and very hurt child is sitting alone and afraid in the bottom of the dark pit all by herself, desperately wanting and needing someone to hold her and to tell her that everything is going to be all right."

I then tried to figure out why she was trying to kill herself and what she needed in order to stop hurting herself. As tears began streaming down my face, I inadvertently blurted out, "My child needs someone to hear her. She needs to feel loved, she needs someone to believe what she was saying about the adults in her life who hurt her, and she needs to connect with someone so the pain will disappear. She also needs to tell all of the secrets she was required to keep, and for it to be okay to share them with someone who won't hurt or judge her. She needs to believe in her heart what has happened to her, despite the fact that her mom won't validate her memories. She needs to believe her own thoughts, feelings, and memories—even if no one else does."

Before I could go any further, David announced, "We're running out of time. Sandy tell your child self that you need to go, but you will return to finish helping her."

I did as he instructed, even though I didn't feel ready to leave this place. As soon as I came back to the present, I realized this was by far one of the most heart-felt and productive sessions we'd had.

The vision I experienced with the mirror technique opened up my unconscious mind, but it also left me feeling guilty and sad. I had no idea why until my mind's eye kept flashing back to the dark bottomless pit where I left my inner child trapped, without hope of rescue. I was overwhelmed with immense sorrow. I wondered why we had left her down there, and why I didn't insist that we get her out so she could feel safe and secure. With these feelings reverberating through my heart, I caught a glimpse that things were going to get worse before they would get better. But, I also had hope.

I was right: the nightmares and night terrors increased, the headaches came back, and I was back to feeling needy. The next few weeks with the mirror technique proved to be interesting, especially with one particular therapy session.

I began experiencing pain in my pelvic area where my uterus used to be before my hysterectomy. In many ways, the pain reminded me of the endometriosis I'd experienced and how my insides hurt after being sexually violated by Gene and all the other men. I then remembered the scientific research articles I had been reading that reported women of childhood sexual abuse had an increased rate of endometriosis and adhesions from the abuse, which lead to an increased number of premature hysterectomies. In my case, the physical problems were now leading to body memories about the abuse and were causing me a great deal of difficulty in being able to cope with the feelings associated with it. I instinctively returned to the child who felt as if she had done something to cause the sexual abuse to happen and I was scared. I tried to push my feelings aside as I arrived at my therapy session an hour early so Tara could continue breaking down my defenses before I saw David. Embarrassed,

I confessed the physical reactions I had been experiencing and how it translated into guilt and shame about the sexual abuse. I was afraid of what she might think of me, so I tried not to go into great detail about anything. Despite my reluctance she continued trying to get me to talk about the abuse.

By the time David came into the office, I was almost to the point of emotional separation and was having a hard time not getting lost in the awful and painful feelings associated with what Gene and Miguel had done to me. He must have seen this as a golden opportunity because he immediately escorted me over to the mirror to begin the difficult journey down the path fraught with sexual violations.

While sitting in front of the looking glass that still reflected what I saw as a bad child, I found it difficult to open my heart to the task at hand. I felt like a complete failure. No matter how much David tried to lead me down this path, I found it impossible to allow myself to feel what Gene and Miguel had done to me, especially Miguel. In my mind's eye, I could see Miguel sticking his penis down the back of my throat and holding my head so tightly that I couldn't breathe. But, it was too overwhelming to feel the emotions that were fused with this severe form of torture. I couldn't allow myself to feel the fear, the hurt, the anger or anything. I then realized that my throat had closed up again and I felt as if I were being strangled.

The closing up of my throat left no way for the memories of my mind and the feelings of my heart to meet so there could be unity and validation that would ultimately set me free. The constriction of my throat wouldn't allow the feelings that were locked away in the crevices of my heart to escape upwards to my mind where I could apply the cognitive techniques, thus I was kept a prisoner to my emotions and body memories. With David witnessing this unrelenting phenomena, he explained, *"You are having trouble accessing your feelings about the abuse because they are the most emotionally laden feelings and experiences you had as a child—especially since they were filled with the fearful possibility of your own death."*

I now understood that my inner child was too afraid to access the emotions associated with the sexual abuse because I had almost died from it. I realized that I needed to convince my tortured child, who felt helpless and afraid, that she needed to allow the feelings about the abuse to come up through her throat and out into the world so the adult part of me could deal with them. As soon as I came to this understanding, I noticed that my thoughts reverberated once again with the need to hurt myself, while my soul desperately cried out for someone to know the pain and confusion surrounding it. I then realized that my wanting to hurt myself was my way of protecting myself—distracting myself from the horrible abuse. Thus, if I concentrated on self-destructing, then I could continue hiding from the overwhelming feelings and could continue burying them below my constricted throat, deep in the crevices of my heart. It was now clear that if I truly wanted to recover, then I was going to have to stop myself each time I felt suicidal and tell myself, "It is okay to feel the abuse. You have to feel it and come to terms with it in order to be all right." I had to give myself the permission that no one else had ever given me.

The next several nights of sleep proved to be extremely disturbing and unsettling. I dreamed over and over again that I had died by suffocating on dirt and then by drowning in the bottom of a deep lake. The dreams were so real that I could literally feel my nostrils and lungs fighting for air, and the panic that only came from fearing one's own life. Not only this, but I had several severe migraine headaches as my mind couldn't stop visualizing the many times Miguel had me on my knees, gasping for air. As each one of these memories and visions blasted its way into my conscious mind, I tried my best to tell my child self that I was safe, and that it was imperative to let these feelings and memories come out in front of David and Tara.

By the time I made it to my next session, I found myself sitting on the infamous blue, red, and gold striped couch, rocking back and forth, and on the verge of dissociating. I was terribly upset because of the dreams and the visions that haunted me.

David quickly pointed out, "You are having dreams about suffocating and drowning because of the nature of the sexual abuse. While Miguel was hurting you and using your body to fulfill his own sick pleasures, you were left feeling out of control, vulnerable and as if you were sitting on the doorstep of death. That's why you're having problems feeling and expressing your emotions about the abuse, and why they are getting cut off at your throat. The body memories and feelings associated with the sexual abuse 'live' in your throat and are causing it to remain constricted and tight, as if an apple were permanently lodged in your esophagus."

He also explained that when I could finally deal with what happened with Miguel and all the other male adult perpetrators, then I would be able to relax my throat and my feelings would be able to flow freely to my mind where resolution could be obtained.

After confessing my unsettling dreams, we went back to the mirror to continue working on the sexual abuse issues, but this time we ended up in a completely different place than we expected. While sitting in front of my reflection, I once again found it necessary to gently place my fingers on my throat so I could find where my feelings were stuck. Almost instantly,

I could see my child self sitting in a corner, with her knees drawn tightly to her chest. I still couldn't see any of her features, but again I instinctively knew it was me. I could feel her pain and a sense of loneliness emanating from her.

David instructed, "Sandy go over and sit next to your child and talk to her."

"A large black wall has suddenly appeared between us," I heard myself wail. The black barrier prevented me from being able to get to her before she slipped out of my sight and I was only able to feel her hidden presence. Without warning, my body began to tense up. I felt like I was starting to disconnect from myself, like I was no longer real. I feared that I was about to dissociate and fall back into old ways of coping. I knew if I did that, then I wouldn't be able feel my little girl's pain or verbalize her secrets. So I tried to keep talking to myself so I could stay present.

"What is the black barrier between you and your child self?" I heard David ask.

I initially thought it was the sexual abuse, but the more I pressed on my throat and the harder I concentrated, I cried, "It's about my mother and how she beat me." I became afraid. I could feel my child's emotional and physical pain. I could see her crouched in the corner with her face hidden, afraid of being hit again. I could feel her confusion about why Mom, whom she loved so much, would be doing this to her. The emotional pain became too much for me to bear—I curled up in my chair in front of the mirror where I unknowingly got lost in my child's pain.

David was left with the task of quickly trying to bring me back to the present. But for some reason I struggled with leaving my child self behind and it made it difficult for me to get back. It was as if I couldn't leave her behind again without helping her.

David began demanding, "Sandy, open your eyes, stand up, and look at yourself in the mirror!" After several minutes of trying to claw my way back, I realized I was standing in front of the mirror. I then saw something unexpected: *I could see that it was me, as an adult in the mirror, but postured in such a way that my hands were curled up close to my chest and my body was slumped over like a frightened child.* Seeing the way my child manifested herself in my adult body was an eye-opener. It allowed me to see and understand that these two parts of myself were incompatible and I needed to help my inner child heal and find a safe place in my heart to live quietly and restfully.

Before leaving David's office that day, I was still having problems not drifting back into my mind. And while I was still partially connected to my little girl, a couple of things occurred to me. I now understood that it wasn't just my need to have my spoken words and my feelings match so I could feel real and validated, but I also needed to have my *internal* words and feelings match. *I not only needed others to see and validate what I was saying, I needed to feel and believe what I knew to be true so I could validate for myself everything that happened to me and embrace everything about me.* Having my spoken words and my feelings match was to provide me with a means of getting validation and nurturing from the *external world (external locus of control)*. Having my inner, unspoken words match my feelings would be the means by which I would obtain validation and nurturing *from within myself*, from my heart and the core of my being *(internal locus of control)*.

While trying these new methods that would help me understand my child self and would hopefully pry open the hatches of my heart about the sexual abuse, God tried to help me out by having my ex-husband, Randy, call me. During the last few years, he and I had only briefly spoken several times on the phone. By now, I hadn't spoken to him in about five months. It bothered me that each of our conversations reawakened the love I had for him. And how I wanted him to still be my partner, because I believed we were soul mates, even though I wasn't at a place where I could even fathom having sex with a man. At the same time, it bothered me because he always remarked that I could do better than him, that he wasn't smart enough for me, and frequently dropped sexual innuendoes. It was the innuendoes that reminded me of the sexual abuse and made me wonder if he learned anything from our marriage.

After realizing that he was triggering the same feelings I had about the sexual abuse, I came up with an idea. "Randy, would you be willing to come up here to participate in one of my therapy sessions?" Without waiting for a reply I continued, "I need you to be the catalyst to help me access the hidden, life-threatening emotions that surround the sexual abuse—how it affects me as an adult, and prevents me from fully participating in intimate relationships." I knew he was the only hope I had left of tapping into these feelings and memories.

With a cautious tone, he replied, "I'll have to think about it."

At my next session with David, I spoke with him about my idea and was relieved when he said, "I agree—it's a great idea—it might be the ticket you need to unleash your feelings about the sexual abuse, once and for all." With his confirmation securely tucked away in my heart, I immediately went home with great hope that Randy would call that night to declare his willingness to accompany me on this journey.

When I got home, Spencer, a friend of mine, was waiting for me on my front porch so we could practice playing our guitars for a big grand opening we were going to play at over the weekend. With all the excitement about finally finding a way to overcome the sexual trauma, I had forgotten all about him coming over.

About five minutes later, the telephone rang. Excited, I ran to the phone and picked up the receiver. I immediately knew something was wrong by the tone of Randy's voice. I didn't have an opportunity to say anything before he exclaimed, "You don't need to be in a relationship with me. You're too smart for me, and I'm not any good in relationships. I'm not coming up to help you with therapy."

In a calm and collected manner, I explained, "Even if you're not interested in a relationship, I need you to come up and help me with the sexual abuse issues."

Randy's voice was condescending and hateful as he went on to declare, "Under no circumstances will I help you!"

With all hope of ever recovering from the sexual abuse waning, I became *aware* that my anger, frustration, and desperation were beginning to escalate inside me, as it usually did when I felt threatened or hurt. I could feel my hurt child wanting to manifest. I wanted to shout at Randy to forget the whole thing, and to declare that I didn't need him or anyone else to help me. Instead, I forcefully, yet politely, said, "Thanks Randy for messing up my life again." I then slammed the receiver of the phone down. I could feel myself wanting to cry in desperation and scream with anger. But, I knew I couldn't afford this luxury since Spencer was sitting in the next room. Instead, I told myself that I had to pull myself together so I could fulfill my obligation to Spencer. The only way I could do it was by not paying attention to what had just happened and to practice the New Perspective Paradigm that included my cognitive phrases. My ability to recognize how I felt and then talk myself into a different activity proved to be extremely beneficial as the music we played that night was the best we had ever played. We were ready for the grand opening and I was happy with my progress.

Later that night as I thought about the conversation with Randy I understood what David had been talking about in relation to how I react when people push my buttons. For the first time, I could see that when I got into a difficult situation that triggered my wounded child self, I immediately wanted to jump into an all or nothing mindset called *splitting*. This was evident with the words that I wanted to say to Randy—that I didn't need him or anyone else. I now saw how those statements left the other person without any available reply, how it sabotaged and ended the conversation right then and there, and how it didn't allow for anything positive to come out of the situation. It was like dropping a bomb and running.

I went to bed right after Spencer left, but I didn't get much sleep that night for thinking about the difficult conversation with Randy. Because I couldn't sleep, I got up early. I then realized that something was different about me. For the first time in my life, I wasn't suicidal or self-destructive after a major confrontation with someone. And it was due to the fact that I *intellectually and emotionally* understood that what happened with Randy didn't have to lead to an all or nothing decision and this situation wasn't about me—it was about him. After I realized this, I called him and asked, "What's wrong with you—what's really going on?"

In a somber voice he replied, "I had a fight with my daughter and, I feel worthless as a human being." With his confession out in the open and my new sense of objectivity, we were able to talk more honestly and freely. We both admitted that our feelings about each other hadn't changed over the years, but we both were afraid of getting hurt again. By the end of the conversation, Randy was going to work and then driving up to my house that Friday night so he could go to therapy with me on Monday.

I now understood that when I could be objective about the situation, could control what came out of my mouth, didn't play the role of the helpless child, and talked about my feelings, this provided the opportunity for further conversation and solutions to arise. It also helped the other person feel less defensive and permitted the relationship to continue, even if in an unexpected direction. With this new approach I didn't find myself back in situations where I made black and white and all or nothing statements that would permanently cut off all interactions and possibilities. I could now stay calm and get my needs met, all at the same time. I was proud of myself because I behaved like an adult, rather than a wounded child. It felt wonderful because this was another sign that I was changing and growing.

For the next two days, Randy called several times with various excuses as to why he couldn't come up. I was disappointed each time he created a new excuse, but I was diligent in maintaining my new adult self. In the end, I got to the place where I didn't care if he showed up or not, and that was further proof of my growth.

He finally made it up to my place around one o'clock on Sunday afternoon. Despite the fact I was really nervous, it was good to see him. We hung out together, went for a picnic lunch, and rented a couple of movies to watch with dinner. Even with the new me trying to stay focused solely on the present moment, my anxiety was so high that I wasn't sure if I would be able to make it through the evening. I was nervous because

I wasn't sure how I was supposed to act, or what I was supposed to do around him. I wanted him to be there, but I didn't want to give him any misperceptions or run the risk of him making a sexual advance.

We successfully made it through the evening without incident. It was now time for Randy to escape to the loft, and for me to retreat to my own room to get some sleep in preparation for the big therapy session the next day. However, I couldn't rest; memories of our failed marriage and the sexual abuse plagued my mind. I just laid there, I contemplating whether I was making a mistake in inviting Randy to the therapy session. I couldn't make my mind shut off, even though I desperately needed all the strength I could muster up for the long day ahead. I wondered what I was going to do. Was I going to tell Randy that his going to the therapy session with me wasn't a good idea? Was I going to send him home, never to see him again because the core of my being that was hurt so many years ago was beyond repair? Or, was I going to do my usual and not say a word, hoping he could read my mind?

Before I knew it, it was time to see David and Tara, hoping we could blast through the defense mechanisms that kept me a prisoner. This proved to be a pivotal therapy session in my recovery and one I will never forget.

Randy and I walked into David's office and sat side by side on the striped couch that had supported me for so many years. David began by carefully explaining to Randy the purpose of the session. He then started explaining my situation, "Prior to Sandy's relationship with you, she had safely tucked away and repressed all of the sexually abusive things that happened to her, deep inside of herself for safe keeping from the world. In essence, she unconsciously hid those terribly overwhelming feelings from herself and avoided intimate relationships in order to protect herself from getting hurt again. Thus, when you and Sandy entered into the intimate aspect of your relationship, the repressed emotions and memories that she had safely folded away, came to the surface all at once."

As soon as I heard his rendition of what had happened to me, and why I emotionally fell apart with Randy, I knew it was the truth.

"Randy, tell me about the first sexual experience you had with Sandy when she emotionally fell apart, and hid in the corner. What's your recollection of this event?" David asked.

It was obvious that Randy was uncomfortable and that he wanted to protect me, but he went on to explain what happened. "Sandy had great difficulty with sexual acts, but at that time I didn't completely understand everything that happened to her and I didn't know what to do to help her."

"Sexual acts between a man and a woman are perfectly normal and your behavior with wanting to have sex with her was normal. However, her inability to handle with a man wasn't normal, but maladaptive because of the sexual torture she'd experienced," David explained.

My mind understood David was right because I felt abnormal; like there was something wrong with me. But, his explanation left me feeling that his siding with Randy and excusing his past behavior and unwillingness to help me work through my childhood difficulties, especially when we were married.

I felt abandoned by David. But I tried to push those feelings aside as he continued asking Randy very frank questions about our sexual lives together, while I sat quietly listening to the embarrassing conversation. I must admit that Randy was very accurate in his responses and recollections, and appeared surprisingly at ease with answering David's questions. I, on the other hand, was so anxious that I could hardly remain seated on the couch. While paying close attention to Randy's perspective about what happened between us, I began realizing that he was failing to mention one very important thing. Frustrated at his omission, my emotions began welling up inside of me until I understood that I had to say something or I would remain forever lost. I had to proclaim, in my own words, what bothered me about my relationship with him and one of the many reasons why I couldn't have sex with him.

Tears began to well up in my eyes as my trembling voice exclaimed, "When Randy and I were together, I needed to have felt like he loved me for who I was, before we ever broached the sexual part of our relationship. I just wanted to feel loved and that he was my best friend before we had sex, so I wouldn't feel like he was only interested in what I could do for him sexually. I needed to believe in my heart that he wasn't just another guy who was going to use me for what he could get from my body. Randy, you never gave me a chance to overcome my past sexual hurts so I could have a normal relationship with you—it was always about you and what you needed."

With my truths hovering in the air, I felt emotionally vulnerable. I was crying uncontrollably. I could *feel* the sexual abuse that had hurt me. I could *feel* how I felt responsible for everything that had happened to me; how I believed that I was to blame for the abuse because I didn't make the perpetrators stop hurting me out of desperation for love and fear of being hurt.

I began feeling like I was about to become the child again who needed to hide somewhere safe inside myself; far away so no one could see her. When I realized this, I became afraid and frustrated because I knew that

I would never be able to resolve this problem if I dissociated now. I desperately looked at David, "I'm begging you—please keep me present and make me deal with what I am feeling."

Since he was all too aware of what was about to transpire, he backed the conversation up so I could get connected again, but in a safe way. When I got reconnected with my emotions, my inner child quickly showed herself with gut-wrenching emotional pain. She wanted to know why those men did that to her. Why did they hurt her? Did I have "Here is a completely deprived and vulnerable child available to be abused" written on my forehead somewhere?

David quickly pointed out, "As a child, you had been a *victim of opportunity* with the adults in your life, especially the men. Somehow they could see your vulnerabilities and thus they preyed upon them."

My child self couldn't understand this concept, or accept that as a reason. Instead, it only left me feeling more overwhelmed and helpless. It was at this point that David tried to convince me, "Nothing that happened to you was your fault. And, even if you had taken off all of your clothes and danced around naked in front of those men, they still were responsible NOT to abuse you because you were the child. You were merely a young girl who had been deprived and desperate for love, and you didn't deserve the abuse you received just because you were desperate. *You weren't the one who was responsible for stopping the abuse because you were just a kid who was too young to know how to make it stop.*"

Even after hearing these things, I still couldn't make the leap from dysfunctional thinking and painful feelings to resolution. There was something important that my emotional child self was still struggling with and I needed to help her understand what it was. As I sat on the couch with tears streaming down my face and my soul buried in the emotional turmoil of the abuse, it dawned on me exactly what was happening to my inner child. She was feeling alone and vulnerable, like she had no one to help her with the abuse despite the fact that there were three other adults in the room with her. Inside, she was crying, screaming and begging for someone to help her with the terrible pain by loving, nurturing and showing her compassion. Then I realized that what I had needed was for my mother to have sat down with me, all those years ago, and to have held me while I confessed what happened to me. Then for her to have loved me and told me that everything was going to be all right, and that none of what happened was my fault. I needed someone, back then, to talk to about what happened to me so I could have felt loved and could have been comforted through it. I needed to have been held and nurtured so I could have healed along the way. I instinctively understood that if my mother would have done that for me when the abuse began, I wouldn't have ended up in the shape I was now in. Consequently, I was left with an eleven-year-old child who needed to sit down with someone and tell them what happened to her while being held and comforted through the whole thing. She needed to walk through the experience with someone who could nurture her and help her to see and feel that none of it was her fault. To help her realize that the fault and responsibility lay with the adults who were in her life at that time.

I now understood that I was a thirty-six year old adult with an eleven-year-old child living in my heart and in the core of my being who needed the love and support she should have received as a child. I was an adult who needed the love of a parent to heal her inner most wounds, but without a way of getting my child's needs met since I was now an adult.

It was at that very moment that I realized what had been different in mine and David's approach to therapy these past couple of years. David was trying to help me *resolve* my problems and I was desperately trying to *heal* from them. The difference was that *resolution was the ultimate goal, while healing was the process that would lead me to resolution.* I wasn't going to be able to reach resolution until I could begin to heal, and there were many steps between healing and resolution. I also understood that my healing could only happen through accessing my emotions. And, it would only continue as long as I followed the New Perspective Paradigm, which incorporated the emotional and intellectual journey by using the cognitive phrases as a bridge between my heart and my mind.

Because of this session, I now understood, and so did Randy, that if I was ever going to have an intimate relationship with another man, or even him, that the person I was involved with would have to do and allow several things. *The person would have to understand what happened to me and allow me to move through the relationship at my own pace. Sexual activity couldn't, and wouldn't, be a part of the alliance until I was the one who said it was time to try it. They would have to become my friend first and I would have to grow to trust that person before anything sexual could ever be a consideration. The person would have to be very understanding and very patient, but also someone who could allow me to direct the relationship. Then, as I felt safe and trusted my companion, I would be able to function normally in the sexual part of the relationship.*

These initial insights gave my heart the first glimpse of freedom from the sexual abuse, as if a terrible burden was being pried from the core of my being. The trick now was finding the remaining insights to completely unlock this Pandora's box and find that special someone who could fulfill the enormous role.

A couple of days after this pivotal therapy session, I gained another piece of invaluable insight. It pertained to my ongoing confusion about whether I was heterosexual or gay. It really bothered me so I spent a great deal of time searching my heart for the answer. I kept coming up with two thoughts and two feelings that were recurrent and, more importantly, that matched. The part of me that wanted to be normal found it desirable to be in a relationship with a man, especially since I needed to participate in something that appeared normal just once in my life. I wanted to know what it felt like for a man to hold me and to take care of me without it being terrifying. To know what it felt like to be treated like a lady and to do things with each other without feeling vulnerable. I also coveted the comfort and the emotional contribution that only a woman could provide; the warmth that came from snuggling and holding hands and that would satisfy the needs of my inner child; the time that would be spent talking and enjoying each other's company; and to be in a relationship that wasn't as sexually complicated and would allow me to feel a deep connection. I truly needed all of the things a woman could give me, even though I wanted to be normal.

It was then that it dawned on me that all of this reflected the same old dichotomy. I finally understood that the part of me who wanted to be normal and heterosexual was my *mature adult self*, and the part of me who wanted the comfort of a woman and the non-threatening aspects of a sexual relationship was my *traumatized child self*. Again there was a paradox between my adult and child, and it was imperative that I resolve this duality and inner conflict.

I brought this insight into therapy and it led to an extensive search for us to see if we could pin down which person I truly was. As David probed me with a barrage of questions, he quickly broke down my defense system until I became extremely vulnerable. Embarrassed, I looked at the floor and confessed, "The idea of being in a sexual relationship with a man still bothers and scares me. When I think about having sex with a man, I'm immediately filled with shame and mortification. My mind's eye suffers with a very strong and pungent visual image of what that means. Having sex means that I have to be in a vulnerable position, with my legs spread open, making me feeling completely exposed. To me, spreading my legs is synonymous with giving someone permission to hurt me again. My child self still believes that my spreading my legs for the sexual perpetrators, even though done unwillingly, was me somehow giving them permission to hurt me. Thus, I still feel like I would be a bad person if I let someone have sex with me. I don't see sex as a consensual act between two people who love each other. Instead, it is something men do to women just to satisfy their own needs without any regard for the woman."

Still looking at the floor, I continued, "I would feel completely ashamed if anyone ever thought I was having a sexual relationship with a man, as this would automatically make me a bad person in my own mind...like I was still letting the abuse continue. I would be the bad child all over again who couldn't make anyone stop hurting her, and who would feel bad because she doesn't know how to make the abuse stop."

Waiting for David's analysis of my words, Tara chimed in with something important. "Because you were a child when the sexual abuse occurred it took away your choice as to whether you were going to participate in it or not." In other words, the sexual abuse was done to me at such a young age that I was incapable of exercising a choice about what was happening to me. I couldn't make them stop hurting me because I had no power as a young girl, especially when my life was being threatened and because my need for love and attention was so great. As soon as my heart heard and understood her brilliant statement, I knew this was a jewel that needed further examination. I believed that if I could just take this wonderful piece of information and internalize it, I could be free from feeling that it was my fault and that I let the abuse happen.

Without hesitation, David looked at me with seriousness in his eyes and proclaimed, "It's all right if you choose to be gay, since being gay seems to be *easier* for you."

I didn't know what it was about his statement, but I immediately became upset with him and declared, "I don't want to be the victim any longer!" I was convinced that I would continue being the victim if I chose to be gay, just because it was easier. It would mean that I gave up trying to be normal and that everyone who sexually abused me won. Saying "I'm going to be gay because it is easier," was like admonishing myself with the idea that it was all right to let my past abuse continue to hurt me and keep me the victim because I wasn't strong enough to overcome what happened to me. At that point in my therapy, I just couldn't live with that. I wanted to be able to choose what I wanted, not settle for being gay because it was too hard overcoming the sexual abuse. I only wanted to be gay if that was who I truly was in my heart.

I also couldn't settle for this because of a statement David had made at the beginning of my therapy: "You are gay because of the trauma, not because you were born that way." His insight with this changed how I saw myself and my sexual orientation. I used to feel proud of the fact that I was gay because it was the only thing in my life that I had ever accepted about myself and felt comfortable with. I wasn't afraid to be open about it and I didn't care what other people thought about it. So now that I knew I wasn't born gay, it was like living a lie, like not being real. I had to know the truth and decide one way or the other who and what I was going to be. At the same time, I also came to understand that *it wasn't so much the gender of the person that was the issue, but the person's ability to take my past into consideration and allow me the work through the relationship at my own pace.*

After I left this session I couldn't get my mind off the statement that Tara made, "Because you were a child, the choice was taken away from you." I found myself mulling this over and over again in my mind until I struck gold and was opened up to a new insight about myself. I was so convinced about my new found discovery that I took it into my next therapy session where I was proud that it led to a flood of new insights that changed my whole perspective about my past.

The insight I took into the session was this: *not only did all of the men who sexually abused me take away my choices, but so did my mother.* When she assigned me the role of being the caretaker of her and my brothers, I was too young to know that this wasn't supposed to be my role—my choice of saying no didn't exist. And since I learned that I didn't have a choice or the power to stand up for myself as a child, I carried it over into my adult life. This was part of what was keeping me locked away in the role of the helpless victim; *still playing the role of the helpless child who didn't have any rights or choices; no way of standing up for myself.*

Not standing up for myself with my mother, and even as an adult, left me living my life the way other people thought I should. Thus, I didn't stand up for myself with my abusers or in any other situation. I allowed others to treat me anyway they wanted without ever expressing my anger or pain. I continued to do things that I didn't want to do out of fear of getting hurt and because I still felt like the trapped child without any choices. *I was still playing the role assigned to me as a child, even though I was an adult.* This sole concept and realization was freeing to my adult and child self. *I now understood that if I could dump my old perspective, stop living as the victim, and claim that I have choices, then I could live my own life where I could avow my own feelings, make my own choices, and stand up for myself.* I had to understand and know that I was no longer the helpless child who couldn't make the abuse stop.

These miraculous understandings led to many more steps of wisdom that were built, like a staircase, one step on top of another, until the landing of recovery and healing was in sight.

The next step of the staircase was laced with the understanding that I not only felt as if I didn't have any choices about how my mother treated me, or what Gene and Miguel did to me, but I didn't have a choice about how I felt about those things. In other words, when my mother assigned me the role of being the caretaker and my insides became overwhelmed with it, I believed that I didn't have the right or the choice to feel the abandonment and anger it left me with. That when my mother was beating me or throwing me out of the house into the cold snow to walk four miles to the nearest town, I didn't have the right to acknowledge that I felt hurt, angry, unloved, and afraid. Even when Miguel was shoving his penis so far down the back of my throat that I thought I was going to suffocate and die, I didn't have the right to feel what that felt like and how that would have made any other person feel. Instead, I was forced to stuff those feelings deep inside the core of my being and not acknowledge them because it wasn't allowed.

This insight led me to understand that when I was playing the role of the caretaker and protector of my mother, *I wasn't allowed to be the child I was supposed to be.* It didn't allow me to feel anything that didn't pertain to taking care of her. It didn't allow me to feel what a normal child would feel: love, safety, and happiness. This led me to understand why I never felt validated.

I never felt validated because my mother never acknowledged what was happening in our family, she wouldn't allow me to behave in a way that signified to other people that I needed to be loved and understood and I was never allowed to feel what was happening to me. This left the abuse seeming as if it were a figment of my imagination, but with physical consequences. I had to be what she and everyone else expected me to be while I felt as if I were dying inside from needing so badly for someone to hear, love, and help me. But, when I felt those bad things, there was no one to listen to me. More so, when I found a rare soul outside of the family who would listen, my mother would tell them I was a liar. So, I grew up believing that what I felt was a lie, and that I had no right to feel the emotions and torment of the abuse. As a result, my child self got locked away in a prison created by my mother, and all of the other abusers, screaming to get out and be heard. *I was expected to divorce myself from my feelings in order to play the roles assigned to me by my mother.*

Having to divorce myself from my feelings was also true of the sexual abuse and it explained why it bothered me so badly. I realized that I ended up separating myself from my *feelings* about what Gene and Miguel had done to me so I could meet their sexual demands and survive it. This was the apex of the emotional impact of the sexual abuse. *They took away my choice by making me do things that I didn't want to do and this became the point of my greatest vulnerability.* As I came to understand this, my heart and soul literally cringed every time I thought about what they did to me and what they made me do to them. I was consumed with total shame, total vulnerability, and felt like I wanted to crawl deep inside myself and die. Almost instinctively, this led me to understand that those feelings contributed to my need to self-destruct and were created by the fact that I didn't have the choice or power to make the sexual abuse stop. It was why I hated, and felt so badly, about myself.

This made it possible for me to understand that it wasn't only the sexual abuse that left me feeling self-destructive. It was also because of people like my mother who forced me to do things that I didn't want to do and *took away my God-given right to be a child who had choices*. She forced me to hide my emotions and my feelings until I was left with nothing but frustration and abandonment.

The question now was what did I need to do to make all of these insights real for my child self? And so real that she could feel and verbalize all the things she had tucked away deep inside her heart that needed to be heard for over thirty years. My adult self understood that all of these revelations were filled with great insight, but my child needed to experience them on a feeling level in order to finally be healed once and for all. I had to get my feelings, thoughts, and words together so they were all in one accord. This led David to illuminating another piece of the puzzle when he proclaimed: *"You need to integrate the thoughts and feelings of your inner child with the insights and cognitive understandings of your adult. The only way you can do this is by accepting the feelings and experiences you had as a child as a part of who you are at this point in your life. And you have to do it without judging yourself negatively."* In other words, I had to understand in my heart and in my mind that I did the best I could with what I had to work with. This, in turn, led to the most useful insight of all.

For the first time, I got a glimpse of the fact that I had to stop self-destructing, running, and hiding from the abuse—I had to *accept* my feelings and experiences that I had as a small and helpless child. By allowing myself to feel and accept the bad things that happened to me meant that I had to allow myself to be willing to *embrace and feel* the abuse without expecting my mother or someone else to rescue me from it. I had to lose the fear that if I faced my thoughts and feelings alone that they would consume me. *I was now the one who was going to have to face me, and what happened to me, and do it without the hope that my mother would rescue me.* I couldn't do it with the expectation that someone was going to help lessen my pain, even when I tried to enlist their help by becoming suicidal or self-destructive. I had to be willing *to feel* all of it on my own, with my own heart, and the new understandings of my adult who was perfectly capable of taking care of my child.

This was an extremely scary insight because I could see in my mind's eye that if I could do this, then I would be cutting loose the strings that bound me and my mother together. The strings of emotional neediness and helplessness that kept me in the role of a helpless child and victim. By cutting loose my ties and my fear of losing my mother, I would finally be free to experience what she did to me and the feelings of abandonment associated with it. I wasn't sure if I was ready for this just yet, but at least I understood what needed to be done.

David then pointed out, "You're not getting rid of your mother— you are merely *separating* yourself from her emotionally so you can feel your pain, grow up emotionally *(individuate)*, and develop a healthier perspective about her." *If I could set my mother aside long enough to face my feelings about her and what she did, then my inner child could grow up emotionally and become an adult who could have an adult relationship with her.* I had to separate, individuate, and then chose how I wanted to reintegrate, if at all, with her.

I looked at David and Tara with tears in my eyes and tried to explain, *"The reason why I have been afraid of claiming and experiencing my feelings is that it will leave me feeling isolated, alone and like an emotionally fragile child all over again."* I was afraid of re-experiencing my childhood and doing it by myself; I was afraid I couldn't go through it again and survive it yet another time.

David explained further, *"You only have to hold onto the feelings long enough to throw them away. If you own and accept the feelings, you take back the right to choose for yourself what to do with them—to throw them away!"*

When I understood I could accept and let my past go, and I remembered all of the insights I had gained, something happened that I had never experienced before. Something in the core of my being was different. I no longer felt as if I were a slave to the old emotions. I felt hope that I would be able to overcome what happened to me and that I might be finished with therapy by the time David retired.

It was also the first time I actually slept a couple nights in a row without remembering what I dreamed. I was on the right track and on the real road to healing *and* resolution, even though there were many more miles to trudge before the ultimate insight was reached that would yield healing and then resolution.

Chapter 32

Healing and Resolution

I BEGAN GRIEVING the emotional loss and separation from my mother and the process of removing the power I had given her so she couldn't ever hurt me again. However, I still hoped that maybe one day I would be adult enough to have a healthy relationship with her.

As I grieved, my heart instinctively came to understand that there were more truths that needed to be uncovered about my mother. I had to figure out how to let her go, not only in my mind, but in my heart. I needed to experience and survive the emotional death of my mother so I would be free to become the person I wanted to become. But I still didn't know how to meet my own needs, and I didn't know how to love and comfort myself when my inner child was hurting. Since my mother had never given me these things, I didn't know how to give them to myself.

I then realized that I wasn't only grieving the loss of my mother and experiencing the gaping wounds of my child that needed solacing, but I was also beginning to agonize over whether I would be able to handle the loss and bereavement of David's retirement. I couldn't bear the thought of losing the only person who had stuck by me. I wanted to hide somewhere deep inside myself so I didn't have to face his leaving me. I could feel the pain and sadness all the way down to the core of my being. It then dawned on me that the feelings about David's retirement were the same feelings I felt about my mother. I loved both David and my mother like a child would love her parents, but his retiring reminded me how it felt when my mother had abandoned me, and I wasn't sure I could survive that again.

At our next session, I explained my insight to David and discussed my fears about his retirement, his leaving me. We explored why his retirement bothered me so much, and realized that his ending his practice could ultimately be a blessing in disguise. Maybe my having to deal with his leaving would simultaneously force me have to come to terms with my feelings about my mother. In essence, if I could survive his retirement when it reminded me of the abandonment by my mother, then I would be free of my mother's emotional hold on me, once and for all.

As we continued the journey that involved trying to access the feelings I wasn't allowed to feel as a child, David utilized guided imagery, while Tara tried role-playing my mother. These techniques only led to frustration because I still didn't feel safe enough to allow my forbidden feelings about my mother to manifest, especially in front of anyone outside of the family. Frustrated and angry, I demanded, "We need to go ahead and call my mother so I can beg her to come to one of our sessions. She is the only one who can make these feelings come out." I was hoping that she would trigger my child's forbidden feelings and allow me the opportunity to verbalize to her the things that had gotten locked away in my heart.

I could tell by the expression on David's face that he was surprised that I would even consider anything like this, especially after what happened in Susan's office when she walked out on me several years earlier. He asked, "Why is it so important to get your mother to admit what she did and acknowledge what happened to you?"

Without thinking I said, "So I won't feel like I was all alone in my misery when I was a child, and so I won't feel as if I'm alone in it now." I didn't know where those words came from, but I knew they were the truth. I needed my mother's help when I was a little girl, and somewhere deep inside I needed her now. Intellectually I understood this went against my former insights, but I was still missing a vital part of the understanding that would force me to finally let go of this thinking.

David finally agreed, but he insisted that he be the one to make the call. He was really sweet about the whole thing as he graciously picked up the phone, dialed my mother's number and implored her to come up to his office to help me. However, the longer he talked with her, the more aggravated and disgusted he appeared until he finally hung up the phone in frustration. He looked at me with sorrow and aggravation on his face as he exclaimed, "Your mother is the most pathological person I have ever spoken to in my entire thirty years of practice as a psychologist! She did everything you said she had done in the past. She tried to play the perfect mother while declaring that you are the one who is lying and the one who is emotionally unstable." His voice then switched to a tone of conviction as he declared, "Your mother is never going to admit what she did or acknowledge what happened to you because she is just plain crazy."

As he verbalized the true nature of my mother, the feelings in my heart that were drowning in a pool of helplessness rushed to the surface as I cried, "There are no more solutions to my problems about my mother."

"The situation with your mother isn't hopeless, but it's up to us to figure out a way to do it without her."

After the unfortunate phone call with my mother, I finally grew to understand that she wasn't ever going to be there for me, much less validate the memories that my family considered to be forbidden and unspeakable. I now knew that I didn't have a mother and I never would, even though I desperately wanted her to be there for me. *As I grew to understand these things, I became angry.* I wanted to call my mother and give her an ultimatum: "Unless you participate in therapy with me, admit what happened to me growing up, and confess your part in the abuse, then you will no longer have a place in my life. I can't continue living with the secrets, and hiding from myself and the world."

David advised against me making this phone call, and said, "Sandy, you need to make this ultimatum to your mother in your heart. *You need to tell yourself that your mother is never going to change, she is never going to admit to anything, and she is never going to be able to love you the way you need her to love you.*"

I knew he was right, but I just couldn't figure out how I was going to be able to do this when what I so desperately needed was for her to love me. We then discovered what was keeping me stuck: *I was continuing to hold on to the hope that my mother would change into this loving maternal figure who would provide me with everything I missed as a child.* And, as long as I held onto this belief and fantasy, I was never going to be able to let go of her, or my pain. So again, the same question arose as to how was I, as a 37 year old adult, going to get the needs of my child self met in a world surrounded by adults who had their own lives to lead? This fundamental and critical question led me, David, and Tara to an important conclusion: *I had to learn how to do for myself what my mother wasn't able to do for me. I had to learn how to re-parent myself.*

The closer Tara got to earning her Bachelor's degree in psychology, the more she and I began having problems in our private counseling sessions. She changed from being the caring and nurturing person she had been, to trying to emulate David's unemotional cognitive approach. She came into our sessions and began acting more like a therapist seeking cold hard facts, as opposed to the compassionate person I was used to talking to. With each session that passed, I began missing the person who sat on the floor with me, holding my hand, and listening to me from her heart. I missed the person my child felt safe enough to come out in front of, and I wanted the nurturing and caring Tara to come back.

Tara and I began getting into the same arguments that David and I used to embark on in relation to therapeutic style and technique. I didn't need her to be my therapist; I needed her to be a friend who would sit and listen to me and help me access my emotions. My old self began rearing its head because I was afraid to tell Tara that I missed her compassionate side. I was too embarrassed to admit what my needs were, so I disguised them by telling her, "I need the old Tara back, please stop playing cognitive therapist with me." In my naïve child-like way, I thought she understood what I was saying, but each session turned out to be the same with me getting hurt and angry because I wasn't getting my needs met.

Tara playing the role of the therapist finally reached a climax one day when I got so angry that I ran out of my session with her, went straight to my car and got a razor so I could cut myself. I just sat and held onto that razor for what seemed like an eternity. I then realized that I was doing what I had always done: I was letting someone treat me however they wanted without standing up for myself and then wearing my pain on my body. So I marched myself back into Tara's office where I exclaimed once again, "All I'm asking is for you to treat me like you used to." But I still didn't specifically state my needs. She continued to proclaim that she hadn't changed and she didn't understand what I was saying. Unfortunately, we didn't resolve this issue before it was time for us to meet with David.

Tara and I continued our debate in David's office. I tried to explain, "Tara has abandoned me." I then tried to verbalize what I needed from her, but I couldn't, I was too embarrassed.

"Sandy, why do you have such a hard time telling people what your needs are?" David asked.

I bowed my head and said, *"I was never allowed to tell anyone what I needed as a child—I'm embarrassed and ashamed that I even have needs. My needs have always made me weak—vulnerable for people to hurt me. I feel like me needing something makes me a bad person."*

David looked at me and explained, *"Unless you can get to the place where you can tell other people what you need, you will always be left unfulfilled and frustrated because people can't read your mind."*

I knew he was right. I had to take a chance at that moment and force myself to divulge my needs. Nervous and afraid, I stared at the floor, and admitted to Tara, "I miss you sitting on the floor with me, holding my hand, helping my child feel safe, and listening to me."

Tara got up, came over and sat on the couch next to me and put her arms around me. I lay my head on her should and cried as she told me over and over again, "Things are going to be all right. You're stronger than your pain, and I'm here for you."

Her doing that led to another insight. It helped me to discover why I thought it was so important for people to show me they loved me; for them to be consistent with their expression of caring; and why I always suspected I had done something wrong when someone was having a bad day. *I was taking everything as a personal offense against me because, up to this point in my life, I hadn't possessed the ability to TELL people verbally what I needed and what I felt. Instead, I SHOWED them how I felt through my ACTIONS, such as suicide, anorexia, alcoholism, and drug addictions.* My unconscious mind thought this was the way everyone communicated and spoke their truths. *No one openly and honestly confessed what they were thinking or feeling, and that people walked around trying to guess and read each other's moods and thoughts through facial expressions and actions.* This distorted thinking led me to believe that if someone didn't call me, didn't hear what I was saying, didn't show me love, or didn't remember something important, like my birthday, that they were telling me through a non-verbal means of communication that they didn't care about me. I didn't trust that the people in my life would tell me what they were truly thinking and feeling about me because I never witnessed it and I was never taught that in my family. So, instead of verbally communicating with other people, I projected my thoughts and feelings onto them through my actions and hoped they could magically understand my covert messages that cried out for help and understanding.

When I realized what I was doing and that no one could understand my hidden messages, it released me from feeling like everything was my fault, that everything was about me, and that no one cared. I could now lay this burden down and let others take responsibility for themselves. I could honestly say to myself and feel in my heart that "People don't do things against me, they do things to meet their own needs." The task remained that I still had to practice telling people my thoughts and feelings so I could communicate with them in a way they could understand and so I could get my needs met.

As I was trying to understand that it was all right to get my needs met, God and the universe were providing me with other means of healing myself and things began happening to show me that I was indeed changing as a person,.

One day, while I was at the local post office picking up my mail, I ran into Lydia. This was the first time I had seen her in a casual way since my suicide attempt several years ago. Surprisingly, she stopped and made small talk with me and inquired, "How are things going?"

I was nervous standing in her presence, but I took this opportunity to paste on my adult face as I said, "I'm doing well, thanks. Actually, I'm going back to graduate school and am looking for extra work." My openness was met with a barrage of enthusiasm as if nothing bad had ever happened between us.

She then openly proclaimed, "I know someone who might be able to give you some temporary work. I also need some work done on my porch—I'll call you with the details."

I was excited about the possibility of making some money so I could afford graduate school and my books, but, unexpectedly, I questioned if I really wanted to be around Lydia again, especially after remembering how she treated me after my suicide attempt and Dr. Russ' death.

About a week went by when I realized that Lydia had never called me about the work she needed done. Oddly enough, I ran into her again at the post office where she stopped and talked to me again. We discussed my continued search for work because none of the leads I had followed were panning out. In an enthusiastic tone of voice, she reiterated that she wanted me to do some work on her porch, but remained rather vague about the details. This was my clue that she was uncomfortable with me, and this was the last thing I wanted. I didn't desire for either one of us to be discomforted or feel awkward around each other. Then I caught myself slipping back into old thought patterns. I automatically began assuming that there was something inherently wrong with me and that Lydia was uncomfortable because I was a bad person and because of the suicide attempt. When I reflected back on what I had done to try to end my life, I felt ashamed and guilty until I began to realize how stupid this whole thing was. This was the old me trying to make me feel bad about myself and trying to force me to assume responsibility for someone else's thoughts and feelings. I was proud that I was finally becoming aware of my thoughts.

Now that I understood that the old parts of me were trying to manifest themselves once again, I made the conscious decision that I wasn't going to let that happen again. I reminded myself that I was an adult and that "I am no longer a wounded and tortured child" and "that was then and this is now." With my new perspective at hand, I decided to call Lydia to clarify that I was a different person now and I wasn't looking to get back into her life, I just needed some work.

With my chest held high and my cognitive phrases whirling around in my mind, I made the valiant effort. I called Lydia to let her know what was on my mind. Unfortunately, all I got was her answering machine.

For a brief moment I panicked as I didn't know what to say, but I quickly remembered my objective and left a message declaring, "I'm not the same person you used to know and I'm not trying to ease my way back into your life." Almost immediately, I got a response from her that resonated with relief and a willingness to treat me as an adult instead of a parent, and a date to begin working on her porch.

I showed up at Lydia's house to work. I was a nervous at the new role that I would now play with her especially since I no longer needed her to be my surrogate mother. As soon as I walked in the door and saw her, it was like we had never spent any time apart. We both seemed to pick up where we left off with our joking around and gossiping. Even though it was kind of strange, it was refreshing.

After working for a couple of hours, Lydia surprisingly invited me in for lunch. I was a little hesitant and uneasy with the thought of this intimate activity because I didn't want an opportunity to arise where I would feel the need to defend myself for the suicide attempt or to ask her why she treated me so horribly when Dr. Russ died. But, since I was trying to practice the new adult me, I accepted the lunch invitation.

We ate lunch together and talked about all kinds of things that weren't threatening. I found this time with her very beneficial. By the end of lunch, I felt something new come over me; an insight. For the first time I understood that I had to forgive Lydia for the things she had done to me if I was ever going to get on with my own life. I was going to have to leave behind the resentments I had held onto for the past several years. I also realized that my heart finally possessed the ability to really forgive someone. And if I could forgive her, then maybe others.

This was the first time I actually felt that I could control my emotions and behave like an adult. I no longer viewed Lydia as my mother, but as another adult female who was important to me. I couldn't believe it— I was finally growing up.

By the end of the day, I completed my work on the porch and it was time for me to leave. I was somewhat saddened that I was leaving my renewed friendship behind. But I was stable enough in my heart to realize that I was an adult, and if this relationship was to proceed, I would have to let it go and allow Lydia to move at her own pace. Lydia then reached her hand out to pay me, hugged me and kissed me good-bye. With this one hug, I felt all my resentments about her disappear and it validated that I was truly different on the inside. I let her go and was now able to deal with her as an adult because I no longer needed to see her as my mother or a person who could fulfill my needs. This was a good thing because our relationship changed and blossomed from that day forward.

We went out to eat together, drove around looking at the beautiful Northeast Georgia mountains, talked on the phone, and had a great time exploring who we were as mature individuals.

It was at this time that I decided to see if anyone else had noticed any changes in me. I found it necessary to test whether or not my interpersonal skills had improved and were carrying over into my life outside of therapy, so I made the decision to step out into new territory by throwing a party at my house to see who would come. I knew having a party would be a good way to determine this since I had attempted a gathering of what I thought to be friends about two years earlier, only to be disappointed because two people showed up. Even though I was afraid that history could very well repeat itself, I found it necessary to pursue this way of defining myself and my progress.

The day before the party, I spent the entire time cooking and cleaning. I set up a bonfire with straw bales strategically placed around it so people could sit by the fire in a warm circle, while others could entertain everyone with their musical talents. As I prepared for the party, I found something different springing up inside me. I discovered that it didn't matter whether anyone showed up or not because I was doing this for me, and I felt good about who I was becoming. For the first time in my life it would have been all right if I was the only person sitting around my bonfire eating my food because I would have been basking in the wonderful feelings I discovered that day.

The party happened on Saturday, November 11, 2000. There was a beautiful full moon, food and drinks precisely laid out on the table, and music softly filled the air. To my surprise, people started arriving at 5:30 in the afternoon. Soon I had a whole house full of people, and I loved every minute of it! About seven people showed up with guitars and ten people with hand drums, while others brought tambourines, shakers, flutes, and their own beautiful voices. For a brief moment, as we sat around the fire, it felt like we were hippies when one woman started singing Janis Joplin tunes acapella.

It felt so good to see all of these people sitting around a bonfire I had made, playing music and having a good time. It was truly great, and my heart reveled with a sense of accomplishment at the new and improved me. For the first time in my life, I truly had friends, and it was evidenced by the thirty people who came and shared in the fun and good food. It was truly a victory that my party was a success and that I focused only on having a great time and enjoying my accomplishment.

Around that same time, I also opted not to pursue school, but took a job as a counselor working in a rural city close to my home. Overall, my new place of employment was working out both positively and negatively. The negative aspect was that I didn't like what I was doing. I was going into people's homes and providing them with counseling that they didn't want because it was mandated by the local social service agency. The affirming thing was that I was receiving a great deal of positive feedback and reinforcement about my skills, not only from my supervisor, but from my professional colleagues. It was wonderful to hear other people say that I was doing a good job, that I was competent, that I was a good counselor, and to ask for copies of my reports because they were professional and helpful. This was the first time in my life that I was truly seen as an important part of a team and where my interpersonal and professional skills were appreciated and held in high-regard.

At my next therapy session, David brought up the dreaded topic of his retirement. This was the final hurdle that needed to be scaled so I could learn how to let him go in an adult manner, and would hopefully settle the final issues pertaining to my mother and letting her go. I wasn't ready to begin the process of facing his retirement and the feelings it would illicit about my mother, but I realized that I would never be ready to face these issues if they weren't forced upon me.

The more we talked about David's retirement, the more my heart began to feel as if it was being ripped out of my chest, torn into a million pieces and left on the ground for everyone to see. My child's feelings and sense of desperation began manifesting itself with tears and gut-wrenching pain that came from the dark side of my soul where loneliness and abandonment resided. I became aware, once again, that the feelings I was experiencing about David's retirement were the same feelings that lived inside me about my mother.

My child self was inundated with overwhelming feelings that David was abandoning me and I didn't understand why he was doing this. I wondered why it wasn't permissible for just one person in my life, who understood me, not to leave me? And, why couldn't David be my dad and love me like a parent loves a child? I felt the desperate need to beg him to please not leave me, like my mother did. I wasn't ready! I wasn't strong enough to lose the only person who never gave up on me, who was my friend, and who I saw as my surrogate parent.

The feelings were very confusing since I knew in my adult mind that I was capable of taking care of myself. But, my child was still desperate, and in too much pain because she hadn't completely resolved the issues around her mother. She still needed someone to love her and care for her until she could love herself, but she didn't understand why she needed this so badly. By the time this session was over, I felt like giving up if I couldn't keep David in my life (or Tara since she was getting married and moving to Virginia). Why did the two most important people in my life have to leave me?

As I was walking out the door, David warned, "I want to talk about this again during our next session to see if we can discharge the feelings around my retirement, and hopefully, discharge the left-over feelings about your mother."

In between these sessions, I forced myself to try and understand why I couldn't let go of David, and fell upon some invaluable insights.

I was trying to figure out what was at the core of my being that wouldn't allow me to be free. I was still afraid that if I didn't figure it out I would end up killing myself at some point after David's retirement. This life-threatening realization forced me to push myself to feel the terrible feelings associated with his retirement and how these feelings led back to my mother. I came to insightfully understand that I was able to deal with my mother appropriately in my everyday life (even though I continued having difficulty accessing my feelings about her) only because I had transferred everything I thought, felt, and needed about her on to David. He had become my parent and I wanted him to do for me what my mother never did: to love me, to understand and comfort me, and to validate what happened to me. As I was viewing him as my only means of getting my needs met, because he was now my parent, his retirement made me feel as if I was losing my mother all over again!

This led me to an additional understanding about how I saw the world, and people in general. I mentioned earlier that I was nervous and fearful around people because I viewed everyone like I did my mother: punitive and always waiting to hurt me. I now understood that there was a double edge to this sword, and it was that *I saw everyone not only as my punitive mother but also as a potential parent who could take care of me.* As a result, I was constantly searching for people to meet my needs, to love me, to care for me, and to treat me like a parent would a child. Unfortunately, *no one understood that I assigned them this role and thus I didn't get my needs met.* Instead, everyone saw and treated me like I was a capable and self-sufficient adult, and didn't know I saw them as my parent. In turn, I was keeping myself in the victim role and sustaining the legacy that no one loved me. I was looking for what I had desperately needed from my mother in other people that now included David and anyone who was a part of my life.

For the first time, I truly understood that I had always seen myself as a child who was hurt, almost beyond repair, and who needed to be taken care by a kind and loving adult. A child who had an adult tucked away somewhere inside her heart who only came out when the child was in trouble with the outside world. I now understood that I was an adult who was helping her child self grow up so she could cope with life on its terms by staying grounded in the present and future, instead of the past. I finally comprehended that I, the adult, was the one with the power and the one who was in control of my own life and how I felt. I understood who I was.

I also figured out why the cognitive techniques hadn't worked as well as David would have liked. It was because the cognitive techniques made me feel just like my mother made me feel when I was growing up: when I tried to tell people what was happening and she would tell them I was lying, and discounted everything I felt and said. Because I was made out to be a liar, I had to deny my feelings, remain silent, and deny what I knew to be the truth.

After I started seeing David, my inner child wanted to come out in front of him, to be heard and to proclaim and *feel* the forbidden family secrets, but he only encouraged me to talk to myself and to use my cards, instead of speaking and feeling my truths out loud. This technique didn't allow my child to feel what she needed to feel, say what she needed to say, or to feel validated. It made her feel as if she had to continue denying and hiding her feelings, just like she did at home with my mother.

David now understood what I was saying, and he understood why I needed to experience and talk about my feelings *before* I could apply the cognitive phrases to change my perspective about what happened to me and how I felt about it. *My child had to be heard so she could no longer be controlled by her feelings.* She had to get rid of her mother who resided in her heart and who kept her in constant pain and in the victim role. It was connecting with these feelings that allowed me to feel real and validated so I could then dispel the old beliefs with the cognitive techniques and phrases.

The next several weeks were spent trying to help me connect with the part of myself that hurt about David's retiring. It was through this process that I figured out the last place my child self was stuck and why I continued to feel the terrible things that happened to me despite the growth and change I had accomplished over the past several years. I finally found the place where my child originated and where she had gotten lost.

The last part of my child's pain was centered around my mother. I knew this was true because it perfectly matched the pain and emotional turmoil that lived in the core of my being. And, much to my surprise, the pain was generated and became stuck in the high point of one particular incident that left me feeling desperate and vulnerable. Those overwhelming feelings became locked away in my heart and were then exacerbated by the later beatings, abuse, neglect, and emotional torture I sustained as a child.

The incident I refer to was when my pink kitty was left at the hotel in Arizona and my mother refused to go back and get it, or to comfort me in the agony of my loss. She knew my pink kitty was the most important thing in my life and it was all I had to hold on to. That I had no one else to love me, to hold me, to help me feel secure, and no one besides my pink kitty with whom I could attach myself as I would have my mother if given the chance. Since I didn't have my mother and there was no one else available who would fulfill my desperate yet basic child needs, I clung to my pink kitty. My pink kitty was my whole world—it kept me emotionally glued together and prevented me from skipping off into the world of insanity. From a psychological and spiritual point of view, it was my only means of survival.

As I lay in the bed at the hotel on that night so long ago, all of the things my child's unconscious mind had been learning from earlier traumas hit me all at once. It was the first time I felt, on a gut level, how alone I truly was. How unloved and how unimportant I was to everyone around me, especially after my eye accident. How I never had a mother or anyone to rely on for nurturing or support. How my father used to hurt me and caused me to feel terrified of him. It was then that I truly felt the hole that was already being honed inside my heart that would eventually become the unrelenting pit of despair and loneliness that caused my self-hatred and self-destruction. I felt my heart and soul retch at the loss of my pink kitty, all the way down to the core my being, where I wished in a very child-like way, that someone would kill me that day so the unbearable pain and agony would have gone away.

Since there was no one to care for me, or about my pain, I was stuck with my feelings of desperation and abandonment, even though I was only eight years old.

Thus, began the place where my child resided; the child who felt the need to hurt herself to relieve her own pain. It was also the place where the culmination of all future abuse solidified in my child that she was a helpless victim in the savage and brutal game of life.

This was the most important insight I discovered because this was the place I had stopped growing emotionally, where I became the victim and was who my inner child was. This incident was where I learned the distorted truths I held as an adult. Where I came to believe: I am vulnerable; the world isn't a trustworthy place; I'm not good enough to be loved; people are mean and uncaring; the world is a cold and cruel place; people are to be feared; I am a victim; there is no place where I can be safe; and that I am somehow different from everyone around me. It was the place where I became fixated on the need to hurt myself out of anger and desperation because no one would love me or help make my pain go away.

As I looked back on this event in my life, I was truly amazed that I not only survived it without going crazy, but that I didn't develop a multiple personality disorder. I was astonished that I was emotionally intact as that day in the hotel room made me feel as if I were going to break into a million pieces from the emotional pain and tormenting feelings of loss and abandonment.

Now that I understood the birthplace of my pain, I understood the origin of my child self and who I truly was on the inside. This was the genesis of my emotional arrest and the child who lived in an adult's body.

David explained why I held onto my child self and all of her memories all of these years and why I didn't develop a multiple personality disorder. "You needed your inner child because she was your only link to the past. Without her and her memories you would never have been able to remember what happened to you so you could heal yourself."

She was my bridge between my past and present; between my child growing up and my current adult self. It was my child who provided all the information and memories I needed in order to heal myself.

It was through this understanding that I was able to free myself of my mother's invisible grasp on my inner child. My mother could no longer hurt me because I now understood how I had been letting her hurt me. I was no longer the quintessential victim, and since I was no longer a victim she couldn't hurt me anymore. I was also free from needing David to love me, as my mother should have. I no longer needed him, or anyone else, to be my parent and take care of me. I was now an adult who had an internal child who needed to be raised with the love, nurturing, and understanding that only I could provide.

The task now was to use the emotional insights I gained from therapy, and the cognitive tools David taught me, to begin re-parenting my inner child from the wonderful child she was before the unconscionable abuse began into the adult she could be without the painful baggage. I was now at a place where I could incorporate what David had taught me, what Tara provided me, and what I forced myself to face and learn.

I also knew I had one very important thing left to do. I had to accept myself for who I was, *all of me*. I could no longer keep trying to kill off parts of me, while trying to build up other parts. *I had to understand that my little girl was going to be with me forever, but I didn't have to allow her to run or ruin my life.* Instead, I would feel her from time to time and I would have to comfort her when she began to hurt again. I had to understand and accept that I was both the child and the adult in one body, but I could now take care of both of us.

Time progressed and all of the emotional insights, especially the one about my pink kitty and my becoming emotionally-arrested then, proved to be helpful on my journey. I was set free from my past and my mother. My once broken and weary spirit was healing and achieving the desired resolution that David and I had fought for with every ounce of our beings for over three years.

The day finally arrived when I had to face the fact that my time with him was over and it was time for both of us to move on. David had been my therapist, my friend, my parent, my mentor, and most of all, my pink kitty. It was time for me to take the things I had learned from both of us and practice them and live by them in my daily life. It was time to walk the walk and to live!

As I hugged David and walked out of his office that one last time, I felt my heart break with the pain of our parting ways. But, I knew my child had to experience this pain because it was through his leaving that I was able to finally grieve my child's past hurts, especially the loss of my mother and my pink kitty. It was my child's opportunity to feel the pain and know that it couldn't kill her, not now or ever. To know that she was finally strong enough to endure the past and the future journey with the caring and re-parenting my adult self would provide her. My adult self intuitively knew that I was going to "be all right" because I had all the tools I needed to be okay and to survive. I had learned what I needed to do in order to face life on its terms.

The next several months didn't prove to be as difficult as I thought they would be, despite the fact I was grieving David's retirement and my child's many losses. For the first time in my life I grieved in a way that was healthy rather than destructive. I finally became the good observer and the good survivor who could say, "So this is how it is," and live.

Sandy Riggin is currently working on the publication of her second book, which outlines the therapeutic techniques she utilizes in her private practices to assist people with recovering from childhood abuse and/or trauma. She is also continuing to conduct seminars and group therapy sessions for survivors. Should you wish to obtain information about her book(s), seminars, counseling practices or contact her for any other reason, please feel free to write or visit her at:

Postal Address: P.O. Box 357
                 Sautee, Georgia 30571

Email Address: spriggin1024@yahoo.com

Web Address: www.sandyriggin.com